Hugh Trevor-Roper was the most brilliant historian of his generation. An expert in the history of early modern Britain and Nazi Germany, he was Regius Professor of Modern History at Oxford University and latterly Master of Peterhouse, Cambridge. He received a life peerage in 1979. He was the author of numerous books, including his famous investigation of Hitler's last days. During World War II, Trevor-Roper served in the Secret Intelligence Service, giving him a remarkable insight into the work of the intelligence services in Britain. His *Wartime Journals* were published by I.B.Tauris in 2012.

Edward Harrison is an historian and writer specialising in World War II. He attended Trevor-Roper's lectures while at Oxford University and has taught history in Britain and the US. He has held Visiting Fellowships at Oxford and an Anthony de Rothschild Fellowship in History of the Churchill Trust. He is the author of *The Young Kim Philby: Soviet Spy and British Intelligence Officer* (2012).

HUGH TREVOR-ROPER

THE SECRET WORLD

BEHIND THE CURTAIN OF BRITISH INTELLIGENCE IN WORLD WAR II AND THE COLD WAR

EDITED BY EDWARD HARRISON

FOREWORD BY SIR MICHAEL HOWARD

I.B. TAURIS

LONDON · NEW YORK

Published in 2014 by I.B.Tauris & Co. Ltd
6 Salem Road, London W2 4BU
175 Fifth Avenue, New York NY 10010
www.ibtauris.com

Distributed in the United States and Canada
Exclusively by Palgrave Macmillan
175 Fifth Avenue, New York NY 10010

ISBN: 978 1 78076 208 1
eISBN: 978 0 85773 703 8

A full CIP record for this book is available from the British Library
A full CIP record is available from the Library of Congress

Library of Congress Catalog Card Number: available

Typeset by JCS Publishing Services Ltd, www.jcs-publishing.co.uk

Printed and bound in Sweden by ScandBook AB

MIX
Paper from
responsible sources
FSC
www.fsc.org   FSC® C007584

Contents

Illustrations

1   Hugh Trevor-Roper: an informal photograph taken in Christ Church, c.1950.

2   Lady Alexandra Howard-Johnston in her gown to meet Princess Elizabeth and Prince Philip in May 1948. She married Trevor-Roper in October 1954. (*Xenia Dennen*)

3   Sir Stewart Menzies, Chief of the British Secret Intelligence Service, 1939–52. (*National Portrait Gallery, London*)

4   Peter Koch de Gooreynd, who kept Menzies company at the bar of White's. (*National Portrait Gallery, London*)

5   Sir Dick White, the only person to become head successively of both MI5 and SIS, and Trevor-Roper's influential mentor.

6   Charles Stuart: Christ Church historian and Trevor-Roper's first recruit to his wireless intelligence unit. (*Christ Church, Oxford*)

7   Rachel and Patrick Reilly, the diplomat who effectively vetoed Philby's becoming Chief of SIS. (*Bodleian Library, Oxford*)

8   Broadway Buildings, located opposite St James's Park underground station, provided SIS with headquarters from 1926 to 1964. (*Westminster Council Archives*)

9   Kim Philby, Soviet spy and British intelligence officer. (*Getty*)

10 Eleanor Philby: the spy's third wife, whom he abandoned in Beirut. She followed him to Moscow, where he left her again. (*Getty*)

11 Melinda Maclean: the American wife of the Soviet spy Donald Maclean. Her relationship with Philby contributed to the collapse of his third marriage. (*Getty*)

12 Michael Straight: an affluent American recruited at Cambridge to spy for the Soviet Union. (*Ramsey and Muspratt, Cambridge*)

13 Admiral Canaris: the head of the German Secret Service from 1935 to 1944. (*Bundesarchiv*)

14 Otto John, the first head of the Federal Office for the Protection of the Constitution, the German equivalent of MI5. (*Getty*)

Editor's Acknowledgements

My first debt is to Blair Worden, literary executor of Lord Dacre of Glanton, who generously invited me to undertake this edition. His thoughtful advice and unfailing encouragement were essential to the book's completion. Also vital was the expert and invaluable help from Judith Curthoys, archivist of Christ Church, who guided me through the Dacre Papers. I have been very fortunate in the scholars who have previously studied Lord Dacre's career, and owe a particular obligation to Adam Sisman and Richard Davenport-Hines. Sir Michael Howard, who succeeded Lord Dacre as Regius Professor of Modern History at Oxford, most kindly agreed to write the foreword.

Rodney Allan painstakingly checked the transcription of *The Philby Affair* and *Admiral Canaris*. I am also grateful to others who have generously provided assistance, in particular Phyllis Acheampong, Anthony P. Adamthwaite, Richard J. Aldrich, Eilish Burke, Susan and William Chater, Joanna Chaundy, E.L. Harrison, Anna Henderson, the late M.R.D. Foot, Laurence Guymer, Patrick Hederman, Roy Hughes, Peter Jackson, Clare Kavanagh, Helen Langley, Vicky Mitchell, Peter Pulzer, Jane Reilly, Alysoun Saunders, Gina Thomas, Martin Thomas, W.E.S. Thomas, John and Christina Harrison, Patricia and Nathan Winter, Danielle Wall and Roberta Wiener.

I wish to thank the following individuals and institutions for their helpful permission to use or consult material:

The Literary Estate of Lord Dacre of Glanton for permission to publish Hugh Trevor-Roper's essays and letters concerning secret intelligence;

The Bodleian Library and Jane Reilly for permission to publish letters of her father, Sir Patrick Reilly, and a photograph of her parents;

Susan Chater and William Stuart for permission to quote from the papers of Charles Stuart and to republish two of his articles;

The Very Reverend Christopher Lewis, Dean of Christ Church, for permission to reproduce an article from the *Christ Church Annual Report* of 1993;

Sir Michael Howard for permission to quote from *Strategic Deception*;

Immediate Media Company London Limited for a licence to republish a
quote and an article from the *Listener*;

The *Independent* for permission to republish an article;

The *New York Review of Books* for permission to republish three articles;

The Warden and Fellows of Nuffield College for permission to reproduce
quotations from Lord Cherwell's papers;

The *Spectator* for permission to reproduce two articles by Charles Stuart;

The Trustees of the Liddell Hart Centre for Military Archives for quotations
from the Liddell Hart Papers;

Xenia Dennen for permission to reproduce the photograph of her mother,
Lady Alexandra Trevor-Roper.

Every effort has been made to trace the holders of copyright in text or
photographs. If any have been inadvertently omitted, acknowledgement will
be made at the earliest opportunity.

At I.B. Tauris, Lester Crook not only helped in the planning of the book
but also read the typescript and suggested invaluable clarifications.
Joanna Godfrey has been an exemplary editor, providing very prompt and
sympathetic support throughout the project. Alexandra Higson oversaw
the meticulous production of the book, which Jessica Cuthbert-Smith copy-
edited with her customary precision and felicity. Zoe Ross expertly compiled
the index and Steve Williamson proofread.

My greatest debt is to Hugh Trevor-Roper himself. When I met him as an
undergraduate his kindness completely belied his formidable reputation. In
later years he sent me most helpful letters clarifying the mysteries of secret
intelligence. Above all I am grateful to him for writing essays which still held
my attention after repeated readings and which provided distraction during
the most mundane of editorial tasks.

Foreword
by Sir Michael Howard

Many British academics served with the Intelligence Services during World War II, but very few breathed a word about their activities. For many there was little temptation to do so. Even those who served in that holiest of holies, Bletchley Park, were often little more than cogs in a machine, knowing as little as anyone else of the importance of the organisation's final output. Few of them had any beans worth spilling, and they returned with relief to environments and activities far more agreeable than any they had experienced in the drab government offices where they had spent the war.

Not so with Hugh Trevor-Roper. Good fortune, his own remarkable talents and, not least, his skill at bureaucratic infighting had gained him a place at the very centre of the British intelligence *apparat*. There his success in thwarting the designs, not only of the Abwehr but – far more satisfying – of his adversaries in Whitehall, provided challenges that made his subsequent academic career, brilliant though it was, something of an anticlimax. This did not make him any less discreet than his less flamboyant contemporaries, but the experience shaped his interests and perhaps moulded his character, in a way that made him unique in his generation.

For most of Hugh's academic contemporaries there was a clean break between their war service and their subsequent peacetime activities. But for Hugh the one led seamlessly into the other in a way that made it difficult for him, even had he been so inclined, to put his past behind him. At the end of the war the intimate knowledge he had gained of the governance of the Nazi regime through his mastery of its communications made him the obvious choice to investigate how Hitler met his end; a matter not just of historical interest but of great political significance at a time when rumours abounded that the Führer had been spirited away by one or other of the Allies for their own nefarious purposes. It was probably for the same *raison d'état* that the government allowed him to publish his findings.

The result was *The Last Days of Hitler* – a publication that made Hugh world famous. It also made it unlikely that he would devote the rest of his life simply to exploring the field opened up by his earlier study of that very different historical character, Archbishop Laud. As it was, his interest was to oscillate between those two very diverse poles. By far the greater part of it was indeed to be dedicated to his work on the seventeenth century, the huge scope of which would not be fully appreciated even by his academic colleagues until after his death. But in the eyes of the general public, alas, his reputation remained that established by *The Last Days of Hitler* at the outset of his career, and would be destroyed by the fiasco of the Hitler Diaries at its end.

If Hugh did any work for the Intelligence Services after the war he left no trace, but it is not likely. His professional colleagues had always resented the wartime intrusion of interlopers and were glad to see the last of them – with the exception, of course, of the deferential and reliable Kim Philby, the only one they wholly trusted. So for two decades Hugh displayed his wartime expertise only in occasional articles and book reviews such as that of the Canaris biography printed in this volume. But in 1967 the scandal created by the defection of Kim Philby, and even more, by Philby's own very explicit memoirs, made it possible for Hugh, with official approval, to set the record straight. So he published his own account of the secret world that he had shared with Philby and provided his own explanation of Philby's treachery.

The Philby Affair, published in 1968, sold widely and served to confirm Hugh's public reputation primarily as an expert on World War II. Being little more than an extended essay, it has been possible to print it here, together with much of the correspondence to which it gave rise. But now that Hugh was 'out of the closet' he could talk, and write, more freely about the Intelligence Services and his experience within them. More important, his study of Philby provided a rare opportunity for cross-fertilisation between his widely diverse interests. As a colleague he had appreciated Philby's urbanity, ironic wit and breadth of interests in company that otherwise consisted, as Hugh himself frequently lamented, of stockbrokers recruited from the bar at White's and retired Indian policemen. But how was it that such a worldly and sophisticated a character as Philby could be not only a communist (easy enough for the intelligentsia in the 1930s), but a fully paid-up Stalinist and a professional agent of the KGB?

Hugh brought to this problem the understanding, not just of a historian, but a historian whose field of study lay in the wars of religion that had ravaged Europe in the sixteenth and seventeenth centuries. Then also there had been 'true believers': men of great learning and civility who had nevertheless closed their minds to everything but dogma enunciated by an infallible moral authority and enforced by a pitiless civil regime; men whose cold ruthlessness had swept away the civilised tolerance preached by Hugh's own hero Erasmus. The mid-twentieth century was seeing just such another war of religion, whose pressures and necessities had moulded very similar types. Hugh could see where Philby fitted in and knew how dangerously effective such men could be. Certainly the thought that Philby very nearly reached the top of the Security Services at the height of the Cold War is enough to chill the blood.

It is hardly surprising that Hugh found the period through which he was living at least as interesting as the past to whose study he had dedicated his life, and he used his knowledge of each to deepen his understanding of the other. It is this amalgamation and cross-fertilisation that makes Hugh's writings about his 'secret world' so important if we are to understand, not only how his own interests developed, but also his significance as a historical figure in his own right. We are very fortunate to have in Edward Harrison an editor with the expertise to guide us through them.

Abbreviations and Glossary

These relate to the United Kingdom unless otherwise indicated

Abwehr	German military intelligence
ACSS	Assistant Chief of the Secret (Intelligence) Service
ADM	Admiralty
Apostles	elite secret society of pre-war Cambridge University
BBC	British Broadcasting Corporation
BEF	British Expeditionary Force (to continental Europe)
Berkeley St	London-based unit for breaking diplomatic codes
BND	Bundesnachrichtendienst: German Federal intelligence service, namely secret intelligence service abroad of the Federal Republic of Germany
Bodden	German code name for deployment of special equipment to monitor ships passing through the Straits of Gibraltar
BSC	British Security Coordination [for the Americas]
C	letter denoting either the Chief of the Secret Intelligence Service or the Service itself
CE	counter-espionage
Cheka	Soviet security and intelligence agency, precursor of KGB
CIA	Central Intelligence Agency (USA)
Comintern	Communist International: an organisation coordinating the activities of national Communist parties in the interests of the Soviet Union
Cossac	Chief of Staff to the Supreme Allied Commander
CSDIC	Combined Services Detailed Interrogation Centre
CSS	Chief of the Secret [Intelligence] Service
DCSS	Deputy Chief of the Secret [Intelligence] Service
DSO	Distinguished Service Order
Enigma	German coding machine
FBI	Federal Bureau of Investigation (USA)

FO Foreign Office

GC & CS Government Code and Cypher School with responsibility for devising British codes and breaking foreign ones

GHQ General Headquarters

GRU Soviet military intelligence

Humint intelligence from human sources

ISBA Intelligence Service British Agents: decrypted and translated German spy messages given particularly restricted circulation as they referred to SIS agents

ISK Intelligence Service Knox: decrypted and translated German spy messages originally enciphered with an enigma machine

ISOS Intelligence Service Oliver Strachey: decrypted and translated German spy messages originally enciphered manually, e.g. with a code-book.

JIC Joint Intelligence Sub-Committee

KCL King's College London

KGB Soviet security and intelligence agency

KO War Organisation: name used by Abwehr offices abroad during World War II

LCS London Controlling Section {for Deception}

MI5 Security Service: agency responsible for preventing espionage, sabotage and subversion on British territory

MI6 Popular name for Secret Intelligence Service

MI8 Military Intelligence department of the War Office

NKVD People's Commissariat for Internal Affairs incorporating the security and intelligence agency GUGB (USSR)

OED *Oxford English Dictionary*

OGPU Soviet security and intelligence agency, precursor of KGB

OSS Office of Strategic Services (USA), precursor of CIA

PCO Passport Control Officer

RIS Radio Intelligence Service: Trevor-Roper's wireless intelligence unit in SIS

RSS Radio Security Service: organisation for intercepting the wireless messages of foreign intelligence services during World War II

SD Sicherheitsdienst: Nazi Party security service within the SS

Section D   Secret Intelligence Service sabotage section taken over by SOE in 1940

Section V   Counter-espionage section of the Secret Intelligence Service

Section IX   Anti-Communist section of the Secret Intelligence Service

Security Service   Usually known as MI5

SHAEF   Supreme Headquarters Allied Expeditionary Force

SIS   Secret Intelligence Service: responsible for gathering intelligence and counter-intelligence outside the three-mile territorial limits of the British Empire

SOE   Special Operations Executive: British overseas organisation responsible for sabotage, subversion and stimulating resistance movements against enemy powers during World War II

SS   Schutzstaffel: protection squad of the Nazi Party

Stasi   East German state security and intelligence service

Ultra   Security classification for intelligence derived from German wireless messages enciphered by the Enigma machine

USSR   Union of Soviet Socialist Republics: the Soviet Union

VCSS   Vice Chief of the Secret [Intelligence] Service

VD   Iberian sub-section of Section V of the Secret Intelligence Service

Vw   Wireless sub-section of Section V

WO   War Office

Z   letter designating pre-war Secret Intelligence Service network operating under business cover

Editor's Preface

Hugh Trevor-Roper was one of the most original and eloquent of historians. Born in 1914 and educated at Charterhouse School, he went to Oxford University to read Classics, but after two years he changed to the full-time study of modern history. His controversial first book, *Archbishop Laud*, was published in 1940 and was followed in 1947 by an international best-seller, *The Last Days of Hitler*. Even amongst a generation of outstanding Oxford historians his talent was so precocious that he was appointed Regius Professor of Modern History at the age of 43. Trevor-Roper's main area of research and writing was the early modern period but he consistently maintained an unusually extensive range of historical interests and wrote about them in a uniquely expressive and balanced style.

Trevor-Roper won fame as a historian, but he also twice made his mark on the secret world of intelligence. During World War II he was an exceptionally thoughtful and vigorous intelligence officer whose expertise on Nazi Germany was so impressive that he was entrusted with the crucial mission of establishing the facts of Hitler's death. After the war he was often tempted away from his principal historical interest in the early modern period to write about Cold War intelligence. Such essays form the core of this book. But Trevor-Roper's contribution to the intelligence world was not just one of intellect and elegant communication. In the world of secret service, brains were not enough. Trevor-Roper had to develop an impressive array of skills as an intelligence officer. Intelligence was a Darwinist world of competing interests and it was essential to be combative. This made him some unforgiving enemies, who surge forward in this book and animate its pages. When he became an intelligence officer in 1939, Trevor-Roper was a promising young historian on the eve of publishing his first book. In his previous experience, intellect had usually triumphed, so he was shocked to discover that reason did not reign supreme in secret service. Issues were not always decided just on their merits, for personalities and jurisdictions also played their part in determining outcomes. Some of the people Trevor-Roper met in the secret world horrified him for life, and in old age he still wrote about their shortcomings with profound distaste and corresponding vigour.

The urgent demands of wartime intelligence also forged exceptionally powerful bonds between Trevor-Roper and those he found willing to cooperate. The life-long friendships he made during the war proved a great asset for Trevor-Roper in his writing about the secret world. He could consult his old friends for both evidence and opinions about the books he was reviewing. There were many such friends, but perhaps the most important were the intelligence officer Dick White, the diplomat Patrick Reilly and the historian Charles Stuart. Trevor-Roper corresponded with all three about intelligence matters for the rest of their lives. His reviews generated further illuminating correspondence with other former intelligence officers. As was the case with many of his correspondents, secret service had provided Trevor-Roper's first experience of working life. It had made a profound impression on him and he later watched the world of intelligence with particular sharpness, expressing his observations to his former colleagues in some of his most ironic and entertaining letters. He wrote and received hundreds of letters about secret intelligence, and some of the most revealing passages in this correspondence are quoted in this book.

Trevor-Roper's intelligence writings sometimes took the form of substantial essays, in which he went far beyond the confines of the literature under review and developed his own ideas on the subject and described the experience from which they were drawn. This was the way in which Trevor-Roper constructed *The Philby Affair*, his most important work on secret intelligence. In this book he explored not only the actions of Kim Philby, the British intelligence officer and Soviet secret agent, but also his mentality. *The Philby Affair* is remarkable not only for its content but also for its style, gaining particular fluency and direction because it was personal and autobiographical. First published in *Encounter* in April 1968, Trevor-Roper expanded the essay and republished it in book form the same year.

In *The Philby Affair* Trevor-Roper recaptured the brilliance and zest that had marked his previous book on the modern era, *The Last Days of Hitler*. Not only is *The Philby Affair* valuable for its personal testimony as to Philby's behaviour, it also provides a controversial critique of SIS during World War II. But *The Philby Affair* has a resonance beyond its immediate focus, as it provides an admirably lucid explanation of secret intelligence. George Kennan, former US ambassador to Moscow, commented that Trevor-Roper's piece on Philby was 'brilliantly perceptive with relation to the western-intellectual captives of the communist movement', and that 'it contains the soundest and most perceptive comment on the role of secret intelligence that I have seen anywhere.'[1] Walter L. Pforzheimer of the CIA recalled that the Director of Central Intelligence, Richard Helms, made Trevor-Roper's 'splendid essay on Philby [...] must reading for all of his senior officers. It was a splendid piece.'[2]

Trevor-Roper wrote some of his best book reviews about the secret world. After reading one of these, Sir John Masterman, Trevor-Roper's former history tutor, wrote to his pupil that 'You have a wonderful power of reviewing a book without fear or favour. No one else in England can do this as well, or half as well, as you do. I trust that your reviews of important books are being collected for subsequent publication. They ought to be.'[3] Throughout his life Trevor-Roper sought to achieve a better understanding of his service in wartime intelligence through conversation, correspondence and extensive reviewing. Although he planned to publish a book of his intelligence essays,[4] other projects intervened. So his most substantial writings on espionage are collected here for the first time.

Some small changes have been made to the original texts to correct typographical errors, for consistency and to modernise some punctuation. In the texts my insertions and minor explanations have been inserted in italics, within square brackets. Trevor-Roper's original notes are presented as footnotes, while my editorial notes appear as endnotes at the back of the book.

Edward Harrison

Editor's Introduction:
Hugh Trevor-Roper's Secret War

How did Hugh Trevor-Roper become an expert on secret service?[1] He joined the Secret Intelligence Service (SIS) by the indirect route of wireless security. In December 1937 the General Post Office was commissioned to build three stations to intercept illegal wireless messages. During a meeting at the War Office on 7 December 1938 it was decided that the detection of illegal wireless should come under Military Intelligence, which received funding for the establishment of a Radio Security Section (RSS) in March 1939.[2]

The outbreak of war with Nazi Germany renewed official interest in Britain's radio security. On 16 September 1939, Lord Hankey,[3] the minister without portfolio, was asked by Prime Minister Neville Chamberlain to investigate the possible leakage of military information to Germany by wireless messages from Britain. Hankey identified numerous ways in which intelligence leaks might take place. Most of these gaps, however, could not be used for passing material quickly. By contrast, short-wave wireless was fast, and MI5 had already found one illicit wireless set used for communication with Germany. Hankey recommended that the Radio Security Section should be revamped and 'that the new organisation should be made responsible for all problems in connection with (i) the interception of illicit wireless [...], both at home and from abroad; and (ii) the detection of radio beacons [inside Britain], which might act as a guide to enemy aircraft raiding this country.' He also recommended that 'immediate steps should be taken to make up the present deficiencies in personnel and equipment'.[4]

The Radio Security Section began to expand rapidly under the executive command of Colonel J.P.G. Worlledge of the Royal Signals, who was known as 'Controller RSS'. MI5 had found wartime premises in Wormwood Scrubs and RSS was installed there as well. It soon hired academics eager to take part in the war effort. In December 1939 E.W.B. 'Gilly' Gill,[5] bursar of Merton College Oxford, was recruited to head the discrimination section of RSS, which guided the work of the whole unit. Gill had served as a wireless intelligence officer during World War I. Afterwards he had lectured on electricity at Oxford, where, in Trevor-Roper's words, 'he was regarded with friendly indulgence by classical dons as one who [...] could mend the wireless set when it went wrong, or the electric light when it fused, but could only by a charitable laxity of definition be included among the educated.'[6] In late 1939 Trevor-Roper was a junior research fellow at Merton waiting for his army call-up. He accepted an invitation from Gill to join RSS instead. The two were given a cell in Wormwood Scrubs and began work. Trevor-Roper got on well with the officers from MI5 in other cells.[7] In particular he made friends with Guy Liddell,[8] T.A. 'Tar' Robertson[9] and Richard 'Dick' Goldsmith White.[10]

Gill examined all the technical evidence and decided that the enemy was not using wireless head beacons, so RSS stopped searching for these. The other part of the RSS brief – namely, the identification of German radio operators in Britain – was also problematic. During autumn 1939 RSS did not succeed in intercepting any radio messages from German spies working in Britain. By December RSS realised that it might be easier to find radio messages made from Germany to spies in the United Kingdom. The agents had to be able to pick up their instructions and so RSS could receive them too. Gill received help from MI5, which controlled a double agent code named *Snow*, who was also working for the Abwehr or German secret service. *Snow* was under guard in Wandsworth prison and his radio was operated for him by a warder. This guard was conscientious and noticed that the German operator also sent messages when *Snow* was off the air. These extra signals gave British intercept stations a vital clue to the communications of a German spy network.[11]

Snow's case officer informed Gill of the type of message agents would probably send, and of a station in Germany to which spies would report. RSS kept a special watch on this station, which was sending messages of the appropriate type to a ship, the *Theseus*, off the Norwegian coast. RSS intercepted the messages and forwarded them to Britain's professional code-breakers, the Government Code and Cypher School (GC & CS) at Bletchley Park. Bletchley replied that the material should be ignored. This did not satisfy Gill and Trevor-Roper, who decided to work on the messages by themselves. Trevor-Roper eventually cracked the cipher in early 1940 while thinking in the bath during an air raid. It was a hand-cipher used by the

Abwehr station in Hamburg to communicate with the *Theseus*, which was sending back reports on neutral shipping.[12]

Bletchley Park was affronted by RSS's encroachment on its jurisdiction. Its executive head, Commander Alistair Denniston, prompted Colonel Butler of MI8, the branch of military intelligence responsible for radio, to tell RSS not to interest themselves in code-breaking. RSS, Bletchley and MI5 held a meeting on 20 March 1940 at which Bletchley agreed to form a separate section for the traffic Gill and Trevor-Roper had discovered. In future, the raw material was to be sent to Oliver Strachey at Bletchley. Strachey[13] was an experienced code-breaker, but his section was initially too small to deal with the traffic. In consequence, despite the ban from MI8, the next four Abwehr ciphers to be broken were cracked in RSS, not at Bletchley.[14]

While British wireless security was improving, the military situation on the Continent was deteriorating sharply. But Trevor-Roper was unperturbed by the collapse of France in June 1940: 'I merely reflected that we had no more speculative allies & knew where we stood.' He was later astonished by 'the serene, effortless confidence with which we accepted, and reacted to, the most colossal of disasters'.[15] The disasters meant extra work for RSS; the Abwehr now planned to send more agents to Britain to spy for Hitler's proposed invasion. In August 1940 RSS discovered German espionage preparations by identifying traffic on a wireless network in northern France. The resulting decrypts showed that the French stations had been set up to work with new sources in Britain. But Bletchley was unable to read other traffic intercepted by RSS, which used better ciphers between Berlin and seven European outstations. The British code-breakers finally broke this traffic in December 1940: it was the hand-cipher used between Abwehr HQ and its chief foreign stations. A few hundred messages in this cipher were decoded each week during 1941 and circulated to a few government departments under the name of ISOS (Intelligence Service Oliver Strachey). ISOS gave invaluable assistance in frustrating Abwehr efforts to establish spies in the United Kingdom. During 1941 information from ISOS was solely responsible for the capture of five of the 23 agents the German secret service sent to Britain. The material was also of great importance in running six of MI5's double agents. By the end of 1942 ISOS would enable the capture of 20 enemy agents out of the grand total of 87 taken prisoner.[16] In April 1942 this invaluable source was betrayed to Soviet Intelligence by Anthony Blunt of MI5, who offered to provide batches of ISOS.[17]

By late 1940 RSS had become so large that it was an unwelcome burden for MI8 in the War Office. In October 1940 MI8 declared that it wished to concentrate on the wireless messages of hostile armies and proposed that RSS, which focused on enemy spies, should be transferred to MI5. But MI5 refused to take over RSS, as the Security Service was responsible for the protection of British territory, and so far RSS had focused on communications between enemy stations abroad. An unfortunate incident during December 1940 reinforced the sense that the arrangements for managing RSS had to be changed. Trevor-Roper used RSS intercepts to compose an intelligence note on the German secret service in Morocco but Worlledge circulated this note too freely for the liking of SIS. In his first brush with Trevor-Roper, Felix Cowgill[18] of SIS counter-intelligence wished to have the compiler of the note prosecuted. Although this was prevented, RSS was excluded from the distribution of ISOS for about ten days. Cowgill never forgot the affair: nearly two years later MI5 considered that it 'probably accounts for the distrust with which Major Cowgill has ever since regarded Intelligence Notes'.[19]

Who was to get a grip on RSS? Lord Swinton,[20] secretary of state for air between 1935 and 1938, was to play a central role in deciding this issue. On 27 May 1940 the War Cabinet had made Swinton chairman of the Security Executive, set up to combat the threats from Axis espionage, sabotage and subversion. He was to supervise the work of MI5 and SIS in Britain and Eire. Swinton decided to ask Sir David Petrie,[21] former director of the Intelligence Bureau in India, to consider the problem of RSS and give advice. Petrie was already advising Swinton on MI5. Indeed he was made its director general from March 1941.[22]

As RSS was a security and intelligence unit, it had to become part of either MI5 or SIS. MI5 was concerned with the detection and prevention of espionage, sabotage and subversion on British territory; SIS was responsible for gathering intelligence and counter-intelligence outside the three-mile territorial limits of the Empire. The basic division between the two organisations was geographical, but radio waves passed with careless abandon across the three-mile limit, and so fell within the jurisdiction of both British intelligence services. RSS business related to both MI5 and SIS. Although MI5 had recently refused to take RSS, since then the radio organisation had become much more significant due to the breaking of the main Abwehr hand-cipher. MI5 wireless was in its infancy; by contrast, Section VIII of

SIS specialised in wireless and overseas communications. Since March 1938 Section VIII had been led by Richard Gambier-Parry,[23] who had previously worked for the British Broadcasting Corporation (BBC) and as British sales manager for an American radio manufacturer. Gambier-Parry reorganised and expanded SIS wireless, and his success influenced the arrangements for control of RSS.[24]

On 30 January 1941 Petrie reported to Swinton that SIS had a 'very efficient wireless installation [...] The logical and right course would be for R.S.S. to be taken over lock, stock and barrel by M.I.6, to be equipped, staffed and run purely as an Intelligence instrument.' Swinton accepted Petrie's recommendation and decided that SIS should take over RSS. Menzies approved the proposed addition to his organisation, as Swinton informed the director of military intelligence, Major-General F.H.N. Davidson, in the first week of February 1941. Swinton told Davidson that everyone else was in favour of the change too.[25] In his reply to Swinton, Davidson accepted the SIS takeover, though he questioned whether MI6 had the organisational capacity to run RSS. Indeed, behind the scenes Davidson was campaigning for Menzies to be replaced, claiming SIS intelligence was appalling.[26]

The War Office transferred RSS to SIS in May 1941. Afterwards, the Radio Security Section came to be known usually as the Radio Security Service. Colonel Worlledge was moved out to a temporary liaison post. Major Gill had been largely responsible for the early successes of RSS, but the new regime did not want him. He was demoted to captain and sent to the Catterick Signals Training Centre.[27] MI5 later commented that 'the chief architect of the work which was now to be the main function of R.S.S. was dismissed unseen. All questions of organisation, policy and personnel were decided by S.I.S., although since S.I.S. had never practised interception, there was no one in S.I.S. who could understand the questions they were deciding. *Hinc illae lacrimae.*'[28]

After its transfer to the Secret Service, RSS came under the wireless section headed by Richard Gambier-Parry. Trevor-Roper later wrote that Gambier-Parry:

> had been educated, up to a point, at Eton and had held a post, as a technical expert, in the BBC until an unfortunate episode with a secretary had led, in those more conventional days – the days of Sir John Reith – to his resignation; whereupon he had moved to MI6 [...] I came to know

Gambier quite well and found him enjoyable company. I have no doubt that he was efficient too.[29]

Gambier-Parry devolved control of RSS to an old friend, E.F. 'Ted' Maltby, who became 'Controller RSS'. Trevor-Roper recalled that Maltby, who

seemed to have started his military career as a colonel – one has to begin somewhere – was also an Etonian, but from a less assured background, and he clearly modelled himself, externally at least, on his patron. But he was at best the poor man's Gambier, larger and louder than his master, whose boots he licked with obsequious relish. Of intelligence matters he understood nothing. 'Scholars', he would say, 'are two a penny: it's the man of vision who counts'; and that great red face would swivel round, like an illuminated Chinese lantern, beaming with self-satisfaction. But he enjoyed his status and perquisites of his accidental promotion and obeyed his orders punctually, explaining that any dissenter would be (in his own favourite phrase) 'shat on from a very great height.' I am afraid that the new 'Controller RSS' was regarded, in the intelligence world, as something of a joke – a joke in dubious taste. But he was so happily constituted that he was unaware of this.[30]

Under Maltby, RSS was located at Arkley View, near Barnet. Trevor-Roper became responsible for RSS intelligence with the symbol Vw (Five wireless) as a member of the counter-espionage Section V of SIS. Although Section V was located in St Albans, Trevor-Roper insisted on staying in Arkley so that he could provide RSS with intelligence guidance.

Most RSS personnel spent their time intercepting the radio messages of the Axis intelligence services. Trevor-Roper guided their interception by studying the call-signs, frequencies and other technical features of Axis wireless. For this work he could draw on intelligence materials such as the interrogation of prisoners and the intercepted radio messages themselves. The deciphered messages gave clues of new enemy wireless networks and forthcoming changes in frequencies and operator procedures. Trevor-Roper soon realised the wider implications of his work. The Axis introduction of new networks could shed light on both their intelligence and indeed their military plans. Furthermore, the intercepts told much about the structure and methods of the Axis secret services, and even about the regimes of which they formed part.

Trevor-Roper's initial intelligence work focused on ISOS, messages decrypted from Abwehr hand-ciphers. But the significance of his role would increase greatly after the breaking on Christmas Day 1941 of the Enigma machine[31] code used for the majority of Abwehr wireless signals. The resulting 'Ultra' decrypts became known as ISK (Intelligence Service Knox), after the cryptographer Dillwyn Knox.[32] By May 1945 Bletchley had circulated 140,869 ISK messages plus 98,710 ISOS and 12,954 from the Security Service of the Nazi Party,[33] whose traffic was known as ISOSICLE. Besides ISOS, ISK and ISOSICLE, smaller quantities of other German secret intelligence decrypts were also sent to the relevant Bletchley Park customers. By May 1945 the Admiralty had received the remarkable total of 271,118 German intelligence messages.[34]

The value of this material was well understood in MI5. B Division of MI5 was headed from 1940 by Guy Liddell, who kept a very detailed diary of his work, with occasional comments on Trevor-Roper and other intelligence personalities. Liddell had much experience of tracking hostile intelligence services and appreciated the astonishing advantage in the secret war won by British code-breakers. In June 1941 he had commented that the hand-cipher ISOS 'material was pure gold and everything should be done to develop it 100%'. According to Liddell, it was 'necessary for all those concerned in its production to increase their staffs'.[35]

As Trevor-Roper's work was intimately concerned with the production of ISOS, during the following year he recruited three new officers. In building his team he turned to his old college, Christ Church Oxford, to which he had a profound attachment. He wrote in his memoirs that everything about Christ Church was 'grand and spacious [...] It has always been a proud college and its members have tended to look down, with an assumption of effortless superiority, on the lesser colleges of the university. This sense of superiority, of being themselves a natural aristocracy, is an invisible cement.' He would tell Dick White, albeit with a characteristic tinge of self-mockery, that 'although sensible people *can* be found who have come from other colleges, I would not take their sense on trust, whereas it is my settled conviction, or prejudice, that one can be sure of Christ Church men. Indeed, in the hour of battle, I really only feel safe if I have a Christ Church Man on my right and on my left.'[36] Trevor-Roper had asked his mentor J.C. Masterman[37] for a first-class young man exempt from military service. Masterman recommended Charles Stuart,[38] a graduate of the Christ Church History School, because of his 'ice-blue clarity of intellect'. Stuart arrived on 30 July 1941. Trevor-Roper remembered Stuart as 'a splendid colleague: so exact, so retentive of detail: he built up, from scraps of evidence, bit by bit, the whole system whose communications and organisation we were studying, knew all the German spies and their controllers [...] they could never elude his vigilant eye and meticulous card-index'.[39] In September the philosopher Gilbert Ryle, also from Christ Church, was added to the strength. He was a close friend who had stayed with Trevor-Roper's family before the war. Ryle had written to Trevor-Roper that he was bored in the Welsh Guards as he was too old for active service.[40] Ryle was an unlikely recruit to SIS, but proved surprisingly effective. Guy Liddell found him 'energetic and extremely intelligent'.[41] With a Christ Church man already to his right and left, Trevor-Roper felt safe in recruiting someone from All Souls College as the fourth member of his team, and the philosopher Stuart Hampshire[42] arrived in January 1942. Hampshire had won his All Souls fellowship in 1936, when Trevor-Roper himself had been an unsuccessful candidate. Trevor-Roper now rescued him from a frustrating job in Freetown.[43] According to Patrick Reilly,[44] who became personal assistant to Menzies in May 1942, Trevor-Roper and his staff formed 'a team of a brilliance unparalleled anywhere in the intelligence machine'.[45]

From 1941 Trevor-Roper and his Vw staff regularly issued short reports or notes of about four pages in length describing Axis secret wireless in particular geographical areas. Each document was compiled by the Vw member who specialised in that region. Forty-six were produced between 31 August 1941 and 9 April 1943, providing a geography of the wireless stations used by enemy intelligence, complemented by an occasional 'Who's Who' of the Axis spies in individual countries.[46] Vw's product was invaluable but highly sensitive and raised difficult security issues. Such matters were controlled within SIS by Valentine Vivian,[47] director of SIS Security, and Felix Cowgill, the head of Section V. Cowgill in particular wished to restrict the circulation of ISOS to protect their security, but MI5 felt that it needed to see as much as possible of the material in order to build up a detailed picture of its opponent. Vw was thus in a very awkward position, as its working interests clashed with those of its own section. Whereas Cowgill insisted on minimising the passing of information, Trevor-Roper's sub-section needed to share material with Bletchley Park, MI5 and the intelligence staffs of the armed service ministries in order to puzzle out the meaning of the decrypts.[48]

MI5 decided a committee was the best way of increasing its influence over the work of RSS. On 19 May 1941 Malcolm Frost, MI5's wireless expert, told Guy Liddell that he and White 'agreed that it would be most helpful to have an informal committee between S.I.S., R.S.S. and ourselves, so that we can from time to time discuss our mutual problems. I suggest that this should consist of Major Cowgill, Colonel Maltby, Dick White, yourself and myself.' The first meeting of the Joint SIS and Security Service (SS) Wireless Committee took place the following day with Liddell as chairman; Trevor-Roper was appointed secretary to the committee. Those present at the first meeting 'agreed that it was the function of the Committee to coordinate the mutual interests of S.I.S. and the Security Service in the Radio Security Section. It should lay down general directives for the operation of R.S.S. to S.I.S. and the Security Service.'[49]

MI5 quickly identified Trevor-Roper as a valuable but unsettled ally on the committee, who wanted a more liberal discussion of ISOS than his head of section Cowgill would allow. On 5 July Liddell spoke with Herbert Hart,[50] the junior officer in his counter-espionage division who initially received the ISOS sent to MI5. Liddell noted that Hart thought 'if Trevor-Roper goes a great deal will be missed. Hart is quite convinced that Trevor-Roper is right and Felix [Cowgill] wrong.'[51] The issues between the security and intelligence aspects of ISOS were fought out at the meetings of the Wireless Committee. Liddell recorded the rows in his diary. Following the meeting on 25 August he noted, 'We had an R.S.S. meeting at which the question of T.R.[Trevor-Roper]'s notes and their circulation were discussed. These notes are excellent value in explaining the significance of ISOS material. For some reason or other Cowgill does not wish them circulated to the recipie[nts] of ISOS.' Liddell had a long talk with Cowgill after the meeting and urged 'the desirability of a very free interchange of information. Cowgill said that he had always been brought up never to pass information [to] anybody unless it was absolutely necessary. I said I thought this was an excellent doctrine but that it all depended on the interpretation of [...] absolutely necessary.'[52]

Liddell found Trevor-Roper almost as intractable as Cowgill. On 1 September Liddell recorded,

Trevor-Roper came to see me. He seems to be very worried by the fact that his work is not given official recognition [...]. The sections in various departments receiving ISOS were [...] ill-informed about its real significance. They could not make a proper study of it unless they considered it in its communications setting [...]. Personally I think that there is much to be said for this suggestion, and were it not for the difficult personality of T-R and his quarrels with Felix the whole matter could have been settled months ago.[53]

Trevor-Roper's basic goal was to ensure the circulation of his team's notes explaining the context of the German spy messages, and this was finally achieved after weeks of wrangling. On 9 September 1941 Liddell commented on another Wireless Committee meeting that:

It was of the usual rather controversial type. It had been arranged some time ago that we should receive a copy of T-R's notes on ISOS, but somehow or other they had never reached us. I asked that the minutes about T-R's notes should be read out and it was quite clear that we should have had them. They had been sent to Section V and had apparently stuck. We are now to get them. Strachey of G.C. and C.S. asked to have them too and stressed their great importance to him in carrying out his work.[54]

By spring 1942 the disputes within British counter-espionage had come to focus on the SIS practice of withholding German spy decrypts to protect the security of its codes or agents. In particular, there was a group of Nazi intelligence intercepts naming British spies which Cowgill instructed Bletchley Park to remove from the flow of ISOS sent to the Security Service and the armed forces. These extracted intercepts, which only went to SIS, were named Intelligence Service British Agents (ISBA). The ISBA series finally amounted to 7,769 messages,[55] which might indeed name SIS agents but could also have information relevant for counter-intelligence or even military operations. Then in March 1942 Hart of MI5 received a list of numbered ISOS on which he noticed messages he had never received. He told White, who reported to Guy Liddell that the messages,

apparently through some typist's error disclose the existence of a series of ISOS messages, known as ISBA, of which we have no knowledge. Upon receipt of this Hart rang up [Kim] Philby[56] and asked for an explanation. He was informed that such messages concern the security of British agents abroad and were therefore not put into general circulation.[57]

Yet ISBA included messages relating to British double agents whose case officers were usually from MI5. These officers were particularly indignant over being excluded from receiving ISBA, as they lacked some information about German intentions which they needed to instruct their agents. Liddell complained to Vivian, who responded by authorising Liddell and White to receive ISBA.[58]

Trevor-Roper himself later suggested that it was not through any typist's error that ISBA came to light, but rather through his own intervention. He strongly believed that if the discussion of ISOS was limited too narrowly by security, less intelligence value would be drawn from the evidence. The best method of understanding the spy messages was by discussing them with other intelligence staffs which could see them from a different institutional perspective. He felt that it was absurd to lock up intelligence within SIS. Isolated items of information had only limited value: the intelligence premium came when such fragments were put together to build a complete picture.[59] Trevor-Roper later wrote:

My recollection of the discovery of Cowgill's silent suppression of ISBA is this. The first evidence came to me by accident, through a misdirection of documents which presented me with a set of ISBA messages with a very restricted distribution list on which MI5 and the Service departments did not feature. I checked the serial numbers and satisfied myself that these were ISOS and ISK messages secretly subtracted from the circulated series. I then telephoned Herbert Hart at MI5, who exploded. After that, I left the fat simmering merrily in the fire, leaving MI5 and the Service Departments to put the heat on C. As I was a member of MI6, I thought it prudent to keep out of the battle.[60]

In the aftermath 'we regularly used the verb "to isba", meaning to try to deprive someone of legitimate information.'[61] Trevor-Roper's account of the genesis of the ISBA row is thoroughly credible. Dick White had thoughtfully invented the typist's error in order to provide cover for his friend, who needed it, as Trevor-Roper was sometimes too careless in expressing his disenchantment with the secret service. He repeatedly felt at the end of his tether and later wrote that he would have 'gone mad' during his time with SIS but for the release he found in fox-hunting.[62]

By early 1942 Trevor-Roper was trying to change jobs. On 22 February he wrote from the Savile Club to an Oxford friend, Lord Cherwell,[63] now Churchill's assistant and statistician, to seek help in finding a new position. Trevor-Roper told Cherwell that he and Gill had built up a system for intercepting the wireless traffic of German intelligence. Although 'the system, as we founded it, is getting, by the methods we devised, over 5000 messages a week [...] this new world of intelligence has now been pirated by the British Secret Service, and I have told you, roughly, the mess they have made of it.' Trevor-Roper complained that 'my position is purely advisory to a technical department which, under the control of gramophone-salesmen and others from the commercial world, generally prefers not to take advice.' Indeed 'the technical service which has pirated our methods is absolute controller of its own policy and has no responsibility towards Intelligence for its results.' Trevor-Roper had demanded that the intelligence heads recognise the defects of technical policy, but in reply was told that he ought to consider resigning.[64]

Trevor-Roper was regarded with suspicion by his superiors within SIS; they felt that he was talking about the business of a secret department to outsiders and stirring up trouble. On 15 April he wrote to Cherwell:

> The storm has broken over my head; but on looking round after it, I find that the damage is slight, and in some places the air is clearer & the countryside more refreshed. I was summoned by Menzies yesterday and accused of having supplied facts to Gill which he had supplied to you and you to Swinton. I am not sacked – indeed I seem to have disconcerted Menzies & Vivian by my lack of contrition; and I told them plainly that I [...] regarded the secrecy of the Secret Service as being a protection for its work, not a cloak for its scandals. The session lasted three hours, & I agreed to apologise to Gambier Parry, on the understanding that this did not involve a withdrawal of my statements; and Menzies has agreed to receive from me a proposal in respect of the organisation concerned (which I had previously been forbidden to submit).[65]

Trevor-Roper's views on the reorganisation necessary were summarised in a document entitled 'Interception and Intercepted Intelligence' which he enclosed in a letter to Cherwell on 10 May. This proposed not only the central direction of all organisations providing intelligence from Abwehr intercepts, but also 'greater co-ordination of all the specialist processes of research, whose relation to each other should be that of cogs engaging each to drive a machine for a definite purpose, rather than (as at present) that of disengaged wheels revolving in their own orbits'. Finally Trevor-Roper requested an office dedicated to the coordination of intelligence about the Abwehr and its intensive study.[66] Although his proposal fell on deaf ears at this stage, its emphasis on centralisation, the coordination of research and the specialist study of the German opponent were all themes which recurred in his later writing on the organisation of British intelligence.

Not content with fighting the chiefs of SIS, Trevor-Roper was also at loggerheads with the leaders of Bletchley Park. The Admiralty had requested RSS to research Italian secret radio. By late March 1942 RSS had discovered a substantial network of Italian wireless stations based on Rome which was named Group 8. Trevor-Roper wanted to visit Bletchley to research Group 8, but his entry was barred by Commander Edward Travis, Bletchley's new operational head.[67] On 21 April Travis wrote explaining his action to Menzies, who was director of the Government Code and Cypher School as well as Chief of SIS: 'Captain Trevor-Roper either suffers from delusions or has deliberately attempted to mislead you [...] he is not a suitable person to whom I should give, so far as I can see for no reason, the run of Huts 3 and 4.' As a compromise, Menzies suggested that Ryle might perform any necessary liaison. Trevor-Roper replied in a letter which swept this suggestion imperiously aside. He pointed out that Ryle was a specialist on the Abwehr in the Middle East:

My liaison is [...] wanted in connexion with Italian secret naval working which has been identified as a result of my liaison in the past, and on which further important work is being held up until that liaison can be resumed. Quite apart from this it is clear that the unstated objections to my liaison with the Naval Hut [Hut 4] are personal, not departmental, and [...] originate from Commander Travis; and since Lieut. Ryle is unwilling to accept a position based on such personal discrimination, I am disinclined to impose it upon him [...] if Commander Travis has made allegations [...] I hope I may be allowed the usual privilege of being made acquainted with them and answering them.

Menzies passed on Trevor-Roper's letter to Travis, describing its author as a 'tricky legal worded young Oxford don'. Travis showed the offending document to his deputy, Nigel de Grey,[68] who commented that 'his own master [Menzies] does not seem to be able to control him. How then can we confide our secrets to him? Anyhow if Ryle is given them he [will] only hand them on to TR [...] TR seems unable to speak the truth even by accident.'[69]

Just when the leaders of Bletchley Park were denouncing Trevor-Roper for his attempts to achieve direct contact, one of their junior officers composed a document which graphically explained why such liaison was necessary. Early in 1942 Peter Twinn had taken over the ISK section working on Abwehr Enigma. On 4 May 1942 he wrote almost plaintively to Travis about the problems caused by working in isolation:

> I wonder if you could arrange some form of liaison between us and Glen Almond [Section V] and possibly any other people who are interested in our results. During the four months I have been in this section, I have had no communication of any kind from outside B.P. and, in consequence, I am quite in the dark as to the relative importance of the various lines which we break [...] I feel that it would be much easier to decide questions of priority and to decide which lines of research to follow up first, if I were told which traffic provides the most important intelligence and which of the unbroken traffic is most likely to be of interest.[70]

Twinn's memo vividly highlighted the problems caused by over-emphasising security at the expense of intelligence.

Although Trevor-Roper's row with Travis simmered down and he was allowed back into Bletchley, Menzies did try to bring his turbulent expert on Axis wireless under tighter control. After visiting Trevor-Roper's section at Barnet on 8 October 1942, Wing-Commander Peter Koch de Gooreynd[71] of Menzies' secretariat recommended a restructuring. In consequence, Trevor-Roper's sub-section (Vw) was now completely integrated into Section V. Charles Stuart would later recall:

> The principle behind this was allegedly to put an end to Trevor-Roper's anomalous position of owing obedience to both Cowgill and Maltby (while obeying neither) and to improve the co-operation [within Section V] [...] Hitherto we had been paid at normal army rates [...] paying full income tax. Now we were introduced to the lush pastures of S.I.S.'s pay system; each month it rained fivers (I now received £40 a month tax free),

save for Gilbert who was forgotten altogether but who was subsequently remembered thanks to T-R and eventually stumped off to his billet one pay-day with fivers sticking out of every pocket.[72]

The shower of five-pound notes could not induce Trevor-Roper to obey Cowgill. He openly defied his boss at the Wireless Committee. At its 38th meeting, on 5 December 1942, Cowgill, with Maltby's support, argued in favour of a proposal from Valentine Vivian that the committee should vote for its own dissolution. Dick White disagreed: 'this committee supplies a body of people all intimately concerned with the current problems connected with ISOS and ISK traffic; it provides opportunities for the general pooling of such material from which valuable discussions and decisions emerge.' Trevor-Roper sided with White, commenting that 'the processes of ISOS interception, cryptography, editing, interpretation, etc. were so interdependent that satisfactory decisions could not in fact be obtained by individual *ad hoc* liaison; they required the simultaneous liaison of representatives of all parties, and such liaison was best guaranteed by the periodical meetings of this Committee.' Trevor-Roper argued convincingly against his boss and then voted against him, as did six of the eight present. It was a humiliating defeat for Cowgill, who took out his resentment on Herbert Hart. Trevor-Roper's minutes noted that 'Lieut. Col. Cowgill wished it to be recorded that he did not believe Mr. Hart's views to be relevant, or that Mr. Hart had a right to vote, not being an original member.'[73]

This meeting was so turbulent even by the standards of the Wireless Committee that in the aftermath Liddell went to Broadway Buildings to defuse the situation. He had an informal talk with Menzies and told him that he hoped the committee would be allowed to continue, indeed that its terms would be extended to cover discussion of the intelligence content of ISOS, very much Trevor-Roper's preferred approach. Liddell noted that Menzies 'seemed to be in agreement and expressed a wish that his personal representative Wing Commander de Goureynd [sic] should be allowed to attend the next meeting as an observer'.[74] Menzies reassured Liddell that 'as a result of our deliberations a whole number of facts had been brought to his notice for which he was very grateful.' Next Liddell saw Vivian about Trevor-Roper. Cowgill had been stoking up the deputy chief against the rebellious wireless officer, and Vivian suggested replacing him as secretary of the committee. But Liddell told Vivian:

if his idea was to get rid of T-R he was making a great mistake. I thoroughly realise that in some ways T-R was a trouble[some] person. At the same time I liked him and had a high opinion of his ability. I thought that he had been badly mishandled. Had his views, many of which were obviously right, been given more sympathetic consideration, many difficulties might have been avoided. Viv. had two alternatives, one to get rid of him altogether, and the other to retain his services and give him freedom of action. To kick him off the [Wireless] committee was no way out of the difficulty and would be highly detrimental to our discussions to which he contributed almost more than anyone.[75]

After Liddell's visit, Menzies gave the subject of the Wireless Committee a good deal of thought and decided that Vivian and Cowgill were mistaken. Vivian had to climb down in a letter to Liddell of 24 December 1942 in which he admitted that Menzies considered 'it is desirable that the officers concerned with ISOS-ISK, from the technical, cryptographical and intelligence aspects, should be able to meet regularly to discuss questions arising out of their work and to make any recommendations which they think will improve the development and use of this traffic.' Even more painfully, Vivian had to tell Liddell that Menzies wished Trevor-Roper to become a full member of the committee, representing Section Vw of SIS, so that a new secretary would be desirable. Liddell replied that 'the expert knowledge of the present Secretary has proved a valuable contribution to our discussions. If he is to become a full member [...] the best alternative choice to my mind in the interest of the work would be Ryle, who has all the necessary qualifications.' Vivian wanted a new chairman, so Liddell suggested de Gooreynd, 'who appears to be in every way suitable, or failing him Dick White'. Vivian replied that 'C.S.S. very much regrets that he cannot spare de Goureynd [sic] for the Chairmanship, which would inevitably take up a lot of his time. He would welcome Dick White's appointment.' SIS agreed to Ryle becoming committee secretary.[76]

On 3 February 1943 Menzies visited Barnet to see the Radio Security Service and Trevor-Roper's team: Charles Stuart entered '"C" 2.30' in his diary and underlined it twice.[77] The same month Menzies agreed with Petrie to reconstitute the Wireless Committee into a 'Radio Security Intelligence Conference'. In addition to the old remit of deciding priorities of interception for RSS, the new conference acquired formal intelligence and advisory roles. It was 'to discuss and if necessary make recommendations upon any problem, whether of a technical, cryptographic or intelligence nature, arising out of [...] material intercepted by R.S.S.' and 'to consider and make recommendations upon any matter concerning the material intercepted by R.S.S. which may be referred to the Committee by higher authorities'.[78] Cowgill's attempt through Vivian to close down the Wireless Committee had completely backfired. Instead, the committee's remit had been extended so that it could now make recommendations on intelligence. Menzies had been drawn into the rumpus, judged the matter on its merits and sided with MI5 and Trevor-Roper.

Although eventually victorious, Trevor-Roper had found this Wireless Committee wrangle so depressing that in December 1942 he once again appealed to Lord Cherwell:

> I am looking round for a job; have you any suggestions? I think as much as can be done in my present position has been done, and a much greater amount that ought to be done will never be done, since no radical change can be expected in a department protected by so much secrecy and mumbo-jumbo. If you think there is any position I could usefully fill, I think I could bring with me two first-rate assistants,[79] which I dare say is something in this time of man-power shortage. I should like, if that were possible, a political rather than a military, and a freelance rather than a departmental position, and would be ready to go abroad. I can give plenty of references from this world if wanted – but you know Denys Page[80] and Masterman, both of whom are familiar with my work. J.C. [Masterman] might say, as he has said before, that it is important that I should stay where I am and hope for a changed policy, but I think I can judge as well as he can whether such a change is obtainable. Are there any prospects in the anti-submarine world?[81]

Cherwell promised to do anything he could to help Trevor-Roper,[82] but nothing materialised. Trevor-Roper stayed in the secret service, and his fortunes began to improve. In early 1943 growing recognition of his work brought an invitation to attend a monthly committee which met in the War Cabinet offices of the London Controlling Section for strategic deception. The aim of the committee was to identify the probable enemy appreciation of Allied intentions for the benefit of deception staffs. It was to puzzle out what the Germans thought the Allies were planning, so the Nazi regime could be misled by deceits they would swallow with a ready appetite. Trevor-Roper's participation gave him an invaluable monthly overview of Nazi strategy and Allied deception policy.[83]

Despite the expansion of his interests, Trevor-Roper was not distracted from his routine work, where he showed a formidable grasp of detail. His approach is nicely illustrated by work on decrypts relating to German and Italian espionage in southern Africa. Paying particular attention to the chronology of events, he tracked items of information from the two principal German agents as they were incorporated first into the German and then the Italian reports. This sequence clearly established the dependence of the Italians on their allies. His scrutiny also identified a crucial mistranslation in one decrypt. The document reported that the most active German agent in the Union of South Africa contemplated sending intelligence about the movement of ships directly to submarines. 'This', read the translation, 'will in all circumstances be done.' If so, the news was alarming. In fact, as Trevor-Roper suggested, the agent had merely proposed to send intelligence to submarines, and the crucial phrase really meant: 'in all circumstances the work will go on.' In other words, the agent was only making a general promise to keep going rather than a specific commitment to provide submarines with intelligence directly. Trevor-Roper concluded that German intelligence was not providing much assistance to Axis submarines off southern Africa, a matter of particular interest to the Admiralty and Foreign Office, which both received his memorandum of 16 March 1943.[84]

The Admiralty and Foreign Office were among the most important clients of SIS, and indeed the very same month another influential client, the Security Service, gave Trevor-Roper some quite remarkable support. Although Trevor-Roper's spirited independence was a thorn in Cowgill's side, his determination to promote cooperation with the other departments of British intelligence greatly impressed MI5 and in particular Dick White. Trevor-Roper's intelligence work during the war won over the patron who would shape his career more than anyone else. From early 1943 White chaired the weekly meetings of the new Radio Security Intelligence Conference. As before, Trevor-Roper was one of the main contributors.[85]

White not only perceived Trevor-Roper's outstanding ability but was determined that others should know about it as well. On 14 March 1943 White told Liddell,

I can think of no single officer, either in M.I.5 or M.I.6 who possesses a more comprehensive knowledge of the Abwehr organisation, particularly on its communications side, than Capt. Trevor-Roper [...] I discussed with Col. Dudley Clarke [the controller of deception policy in the Middle East] ideas put forward in a recent paper by Capt. Trevor-Roper [...] He expressed the greatest interest in them and specifically said that help of that kind was of the greatest importance to him.

White urged Liddell to ask Menzies to send Trevor-Roper to the Middle East for three months so that he could 'introduce a wider perspective into the otherwise somewhat parochial outlook of Counter Espionage workers in the Middle East'. As there was no representative of Vw in the region, those concerned with Abwehr communications 'should reap a very considerable advantage from working with Capt. Trevor Roper'.[86]

Guy Liddell took up White's suggestion and wrote to Menzies on 22 March 1943. He included much of White's enthusiastic document verbatim and suggested that 'a representative of Section V.w., preferably Captain Trevor Roper himself, would be a great asset at least for a short period to all the various C.E. workers in the Middle East.' Trevor-Roper was to assist the MI5 staff and other counter-intelligence personnel in the region. Menzies had been forced to swallow much criticism from MI5 during the previous year. It made a most welcome change for a very senior officer in the Security Service to praise one of Menzies' staff to the skies and ask for him to be sent to assist all the counter-espionage officers in the Middle East. Menzies was on good terms with Liddell and could hardly fail to be impressed by his high opinion of Trevor-Roper, though in the event the latter did not visit the Middle East until early the following year.[87]

Trevor-Roper's rise had now become irresistible. The Security Service was urging Menzies to strengthen RSS because of its analytical contribution. Trevor-Roper had acquired an influential ally at court in the form of Patrick Reilly, who recalled in 1993 that he had briefed Menzies, 'giving him a much more fair account than he had from Cowgill and Vivian'. As a result, Menzies had enhanced Trevor-Roper's position within SIS. In May 1943 Menzies decided that in future Trevor-Roper would no longer be subordinate to Cowgill but would come under C's own control. On 13 May Trevor-Roper's unit was removed from Section V and established as the Radio Intelligence Service (RIS), which was responsible via Koch de Gooreynd and Reilly directly to Menzies. The same day Koch de Gooreynd and Reilly visited RIS at Barnet to launch the new section.[88]

Trevor-Roper's new autonomy was clearly illustrated when he attempted, admittedly in vain, to arrange for the sharing of radio intelligence on German spies with the Soviet Union. In June 1943 SIS posted Lieutenant Cecil Barclay as an avowed representative to the British Military Mission in Moscow to improve the exchange of information with the Soviets. In particular he was to discuss operations conducted by the Abwehr behind Soviet lines and urge improvements in the Russian use of ciphers.[89] Later that summer RSS located German agents transmitting from Russian territory. Trevor-Roper promptly sent a telegram to Barclay: 'R.S.S. have identified several new transmissions from Russia to Stations in German occupied territory [...] Traffic is not read here but WTI [Wireless Telegraphy Intelligence] indicates that it is from German controlled Russian speaking agents behind Russian lines [...] does this fit in with anything known to the Russians.'[90]

This telegram caused a bigger stir in London than in Moscow, drawing the attention of Gambier-Parry, Maltby, Cowgill and Koch de Gooreynd. Maltby wrote to Cowgill that,

> Gambier decided that it was best not to take any action (against Trevor-Roper) at the moment. You of course may not concur in this but it does seem to me that nothing but good can have come from passing this information on in view of the extent to which 'Y' information is, I believe, now to be exchanged with the Russians, although you must realise that I have no first hand knowledge of policy in this connection.

Cowgill replied to Maltby by pointing out that 'I am not much concerned with the rights and wrongs of giving this information to the Russians. What I am concerned about is whether, as a matter of principle, it is right for R.S.S. to send such telegrams without reference to you or me.'[91]

Maltby now approached Koch de Gooreynd, who replied in a note,

> I spoke to PA/CSS [Reilly] who told me that when RSS asked him if it was in order to send out attached CXG49 [the offending telegram] he told Trevor Roper that as long as he did it in conjunction with RSS & asked [Section] V he saw nothing against it. TR is away as you know for the moment but it looks as though he did not ask Sec[tion] V: as he was told to do by Reilly. However he will be asked when he returns.

Maltby passed on Gooreynd's note to Cowgill with the comment,

This is personal and private and, for the present, off the record, although we can very soon put it on the record it it seems advisable [...] Undoubtedly T-R consulted R.S.S. who were only concerned with the facts of the matter, but it now looks as if he altogether omitted to consult you, whose approval he was told was essential. T-R will be tackled on the matter on his return from leave, but I should be grateful if you would make quite sure that he did not consult any of your heads of sub-sections, or take any other action which might be construed as obtaining V approval. Let us be absolutely sure of the position for a start and we can then discuss action when we next meet – I will give you a ring.

Cowgill replied, 'Neither V/PA [his assistant] nor I nor anyone in the appropriate geographical subsection was aware that this telegram was in the wind. None of us were consulted before it was dispatched.'[92] Yet, despite their best efforts to undermine Trevor-Roper, Maltby and Cowgill's petty campaign fizzled out. Trevor-Roper had now eluded their grasp and could act without consulting Cowgill at all and get away with it. It seems that nothing came of his attempt to share intelligence with the Soviets, though Barclay himself was given some captured Nazi code-books in November 1944.[93]

Trevor-Roper's enhanced status meant that in June 1943 he could finally issue, as 'Radio Intelligence Service 1', a paper on 'Canaris and Himmler'. Although Stuart Hampshire was the original author, Trevor-Roper endorsed his conclusions. Philby had previously blocked circulation of this document and even now he watered it down before it was sent out. In the paper Hampshire explored the relations between Canaris's Abwehr and Himmler's Sicherheitsdienst (SD) or Security Service. Hampshire wrote that because the SD had become active in counter-espionage and sabotage, the Abwehr was concentrating increasingly on an indispensable function where the SD could not compete, namely the supply of operational intelligence to the Wehrmacht:

The keystone of the Abwehr reporting-system is the observation of ships and aircraft in the Straits of Gibraltar...this explains the extraordinary importance which Canaris attaches to his relations with highly-placed Spaniards [...] It is Canaris' policy to concentrate Abwehr resources on supplying immediate operational information for Commanders in the field; it is by his success or failure in this that he will be judged; his Spanish contacts are his main support.[94]

Hampshire argued, 'In our sources, the subordination of the Abwehr in counter-espionage has been most evident in Norway; there has been a steady increase in the instances of the S.D. taking over cases from the Abwehr.' However, 'the outstanding encroachment is in the sphere of sabotage and subversive activity of all kinds. The sabotage and insurrection department of the Abwehr, Abteilung II, has been remarkably unsuccessful, and we have abundant evidence of its incompetence in Western Europe; Canaris seems to have little interest in its work.' Meanwhile, the SD had become 'the active promoter of sabotage and insurrection'. In political intelligence the SD also had the upper hand, as Himmler took a personal interest in its reports and passed significant material directly to Hitler: 'This easy access to Hitler is a source of great strength to the S.D. [...] [by contrast] We know of only one recent instance of a report from Canaris being passed to Hitler.'[95]

L.R. Palmer[96] of Bletchley Park vigorously challenged the RIS conclusions. He denied both that there had been any basic change in the Abwehr's operations, and that it was now concentrating on operational intelligence. Canaris's visits to Madrid, maintained Palmer, were an old habit, not because he was nervous of Himmler. Palmer also contradicted the RIS conclusion that Canaris had little interest in sabotage and insurrection, claiming there was 'Strong Abwehr interest in this section of its work' and Canaris had protested against SD subversion in North Africa. As far as counter-espionage was concerned, Palmer wrote that there was 'copious evidence of close collaboration' between the Abwehr and the SD, which acted as the Abwehr's executive. Palmer disputed the Norwegian evidence and claimed that Abwehr counter-espionage was 'functioning quite normally'.[97]

Although Palmer disagreed with RIS, such discussion between experts over the meaning of intercepts was exactly what Trevor-Roper wanted. Multilateral appraisal was the best way of extracting the maximum from the sources. So his reply was conciliatory: 'There is certainly room for another view of the evidence, and I found Palmer's document very useful. The R.I.S. paper is certainly, as I have explained, the most speculative we have issued, and it was for this reason that I asked you to emphasise the tentative nature of its conclusions.' Nevertheless, Trevor-Roper pointed out, 'our material supports the view [...] that Canaris is interested mainly in operational intelligence.

It is noticeable that Canaris, in his frequent journeys, only visits the Abt.I [Intelligence] offices; I don't think he has ever honoured Abt.II [Sabotage] or III [Counter-Espionage] with a personal inspection on his numerous tours.'[98]

Guy Liddell was much impressed by the RIS document and noted that 'T-R has written an extremely interesting memo on the struggle between the Abwehr and the SD. Himmler is gradually muscling in on Canaris's preserves.'[99] Trevor-Roper and his team were right to identify power struggles within German intelligence. Although the Abwehr and SD sometimes cooperated effectively in the field, relations at the senior level in Germany were increasingly marked by suspicion. Indeed, RIS sensed structural changes which were already taking place within Germany. At a meeting on 18 May 1942 the Abwehr had been forced to concede that henceforth political espionage abroad would be exclusively a matter for the SD. Indeed, in future the SD would even carry out counter-espionage. Canaris was weakened by Gestapo suspicion of his deputy Colonel Hans Oster, who led a group of Abwehr officers actively conspiring to overthrow the Nazi regime. After the Gestapo arrested three of Oster's closest collaborators in early April 1943, Canaris dismissed his deputy. The Abwehr had failed to forecast the Allied landings in North Africa in late 1942; it failed again over the invasion of Sicily in July 1943. Canaris's special influence in Spain had dissipated in the face of Allied victories by the end of 1943 and he could no longer facilitate German espionage there. The final straw came with the defection of three Abwehr members in Turkey to the British on 10 February 1944. The next day Hitler commissioned Himmler to take over the Abwehr and commanded him to create a unified German intelligence service. Canaris was suspended. At the end of February 1944 he was removed as Abwehr chief.[100]

In March 1944 an SIS agent in Stockholm reported 'a definite revolutionary atmosphere among the [German] Generals'.[101] A wide range of Abwehr officers were involved in the military plot to overthrow Hitler which came to a head in the failed assassination attempt of 20 July 1944. Afterwards RIS commented caustically that Department 2 of the Abwehr 'has not an impressive record in pure sabotage; it is not surprising that Stauffenberg's bomb destroyed Hitler's trousers but not his person if, as has been suggested, it was supplied by Freytag von Loringhoven, head of Abteilung II; it is fitting that Abteilung II's last and most glorious exploit should be a near-miss.'[102] The RIS conclusion that Canaris and the Abwehr were incompetent found a strong echo in Trevor-Roper's later publications.

In late 1944 the whole intelligence struggle took on a new dimension as the Allied armies captured increasing numbers of Nazi intelligence officers and it became possible to search for others in territory lost by the Wehrmacht. To cope with these new opportunities it was decided to set up a War Room of Allied Counter-Intelligence in London. Also known as the German War Room, this was to be a centre for collating incoming material on the German secret service and initiating further action. It would provide expert advice on the organisation, operations and personalities of Nazi intelligence to counter-intelligence officers with Allied armies in the field. As MI5 realised, the great advantage of the arrangement was 'that information from all sources would for the first time be effectively brought together'.[103]

There was much discussion within Allied intelligence over who should head the German War Room. Dick White, perhaps the most obvious choice, was unavailable because he was working at General Eisenhower's headquarters, where he was considered indispensable. Trevor-Roper told Liddell that nominal control should go to Menzies because he was responsible for the security of ISK, but that someone from MI5 should be put in charge of the actual work. Liddell noted in his diary that 'T-R wants to exclude Felix and takes the view that SIS must control the secret sources.' In a discussion recorded by Liddell, senior MI5 staff agreed that 'Tim' Milne[104] 'quite definitely we did not think was a big enough weight. As regards Dick [White] we were quite certain that he should remain at SHAEF[105] for the time being. To remove him would merely be pulling down one house to build another.' Menzies himself wanted an acquaintance from White's, whom he had occasionally seen at the Joint Intelligence Sub-Committee (JIC), but admitted to Liddell that 'Tar' Robertson of MI5 might be very good. 'Tar' was confirmed as head at a meeting of senior Allied intelligence officers on 15 January 1945.[106]

Robertson directed the German War Room from 1 March 1945. It included a publications section, though its reports on German intelligence were classified secret and circulated only to relevant officers within Allied intelligence, whose attention was drawn to particular gaps in Allied knowledge and the methods by which they might be filled. The section comprised three officers brought in from SIS, namely Trevor-Roper, Hampshire and Stuart. The publications section had access to all the information which came into the War Room, such as decrypts, captured documents and prisoner-of-war interrogations.[107]

Such a concentration of evidence was something Trevor-Roper had long wanted. All the same, he had nearly been excluded from this promised land until Menzies intervened. On 5 February 1945 Liddell recorded in his diary that 'Tar' Robertson had seen Menzies and,

> it has been agreed that T-R shall run the research side of things. TAR had been doubtf[ul] about employing him as there had been so much opposition from Section V officers. C [Menzies] with whom I discussed the point said that if there was any difficulty with Section V he would deal with it. He said that he had always backed T-R and that it would be a great mistake to leave him out of the organisation.[108]

The attempt to keep Trevor-Roper out of the War Room may have been Cowgill's parting shot before he left SIS in the second week of February 1945. More than 40 years later Trevor-Roper denied reciprocating Cowgill's

> petty private resentment. My complaints against Cowgill were not of this kind, and so far from feeling any resentment against him, I have always, ever since I was emancipated from his oppressive control, felt rather warmly towards him. I always regarded him as a fundamentally honest & hard-working man [...] who was unfortunately placed in a job for which his background, his character and his very virtues disqualified him.[109]

After Cowgill's departure, Trevor-Roper entered the most productive period of his intelligence career. War Room staff advised those questioning captured German intelligence officers and also took part in interrogations themselves, giving Trevor-Roper opportunities to develop his interrogation skills and his knowledge of the German opponent.[110] During the summer of 1945 he summarised his conclusions about the enemy's secret service in his most significant wartime paper, which he entitled 'The German Intelligence Service and the War'. At the height of his expertise on the subject, his report not only examined the successes and failures of German espionage but also explored their wider significance for the use of intelligence.[111] The document reflected the themes and evidence of previous Vw and RIS reports and so drew on the research of Trevor-Roper's immediate colleagues as well as his own. Although Trevor-Roper later ironically attributed the authorship to Charles Stuart, in more serious vein he made it clear that it was his report. He noted,

I was then expecting to be demobilised [...] in September 1945, so it was, in effect, my testament, or *relazione*, on terminating my war service [...] When I wrote it I was not unaware that some of my criticisms of the German Secret Intelligence Service might equally apply to our own. [I] never heard of any reaction to it. It dropped, as far as I knew, into a bottomless pit of oblivion.[112]

In his valedictory paper Trevor-Roper argued that German intelligence was 'successful in its own territory and a complete failure in Allied territory'. The Abwehr was active not only in espionage abroad, but also in counter-intelligence, sabotage and subversion. Trevor-Roper wrote that its principal successes in sabotage and subversion had been achieved in Yugoslavia in spring 1941:

by penetrating and controlling various dissident or wavering groups, the Abwehr succeeded in sabotaging the mobilisation of the Yugoslav forces, and in preventing the demolition of bridges, etc. to an extent which materially assisted the advance of the German armies, and which affords a strong contrast to the ineffectiveness of its operations in the same area when the German armies were in retreat.[113]

The paper argued that Department 3, which handled counter-espionage, 'was the most consistently successful of Abwehr departments, although it is not always easy to distinguish between its operations and those of the Gestapo'. After the German conquest of France and the Low Countries, Department 3,

was able to penetrate the local resistance movements, and, through them, the Allied agencies which relied on them. The penetration of the Dutch resistance movement in 1944, after the Allies had already landed successfully in France, shows that [Department 3] continued to act with vigour and success, later than any other Abwehr department. It is interesting to note that, in the various purges to which the Abwehr was subjected in 1942–44, [Department 3] alone kept its personnel and constitutions almost intact – a strong argument that its efficiency was admitted.[114]

By contrast, Trevor-Roper considered that Department 1 of the Abwehr, which provided positive intelligence, was throughout the war the most unsuccessful of Abwehr departments, and this was in a very large measure due to the character of Canaris himself, although there are also independent reasons for its failure, inherent in the work itself. It was in positive espionage that Canaris took most personal interest (he showed little interest in the other departments of the Abwehr) [...] Canaris interested himself personally in naval espionage; and it was the naval section [...] which (though it had one significant success) enjoyed in general, the most consistent record of inefficiency and corruption. The explanation is, to a large extent, that Canaris was firstly, a bad judge of men and secondly, himself a professional intrigant rather than an organiser. In consequence of the first fault, he chose worthless officers; and in consequence of the second, he gave them practical independence [...] The Abwehr was filled, in its higher ranks, with personal friends and dependents of Canaris, and they were (in general) idle and corrupt [...] The Abwehr was thus a loose and irresponsible collection of worthless characters whom Canaris refused to dismiss. Instead of organisation, Canaris relied on personal astuteness. This saved himself longer than some of his officers, but not much longer.[115]

Despite all its shortcomings, Abwehr espionage did achieve some conspicuous success in Spain. Trevor-Roper explained,

Canaris enjoyed a highly privileged position in Spain and Spanish Morocco, and this privilege embraced the Abwehr also, not as the Abwehr, but as Admiral Canaris' personal bureau [...] an elaborate and successful system of reporting the passages of British warships through the Straits of Gibraltar was perfected with Spanish assistance. This [...] was the most successful undertaking carried out by [Department 1] [...] it was a personal success for Canaris. The German naval and air authorities are unanimous in regarding it as the most important contribution made by the Abwehr to the conduct of the war.[116]

Although the Abwehr was successful under favourable circumstances on Spanish territory, it failed to forecast accurately the Allied invasions of 1942–4, the occasions above all others when the German armed forces really needed good and timely material. Instead, the Abwehr drowned the High Command of the Wehrmacht 'with mis-information, sometimes invented, and often deliberately supplied by the Allies'. Trevor-Roper wrote that the Abwehr:

sent its reports on to service departments for evaluation; but these service departments lacked the means of discriminating between Abwehr reports. This lack of centralised evaluation, on the basis both of the quality of the source and the quality of the material, was harmful in both directions. This lack of centralisation was not particular to the Abwehr; it obtained throughout the German intelligence world.[117]

Trevor-Roper saw the lack of centralisation in German intelligence as:

one aspect of a phenomenon which was of much wider relevance in Nazi Germany. For although in theory the structure of the administration was 'pyramidal' and centralised, in fact the apex of the pyramid, or the centre of the circle, was not a unitary structure at all but a vortex of competing personal ambitions. Thus all German politicians of consequence sought to set up their own information bureaus (just as they sought to establish private armies) as additional supports for their political authority; and it was essential to the purpose of these bureaus that their results should be the private property of their chiefs, and not pooled at an administrative level [...] Cryptography, the surest and most vital of all sources of intelligence, was dissipated among [...] various offices [...] This system led, not only to the stagnation of intelligence in private pools, but also (as was inevitable in a subject so dependent on central research as cryptography), to technical inefficiency.[118]

Trevor-Roper believed that the general failure of German intelligence 'was not solely due to the effectiveness of Allied counter-measures based on the central exploitation of special sources [Ultra]'. It also lay in German intelligence methods, which 'were never the subject of informed and objective criticism by a higher authority'. Trevor-Roper drew three main conclusions from examining these methods and their results. First, 'That penetration and deception, properly used, are both more productive and more reliable than the use of individual agents in enemy-occupied territory'; second, 'That such individual agents are not only of very limited value, but can be a positive and serious danger to their employers. This was especially so in the G.I.S. [German Intelligence Service], where the undue credit given to agents unchecked by other sources was the cause of significant strategic errors by the German General Staff [...] Third and last, Trevor-Roper concluded 'that information obtained from secret sources is only comparable in reliability with that obtained from "open" sources when they are centrally evaluated, in conjunction with the results of cryptography.'[119]

Trevor-Roper's document provided a remarkably clear and searching analysis of German intelligence, anticipating comment and analysis he later provided in *The Last Days of Hitler, Admiral Canaris* and *The Philby Affair.* It brought out the principles on which he believed intelligence should be conducted: the need to check secret against open sources; scepticism about human agents on foreign territory; his preference for evidence from code-breaking. More fundamental was his conviction that the study of intelligence material should be centralised and conducted in a critical spirit. For Trevor-Roper it was not the cloak and dagger which decided the struggle between secret services, but intellect. While this was no doubt true, Trevor-Roper was unduly sceptical about traditional agents, perhaps because it was the aspect of SIS work with which he was least familiar. Trevor-Roper was expert on German offensive espionage rather than its more effective British counterpart. Indeed, individual spies could still exert a decisive influence on the international strategic balance, as Trevor-Roper would later himself show in *The Philby Affair*. In that work he would also enunciate a further principle: that the secrecy under which intelligence services worked tended to have a cumulative effect in impairing their focus and that this process was only arrested when some external disaster imposed correction.

The esteem which 'The German Intelligence Service and the War' brought Trevor-Roper among its limited readership had a large consequence; it was thanks to the paper that he was charged with solving an ominous and urgent problem which emerged following the Allied occupation of Germany. Dick White later told Trevor-Roper's wife Xandra that it was because he was so impressed by the document that he had chosen her husband to investigate the fate of Hitler.[120] The chaos and devastation which accompanied the siege of Berlin in April 1945 had made the circumstances of Hitler's death mysterious. Uncertainty would distract the German people from the task of reconstruction. By June Stalin was claiming that the Nazi dictator was still alive, and the Russians accused the British of hiding the Führer and Eva Hitler. It was politically necessary to silence this accusation by solving the mystery of Hitler's end. Dick White, then a brigadier in charge of the Counter-Intelligence Bureau in the British zone of occupation, recalled in 1985 that 'this seemed to me important at the time for the general security and stability of the occupied zones [...] The idea of an enquiry into Hitler's fate was wholly mine.' As White regarded Trevor-Roper as the foremost German expert in British intelligence, he was the obvious person to investigate the problem. Trevor-Roper later recalled the occasion in September 1945 when White sounded him out: 'it was when I was drinking hock with Dick White [...] in Bad Oeynhausen [headquarters of the British 21st Army Group] that my researches were first instituted [...] over the third bottle of hock [...] Dick [...] asked me if I would accept the job, and of course I said yes.'[121]

Before tackling his new mission, Trevor-Roper had to be released from his War Room duties. On 10 September 1945 White wrote to 'Tar' Robertson, mentioning,

> a considerable amount of comment in the Press on the subject of whether or not HITLER is still living [...] the chap who has kept the closest tabs on the matter appears to be Trevor-Roper. I am, therefore, anxious that he should prepare a brief [...] subject to your agreement [...] a job like this, unless it is done now, will never get done and unless it is done by a first-rate chap, won't be worth having [...] it should I think be a work of some considerable historical interest.

This last comment was remarkably prescient. Robertson was initially reluctant, but Trevor-Roper succeeded in winning his permission to undertake White's task.[122]

This new intelligence mission was a great responsibility. How did Trevor-Roper carry it out? His status as a British intelligence officer afforded considerable advantages. He had access to much captured documentation, such as the papers of the Doenitz government, which briefly succeeded that of Hitler. Relevant evidence from British and American interrogations or bugging of prisoners was circulated to the War Room in London or the Counter-Intelligence Bureau in Germany and routinely passed to Trevor-Roper. In contrast to his wartime team work, Trevor-Roper's Hitler mission was a solitary one. In 1985 he recalled,

> There was no 'team' of investigators appointed at a high level in London. I had no assistants at all, but worked entirely as an individual, though I was authorised to give instructions to, and call for documents from, military intelligence, Prisoners-of-War camps, Field Security Police, in both the

British and American Zones. I carried out the investigation personally, on the spot.[123]

Trevor-Roper was able to call on British and American agencies to carry out inquiries or interrogations on his behalf, and so he could deploy an army of research assistants armed with the powers of arrest over the defeated Germans, who were quite at their mercy. Usually the witnesses did not want to be discovered, but if they came to the attention of the Anglo-American occupation forces Trevor-Roper could request the results of their interrogation or question them himself. His major handicap was that the Russians refused to help, a stance which denied him access to a number of important witnesses.[124]

Trevor-Roper successfully located seven witnesses to help him reconstruct what he called the 'dark period' between 22 April, when much of the Nazi elite left Berlin, and 2 May, when the Russians occupied Hitler's bunker. Trevor-Roper treated their evidence with scepticism, as he later explained:

> It is quite impossible to arrive at a complete estimate of events if one begins by accepting any individual statement as accurate throughout. All witnesses in the present case are fallible, as is only to be expected at this distance of time. They are particularly fallible in the matter of dates: they could not possibly be otherwise, living as they did, perpetually underground, not distinguishing night from day, in circumstances of siege and bombardment, and only asked to remember the details at least five months later [...] All the dates which I have given are based on external evidence.[125]

In the report on his inquiry Trevor-Roper conceded that 'the only conclusive evidence that Hitler is dead would be in the discovery, and certain identification, of the body.' However, he concluded that the evidence for Hitler's death was 'positive, circumstantial, consistent and independent. There is no evidence whatever to support any of the theories [...] which presuppose that Hitler is still alive.'[126] There was only one significant error in Trevor-Roper's report. He stated that Eva Braun had married Hitler on 30 April, whereas the wedding took place the previous day. This fact emerged from the discovery of Hitler's wills, marriage certificate and the messengers who had been entrusted with the documents. Trevor-Roper later recalled, 'at the end of November 1945 a document purporting to be Hitler's will was discovered in the coat-lining of a suspect [Heinz Lorenz] detained by the British authorities at Hanover and I was asked to return to Germany and investigate this matter too.'[127]

Lorenz was carrying Hitler's personal and political testaments. He had been a senior editor at the German news service with responsibility for collecting news typescripts and bringing them to the bunker. On 29 April 1945 Martin Bormann, the head of the Nazi Party chancellery, gave him the wills, which he was to take to Munich. According to Lorenz, Wilhelm Zander, a chancellery official, was also given copies of the personal and political testaments which he was to take to Hitler's designated successor, Grand Admiral Doenitz. Lorenz also said that Major Wilhelm Johannmeier, Hitler's army adjutant, was given the political testament to take to Field Marshal Schoerner, Commander of Army Group Centre in Bohemia. In his will Hitler appointed Schoerner Commander in Chief of the Army. Although the three messengers succeeded in escaping from Berlin, they soon realised their tasks were hopeless and abandoned them.[128]

On 14 December 1945 Trevor-Roper left for Germany on his new mission, and stayed for three weeks. Lorenz and his documents were in British hands. Trevor-Roper set out to locate Zander and Johannmeier and find their documents. Johannmeier was living in the British Zone, but claimed he was merely escorting the other two messengers. Trevor-Roper was not wholly convinced, but decided to locate Zander before questioning Johannmeier again. The vital breakthrough came when an American intelligence officer learned that Zander had been treated under an assumed name in a hospital near Munich for injuries sustained walking from Hanover to Bavaria. With the help of the American Counter-Intelligence Corps, Trevor-Roper tracked down Zander to an address near Passau. As he later recalled:

> having motored all day and all night in a jeep, through mud and sleet and snow, I stood, at 3.0 in the morning, in the village of Aidenbach, near the Austrian frontier, and posting a man with a revolver at each corner of the crucial house, since no one answered on knocking, I sent a German policeman to climb through a window and open the door. Then I went in and broke into a bedroom; and from the bed saw emerging [...] a giant nose, the unmistakable nose of Bormann's assistant, SS Standartenfuehrer Wilhelm Zander.

Zander's arrest was quickly followed by the surrender of his documents.[129] Zander confirmed that Johannmeier had also been given a copy of Hitler's political testament. On 1 January 1946 Trevor-Roper re-interrogated Johannmeier, saying that the others had already given the game away and all the relevant information was against his story. For two hours Johannmeier firmly resisted. He did not have any papers, and so could not surrender them. Trevor-Roper was relentless and urged Johannmeier to see reason. The British did not want to hold him captive, but had no alternative as long as he refused to cooperate. Then Trevor-Roper took a break, and this allowed Johannmeier to catch up with the argument and realise the futility of his silence. After making sure he would not be punished, he admitted to his interrogator: 'I've got the papers.' He now led Trevor-Roper to a corner of his garden in Iserlohn. Trevor-Roper was apprehensive lest his prisoner use the cover of darkness to resort to violence, but all went well. Johannmeier dug up a bottle containing, as expected, Hitler's political testament and a covering note from General Wilhelm Burgdorf, the chief Wehrmacht adjutant, to Schoerner. Johannmeier bore no resentment for the surrender Trevor-Roper had cajoled from him. Many years later Johannmeier welcomed his former interrogator as a long-lost friend.[130]

The tracking down of Hitler's wills was Trevor-Roper's greatest success as a British intelligence officer. It was far more than the performance of a wartime amateur: this short mission showed that he could interrogate witnesses and hunt down suspects with a skill and tenacity worthy of an exceptional intelligence professional. Afterwards Peter Ramsbotham,[131] who worked at British Army of the Rhine Headquarters, wrote that 'everyone [...] is full of admiration for the speed and efficiency with which your investigations were concluded.'[132] From the inception of Trevor-Roper's mission Dick White had seen its potential for a book. This possibility did not influence Trevor-Roper during his conduct of the inquiry, for he assumed that publication would be forbidden. In January 1946 Trevor-Roper took up a teaching appointment at Christ Church Oxford. It was then that White proposed that Trevor-Roper should write up his findings as a book. It would need the authorisation of the JIC, the body which coordinated British security and espionage, but White advised Trevor-Roper how to skirt that difficulty. He should not approach the JIC directly, for 'No government agency will ever sanction a proposal of which they cannot foresee the effect [...] But if you were to write it first, and take the risk of their decision, then they would at least see the limits of what they were allowing.' It proved sage counsel.[133]

Spurred on by White's encouragement, Trevor-Roper worked on *The Last Days of Hitler* at an astonishing tempo. He wrote more than two-thirds of the book in less than a month during his first term as an Oxford tutor, between 18 February and 15 March 1946. The main text was finished by 22 May. It was a work of remarkable historical insight, but it was also the product of an intelligence mission, and so required official approval.[134] White submitted a minute about the book to the JIC, which discussed the matter at its meeting on 14 June 1946. Colonel 'Tim' Milne of SIS pointed out,

> whereas Mr Roper was in SIS at the time, the material for his book had not been obtained as a result of his SIS work. Nevertheless, while agreeing to publication as far as subject matter and security sources were concerned, 'C' [Sir Stewart Menzies] disclaimed any responsibility for authorising the publication for commercial gain of material which had been obtained in an official capacity [...] Subject to this, 'C' had no objection to one of his officers publishing such a book after demobilisation.[135]

The Last Days of Hitler was published in March 1947. Dedicated to Dick White, the book enjoyed worldwide success and has remained in print ever since. Few intelligence missions have resulted in such a contribution to historical literature. Patrick Reilly wrote to his old colleague that the book was a 'fine conclusion to your intelligence career'.[136] It was indeed a spectacular culmination to Trevor-Roper's challenging but highly creative period on secret service.

1

Sideways into SIS

More than 50 years after his entry into the Secret Intelligence Service, Trevor-Roper published a revealing account of how it took place:

'Sideways into S.I.S.'[1]

How did I come to be in the British Secret Service – *alias* M.I. 6, *alias* S.I.S. – during the war? How does anyone come to be in any Secret Service? Such a service cannot recruit by open means. Patronage and accident are the only ways in. I had no patron there. I did not belong either to London clubland or to the Indian police, its two chief recruiting grounds. So I came in by accident, and sideways; not personally, but as part of a package. The episode itself has some significance: it forms a small chapter, or at least a footnote, in the history of S.I.S.

Certainly I never envisaged myself in that mysterious organisation. Such training as I had to be an officer was as a horsed cavalryman. Just before the outbreak of war, I had served an attachment to the still unmechanised Life Guards, pounding on a steaming black charger up and down sandy knolls in Surrey. When war was declared I was in Oxford, awaiting orders. Then the Bursar of Merton College, of which I was a Junior Research Fellow, told me that he needed a junior officer and bade me follow him. He had served in the first World War, in the Royal Engineers (Wireless Intelligence) in Egypt and Salonika and was determined not to be left out of the second. His name was E.W.B. Gill, a genial philistine with very little respect for red tape, hierarchy, convention or tradition. In Egypt he had used the Great Pyramid as a mast for wireless interception, and in Oxford he had jolted his college into modernity by introducing electric lighting into its quadrangles. He had written a book about his experiences in the previous war, entitled *War, Wireless and Wangles*. Now that war had come again, he was returning to wireless and wangles. I was tired of waiting and I followed him.

He had found himself a niche in a very small unit called [*the*] Radio Security Service (R.S.S.), or more formally, M.I.8(c), a section of M.I.8, the newly formed communications department of the War Office. The declared purpose of R.S.S. was to seek out unidentified radio signals which might emanate from German spies planted in our midst, to act as 'beacons,' directing enemy bombers to targets in Britain. If such were found, our next duty would be to locate the secret radio transmitters. This was to be done with the help of the Post Office, which had a fleet of direction-finding vans, normally used to hunt down unlicenced operators. The spies thus found would then be dealt with by the internal security service, M.I.5, which at that time was housed in Wormwood Scrubs Prison. I was told that the prisoners, who had been evacuated to a safer, rural prison, greatly resented their dislocation. Gill and I thus began our work in a very old-fashioned and insalubrious prison-cell.*

M.I.5 itself was also rather old-fashioned at that time. Its Director-General was Sir Vernon Kell, who had been its first head during the Boer War,[2] and had ruled it ever since. He could be seen in the coffee-break after lunch, expatiating in the area normally used for prisoners' exercise: a fine figure of a man, casting an appreciative eye on the secretaries, who tended to have elegant figures and aristocratic surnames. It is said that they were chosen, like race-horses, for their legs and their breeding. I found the officers of M.I.5 very agreeable: conversation with them was much easier than with my two or three colleagues in the R.S.S., whose technical jargon I did not understand. At one time another intelligence officer was needed, and I suggested an Oxford friend, Harry Fisher, afterwards a High Court Judge and President of Wolfson College, Oxford. He was interviewed, but turned down because he could not define a heterodyne.[3] Nor indeed could I, but I was already in.

As it turned out, the entire original purpose of R.S.S. was misconceived. We were hunting a quarry that did not exist. There was in fact only one German spy active in Britain when the war broke out, and he was controlled

---

* It is often said that R.S.S. was part of M.I.5, or subject to it: 'M.I.5's intercept station,' etc. E.g., F.H. Hinsley et al., *British Intelligence in the Second World War, Vol. I* (London: HMSO, 1979), pp. 120n. 131, 272, 277. This is incorrect. R.S.S. was never controlled by M.I.5. The position was correctly stated in M.E. Howard's vol. 5 in the same series (1990). Nigel West's statement in *The Faber Book of Espionage* (London: Faber & Faber, 1993) p. 253, that I am 'one of those unusual individuals who have served in both M.I.5 and S.I.S' presumably rests on the same error, although in his earlier book *M.I.5* (London: The Bodley Head, 1981) p. 159, he correctly places R.S.S. under M.I.8.

by M.I.5; and the German bombers were not led forward to their targets by head-beacons in England but directed from behind by tail-beacons in Germany. However, this was not known at the time, and so we dutifully combed the evidence for suspicious signals. This evidence came to us from three main sources. First, we had under our direct control three small intercepting stations at the three corners of the kingdom at Land's End, John O'Groats, and on the cliffs of Dover: the widest base we could get in our narrow island. Secondly, we had the unidentified material rejected by the monitoring services of the Armed Forces, the B.B.C., and cable companies. Finally, we had a network of 'voluntary interceptors' – enthusiastic amateurs throughout the country, mobilised for the purpose by one of our original officers, Lord Sandhurst, in peacetime a wine-merchant. However, in this indiscriminate flood of material we did ultimately discover some mysterious signals which, from the accompanying operators' chat, we knew to be German, and this we dutifully sent to the cryptographers of the Government Code & Cypher School, or G.C. & C.S., recently installed at Bletchley Park.

Bletchley, which would afterwards become so famous, was not then fully organised, and our liaison with it was not yet regular. What exactly happened at this point I am still unsure. At the time we were given to understand that our stuff was not wanted: it had been identified as harmless, and could be ignored. In retrospect I think that this may have been a misunderstanding, or an evasion. But the message delivered to us was unambiguous. We understood that we had been rebuffed and that no more of the material was to be sent.

Gill was not satisfied with this rebuff, and so we decided to prove our point by working on the material ourselves. He had some experience in cryptography and I knew German. So in those blacked-out evenings, in the flat we shared in Ealing, we worked on it and, in the end, succeeded in breaking the cypher: which I hasten to add, was not of the highest class. When we read the messages, we found that we had stumbled on a great treasure, the radio transmissions of the German Secret Service, or Abwehr, in particular its stations in Madrid and Hamburg, the former conversing with its substations in Spain and Spanish Morocco, the latter with its agents on the Baltic and North Sea coasts, some of whom were preparing to land, by boat or parachute, in Britain. There was also a station at Wiesbaden, which seemed to concentrate on training spies for such adventures, and whose laborious initiation of its pupils gave us some valuable hints. We were naturally excited by this coup, and so, when we reported it to him, was our Commanding Officer, Colonel Worlledge, an old-fashioned, honourable but perhaps not brilliant regular signals officer from the first World War, recently imported from Sarafand in Palestine to take charge of us. He ordered me to write a document about it, which I gladly did, and which he then – rather naively, I fear – circulated to his normal customers with a covering note stating that this document, by Lieutenant Trevor-Roper, seemed to deserve distribution. No doubt he expected to hear a general purr of approbation. R.S.S. might not have discovered any radio spies in England, but clearly it was earning its keep.

He was quickly undeceived. When the document reached M.I.6, there was an explosion. The chief of its counter-espionage section, Major Cowgill, newly arrived from the Indian Police in Calcutta, declared roundly, and apparently more than once, that 'Lieutenant Trevor-Roper ought to be court-martialled.'* At the same time, Colonel Worlledge received a rocket from his superiors in M.I.8, to whom presumably, M.I.6 had complained. We were gravely reprimanded for having deciphered the documents and formally forbidden to do so again, 'since that was the province of G.C. & C.S.' We did not take any of this very seriously. After all, as we understood, G.C. & C.S. had refused to handle the stuff, and I was merely obeying the orders of my commanding officer. Relations with G.C. & C.S., at our level, were soon mended and the position regularised. The raw material was now sent regularly to them, and the deciphered texts were distributed to a much more limited list of recipients, under the acronym ISOS, i.e. 'Intelligence Service, Oliver Strachey,' Strachey, the elder brother of Lytton Strachey, being, from now on, our regular contact at Bletchley. He was a long-serving epicurean professional cryptographer, not easily ruffled by such passing inconveniences as the outbreak of war. Later he was succeeded by my former classical tutor at Oxford, Denys Page, which made things easier still.

---

* Cowgill's statement was reported to me at the time. It is also recorded by Kim Philby, *My Silent War* (NY: Grove Press, 1968), p. 57, who presumably heard it after his arrival in Section 5 of M.I.6. [*Trevor-Roper later wrote on an offprint of this essay he sent to me:* 'This is an incorrect deduction. Cowgill's own statement to Antony Cave Brown in 1985 shows that Cowgill demanded that I be court-martialled on a second and distinct occasion, on a different allegation (never revealed to me) in 1943; and it was presumably to this second occasion that Philby was referring. Cowgill's statement to Cave Brown is in A. Cave Brown, *Treason in the Blood* (1994).']

However, the explosion was not confined to our little world. Its reverberations continued far above our heads and precipitated a much greater upheaval. Basically, the issue was simple. R.S.S. had been set up for one purpose, which it had not fulfilled – indeed could not fulfil since the objective circumstances which it presupposed did not exist. Instead it had unexpectedly fulfilled another, which had not been forecast: instead of catching German radio spies in England, it had opened a window into the very council chamber of the enemy secret service. This discovery was potentially of great importance: so important that it must be kept a closely guarded secret. And yet what had happened? Colonel Worlledge, a simple signals officer, uninitiated unto the mysteries of 'most secret intelligence' and high security, had naively revealed it, not only to his official contacts in the Armed Services intelligence departments (which, in the eyes of M.I.6, was bad enough) but also (horror of horrors!) to the civilians of the Post Office. He had thus put at risk a valuable source which was just beginning to flow. In retrospect I have to admit that Major Cowgill, on this occasion at least, had every right to explode.

There was also another circumstance which added piquancy to the affair. M.I.6, at that time, was desperately in need of some success. At the very beginning of the war, it had suffered a humiliating reverse. Its two chief officers in the Hague, Major Stevens and Captain Best, who controlled the relics of its already damaged organisation in Western Europe, had been lured to Venlo, on the German border, for a pretended meeting with important German dissidents, and had there been kidnapped by the Gestapo. In prison in Berlin, they had revealed all and M.I.6 knew it, for their revelations had been published in the German press. Thus the whole organisation of M.I.6 in Western Europe, already half-rotten, had collapsed. In these circumstances the penetration of the secrets of the Abwehr offered a double benefit: immediately, compensation for a dreadful failure, and, ultimately, a far more trustworthy source of information about German espionage.

However, if they were to appropriate and exploit these benefits, the rulers of M.I.6 saw that they must secure control of R.S.S. itself. This it must be admitted, in view of the changed role of R.S.S., was logical. It would also enable M.I.6 to impose its own rules of security and thus prevent further leaks to the Post Office, or indeed to its own closest rival, which it regarded with almost equal suspicion, M.I.5. Which is what now happened. Naturally I was not privy to the discussion, which must have taken place at a high level, far above my head. But the result soon showed itself. In May 1941, R.S.S. was detached altogether from the War Office and M.I.8, removed physically from the embrace of M.I.5, and transferred to M.I.6. While it kept its old name, its original function dwindled into a sideshow, and its accidental discoveries became its main purpose. Liberally financed, and equipped with a completely new and central radio-receiving station at Hanslope Park in Buckinghamshire, it became the whole-time intercepting station of M.I.6, which hitherto had had no such thing. The Abwehr, all its schedules known, was now monitored round the clock and the volume and regularity of the material thus obtained enabled G.C. & C.S. to achieve one of its great triumphs. In December 1941, the Enigma cypher of the Abwehr was broken and the window through which we had peeped was thrown wide open, giving a continuous view of events within. This was a great help to our operations: in particular, the success of our double-cross system would have been impossible without it. So the disaster at Venlo was more than compensated. Indeed, in retrospect, I regard that disaster as a blessing in disguise. It swept away a rotten system of venal spies which, had it been maintained, would have been controlled by the Germans just as their spies were controlled by us – though less effectively, since they had not an open window like ours.

So ended that brief chapter in the history of British Intelligence. The personal consequences for me were that I too, as part of the package, found myself taken over by M.I.6. I was junior enough to threaten no one's prospect of promotion and perhaps it was thought best to keep me under control. Others were not. Takeovers are commonly ruthless affairs and this was no exception. The grandees of M.I.6, in annexing R.S.S., had no intention of encumbering themselves with the directors of the old firm. So Colonel Worlledge, having vainly resisted the change, was quietly dropped and retired to his castle in Ireland. The real genius of the affair, Major Gill, was also deliberately overlooked. Left to find other employment, he became a radar officer and an expert on captured German equipment. Under the new regime, his name was never mentioned. Although I do not think that he would have found himself at ease among the self-important mandarins of S.I.S., the manner of his extrusion seemed to me rather shabby. After all, he had thrown them a lifebelt which, after they had run their own ship aground, had enabled them to be winched to safety and afterwards, on dry land, to congratulate themselves on what they would claim as their achievement.

Section V of SIS

SIS collected information for the British government on foreign territory, if necessary by illegal means. Its headquarters was divided up into sections, many of which in Trevor-Roper's time had offices in Broadway Buildings opposite St James Park underground station. 'G' sections organised the work of SIS stations overseas, whereas 'circulating sections' for the most part distributed intelligence from abroad to the relevant Whitehall departments and received their requests for particular information. During the war there were up to ten circulating sections, each known by a Roman numeral. Sections I to IV passed on political, air, naval and military intelligence, respectively. Section V, Trevor-Roper's new employer, both collected and distributed information about enemy secret services obtained on foreign territory. Section VI dealt with economic matters, Section VII prepared for the eventuality of a German invasion and Section VIII handled communications. Until the summer of 1940 Section IX fostered special operations and was also known as Section D; from May 1943 Section IX focused on Communism. Section X tapped the telephone lines of embassies in London.[4]

During the war Section V expanded more than 50-fold, from three officers in 1939 to 163 officers in 1945.[5] *It was swamped with work when Trevor-Roper arrived. Officers had little opportunity to train newcomers, and so it took him some time to find his feet, as he explained in an unpublished manuscript in his papers which has no title.*[6]

Once I had discovered my way round the Secret Service – which was not easy, for nothing was ever explained and questions were not encouraged – I found many aspects of it very strange. In some respects it was very archaic. For instance, there was no section responsible for radio interception. That, after all, was why we had been brought in. This was not because SIS had not discovered radio. It used radio for its own communications. These communications were serviced by its section VIII. But it had not thought of intercepting those of potential enemies. The Army, Navy and the Air Force had their interception services, but SIS had none. It might of course have relied on those services to pass interesting or mysterious information to it, but it had no means of analysing such material if it should come to it.

Indeed it had very little mechanism for analysis of any kind. The function of the service as a whole, it was explained, was to receive information, not to evaluate it. It was a passive organisation, receiving reports from its agents abroad and passing them on to 'user departments' with little or no comment – a mere qualification of the agent concerned as 'reliable', 'generally reliable', 'believed to be reliable' or 'as yet untested'. Analysis in any depth of intelligence, however obtained, was no more the business of SIS than the interception of enemy radio traffic. The idea that it could be, and should be, was a by-product of the war and grew, effectively, out the absorption into to it of RSS. For the material collected by RSS and deciphered by GC & CS was already, in 1941, a regular coherent stream; after the destruction of SIS agents on the continent it was the only continuous and reliable stream; but because of its technical nature it required analysis. It was not enough to pass such material, as it came, to the 'user departments'. Nor was it reasonable to expect the user departments – the relevant sections of the Service Depts and MI5 – to make their own analysis. That would have required unnecessary duplication. Analysis should, in this case, be centralised, in SIS.

Another surprise to me was the discovery that MI6 & Sec V in particular, had no German department.[7] Since the war was against Germany this seemed to me odd. The explanation given to me also seemed rather odd, at least once we had this new source of information. The service, it was explained, depended on personal presence in foreign countries. An officer of the service had to be responsible for info. collected there. But where was that officer to be posted? Normally he was attached to the embassy, disguised as a Passport Control Officer. Or, in a war theatre, to the army command. But in 1941 the German armies had left very few British embassies and no British armies in Europe; British espionage in Germany had been withdrawn to the Hague and, with the disaster at Venlo, had been totally wiped out – indeed, since Stevens and Best were now telling all they knew in Berlin, had been converted into espionage against Britain. For information about Germany SIS was dependent on the intelligence services of exiled governments in London, which, naturally enough, insisted on using their own communications [...] When I considered this great lacuna in our intelligence it seemed to me that it could, in part, be filled by careful analysis of the new material now coming in through radio interception. This was limited indeed – a secret service, as was only too clear from a study of our own, is not of central importance, but at least its evidence was hard:

its communications, if properly interpreted, showed something of what was really happening in Germany, it did not come through the fallible or deliberately distorted medium of personal spies, and so it might contribute to a true understanding of the intelligence war against us. Since my section was baptised the Radio Analysis Bureau I considered my function to be not only the guidance of RSS in its search for the communications of the enemy intelligence services, which I could do having the advantage of the ISOS decrypts, but also the analysis of those decrypts in order to understand the whole structure and work of those services.

Unfortunately (as I thought) I was not given an opportunity to do this, because I was placed under the authority of Cowgill, [*who,*] to put it bluntly, did not believe in intelligence. He was a policeman and he required from ISOS only the names and movements of enemy agents abroad so that they could – where we had the means – be thwarted in their activities. In intelligence proper he had no interest. Moreover, he had a deep distrust of those who thought otherwise than he did in this matter. By an agreement made between the heads of departments concerned, ISOS decrypts were sent, as of right, to the Secret Intelligence departments of the three services, and to MI5. Cowgill distrusted them. Especially he distrusted MI5. What business had MI5, he asked, to read the evidence which had been given, as a monopoly, to him? They had a legitimate interest, of course, in receiving advance notice of spies coming from the Continent to Britain, whose movements were being planned in Lisbon and revealed by ISOS; and they needed ISOS in order to formulate the policy and the detail of deception, which remained under their control; but why so much curiosity about the background of the material? To Cowgill such an interest was unnecessary, indeed unsafe; every document shown to an outside department was a risk to its security; he was the judge of security, and of relevance; MI5 and the services should be content with the material which he, as ultimate arbiter, would allow them to see. The fact that the authorised recipients of the materials outside SIS were better judges than he of its relevance to their own work did not occur to him. Nor did it occur to him that they were all more intelligent than he. They were intellectuals. He was a hard-working conscientious official who distrusted intellectuals. There was something pathetic in the spectacle of this obsessed and sometimes paranoid policeman seeking, with the best of intentions, to control the thinking of persons so much better educated and more sophisticated than himself.

The problem was stated succinctly by the man who became Cowgill's most trusted officer, his <u>guru</u>, the real author of the successes – for there were considerable successes – of Section V. Writing not of Cowgill or of his Section but, quite separately, about the appointment of a policeman, Sir Percy Sillitoe, as head of MI5 in 19[46], instead of Guy Liddell, Philby writes that Liddell 'like most of the MI5 professionals, maintained that MI5 was an intelligence organisation, not a police outfit. The techniques for combating espionage were different from those adapted to crime. Since spies are backed by the great technical resources of govts, while criminals are not, there is clearly much to be said for that view.'

In these circumstances my attempts to persuade Cowgill as my superior officer of the intelligence value of ISOS fell on stony ground. I could of course have appealed from him to his superior, Colonel Vivian, but Vivian was another ex Indian policeman. He was also a feeble creature, frightened of Cowgill, who had replaced him and despised him. There was no hope in that direction.* Above him was only C.[8] But C was remote and inaccessible. Unless one happened to be a member of White's, a junior officer had very little chance of contact with him, especially if he was not placed in Broadway.

Trevor-Roper provided vivid recollections of his SIS superiors in the following passages, which he drafted with memoirs in mind.[9] First he commented on Cowgill, who:

[...] withheld material from authorized recipients 'because I didn't like the look of some of the people it was going to' [...] The external recipients of whom he did not like the look were all, to say the least, far more intelligent than he: Liddell and White in MI5, Ewen Montagu,[10] afterwards a judge, in the Admiralty; my cousin Brian Melland,[11] afterwards in its Historical Section, in the War Office; John Pope-Hennessy,[12] afterwards Director of the British Museum, in the Air Ministry. These men were naturally impatient

---

* It was useless to appeal from C[*owgill*] to V[*ivian*]. One might as well appeal from an angry crab to a frightened jellyfish. [*separate note by Trevor-Roper*]

of a department which they saw as little more than a stopper on the flow of essential information. Consequently they became a kind of freemasonry which pooled intelligence by direct contact without asking leave of the headmaster of the private school in St. Albans [*Cowgill*].

To serve this freemasonry my section compiled periodic papers giving background information on the German secret services. One of these, on the structure, organisation and personnel of the German secret services, had an indirect effect on my later career. Many years later, Dick White told my wife that it was the memory of this pamphlet which had caused him, in 1945, to invite me to investigate the fate of Hitler. The pamphlet was however a collective work by my section and I should not have been given sole credit for it. Another of our documents had a more immediate effect. It was entitled 'Canaris and Himmler' and was written in November 1942.

Admiral Canaris was head of the Abwehr, but his record, so far, had not been very glorious, and we had evidence that he was being criticised not only for failure to produce reliable intelligence but also for lack of enthusiasm for the Nazi party, even for suspicion of treason in his ranks; and it is true that his chief of staff, Hans Oster, was an active opponent of Hitler, prepared to commit treason. From various sources we were convinced that Himmler's SS, the real and ever-expanding engine of Nazi power, was gunning for him. The SS had its own secret intelligence organisation in the sixth department of the *Sicherheitsdienst* under Schellenberg. But Canaris had a power base of his own: the General Staff, to which the Abwehr was responsible, supported him, and he had valuable personal connexions with General Franco's ministers in Spain. He frequently visited Spain, and since his travel arrangements and political appointments were made for him by the local Abwehr office and reported in *Ultra*, we were familiar with them. This Spanish connexion was a valuable protection to him as long as it lasted. In our paper we set out the facts known to us, and their implications: that a struggle for power between the High Command of the Armed Forces [*and the SS*] was visible below the surface in Germany; that the struggle for control of secret intelligence was a symptom of it; and that the position of the Abwehr, and of Canaris himself, though sustained by his Spanish contacts, was in danger.

When we were about to circulate our paper within the approved freemasonry of the *Ultra* world, a copy was sent to Philby. He instantly – as Cowgill's deputy – banned the circulation. We asked for his reason. He would give none (on such occasions his stammer was always a great help). I sent two members of my section – Charles Stuart and Stuart Hampshire – to discuss it with him. He would still give no reason, merely objecting that the argument was 'speculation.' When they returned, they were indignant. Till then we had always regarded Philby – rightly – as by far the most intelligent and rational member of Section 5, but now he was obstinately refusing to listen to reason. However, we had to admit failure. The paper was not circulated.[13]

We were unjust to Philby in thinking that he had no reason for his action. Twenty years later his true loyalty would be made clear when he fled for protection to Soviet Russia, and in his memoirs, published in 1968, he gave – in another context – his general explanation. The revelation of possible disloyalty in the General Staff, of an embryonic struggle for power between the generals and the SS, might suggest the possibility of contact with the German military opposition. That would not suit: the Russians would not approve any sign that we were 'dickering with Germans.'

It happened that some time after this I had a conversation with the Prof – Professor Lindemann, now Lord Cherwell: I forget whether in Oxford, to which he would return occasionally at week-ends or in London, where I sometimes had lunch with him at the Carlton Grill; for it was only there, he maintained, that the chef could prepare his white of egg and lettuce exactly to his taste. I told him that we had detected signs of an incipient power-struggle in Germany. He expressed interest. I mentioned our suppressed paper; and he asked me to send him a copy, which I did. I then forgot about the matter. I had certainly forgotten about it by May 1943,[14] when I was telephoned by Miss Pettigrew, Menzies' secretary, saying that the Chief wished to see me at 3.0 o'clock one day in the next week, for I was pleased with this sudden notice. 'About time', I said to myself, for I assumed, complacently, that he wished to consult me on some grave matter of policy. So, on the appointed day, I went up to London, took the opportunity to have a proper lunch, with half a bottle of Montrachet, and then went on to Broadway Buildings, the headquarters of SIS. I noticed, on entering Miss Pettigrew's room, that she did not seem as deferential as I had expected, and no words were exchanged as I waited. Then the green light went on, and I entered C's office, where he sat under a portrait of his supposed father King Edward VII.

The atmosphere was formal. He was sitting at a table. Beside him, also at the table, was Colonel Vivian. It became apparent, very soon, that I was not there to be consulted but to be tried. Not that any particular charge was made. The process was inquisitorial, with Vivian the inquisitor: he seemed to be fishing for evidence. As I had been given no notice of the intention, I had to keep my wits about me to respond to questions without inadvertently giving answers which might be used to support unspecified charges, so my memory of the detail is hazy. I was asked whether, and if so how, I knew Lord Swinton. I replied that I did not know him, but he had invited me to lunch, over a year ago, and I had accepted. I was pressed about our conversation, but had fortunately forgotten any indiscretions. And how did I know Lord Cherwell? That was easy: he was an old friend. Had I passed a paper to him? That could not be denied, but it could be defended. Fortified by the Montrachet, I defended myself with confidence, and Vivian started to fumble. 'Of course, sir', he said, on two occasions, 'whatever the outcome, it is impossible for Trevor-Roper to remain in the organisation after this.' The fishing expedition went on, it seemed, for a long time, but the fish wriggled out of the net. Then there was a knock on the door and Miss Pettigrew entered, carrying a china tray with a tea-set on it, and put it before the Chief. 'Do you take milk and sugar?' he asked me, and at that moment I felt the balance turning: from a prisoner in the dock I had become a guest at a tea-party. Vivian felt it too: he fell silent.

After tea I was told to withdraw and Menzies and Vivian were closeted together for a short time. Then Vivian came out and walked past me with averted eyes. The green light went on, and I re-entered Menzies' room. 'I sent for you', he said, 'to sack you. I thought I had no alternative. But I have changed my mind.' Then he pronounced sentence. I was to write him a letter of apology for communicating with Lord Cherwell. But from now on the position of our section would be changed. It would no longer be subject to Counter-Espionage – to Section 5, to Cowgill, to Vivian. It would be re-named the Radio Intelligence Service (RIS) and placed directly under Menzies' personal office. Its function would be unchanged. If I had any problems, I could take them direct to Menzies himself. When I arrived back at Arkley I was still slightly shaken by this unexpected experience, but they pulled me together. 'You don't seem to realise', they said, 'that you have won a great victory,' and it dawned upon me that I had. From now on our position was radically changed. We never had any further trouble. As the first fruits of our freedom we circulated the document 'Canaris and Himmler'. Its 'speculation', as Philby called it, proved correct. In 1943 the credit of the Abwehr with the Nazi leaders sank rapidly. The heads of all its three departments were dismissed. In February 1944 Canaris himself was sacked. Franco had decided to invest in an Allied victory and had declined to allow Canaris back in Spain. Three months later the Abwehr was taken over by the SS.

2

Admiral Canaris

*Trevor-Roper chose a biography of Admiral Wilhelm Canaris (1887–1945)
by Karl-Heinz Abshagen for the first book review he wrote on the subject
of secret service. Appointed Hitler's intelligence chief in 1935, Canaris
could gush with enthusiasm for Nazism in print. In 1938 he declared,
'The officer must exemplify national socialism and make the German
Wehrmacht a model for the realisation of the national socialist world view.'
The Wehrmacht should show 'unconditional political loyalty', as 'The
soldier and officer is once again bound to his supreme commander through
a personal oath to which God Almighty is witness. Any doubt as to this
loyalty or its national socialist reliability would be a most serious insult to
the Wehrmacht and its officer corps.'[1] Such sentiments on the part of Canaris
were not mentioned in Abshagen's stylish and thoughtful book, which
Trevor-Roper originally reviewed in 1950. This review's first appearance
was in German for the American-funded publication* Der Monat; *an
English version was later published in the* Cornhill Magazine.[2]*

The essay on Canaris was reproduced in* The Philby Affair *(1968),
published by William Kimber. This Kimber version is used for the present
volume. In preparing it, Trevor-Roper made numerous small changes
to the 1950 text and also added paragraphs or groups of sentences.
These larger additions are identified in the endnotes. In particular,
Trevor-Roper included more detail of German and British intelligence
activities. He revealed that the Allies controlled Germany's spies and
supplied them with misleading information to achieve deception prior
to the invasion of Normandy. He also mentioned the British deception
of the Germans over the invasion of Sicily. This operation had become
widely known through the publication of Ewen Montagu's book,* The
Man who Never Was. *One added passage, which passed unnoticed
at the time, mentioned British success in breaking German machine
codes.[3] Bletchley's achievement only became general knowledge in 1974,
with the publication of* The Ultra Secret *by F.W. Winterbotham.*

Trevor-Roper added two footnotes to this essay, which the editor has supplemented with endnotes.

Foreword[4]

I served in British Intelligence (during the war of 1939–45) and found myself, by a curious accident, studying at the same time two opposite organisations: the British Secret Service, in which I worked, and which I saw working around me, and the German Secret Service, which we watched and, I may say, penetrated, from afar.[5] I soon discovered that these two services, so different in their myth, were remarkably similar in their reality. We even discovered, in the German Secret Service, or *Abwehr*, personal correspondences and recognised, across the intervening fog of war, old friends of Broadway or Whaddon Hall transmuted into German uniform in the Tirpitz-Ufer or at Wannsee.[6] This was a valuable lesson in sociology as well as an agreeable topic of diversion.

One member of our organisation, however, was very different from his opposite number. Between our Chief, Sir Stewart Menzies, and the head of the *Abwehr*, Admiral Canaris, no parallel could be drawn. We soon became aware that 'the little Admiral' was a far more complex and controversial character than we had supposed. As the incompetence of his organisation was progressively revealed to us, we discovered, or deduced, something of the politics in which he was involved, and we noted his feverish travels, in every direction, but especially to Spain, which distinguished him sharply from our own more sedentary chief.[7]

My interest in Canaris survived my work in S.I.S. Immediately after the war, when I was in Germany, I met several of Canaris's surviving colleagues and read much material concerning the Plot of 20 July. I then wished to write a short study of Canaris, but was inhibited, because so much of my knowledge came from unavowable experience. However, the publication, in 1949, of Herr Abshagen's biography of the Admiral gave me an opportunity, and I published a review article on the subject in the *Cornhill Magazine*, Summer 1950. For this article I drew on three main sources: Herr Abshagen's book, the documents concerning the German Opposition with which I had become familiar, and my own experience of Canaris's organisation during the war.

I have made certain small changes to the text. Sometimes I have corrected an error or improved the sense. Sometimes I have recognised that details which were secret in 1950 are no longer secret in 1968.

* * * *

Hitler's rule in Germany began, in appearance (as it remains in the sterile vocabulary of the left), a conservative rule. It ended, after twelve years of silent internal revolution, as a Jacobin dictatorship. The beginning of that period saw the secret pact between Hitler and the General Staff which culminated in the liquidation of his own left wing and his acquisition of supreme power, legal and actual, in the State; the end of it saw aristocrats and generals banded together, even the slowest and weakest of them, in a last attempt to remove by assassination the radical monster they had so disastrously helped to power. This mutation of Nazi power is the background against which every conscientious German had to adjust his life. Every life was different in the pace and stages and methods of its adjustment and no easy formula can comprehend them all; but without an understanding of that mutation they are all equally unintelligible. The most interesting cases are those of the conservatives themselves. Liberal men hated Hitler throughout, and the mutation of his power, the change of his political direction, though it might alter the degree of their contempt, did not entail the same crisis of conversion or burden of remorse. For conservatives the psychological consequences were far more painful, the political difficulties far more complex. It is for this reason that the diaries of Ulrich von Hassell[8] are so interesting. The same reason gives an even greater interest to a more complex personality in a more central position: Admiral Canaris, for nine years head of the German Secret Service, or *Abwehr*.

Canaris held office from 1 January 1935 – the morrow of the purge[9] which seemed to establish Hitler as a conservative agent. For the next nine years his work, as head of the *Abwehr*, was naturally enveloped in deep secrecy – on which, however, the success of Hitler's policy, both in diplomacy and war, shed a romantic, iridescent but un-illuminating glow. Canaris was envisaged, as the heads of secret services are so often envisaged, as a master-spy, an impersonal genius at the centre of an invisible spider's web. Then suddenly, in February 1944 – on the eve of the conservative rebellion against Hitler – he was put aside. Within a few months he had disappeared altogether from sight. The *Abwehr* disappeared soon after him, and a new organisation – the *Militärisches Amt* of Himmler's *Reichssicherheitshauptamt* (RSHA) – supplanted it.[10] For a time no more was heard of the Admiral who had so long seemed the *éminence grise* of German world-wide intelligence. Only afterwards did the news of his fate gradually leak out. Imprisoned, but untried, moved from prison to prison, within a month of Germany's final collapse he had been secretly executed in the Nazi extermination-camp at Flossenbürg.

What was the crime for which Canaris perished? At Nuremberg his ghost appeared and through the lips of a series of witnesses gave evidence in that still incredulous court-house. One by one, witnesses on both sides found themselves referring to Canaris. Whenever the opposition to Hitler, 'the other Germany', was mentioned, Canaris seemed to be the directing brain behind it. The angry defenders of Nazism denounced him as the traitor who, from his central position, had stabbed in the back a system which might otherwise have conquered the world. A wraith-like figure from the concentration-camp, Erwin Lahousen,[11] himself a former member of the *Abwehr* (and of the imperial Habsburg Secret Service before it), described Canaris as 'a pure intellectual', the secret genius of opposition, and 'the Canaris inner circle' as the very cabinet of resistance. And yet, however insistently that ghost hovered in the court-room, it remained very ghostly. What had this genius of opposition done? Whenever that question was asked, the phantom slid away, leaving no evidence that it was not an illusion. He had written diaries, it was explained – a vast and conclusive indictment of the regime specially prepared for posterity. But even these diaries have proved as elusive as his personality. There is no doubt that they existed, but intelligence officers and historians have vainly sought them. Most of them had already been found by the Gestapo and burnt to cinders in a Tyrolean castle; the rest, it seems, were buried, no one now knows where, in a deserted spot on the Lüneburg Heath. Only a few fragmentary notes survive to suggest their tenor, and these notes are not in Canaris' hand. The personality of Canaris was made more interesting at Nuremberg, but no less elusive.

What kind of man was Canaris really? There is no real mystery. Hundreds of people knew him personally. Many of them have given accounts of him. One of them, Karl Heinz Abshagen, has just published his biography.* It is

---

* Karl Heinz Abshagen, 'Canaris, Patriot und Weltbürger' (Stuttgart, Union Deutsche Verlagsgesellschaft, 1949).

true Herr Abshagen has relied mainly on the recollections of personal friends and on published evidence – he was himself in the Far East during the war, and is less qualified than he supposes to dissent from those who could watch the operation of the *Abwehr* more critically and more closely. But he can and does give a convincing portrait of the man; and as for Canaris's work – that is now no more secret than those other ruined institutions of Nazism. Let us then consider Canaris and his work as they emerge from the evidence that has thus accumulated.

Canaris was a regular naval officer. He was forty-eight years old when he became head of the *Abwehr*. He came neither from the South German lesser bourgeoisie who formed the basis of Nazism, nor from the Prussian aristocracy which, after shifting politics, manned the last citadel of opposition to it. His family were Rhineland industrialists, 'national liberals' opposed originally to both those groups. But as the age of Wilhelm II proceeded, the industrialists and the Junkers of Germany, the 'national liberals' and the conservatives, drew together; and by 1914 were, together, the firmest supporters of the monarchy.

There were differences between them, of course. The Junkers, traditionally, looked east: they were a ruling, 'colonial' class, accustomed, whether as landlords or as soldiers, to command. The Western industrialists, whatever Prussian characteristics they might have adopted, were the heirs of an international class, of the old *entrepreneurs* of that congeries of free cities on the Rhine. Their ideas, even when they had become conservative, remained European. Even in the 1930s something of this distinction survived. Canaris, like Ludwig Beck[12] and Carl Goerdeler,[13] whose fate he shared, belonged to the more sophisticated, more cosmopolitan, and – one must add – less effective wing of the conservative union.[14]

Canaris's training in the Navy further cemented him to the conservative classes. In it, he led an ordinary routine life, with some adventures. He took part in the Battle of the Falkland Islands, serving on the cruiser *Dresden*, the only German ship that survived that disastrous defeat. Taking refuge in Chile, he was interned, but escaped back to Germany, even passing through the British control at Plymouth as a Chilean citizen. He was then sent to Madrid on a secret naval mission, commanded a submarine, and held a variety of naval appointments. So far there was nothing exceptional in his career: it might have been the career of any naval officer. Nor was it exceptional that his activities after the war became political. The German armed forces were a political party in the Weimar years. Canaris toed his party line, supporting the socialist Noske[15] against revolution from the left in 1918, supporting revolution from the right against Noske (though himself on Noske's staff) in 1919. He compromised himself in the court-martial which acquitted the murderers of the communists Liebknecht[16] and Rosa Luxemburg,[17] assisted in the evasion of the naval clauses of the Versailles Treaty, and welcomed the advent of Hitler in 1933. All this was what any other regular officer would have done: it was the party line of the General Staff. And Canaris was rewarded at the end of 1934 when, instead of finishing his service as commander of the naval garrison of Swinemünde, and then going into retirement, he was put in command of the German Secret Service – not because of great experience or great hopes, or mysterious qualifications, but because his predecessor – also a naval officer – had proved somewhat unaccommodating towards the Nazis, and his commander-in-chief, Admiral Raeder,[18] wished to keep the job in the Navy. Thus Canaris's appointment was once again a routine appointment, of no deliberate significance. Its significance was accidental, due to the time at which he was appointed and his own peculiar character.

For the years following 1935 were the years in which Nazism betrayed its conservative promises. Those were the years of the 'nazification' of the Army, of the leftward trend of the Nazi Party, of planned aggression and ambitious foreign policy. For such a policy Hitler needed an appropriate Secret Service – efficient, aggressive, world-wide. How far could Canaris, the conservative naval officer casually jobbed into a routine position, supply such a demand?

To put the question thus is perhaps to put it in over-dramatic terms. The readers and writers of spy-novels and novelettes have indeed created a picture of secret services as mysterious, almost miraculous, organisations: systems animated by powerful and adventurous personalities who penetrate the darkest recesses and emerge with breathtaking scoops. But educated people know that this is not so. They know that apparently miraculous achievements are the result not of miraculous organisations but of efficient routine. They know that the head of an intelligence service is not a super-spy but a bureaucrat.[19] His empire may be somewhat loose: subordinates may sometimes conveniently ignore their superiors, just as superiors sometimes necessarily ignore their subordinates; but it is still a bureaucracy subject to the ordinary rules and weaknesses of that fallible organisation. But in this case we must recognise the illusion as well as the reality, for we are concerned not with educated people but Nazi politicians.

The Nazi politicians were not educated men. They probably believed more abject rubbish than any other ruling class in Western history – including the darkest of the Popes and most bigoted of the Bolsheviks. They also seem to have been indefatigable readers of novelettes, especially about the British Secret Service – that Machiavellian institution which, they believed, had built up the British world-empire. The official, secret, numbered handbooks on this subject which were distributed to trusted officials in Germany might have been written by an enthusiastic Babu[20] Indian trying to rival the Baroness Orczy or E. Phillips Oppenheim.[21] Had I not myself heard a captured *Abwehr* officer seriously describing the researches of which these books were the fruit, and myself discovered numbers of such books in the bombed ruins of the Gestapo headquarters in Prinz Albrechtstrasse, Berlin, I would never have believed that such grotesque rubbish could have been consecrated as doctrine by any bureaucracy. Even now my belief sometimes falters, and has to be confirmed by recourse to my book-shelves, which still contain those bizarre trophies.[22] And such illusions – modified no doubt, here and there, by experience – were entertained throughout the Nazi Party. They were entertained by Hitler himself. Entertaining them, he was determined that he, too, should have a Secret Service of the same kind, for the conquest of his world-empire. He was therefore prepared to allow Canaris unlimited funds, and to expect from him unlimited results. This was a somewhat tall order to a middle-aged naval officer of respectable life and bureaucratic training, who would anyway find himself in opposition to the whole radical policy now in fashion.

Canaris failed. He did not provide Hitler with the exotic Secret Service that he demanded. Indeed, he came to hate Hitler and to hope for his ruin; but with all the opportunities of his position, he failed in that also.[23] His failure was thus complete; and since he was fundamentally, like many traditionalists, a decent and high-minded man, and since his failure sprang ultimately from his character, it has a tragic quality. To explain it, we must look closely at his character.

Already by 1935 this character is discernible between the lines of his somewhat reluctant biographer. Incorruptible, of simple tastes, in many ways conventional, though an inveterate dabbler, he was by ultimate conviction a European conservative and a German monarchist. He admired England

and the English parliamentary system – as long as it was not exported from England. He admired it there, because there it worked; but with a pessimism which suffused his whole philosophy he concluded that such a system, however admirable at home, would never work on the Continent. It is unlikely that this despairing conclusion caused him much regret, for in fact he was anyway a traditionalist. He would really have been more happy in Metternich's Europe than in Liberal England. What impressed him about the English system was its durability, its flexibility. Germany, he felt, could never compete with that. Certainly – as the First World War had shown – Germany could never defeat England in war: it could only defeat itself.

Unenvious of English liberalism, despairing of German conservatism, Canaris found his ultimate spiritual home in Franco's Spain. He had long been familiar with Spain, and the rule of Franco particularly endeared it to him. Hitler made him his personal ambassador to Franco; he was a close personal friend of Franco's ministers, the Foreign Minister Count Jordana, the Air Minister General Vigon, the Chief of General Staff General Martinez Campos; a great signed portrait of Franco dominated his austere office on the Tirpitz-Ufer; and it was in journeys to Spain that he sought rest and consolation in every crisis of his mind. The genuine affection which this genuine anti-Nazi continued to feel for Franco and Spanish fascism plainly perplexes his biographer, who is reduced to arguing that it was only the 'cruelties and illegalities', not the politics, of Hitler that he hated. This seems unfair to Canaris and a misunderstanding of politics. And, anyway, has Franco committed no cruelties, no illegalities? In fact, the problem can be explained. May not Canaris have admired Franco while hating Hitler for the same reason which Goebbels, who admired Hitler, hated Franco: because Franco, fundamentally, is a conservative? Between Hitler and Franco there are indeed superficial resemblances: resemblances of style – they spoke the same political language; resemblances of method – they both used violence and persecution and concentration-camps. But their ultimate aims were opposite. Franco used that language and those methods to preserve, isolated behind seas and mountain barriers, in a sort of European Tibet, a form of society elsewhere obsolete, an unchanging feudal dominion of landlords and priests. Hitler, after 1935, used them to destroy the last vestiges of that old society, whose agent he had once appeared to be, and to set up instead of it, in the industrial centre of Europe, the dictatorship of the German lower middle class.[24]

Like so many conservatives in the 1930s, Canaris both idealised the past and despaired of preserving it. In 1932–3 he had no doubt seen Hitler, as they did, as the man of order, the disagreeable but necessary agent of restoration. After 1936 he no doubt, like them, began to see his error. With the sharp eyes of disillusion he then saw Hitler heading for the abyss; with the weak hand of despair he barely sought to stay him. He was convinced that Hitler meant war, equally convinced that he would lose it – or, if not, he knew that victory in such a war would be even more disastrous than defeat. War against the European order, he was convinced, would be war against England, and war against England would be *'finis Germaniae'*. It would also, perhaps, be the end of Europe – certainly of that conservative, monarchist central Europe which, however precariously, had managed to survive its monarchs in 1918. War against Russia, evidently, did not seem so alarming (or at least so wicked) to this Rhineland conservative. Here again he differed from the Junker conservatives of the East.[25]

What then was he to do? To such a question there are always two answers: there is the life of action, which forestalls destiny by creating new alternatives, and there is the fatalism of those who accept in advance their defeat. Action requires faith: fatalism is the absence of it. Canaris lacked positive faith and, lacking it, disqualified himself for the former course. He therefore plunged into the latter, and clouded his mind with metaphysical gloom. Brought up in the Evangelical Church, he deviated into a vague Catholic mysticism, more consolatory to the desperate soul. In Spain he would wander alone, in circuitous meditation, through those vast Catholic cathedrals. A peculiar religious melancholy inhibited him from action. Nothing seemed of any avail in the world: his own hypochondriac restlessness led him nowhither. In the end he sank into a fatalist conviction 'that he, too, though guiltless, must atone for the evil that Hitler had brought into the world.' However understandable, such an attitude is not very helpful in the practical world. How did it affect Canaris in his double role as head of the Secret Service and anti-Nazi conspirator?

But first, were these two roles compatible? If Canaris was sincere in his opposition, was it not his positive duty to be inefficient as a Nazi intelligence chief, or at least to be efficient with a difference – not to serve, but to ruin his masters? This was the charge that the unrepentant Nazis made against him at Nuremberg: the charge of a new 'stab in the back'. Herr Abshagen is eager to vindicate him from any such charge. Again and again he reverts apprehensively to the problem. Canaris, he insists – though he hated Hitler and dreaded a German victory – nevertheless worked conscientiously and efficiently to secure such a victory. 'In spite of all these mental doubts, the *Abwehr* under Canaris did its duty in full: it supplied the German military commanders with intelligence from behind the enemy lines, about the enemy's strength, his plans, his preparations ...' In its own field the *Abwehr*, he assures us, was a great success; Canaris was responsible for its success, and proud of it. He refused indeed to use the *Abwehr* as a terrorist organisation, but he never refused to fulfil his duty. It was not his fault if the General Staff failed adequately to evaluate or exploit its achievements.* All this may sound very inconsistent, but Herr Abshagen would rather make Canaris inconsistent than disloyal or insincere, or even inefficient.

That Canaris was inconsistent can easily be conceded; that he was loyal is probable; that he was sincere and resisted Hitler and Keitel in their attempts to perpetrate atrocities through the *Abwehr* is certain; but he was also incontestably inefficient. The facts are known beyond dispute, nor does Herr Abshagen give any evidence of any achievement of the *Abwehr* which can counter them. Its boasted agents behind enemy lines were, almost without

---

* This excuse – that the *Abwehr* supplied good information, but that the General Staff failed to evaluate it – appears to have been the standard defence of the *Abwehr*. An entry in the Goebbels diary shows that Canaris himself used it to Goebbels. On 9 April 1943, Goebbels records: 'Admiral Canaris reported to me about the work of our *Abwehr* service. From this I gather that the *Abwehr* has operated better than I had supposed. Unfortunately the results of its work have not been properly evaluated. For instance, it reported the Anglo-American operation in North Africa and the Casablanca meeting in good time, but these facts were not reported to the Führer with sufficient emphasis.' 'I have arranged with Canaris', Goebbels adds, 'that in future we shall work more closely together. He will now make regular reports to me so that I in turn can work on the Führer. In general Canaris makes a good impression – or at least, better than I had expected.'

This entry largely explains itself. After its North African failure, the *Abwehr* had come under heavy criticism, and Canaris was desperately seeking to defend it. He could indeed produce reports pointing to a possible invasion of North Africa. But he could equally have produced reports pointing to possible invasions everywhere else. Before the invasion, these self-contradictory reports – none of which were 'hard' – were useless; afterwards, those of them which happened to have guessed right could be selected for retrospective justification. Such a technique might impress a politician. (I have seen similarly selected reports used to impress a far greater statesman than Goebbels [*Churchill*].) It would not impress a general staff.

exception, controlled by the enemy. Its 'intelligence' about the enemy's strength, plans, preparations, was deliberately supplied by the enemy. On every important occasion – the invasion of North Africa, the invasion of Sicily, the invasion of Normandy – the *Abwehr* failed in its intelligence. On several occasions the information which it supplied to the General Staff was accepted – with disastrous results. It was thanks to misinformation successfully planted on the *Abwehr* that the Germans, in 1943, sent reinforcements to the Peloponnese instead of to Sicily and, in 1944, mistook both the force and the place of the great Allied cross-Channel invasion.[26]

The reasons for this inefficiency were partly technical: the fact that all *Abwehr* hand-cyphers were read by the British from the beginning of 1940 and machine-cyphers – which were clearly thought to be invulnerable – from 1942.[27] Against this overwhelming disadvantage no organisation could be proof. But every organisation reflects, to some extent, the personality of its chief, and some of the *Abwehr*'s weaknesses must also be ascribed to the personal faults of Canaris.

Canaris (it appears clearly between the lines of Herr Abshagen's book) was by nature a somewhat oblique character. This was not a consequence of his profession but of his personality: it was already plain long before he had accepted the post which made him famous. In his early letters he loved (though for no real purpose) to use false names and secret inks. His social manners were full of elaborate innocent make-believe: he pretended – for no other reason than mere whimsicality – to be Greek (his family was of Italian origin, settled in Germany for centuries), and kept a statue of the Greek liberator Canaris in a niche in his home. Afterwards his secret work in Spain, in naval politics, in the evasion of the Versailles Treaty, emphasised and encouraged these tastes. He was known habitually as 'the old Fox', and some disliked him 'especially because of his sly, indirect manner'. It was not for particular purposes that Canaris developed this somewhat tortuous character: it was his nature. 'By his very nature Canaris always took a lively, though in general purely playful interest in the colourful, exotic methods of oriental politicians.' – 'The old man cannot stop playing at Red Indians,' was the comment of one of his subordinates.

In fact, Canaris qualified for the popular conception – the conception of the Nazis and the novelettes – not for the real duties of the office. He was a personal spy, always on the move, always in disguise. He also had other personal recommendations. A man of diplomatic skill, who was able to manage even Hitler in his rages, he had a cosmopolitan outlook, foreign friends, and unrivalled intimacy with those Spanish politicians whose attitude, in 1940–1, might possibly have determined the war. But the popular conception, I have suggested, is wrong. The chief of a secret service is not a super-spy, but a bureaucrat; and as a bureaucrat Canaris was a failure. He was unable to organise his office, unable to control those distant stations where subordinates of dubious loyalty yielded easily to profitable temptations. 'Like many Germans,' Herr Abshagen admits, 'he lacked the gift of delegating responsibility. He centralised all decisions in himself, and consequently the burden on his shoulders soon became humanly intolerable.'

The result was inevitable. Not only was the burden humanly intolerable to him: while Canaris flew in perpetual feverish motion from capital to capital, or plunged into Spanish cathedrals to relieve his melancholy, painfully resolving insoluble enigmas, the *Abwehr* lost all cohesion, all discipline. Among its own members it became notorious, a mere comfortable family concern, not to say a family racket – 'the Canaris Family Ltd.', as one captured *Abwehr* officer described it – and in the Nazi Party it was despised as incompetent long before it was suspect as disloyal. By the end of 1942 (when it was completely surprised by the Allied landings in North Africa), it could only be a question of time before Himmler's rival organisation would destroy it. In 1943 the heads of the two most criticised departments – Colonel Pieckenbrock,[28] head of the intelligence section, and Colonel Lahousen, head of the sabotage section – were removed. 'In both cases,' says Herr Abshagen, 'the dismissal had no political background'; but the fact remains that the *Abwehr* had failed, and failed conspicuously, in both these fields. The third section, the counter-espionage section, had been relatively successful, although its head, Colonel Bentivegni,[29] was scheduled for departure, too. If Canaris himself survived, that was surely not for his efficiency but rather for his personal value in Spanish affairs.

When the next winter came, further blunders were crowned by the loss of that last personal asset. General Franco was by this time manoeuvring himself cautiously from non-belligerency[30] to total neutrality: the presence of Allied forces in North Africa had made such a change both necessary and desirable. At the same time pressure from the British Government was interfering with the work of the *Abwehr* in Spain. In the course of 1943 the most ambitious project there – the so-called *Unternehmen Bodden* for the reporting of ships sailing by night through the Straits of Gibraltar – had been totally dismantled as the result of British pressure on Franco.[31] By the beginning of 1944 Canaris judged that another personal visit was necessary to save the situation. It would be easy, he assured himself; he had done it so often before: a visit to Madrid, a talk with his friends, and all would be well ... But this time an extraordinary thing happened. Unconcernedly, under his usual alias, Canaris set off on his journey, only to be told from Madrid that this time he might not come to Madrid. He might not even cross the Spanish frontier. He never even saw his Spanish friends – for General Martinez Campos declined an invitation to meet him in Biarritz. Herr Abshagen does not mention this significant incident. Perhaps he does not know about it. But it is what convinced those of us who could appreciate it at the time that the fall of Canaris, already overdue, would now no longer be delayed.

Canaris fell in February 1944. The immediate cause of his fall was the defection to the British, in Istanbul, of an *Abwehr* couple, the Vermehrens.[32] But this was merely the occasion of dismissal. The real cause lay deeper. The Vermehren episode did but illustrate it. It was the universal, proved incompetence of the *Abwehr* which, after his subordinates, brought the Admiral himself down.

But what of Canaris's other activity – his anti-Nazism, to which he had not indeed sacrificed or subordinated his official duties and opportunities, but to which, now that his official duties were over, he could at last bend all his energies? Throughout the period of the war, and epecially in the period of defeat, the *Abwehr* in general, and the 'Canaris family circle' in particular, had been a consistent centre of anti-Nazism. The headquarters of the conspiracy was the *OKH*, the Army General Staff; but the *Abwehr* as a service organisation was the natural organ of the military conspirators. When agents of the conspirators needed to communicate in secrecy, or travel abroad, or go into hiding, it was the *Abwehr* which gave them codes or passports or travel facilities, opportunities of disappearance or disguise. Canaris himself constantly talked treason. He constantly put up projects for seizing power, for kidnapping and imprisoning Hitler, for concluding a separate peace with England. In February 1940, he sent an officer to Rome to propose a conservative, 'monarchical' settlement, repudiating Hitler while preserving his territorial gains. In 1943 he sent secret emissaries to Spain and Portugal, vainly seeking contact with England. And these projects of conspiracy and revolt were not merely opportunist: they were inspired by genuine moral revulsion against a hideous tyranny. Canaris was sickened by Hitler's brutality. He expressed a generous contempt for the generals who washed their hands and allowed the S.S. to carry out mass murder in the East. Nazism to him, by 1940, was not only a political disaster: it was also a moral pestilence.[33]

And yet, in that great conservative revolt which was slowly prepared in 1943–4 and which was the only positive attempt to rescue Germany from its ruinous leadership, Canaris took no personal part. Genuinely hating Hitler and Hitlerism, the friend and confidant and tacit accomplice of all the conspirators, conspiracy swirled all around him, but he, the centre of the vortex, was silent and still. So, when the net of the Gestapo began to close, it was on Canaris's chief supporters – Oster, Dohnanyi,[34] Bonhoeffer[35] – that it closed, but not on him. Discredited indeed by the evident disloyalty of his subordinates, he retired, when dismissed for incompetence, not to prison, but to a dignified sinecure on the Economic Warfare Commission, with an office in Eiche near Potsdam, that none might deduce too disastrous consequences from his fall. Meanwhile the remaining plotters continued to plot. His successor, Colonel Hansen,[36] flung himself eagerly into the conspiracy. Finally, on 20 July 1944, the bomb exploded – a captured English bomb, supplied from *Abwehr* stores – and the German generals made their only attempt to seize power in the State. How narrowly they failed we now know.

In the recriminations which followed their failure – and have never ceased to follow each other – there were many critics of Count von Stauffenberg, his friends and his methods. The muddle-headed conspirators like Rommel,[37] the ineffectual conspirators like Schacht,[38] their friends and supporters, have long and loudly protested that those who threw the bomb and planned the coup made a very serious mistake in seeking to murder Hitler. If only they had not been so headstrong, if only they had listened to sager, older men, or awaited the inevitable unfolding of events, then (say these apologists) other more statesmanlike conspiracies would have matured and all would have been well without the risk of failure or revenge, or the dubious imputation of tyrannicide, so contrary to the best theological advice. Herr Abshagen is one of these apologists. 'In the plans of that time,' he says (speaking of earlier, ineffective plans to put Hitler under house-arrest), 'a whole series of errors was avoided into which the unsuccessful plotters of 20 July 1944 afterwards fell.' And yet, since those sager, more statesmanlike plotters had been plotting sagely away for five years and had never yet found the time ripe for any action at all, I find it difficult to prefer them to that 'headstrong' group which, at the very last moment, did at least attempt something, and so nearly succeeded.

Canaris, it need hardly be said, was not one of that group. To the end he was one 'who never completely overcame his conscientious scruples against the attempted assassination'. Herr Abshagen would persuade us that Canaris was both a brilliant head of the Secret Service who yet contrived not to serve Hitler's ambition and a brilliant anti-Nazi conspirator who yet neither wanted nor furthered German defeat. It is a desperate attempt, and even his own evidence destroys it. Canaris was a psychological case. A despairing conservative, a fatalist without faith in the future, mechanically he carried on his work; and since he had faith neither in victory nor defeat – for either would be equally fatal to the world he cherished – and lacked the stamina to prevent that dilemma, he ended by perpetually marking time, as ineffective in conspiracy as in intelligence.

The consequences nevertheless flowed. A month before the plot of 20 July had revealed its corporate disloyalty, the *Abwehr* had paid the price of its proved inefficiency: its relics had been wound up. The hopes which Hitler had once entertained that Canaris would provide him with a gigantic, ubiquitous, infallible secret service, like the British Secret Service of his imagination, had not been fulfilled, and now there was a new claimant for that task: Walter Schellenberg.[39]

Schellenberg was an ambitious young man, determined to rise fast and high under the patronage of Himmler. He saw himself as the intellectual of the S.S., the *éminence grise* of his grim master. At the beginning of the war, when he was a Gestapo officer, he had drawn attention to himself by his famous coup at Venlo, in Holland. There he had lured two important officers[40] of the British Secret Service to the German frontier, to be forcibly kidnapped, with the disastrous consequences to their rickety organisation. Now he was head of the Intelligence Section (Amt VI) of the *Reichssicherheitshauptamt*, the organ of Himmler's secret power. He had long had his eyes on the rival organ of the General Staff, whose inefficiency had long been criticised and whose treachery was now clear. And he was intellectually prepared for the takeover. He, too, had fed his mind on novelettes and believed in the miraculous methods of the British Secret Service. Now, with the dismissal of Canaris, the way seemed open. Canaris's official successor, as head of the *Abwehr*, Colonel Hansen, had but a brief reign. On 15 May 1944, in the *Kursalon* at Salzburg,

Schellenberg received his commission to set up a new 'totalitarian' secret service from Himmler, now the all-powerful minister and arch-crackpot of the regime. It is true, the new service was to prove no more successful than the old: but then perhaps Schellenberg had also misconceived not only the answer, but the problem.

Thus perished Canaris's work. He himself followed. His ineffectiveness did not save him. Even if Stauffenberg had not telephoned on the afternoon of 20 July to tell him that Hitler was dead; even if the Gestapo had not recorded that fatal telephone-call – he still had to atone for his thoughts, and it is difficult to suppose that the great holocaust of Hitler's revenge on the upper classes, which spared so few, would have spared him. He was arrested at once. There was no evidence against him, for he had done nothing – only felt and thought and been inhibited from action. Consquently there was no trial. But there was no intention that he should escape. For seven months he remained a prisoner, while his friends and colleagues were pressed for evidence against him. None came; and his old subordinates – Marogna-Redwitz,[41] Freytag von Loringhoven,[42] his successor Hansen – went one by one to the gallows, leaving him behind. Finally, after seven months, Hitler resolved to deal with the last of them. Early in April 1945, when the collapse of Germany was imminent, Hitler (we are told) was shown the Admiral's newly discovered and now lost diaries. That was enough; and on 10 April, with his colleagues Oster, Dohnanyi and Bonhoeffer, Canaris was taken from his cell at Flossenbürg and quietly exterminated.[43]

It was the end of a life fatally nullified by its own lack of clarity or conviction. Canaris, like so many of the conservative opponents of Hitler, was inhibited by the contradictions, perhaps – in the purely psychological sense – by the 'guilt' of his class, and weighed down by the dead burden of a conservatism no longer capable of conserving. If his ghost haunted the court-room at Nuremberg, it was not because his life had any permanent significance: it was because he had never really been more than a ghost and any re-creation of him necessarily revived his ghostly features. Herr Abshagen, summing him up, compares him with Talleyrand. In an interesting, conscientious but sometimes perverse book, this seems to me the most perverse judgement of all. What possible link can bind together the inextinguishable old rake and sceptic who survived, with such éclat, every stage of the French Revolution – the courtier who contrived indifferently to shine as a bishop of the *ancien régime*, a republican oligarch, a usurper's minister, an imperial prince, the statesman of legitimacy, and the ambassador of the bourgeois monarchy – with this solemn fatalist, the martyr of a faith which he already knew to be dead? Canaris might perhaps have echoed Talleyrand's observation that only those who had lived under the *ancien régime* could know the meaning of *douceur de vivre*; but it is difficult to imagine the ci-devant bishop of Autun wandering dismally through dusty baroque cathedrals in mental search for that vanished elixir. No – the predicament, like the temperament, of Canaris was far more serious. His parallel is not in history but in literature. He was the Hamlet of conservative Germany.

3

The Philby Affair

Kim Philby, Trevor-Roper's former colleague in SIS, had been under suspicion by MI5 since 1951 when he sent a warning to Donald Maclean that he was about to be arrested. In 1955 the suspicion became public knowledge when Philby was accused in Parliament of being the sinister 'third man' who had tipped off Maclean. In 1963 Philby finally defected to Russia, but public curiosity about his career was not satisfied. By 1967 the Insight Team of Sunday Times *journalists led by Bruce Page were gathering evidence which suggested that Philby was a particularly damaging traitor. At that time the* Observer's *Patrick Seale was also working on the Philby story, and his paper was due to publish the memoirs of Philby's third wife, Eleanor. Both Bruce Page and Patrick Seale wrote to Trevor-Roper about their projects, and Dick White, now Chief of SIS, suggested that Trevor-Roper should write about the notorious spy himself. Once again it was White, the moving force behind* The Last Days of Hitler, *who appreciated that Trevor-Roper possessed both special insight into a topical problem and the literary skill to do it justice.*

Trevor-Roper's The Philby Affair *first appeared in a cultural magazine and then as an independent book. Like* The Last Days of Hitler, The Philby Affair *would never have been written without White's prompting. His suggestion was part of a wider effort by British intelligence to deploy historians to offset the damage caused to the intelligence services by the media spotlight on security failures. By 1968 an official publication was already under consideration, and the first volume of F.H. Hinsley's official history,* British Intelligence in the Second World War, *was published in 1979.*

In January 1968 White wrote to Trevor-Roper, expressing his confidence that both MI5 and SIS were able to understand and deal with the Soviet danger. White urged Trevor-Roper to emphasise the national aspects of intelligence in his Philby piece – in other words, its role within British government. Such an approach would offset the melodramatic notions in

*circulation, such as the thesis, favoured by novelists, that Philby should
have been eliminated. White wrote that doing away with Philby in Beirut
would have been a doubtful proposition, and that no democratic politician
would want to incur the responsibility for such action.*[1]

*The Philby mystery captured Trevor-Roper's attention. From 1941 to
1944 Philby had been head of the Iberian sub-section of Section V of
SIS. His counter-espionage against the extensive German spy networks in
Spain and Portugal had brought about frequent liaison with Trevor-Roper
and his team. Trevor-Roper had found Philby competent and pleasant
but also evasive. He was disappointed that their acquaintance remained
superficial: 'Except for one reference to Marx, he never mentioned a book in
my presence, nor could I get him to talk on serious topics: he would always
keep conversation on a superficial plane, in ironic, Aesopian language, as
if he knew of the differences which would divide us should we break the
surface on which, till then, we could happily and elegantly skate.'*[2]

*As the story of Philby's treachery slowly seeped out, Trevor-Roper became
increasingly fascinated by his mysterious former colleague. As he wrote
to Leonard Russell, associate editor of the* Sunday Times *in January
1968, 'I particularly wanted to publish my views on this subject. I was
prepared to publish them elsewhere, but I decided that it was my duty
to offer them first to the* Sunday Times.[3] *You generously accepted and
gave me carte blanche.' But his understanding with Russell unravelled
because the editor of the colour magazine knew nothing about it and made
alternative arrangements. Trevor-Roper was on friendly terms with the
editor of* Encounter, *Melvin Lasky,*[4] *who had organised a 'Congress for
Cultural Freedom' in Berlin which Trevor-Roper had attended in 1950.
Although Trevor-Roper had deplored the Cold War hysteria of Lasky's
conference, by late 1967* Encounter *was a promising outlet with a
circulation of 40,000. In late January 1968 Trevor-Roper arranged to
publish his Philby essay with* Encounter.[5]

The choice of Encounter *was not without irony, as Philby himself seems
to have been involved in the discussions held early in 1951 between the CIA
and SIS which eventually let to the establishment of the anti-Commmunist
magazine. By 1952 it was agreed that the salaries of* Encounter's *British
staff would be paid from the Foreign Office, as it would be improper for the
CIA to pay them. Once the magazine was established in 1953, regular
brown envelopes arrived in* Encounter's *office from the Information*

Research Department of the Foreign Office. More important financially were heavy subsidies from the CIA for the magazine, which could not have survived without them. Although Encounter *published many essays of remarkable quality, they seldom criticised American policy. Only in the spring of 1967 did the British co-editor Stephen Spender establish that his magazine was funded by the CIA. Thereupon he resigned, leaving* Encounter *in Lasky's hands.*[6]

Goronwy Rees,[7] *who wrote a monthly column for the magazine, told Trevor-Roper that* Encounter *was delighted by his essay.*[8] *It was published in the April issue, which went on sale in late March. Trevor-Roper received some very enthusiastic comments. His former pupil, the politician and diarist Alan Clark, wrote to say 'how delighted I was by your piece in* Encounter *on Philby. So true, and so gracefully written, no-one can quite achieve that combination as you do.' Noel Annan, provost of University College London, praised 'a most masterly article' with its 'splendid passages of irony about some of the extraordinary people who graced MI6 during the war' and thought it would 'put an end to the awful crude journalistic generalisations about the Establishment and the operations of Military Intelligence'. Annan later told Trevor-Roper, 'You wrote by far the best piece about MI6 that has ever appeared.' The Dutch historian Louis de Jong thought the article 'magnificent'. One colleague saw an opportunity for malice: Geoffrey Grigson, who had been at school with Cowgill, told Trevor-Roper, 'What a devil you would be if you only wrote a little better, perhaps as well as Taylor.' Trevor-Roper marked this letter, 'no reply'.*[9]

The Chief of SIS was very pleased with Trevor-Roper's article in Encounter. *Trevor-Roper had not only performed a thorough dissection of his subject, he had also stressed the revitalisation of SIS under White's leadership. White wrote that, 'although everything you write merits commendation, I feel I must drop you a line to say how much I enjoyed and admired your piece about Kim. I am about to go to a N.A.T.O. meeting in Brussels where I have no doubt I shall be pestered by my European colleagues on this subject and I shall have no hesitation in referring them to your article. If this puts up the sales of* Encounter *so much the better.'*[10] *In addition to Dick White, during 1968 Trevor-Roper was also in regular contact with another intelligence officer, Richard Thistlethwaite, who had served as MI5's first security liaison officer in Washington.*[11]

Trevor-Roper did not find a publisher for the book form of The Philby Affair *immediately. It had been initially proposed to his usual publisher Macmillan in February 1968 as a small pamphlet to be published very soon after its appearance in* Encounter, *but Tim Farmiloe of Macmillan felt that, though keenly interested, they were unable to publish 'the cheap instant pamphlet that is obviously desirable in the present case'.[12] Farmiloe approached Pan Books, which was then jointly owned by Macmillan, but Pan had recently published Eleanor Philby's book about her notorious husband and could not make an offer.*

Trevor-Roper eventually placed his book with William Kimber, who specialised in intelligence and military history. Kimber had worked at Hutchinson for many years before setting up his own firm in 1950. In 1966 he had published British Agent, *the memoirs of Leslie Nicholson, a career officer in SIS, who wrote under the alias of 'John Whitwell'. The British government had made no effort to stop the publication of* British Agent,[13] *and SIS knew Kimber's publishing interests. Although Dick White moved from SIS to become intelligence coordinator in the Cabinet Office on 1 April 1968, he may have done yet another service for his former protégé by bringing together Trevor-Roper with Kimber, who was willing to publish in one volume both Trevor-Roper's essay on Philby and his earlier piece on Canaris.*

Trevor-Roper described Kimber as 'a worrier, who minds about the truth in the books that he publishes'.[14] Kimber had promised to get the new book out within two months of receiving the revised essays on Philby and Canaris. As when he had written The Last Days of Hitler, *Trevor-Roper's engagement with his subject produced rapid writing. Early on 6 August Trevor-Roper had a meeting with Thistlethwaite, presumably so that the latter could check his typescript from a security perspective. Next he had lunch with a friend Gerald Kidd at the Travellers' Club. Then Trevor-Roper delivered the text to Kimber in the afternoon.[15]*

Trevor-Roper later wrote to Isaiah Berlin, 'In 1968 I published a little book on The Philby Affair. *It is true, I wrote this book (as I wrote* The Last Days of Hitler) *at the explicit suggestion of Dick White, then head of MI6 – who, however, did not see it, and did not want to see it, before publication.'[16] Dick White responded enthusiastically to* The Philby Affair *and obviously valued its contribution to the efforts to spike Philby's guns: 'I was very happy indeed to receive your book on the*

Philby case & still more happy that it came out in time to be reviewed simultaneously with the P. memoirs [My Silent War] *{...} Graham Greene's preface {to the memoirs} was even more nauseating than the Philby book.'*[17] Conceived by the Chief of MI6, and baptised by MI5, Trevor-Roper's book was published to the accompaniment of much secret encouragement.

The book form of The Philby Affair *published by William Kimber in 1968 and reproduced below differed significantly from the original* Encounter *essay. Although many paragraphs were reproduced verbatim, others were heavily rewritten and completely new paragraphs added as well. Significant variations are mentioned in the editorial endnotes, but the main source of new material was* My Silent War, *which appeared between the two publications of Trevor-Roper's essay. The footnotes were included by Trevor-Roper in the Kimber edition.*

Foreword[18]

The true facts about Kim Philby's treachery, though long known in Whitehall and by his former colleagues, were only made public in 1967. Their publication, by enterprising journalists, naturally caused a sensation. But facts, even if correctly stated, can be misleading if detached from their context, and it seemed to me, when I read the published accounts, that the context, as described by writers who were themselves unfamiliar with it, sometimes distorted the truth. I therefore decided, since I knew Kim Philby well and still look back with pleasure to the time which I spent in his company, to write my own account of that strange episode which, when the dust of controversy has subsided, will still remain an interesting illustration of the European crisis of conscience in the 1930s. My article on 'The Philby Affair' was published in *Encounter* in April 1968.

In the story of Philby there are [...] some details which I would now like to add, for they do credit to my friends; but alas, my friends forbid it: so these crowning touches must wait, perhaps, for another eighteen years. Meanwhile, I hope that one of those friends [*D'Arcy Patrick Reilly*] will accept the dedication of this small volume, as a reminder of our special relationship [...]

To D. P. R.

'Many swift arrows have I beneath my bended arm within my quiver, arrows that have a voice for the wise, but for the multitude they need interpreters'[19]

'KIM' PHILBY is familiar to all of us now. His name has become a household word. Certainly he was one of the most remarkable double-agents who have been exposed in our time. For ten years, from 1941 to 1951, he was a universally trusted member of the British Secret Service.* During those years he had access to some of its most jealously guarded secrets, and rose to a key position in it. For the same ten years, and longer, he was a Russian spy, having been a secret communist since 1933.[20] In those ten years he preserved this double position with remarkable poise. He never incurred the suspicion of his superiors. He won the devotion of his subordinates. During the war he was regarded as one of the most efficient of counter-espionage officers, controlling our operations in the Iberian Peninsula. At the outbreak of peace, when the other wartime 'amateurs' left the Service, he was one of the few who were pressed to stay in it; and he stayed in it in a vital position, first as head of the section dealing with communist affairs, then as liaison officer with the American Intelligence Services in Washington. If he was extruded from the Service in 1951, this was not through any suspicion of his true role. It was another's treachery, not his own, whose exposure forced his resignation, and the Service released him apologetically, with golden handshakes. Even five years later, when suspicion was closing upon him, he was publicly vindicated by the Foreign Minister in the House of Commons, and thereafter crept back into the outer fringe of the Service. To the end he preserved his remarkable self-confidence. He never doubted his own capacity to cover his traces. Only the defection of a fellow communist finally exposed him and drove him, in 1963, to take refuge in Moscow – to go, as he expressed it, 'home'.[21]

Such a career of duplicity inevitably raises general questions. First there is the personal question. How was it possible for such a man – favoured

---

* Technically, Philby may be said to have joined the Secret Service in June 1940; but his activities in Section D were peripheral and temporary. His effective and continuous service dates from his recruitment, from S.O.E., to the bureaucracy of S.I.S. in the summer of 1941. [*Section D of SIS was its sabotage unit. The Special Operations Executive (SOE) absorbed Section D and Philby in the autumn of 1940.*]

by society, liberally educated, regarded by all who knew him as intelligent, sensitive, and transparently 'sincere' – to become not only a traitor but a traitor of a particularly despicable kind, lying, deceiving, breaking oaths, abusing confidence and destroying friends in the service not of a natural patriotism nor even of a consistent ideological doctrine but of a particularly revolting tyranny? For Philby's treachery cannot be excused by a transcendent faith in Marxist doctrine. He was not a distinterested or conscientious idealist. Idealists proclaim their faith and guard its purity, even if they must suffer for it. They are sensitive of its betrayal by the egotism and expediency of politicians. They end, too often, as martyrs: martyred not by the open enemies but by the official patrons of their doctrines. The history of communism is rich in such martyrs, and no tyrant slaughtered so many of the faithful on the altar of his own outrageous vanity and cynical political expediency as Joseph Stalin. But Philby never suffered any intellectual discomfort on that account. This subtle, sophisticated man was an undeviating stalwart of the changing party line. From the moment when he decided to serve the leaders of the Russian communist party, his critical spirit, his intellectual purity, his moral conscience, were dead – sacrificed not to faith or truth but to Stalin's politics.

Undoubtedly he chose a lonely and a difficult path, and some respect is always due to those who, through conviction, choose to live dangerously. But if we respect the act of worship we cannot overlook the god who is worshipped. Today Philby may protest about his 'humane' convictions. He may even – now that it is not only safe but orthodox to do so – express retrospective reservations about Stalin's policies. But the fact remains that, so long as Stalin was alive, he laid his offerings of broken trust, a deadened mind and poisoned human relations, on the altar of a cannibal god. It was in the very years of Philby's most active service – from 1933 to 1951 – that Stalin's reason of state was most odious. Those were the years in which he was carrying out the great purges in Russia, was murdering his anarchist allies in Spain, was making his cynical pact with Hitler,[22] was sending assassins to destroy Trotsky in Mexico, was liquidating Poles and Balts, was finally carrying his wholesale purges into the heart of Europe. For a highly intelligent man to be able to make such a sacrifice demands, in the first instance, a religious conversion of blinding force. To continue to make it for thirty years without apparent disillusion suggests an arrest of the mind barely compatible with day-to-day intelligence. And to combine such active devotion to one cause, for ten years, with the equally active performance of opposite duties, without ever showing a sign of strain, argues an almost inhuman self-control.[23] Behind the unruffled mask which he showed to the world, Philby's personality was obviously of complexity impenetrable by ordinary men. It was also of unbreakable strength. The source of that strength, the structure of that complexity, is a psychological problem beyond easy resolution.

Secondly, there is the institutional problem. How did Philby, having once decided on his destructive mission, contrive to enter into the most closely guarded citadel of the British bureaucracy, and to stay in it, and to rise within it, undetected and unsuspected, for ten years? For it must be emphasised that in one respect at least Philby should not have been able to deceive the official world. That he had been a communist in the 1930s was well known – or at least easily ascertainable – in 1941, when he was accepted into the bureaucracy of the British Secret Service. Such an allegiance would normally have debarred any man even for consideration for such employment. But not only was Philby not debarred by it: he rose, in spite of it, and was afterwards placed in the very position in which an active communist could do incalculable damage to the country which employed and trusted him. In order to face this problem it is not enough to consider Philby's personality, or his skill in deception. We must consider the personality of his whole generation, the generation which was young in the 1930s, and the social attitudes, which, at that time, were preserved in the protective, airtight bottle of the British Secret Service.

Thirdly, there is the purely factual problem. What did this remarkable agent actually do? His personality and achievement have recently enjoyed a great deal of publicity and excited a great deal of interest and speculation. But we must control our speculation. Philby's career was undoubtedly spectacular by virtue of the official post that he held and the higher posts to which he might well have risen. But what did he, as a traitor, achieve? How materially did he help the Russians, whom he served, or hinder the British, whose money he took? And what were the long-term effects of his career on the Service which his treachery had corroded? Did he fatally damage a working institution? Or did he perhaps only hasten the salutary destruction of an infected organ, and thereby, unintentionally, allow, thereafter, a return of health?

Finally, we cannot avoid a more topical question. In recent weeks Philby has reappeared before the public. Having disappeared, in 1963, under the water of the Eastern Mediterranean, he has now come to the surface, and spouted vigorously, in his safe northern harbour. Encouraged by the publicity which he has enjoyed, he has announced the completion of his memoirs, and has offered to withdraw this allegedly explosive document in return for a treaty of exchange which the Russian Government has, for years, been vainly seeking to extort by other means. The idea of such a bargain, he naïvely says, is his own. But, of course, no one is deceived. Every detail of Philby's re-emergence, every interview that he gives, every statement that he makes, is nicely calculated in advance by his masters in the K.G.B. Nothing that he says is to be accepted on trust. We must always look behind it for the purpose; and that purpose is not personal, it is political. Our final question therefore is, what Russian policy is served by this new emphasis on Philby, this deliberate attempt to build up a now exploded agent as the super-spy of the century?

*　*　*

None of these questions admits of brief or easy answers. Psychological interpretation is always speculative and the operations of a secret service are necessarily secret. Nevertheless, the attempt should perhaps be made, especially now that Philby has become a public figure, and is in danger of becoming a legend. Already three books have been published about him, and a fourth, we hear, is on its way. Meanwhile his own memoirs have appeared in America. The effect of these books, and the purpose of some of them, may be to foster the Philby legend; but they also contain truth, and perhaps even the means whereby the legend may be corrected.

Of the three published books about Philby, the most ambitious and complete is undoubtedly that of Messrs. Page, Leitch and Knightley, the 'Insight' team of the *Sunday Times*. It can be described indifferently as instant history or as high-class journalism, and has both the virtues and the faults of this, to me, unattractive genre. That is, it has behind it the ample resources of high-powered journalism; it is enlivened by the products of interviews with living witnesses; and it is presented in an efficient, readable, if impersonal style. On the other hand, it lacks dimension: it has no corrective background, no reflective depth.[24] The authors have certainly established the details of Philby's career with substantial accuracy – he himself has admitted that – though they persist in some questionable assertions. But they have made no attempt to reconstruct the context within which he operated, either as a British or as a Russian agent. In particular they overlooked his solid work against the Germans in 1941–5, which was the real basis of his rise within the Secret Service. For this rise they have preferred to find naïve sociological explanations. Philby himself knew better than that: he knew that 'solid and conscientious work' was the only real way to rise.

Mr. E. H. Cookridge's book is different in every way. In many ways it is much worse. It is far less accurate in detail, it omits important episodes, and some of its confident assertions are hopelessly wrong. Nor is it so professional, or so lively, in presentation. On the other hand, the author, who has studied the world of espionage a good deal longer than his rivals, does provide some background to the story. He has conducted fewer interviews, but he has done more homework among the documents. More humane as a biographer, he also sees that mere personal biography is not enough. A career of treachery needs an outside explanation. And in one area at least he gives valuable personal evidence. Mr. Cookridge was brought up in Austria; he became a social democrat; and as a journalist for a social democratic paper he witnessed the Putsch of 1934 by which the Austrian Chancellor Dr. Dollfuss destroyed the social democratic party and established his own 'bourgeois' dictatorship. On that occasion he claims to have met Philby, who was then acting openly with the communists. Since Philby contrived afterwards to bury his communist past, this glimpse of the only period in which he revealed his loyalty is of great importance, and Mr. Cookridge's otherwise shaky book seems to me worth reading for this episode alone.[25]

If Mr. Cookridge casts a narrow beam of light on the dark beginning of Philby's career as a spy, Mrs. Philby sheds a dim diffracted glow over the end of it. She was his third wife – American like her predecessor and successor – and they first met in the Middle East, after his fall from power in S.I.S. Politically naïve, personally incurious, she apparently never learned or guessed anything about his real character till he suddenly and secretly disappeared, leaving her stranded and bewildered in Beirut. Hers is a simple personal narrative which nevertheless has value as well as pathos and charm. She describes Philby's state on the eve of his flight, her own predicament thereafter, her journey to Moscow to join him, and their life there until she discovered that she preferred the West and he preferred Mrs. Maclean.[26] But the book is also valuable for the light which it sheds on Philby's character, and particularly on the unquestioning, all-absorbing egotism which guided him in all his actions, even in the most intimate relations. This egotism would be incredible did we not know of the even more extreme instances in that narrow, ruthless, power-hungry world of communist conspirators: a world in which wives have sent their husbands, and children their parents, unhesitatingly, even smugly, to the prison, the torture-room and the gallows. The fourth book on Philby, which is still to come, is by Mr. Patrick Seale, one of Philby's colleagues on the staff of the London *Observer*.[27]

Inevitably, these published books* – all hastily compiled – differ in detail. Some of them differ materially. Was Burgess an important spy in his own right, whose disappearance was judged necessary by Philby, and planned by him and the Russians, no less than that of Maclean? This is the view of Mr. Cookridge, who can appeal to the published evidence of the Russian Filip Kislitsyn as reported by the K.G.B. defector Vladimir Petrov.[28] Or was he, as the 'Insight' writers prefer, fundamentally unimportant and only accidentally, impulsively, and at the last minute, involved in Maclean's flight? Philby himself supports Mr. Cookridge on the first point, the 'Insight' writers on the second. Again, who was the communist defector whose evidence finally clinched the case against Philby? Was it, as the 'Insight' team suggest, Colonel Michael Goleniewski,[29] a high official in Polish Intelligence, who defected in Berlin in 1961? Or was it, as Mr Cookridge says, the Russian K.G.B. officer Anatoli Alexeyevich Dolnytsin,[30] who defected in Berlin in 1962? Or was it even neither of these, but some third person, still unnamed?[31] And how did Philby travel from Beirut to Moscow? By eastern Turkey and Soviet Armenia, as the 'Insight' writers suggest; by foot over the Lebanese border and by air from Syria, as Mrs. Philby more plausibly supposes; or more comfortably, by sea from Beirut to Odessa in the Polish cargo-ship *Dalmatova* [*sic*], as Mr. Cookridge confidently states?[32] I do not pretend to resolve these differences, which are useful reminder of the fallibility of instant history, especially in secret fields. I have no doubt that I too may be found, in this essay, to be sometimes in error, treading after them over the buried glow of treacherous embers.

Finally, there is Philby's own book. This, of course, is a work of careful and skilful propaganda. He calls it 'a plain, unvarnished tale', but in fact it is

---

* *Philby: The Spy who Betrayed a Generation*, by Bruce Page, David Leitch and Phillip Knightley, André Deutsch, 30s. *The Third Man*, by E.H. Cookridge, Arthur Barker, 30s. *Kim Philby: The Spy I Loved*, by Eleanor Philby, Hamish Hamilton, 30s, Pan, 5s. *My Silent War*, by Kim Philby, Grove Press, New York.

highly selective, and the reason for this selectivity is, at one moment, candidly given: he intends to reveal nothing to the public which is not already known to 'the British and American special services'. In other words, it is only their secrets, not his own or those of the Russians, which he proposes to reveal, and he reveals them, naturally enough – in spite of pious disclaimers – in the hope of embarrassing the West, sowing distrust between London and Washington, and furthering the aims of Moscow. However, when this has been said, it must be added – and my own experience enables me to add it with confidence – that factually his account, as far as it goes, is reliable.[33] Philby's judgement of situations is perceptive and sound. His pen-portraits (some of which are devastating) are – except where his own purpose is involved – exact and just. His historical narrative is accurate. In addition, he writes with art and charm. His account may not add substantially to that of his competitors – he would have failed in his purpose if he gave away any real secrets – but he supplies rich decorative detail, and presents it with an understanding and a subtlety which is far beyond their reach.

As my own qualification for entering this difficult competition and treading the same burning embers, I am tempted to say that I knew Philby personally. For five years I was a member of the British Secret Intelligence Service and found myself living, in time of war, in that strange, twilit world. Inevitably, during those five years, I saw much of Philby. But did I 'know' him? How can anyone claim to have known him, since he deceived us all? Even his third wife, to whom he seemed so devoted – she writes, even now, of 'a divine husband' and 'a perfect marriage' – admits that she can never have known him; for even in his most intimate relations he always wore a mask. The most I can say, therefore, is that I was familiar with his outer form, that I enjoyed its company and the conversation which issued, with apparent sincerity, through the friendly mask. I enjoyed it the more because, in that curious, artificial vivarium of the wartime Secret Service, he seemed an exceptional person: exceptional by his virtues, for he seemed intelligent, sophisticated, even real. In retrospect I see that he was far more exceptional, and far less virtuous, than I had supposed; and that I never penetrated to his reality. I therefore think it more prudent to write simply as an external observer who has had the opportunity to study, with a certain involvement, and yet also a certain detachment, both Philby himself and the world of British Intelligence within which, for a short time, he operated and which he sought to destroy.

The New Machiavel

I first met Philby in 1941, when he arrived in the same branch of M.I.6 (*alias* S.I.S. or the Secret Service) to which I had preceded him by a few months. My own recruitment to that body had been an accident. I had been incidentally included in a package-deal whereby a section of M.I.8, having made some important discoveries, was transferred, in order to control those discoveries, to the Counter-Espionage section (Section V) of M.I.6. Philby's recruitment was more deliberate: indeed, well before his arrival, I had heard of him in expectation, for he had been cried up in advance as the man who would bring order into the chaos of the Iberian department of the same Section V. I had looked forward to his arrival, partly because I, too, wished to see order in that department, and partly out of curiosity: for his name had long been familiar to me. As an undergraduate at Oxford I had heard admiring accounts of him from a friend who often travelled with him in vacations. And sure enough, while we were still waiting for Philby, my old Oxford friend himself appeared in Section V as a herald of the coming hero, a John the Baptist to the new Messiah.[34]

No one spoke more hopefully of this Messiah than the head of Section V, Major Cowgill,[35] a conscientious but worried official who sorely needed an efficient deputy in the private empire which he jealously, not to say fanatically, defended against every supposed rival or critic. It soon appeared that Major Cowgill based his hopes not on personal knowledge but on the enthusiasm of his own immediate superior in the mandarinate. This superior officer was Colonel Vivian, who now, having outmanoeuvred his rival Colonel Dansey,[36] sat at the right hand of 'C' himself, with the glorious title of DCSS and the right to sign his ideogram in red ink. At that time Colonel Vivian took a good deal of credit for discovering Philby, whose father, it seems, was an old friend. Kim was a clever young man, he said, an intellectual – but not one of those unsound, irreverent intellectuals who gave so much trouble ... So he had recommended his employment; and 'C', the Chief of the Secret Service, Sir Stewart Menzies, had duly endorsed the recommendation of *DCSS* in his own ritual ink, which was green.

I admit that Philby's appointment astonished me at the time, for my old Oxford friend had told me, years before, that his travelling companion was a communist. By now, of course, I assumed that he was an ex-communist; but even so I was surprised, for no one was more fanatically anti-communist, at that time, than the regular members of the two security services, M.I.6 and M.I.5. It was quite inconceivable, in ordinary circumstances, that M.I.6 would want to employ anyone who had ever been a communist, or that the department of M.I.5 which supplied the 'trace' (i.e. checked the back history of every new employee) would clear him for such employment. And of all the anti-communists, none seemed more resolute than the ex-Indian policemen, like Colonel Vivian and Major Cowgill, whose earlier years had been spent in waging war on 'subversion' in the irritant climate of the East. That these men should have suspended their deepest convictions in favour of the ex-communist Philby was indeed remarkable. Since it never occurred to me that they could be ignorant of the facts (which were widely known), I assumed that Philby had particular virtues which made him, in their eyes, indispensable.[37]

I hasten to add that, although I myself knew of Philby's communist past, it would never have occurred to me, at that time, to hold it against him. Indeed, I was rather cheered than depressed by this unusual recruitment. My own view, like that of most of my contemporaries, was that our superiors were lunatic in their anti-communism. Many of our friends had been, or had thought themselves, communists in the 1930s; and we were shocked that such persons should be debarred from public service on account of mere juvenile illusions which anyway they had now shed: for such illusions could not survive the shattering impact of Stalin's Pact with Hitler in 1939. We were therefore pleased that at least one ex-communist should have broken through the net and that the social prejudices of our superiors had, on this one occasion, triumphed over their political prejudices.[38] For, of course, we were quite satisfied that it was social prejudice, not political enlightenment, that had brought Philby to us. Was not his father – Colonel Vivian's friend, the Arabian explorer H. St. John Philby – an ex-Indian Civil Servant of impeccable right-wing (not to say, fascist) views, who had just spent a brief time in Brixton Prison under Regulation 18B?[39] I did not know, at that time, that Kim Philby himself had outwardly atoned for his former communist views by overt 'fascist' activities: by membership of the Anglo-German Fellowship[40] and by service as a war correspondent with General Franco's army in the Spanish Civil War. Nor did I ever suppose – what now seems to have been the truth – that the evidence of Philby's communist past, which was so well known to his contemporaries, had altogether eluded the Registry of M.I.5.[41]

One part of our reasoning, I now believe, was wrong. We misunderstood the true character of communism. In particular, we did not appreciate the concealed but impassable gulf which separates it from the next most radical doctrine in the political spectrum. This was a common liberal illusion of that time – the time of the Spanish Civil War and the Popular Front against the mounting aggression of Hitler and Mussolini. In those days many of us believed that the communists were merely the most radical of our allies against fascism, the militants on the extreme left of an equal coalition in which men agreed to differ with mutual respect. Some of them doubtless were – naïve idealists who would afterwards return to the liberal fold. But we failed to realise that others were not.

For if communism may be a political nuance to some, to others it is a religion – perhaps the only religion which can still totally paralyse the mental and moral faculties of its converts and cause them to commit any turpitude, and to suffer any indignity, for its sake. This, I believe, is a psychological fact, which we must recognise if we are to understand the behaviour of men in periods of ideology. Political conversion in the present is sometimes most intelligible if we remember the religious conversions of the past.

For the communist fanatic of today has not always been a fanatic. Like the inquisitors and martyrs of the ages of warring religion, he has often begun as a sensitive, intelligent, cultivated man. He may even have been a sceptic, wandering in the beguiling labyrinth of doubt. But conversion ends all that. For ideological conversion is often a form of intellectual cautery: the intensity of the experience burns out a part of the mind so that it can never be restored. So the culture, the urbanity, the sophistication of such men may remain untouched elsewhere; but where the faith is involved they are moral and mental automata. The sixteenth-century Jesuit, ex-humanist and new machiavel, poet and assassin, equivocator and saint, has his successors in a new age of ideological strife. Such men may seem to us almost schizophrenic. They live in two worlds, operate on two levels at the same time. In fact, one life has overtaken another, devouring the heart while leaving untouched the habits of the mind.

Since the war we have become familiar with this phenomenon; but before the war it was new to us, and we did not appreciate it. In our insularity, we had not yet caught up with the ideologies of the Continent or appreciated their distorting effects on the minds of men. We recognised that communism could seduce liberal men, but we supposed that such seduction was a merely intellectual experience, so that converts, once disillusioned, could recover their past liberalism. We did not realise that some conversions change not only the direction but the quality of the mind. Our more conservative colleagues[42] erred in the other direction. They saw communism as mere 'subversion', the doctrine of subject classes and peoples. They underestimated its power to convert English gentlemen. They also believed that there was no way back for any convert. We thought that there were no Philbies; they insisted that all who had tasted communism were Philbies – except Philby himself. We believed that communist doctrine could not prevail over humanity. They believed that it could not prevail over class. We were all wrong.

That Philby was a communist of this kind I do not doubt. When I first knew him I was perplexed by his character. He was, I believed, an intellectual; and yet he never seemed willing to discuss any intellectual subject. How one longed, in those drab, mechanical days, to escape from routine work and routine postures and to discuss ideas! And yet Philby, who seemed so intellectual, so sophisticated in his outlook, who was so different from most of our colleagues, and whose casual, convivial conversation I found so congenial, never allowed himself to be engaged. In the end, I sometimes wondered whether he was really an intellectual after all. Did he really read books, or think, or talk freely in any circle? Never having been in his house or seen his book-shelves, I could not answer this question. But today I feel that I can. The problem that perplexed me has been illuminated for me not only by his own past history, since revealed, but also by that of other communist intellectuals whom I have known. From the moment of their self-immolation, of that *sacrificio dell' intelletto* which was made by the Jesuits of the sixteenth century, the sublety of their minds does not entirely evaporate, but it is withdrawn from the world of ideas. It is exercised only at surface-level, on trivialities, outside the area of real thought. At the heart, in the mind, on all real topics, it is closed for ever: frozen, sterilised, sealed up.[43]

* * *

This contrast between the death of the mind, where real problems are concerned, and its continuing activity, even subtlety, in trivial, peripheral areas, often leads to bizarre results. Nothing has seemed to me so grotesque, in Philby's recent Moscow utterances, as his presumption in judging the modern world whose real nature, for the last thirty years, he has not even noticed. How can any observant adult, after thirty-five years, rage at the 'betrayal of socialism' by Ramsay MacDonald and yet bow, in mute adoration, before Stalin? 'The politics of the Baldwin–Chamberlain era', says Philby were 'evil', but the great purges of Stalin were merely an 'aberration'. The lack of proportion, even of plain common sense, in such an observation is staggering. Nor is it only the modern world to which Philby is so smugly impervious. He expresses views on history too. 'I regard myself,' he told a Moscow correspondent of the *Daily Express*, 'as wholly and irreversibly English and England as having been perhaps the most fertile patch of earth in the whole history of human ideas.' His 'humane contempt', he says, is reserved not for the essential England but for certain 'temporary phenomena' which prevent England from being itself. The fatuity of these remarks, the suggestion that all English intellectual history directs 'humane' men onwards and upwards to the ideals of the K.G.B., leaves the reader aghast. I am reminded of a remark by George Savile, Marquis of Halifax: 'The impudence of a bawd is modesty compared with that of a convert.'

And then there is that other, more positive force which is so often the real motive of the communist intellectual: love of power. However such a man may have come into the party, it is love of power that keeps him in. Once again we are reminded of the Church, in the age of faith – and not only the Catholic Church, for many a petty Calvin has trod the same narrowing, upward, beckoning path. The communists who joined the Party in the 1930s no doubt began as idealists. They believed that, by joining the Party, they would fight the battle of the poor and the oppressed. But they soon decided that their own battles were more urgent and more exciting. The poor and oppressed must be saved from other, rival, heretical leaders before they could be led, united, against their enemies. Social democrats, anarchists, Trotskyists must be destroyed, for it is better for the poor and oppressed to sink under new fascist oppressors – as they did in both Austria and Spain – than to find salvation outside the true Church. If we can believe Mr. Cookridge, Philby quickly reached this second stage of conversion. Within a few days of supporting the 'popular front' of the Viennese workers against the artillery of Dr. Dollfuss, he was appearing again as a communist agent, trying to destroy the social democratic organisation. For the rest of his life he sought not so much a new society (to which there are many alternative avenues) as the exquisite relish of ruthless, treacherous, private power.

Power for what? Perhaps the question is irrelevant. To many men, power, or the sense of it, is an end in itself. But for Philby, it seems, power was not constructive. He may speak of building a communist state, but the phrase is a cliché only. It is noticeable that the terms of approval which he uses today are but empty, canting generalities, while the hatred he expresses is concrete and real. He applauds 'the principles, of the Revolution', 'the communist idea'; he denounces 'the expense-account lunch', 'the Beaverbrook Press', 'Mr. Wilson and Mr. Heath'. All through his career this negative character is apparent. Philby touched nothing which he did not destroy – from within – while Russia, which alone he served, he did not touch: it remained a remote, unknown abstraction. While the policy which he served veered and shifted, his destructive zeal remained constant. Institutions, persons, friendships, marriage, all crumbled around him. His career illustrates yet another aspect of that intellectual nihilism which seems to be a feature of this century: which was prominent in nazism as well as in communism, and which, detached from all ideology, is with us still.

Finally, there is another force which seems to me, in retrospect, to have dominated Philby's character and determined his lonely and difficult course. I refer to his truly extraordinary egotism and complacency. Mrs. Philby's book gives us some evidence of this. Her account of their 'perfect marriage' is lyrical, and she still evidently looks back to those days with melancholy pleasure. There were, she thought at the time, no reservations, no secrets between them. But, in fact, Philby not only deceived her throughout that time. He not only – as he afterwards admitted – invariably put his loyalty to the Party before her. He also assumed that she would blindly submit to whatever change of life might be entailed by this prior, unrevealed commitment. When she did even this, following him, after harrowing suspense and grim experience, to a squalid and isolated life in Russia, he never thought it necessary, or even reasonable, to offer any explanation. 'He never once said to me, "I've landed you in a situation you perhaps did not anticipate when you married me."' Subtle and sophisticated though he is in external matters, where he himself is involved, Philby is totally, blindly egocentric. Only thus, perhaps, could he have been so constant in his uncritical devotion to the career which he had chosen.

This same characteristic emerges from his own memoirs. Throughout his active career Philby has deceived his friends, his confidants, his colleagues, just as he deceived his wife. Trust has been given to him only to be abused, secrets entrusted only to be divulged. Such treachery is seldom, if ever, forgiven. Mrs. Philby is aware of this: she felt deeply their pariah status in Moscow, their inability to meet those whom they once had known and respected. But Philby, who clearly values the respect of his former friends, seems quite unaware that he has now lost it. In his memoirs he regularly assures his old colleagues of his continuing 'affection and respect' for them. For his old chief, Sir Stewart Menzies, he expresses 'enduring affection'. He protests that he does not wish to 'embarrass' any of them. He seems to assume that if he spares them 'embarrassment' they will return his respect. He even solicits sympathy from those whom his revelations may embarrass by explaining that 'I too have suffered personal inconvenience through my connexion with secret service'. If bigotry has formed, egotism has protected the deadened mind of this still subtle, charming and superficially intelligent man.[44]

Philby's secret history, and the secret quality of his mind, were unknown to me when I first knew him in 1941. More surprising, it was evidently unknown to M.I.5 and M.I.6 too. But in retrospect I am satisfied that such was Philby's character when we met in S.I.S. Our careers in that organisation ran almost parallel, but with differences. I was, I fear, distrusted by our superiors, who suspected me, with some justice, of irreverent thoughts and dangerous contacts. I was secretly denounced as being probably in touch with the Germans, and more openly – and more justly – accused of consorting with the more immediate enemy, M.I.5. I was once summoned to be dismissed. How well I recall that 'trial' – *in camera*, of course – with Colonel Vivian as prosecutor and '*C*' as judge! It was a narrow squeak. I have always felt grateful to '*C*' for his ultimate rejection, on that occasion, of the argument of *DCSS*, who maintained with increasing urgency, and in lamentable tones, that whatever the merits of the case it was quite impossible, after this, for me to remain in the organisation. However, thanks to '*C*', I did remain: indeed, the organisation was afterwards adjusted to separate me from Section V in which I had been an indigestible particle. This separation certainly made things much easier all round.

My own passage in the Secret Service being so stormy, I could not but admire the calm and steady course of my friend, and, in a certain sense, my rival, Kim Philby.[45] Of course, I was quite sure that he, being an intelligent man, was no less critical of the organisation than I was. But he never uttered his criticism. It was always unspoken, implicit only in his benign, distant Aesopian irony. Consequently, he prospered. No one ever suggested that he was in touch with any enemy. No one suggested that it was impossible for him to stay in the organisation. On the contrary, it seemed inconceivable that he would ever be allowed to leave. Colonel Vivian doted on him; Major Cowgill clung to him. He was the blue-eyed boy of the establishment, the one 'amateur' who was appreciated by the 'professionals', the only one to receive, at the end of the war, a decoration.[46]

For all through the war, among the numerous internal tensions of S.I.S., a natural distrust divided these two groups: a distrust partly to be explained by the different social and educational background from which they came. The amateurs regarded the Service as existing to help win the war. It was this need alone which had brought them into it, and naturally they did not look beyond that immediate aim. Consequently, they were impatient of the mandarins with their complacent airs and their sacred 'procedure'. The professionals, on the other hand, preened themselves on their 'long-term views'. They looked beyond the war. Indeed, it seemed to us, they sometimes regarded the war as a dangerous interruption of the Service; and they sighed for the time when they would get rid of those irreverent amateurs with their disruptive 'short-term' views, their carelessness of the delicate health of a venerable system. No doubt, in the end, the Service would have to absorb some of these immigrants; but it was clear that it would absorb only those who would sustain, not imperil, the old fabric. Often, as peace loomed ahead, we asked ourselves who, among the amateurs, would be absorbed. Our answer was always clear. We never doubted that there would be a great sight of relief as the rest of us were released to civilian life. Equally, we never doubted that Philby – that tireless, uncomplaining prop of an exhausted establishment – would be pressed to stay.

He duly was. Indeed, even before the end of the war, the decision was taken. In the summer of 1944, when the Allies landed in Normandy, the end of the war against Germany was already in sight. From that moment Kim and I went different ways. I moved gradually, through Germany, to civilian life. He moved, first upward towards the summit of Section V, then altogether out of it to become head of the new anti-communist section of S.I.S., which was soon to absorb the old Section V. So he established himself at the very centre of the Service on the eve of the new struggle which was already threatening to break out: the Cold War.

In secret, how he must have relished that triumph! It was the ironic climax of his career. His Russian masters, too, must have smirked, a complacent, machiavellian smirk, as they saw their chosen agent moving into this central post.[47] Once again, it was the innocent Colonel Vivian who had engineered the appointment. Major Cowgill, it seemed, had opposed it strongly. Philby was too valuable to spare, he said, and besides, he wanted the post himself: it was his, he thought, by right. But he had been overruled and hatcheted for his pains. Philby and Vivian agreed between them to dispose of him. 'And to think, Kim,' said the Colonel, as he signed the death-warrant, 'that only yesterday I was recommending him for the C.B.E.!'[48]

The intrigue whereby Philby secured the elimination of his own commanding officer, and himself stepped into the vacant place, has been described in detail, and with retrospective relish, in his own memoirs. I found it a fascinating account; for the inner mechanism of this secret history was unknown to me till I read it there. It is full of dramatic irony, too.[49] We all, at that time, welcomed the removal of Cowgill, who had long been impossible. We all allowed that, if he went, Philby would be the natural successor. We all expected a general improvement from the change, when it occurred.[50] What none of us realised was that our Russian allies expected an even greater improvement: that it was they who, through secret contact, had instructed Philby that he 'must do everything, but *everything*', to ensure this happy result – happy for us, happier still for them.

I never had an opportunity of discussing Philby's new work with him. Indeed, for a long time I did not see him again. But from the moment when the unfortunate Major Cowgill was 'released', I never doubted that, within the Service, Philby was the man of the future.[51] Nor did I doubt what his future would be. I was convinced (and still am) that he was destined – indeed that he was being groomed – to head the Service: that he would have been, in the 1950s, the new 'C'.

Sir Stewart Menzies, I know, has denied this, maintaining that Philby held only minor posts. But I am afraid that I regard this as a routine denial, such as any official must sometimes make in the course of duty. And anyway, Philby's posts were not minor: far from it. They were posts of great responsibility and promise, clear auguries of future promotion. So I stand fast by my conviction which, at that time, I based on several grounds. First, Philby was undeniably competent: the most competent and industrious man in that generally lax organisation. Secondly, though conspicuously abler than they, he never showed any trace of impatience or disrespect towards the established leaders of S.I.S. Consequently, he was regarded by them as the hope of the future. Thirdly, his successive posts in the Service gave him, as no one else, a direct understanding of all the branches of it and thus fitted him to command it all. Finally, who else, of his generation, was there? The importation of an outsider into that carefully guarded preserve seemed unlikely. How could anyone who had not been bred in the Service understand its labyrinthine 'procedure'? But within it, who could possibly compete with Philby, trusted by all, favoured by his superiors, experienced in both war and peace, in counter-espionage against both Germany and Russia, tested in both the office and the field, strong in his contact with the American secret services? I looked around the world I had left, at the part-time stockbrokers and retired Indian policemen, the agreeable epicureans from the bars of White's and Boodle's,* the jolly, conventional ex-naval officers and the robust adventurers from the bucket-shop;[52] and then I looked at Philby. I was reminded of Tiresias among the ghosts of Hades. He alone was real: they flitted like shadows in their crowded *coulisses*.

Besides, Philby seemed to have acquired so completely the protective colouring of the office. That air of weary cynicism, that pose of the unhurried, sophisticated, worldly politician

Who sees through all things with his half-closed eyes,

had become, as it seemed, entirely natural to him, as if he, too, had drunk from the drugged chalice of that secret church. I remember the comment of a friend who had visited him in Istanbul after the war. Kim, I was told, had now been entirely corrupted. He lived an agreeable, self-indulgent life, in a pleasant villa on the Bosphorus, with a private lobster-harbour, in lotus-eating ease. All passion, it seemed, was spent. He had become a *routinier* and a voluptary – but still an efficient *routinier* and an agreeable voluptary. He would ensure professional standards; but would not disturb the ancient habits of the professionals. He was both efficient and safe. What more could be asked of the head of S.I.S.?

---

* I fear that it may have been this innocent phrase which, when first published, provoked a stud-farming baronet to send me, from Boodles, an insulting letter. I had not realised that he, too, had been in S.I.S. [*The baronet was Sir Humphrey Clarke (1906–73), who served in British Security Coordination in North America.*]

This last quality, this love of comfort, of epicurean *douceur de vivre*, has often struck me when I have reflected on Philby's career.[53] He himself has never denied it. Indeed, in his Moscow interviews, he has dwelt with some relish on his taste for oysters and caviar, his capacity 'to enjoy life to the full whenever duty permitted'. By 'duty', of course, his duty to his Russian masters. But 'to the full'? Most people will find the phrase, in his circumstances, rather odd. For after all, even for the epicure, oysters and caviar are not a self-contained and complete form of pleasure. Their savour depends, for its fullness, on less material circumstances: on peace of mind, good company, free conversation, unreserved friendship; which, for a secret traitor, are not. Did Judas enjoy the Last Supper? I rather doubt it. And if even the epicure is thus limited in his pleasures, how much more the pretended stoic, the iron-willed, austere devotee of a distant, immutable virtue? However, as I have said, I cannot accept Philby's pretence of idealism. Idealism may have governed him in the moment of surrender. I readily believe that it did. But his surrender, once made, was not to an ideal, it was to a discipline; and whether that discipline served a constant, impersonal purpose or merely a changing, cynical reason of state he no longer asked, or could ask, for his critical faculty had long ago perished. To me, therefore, this epicureanism, so far from being the enviable relaxation of conscious virtue, as he now maintains, seems rather the mere physical escape from the strain of discipline: a relaxation no less mechanical and mindless than the obedience to that discipline. Such relaxation is no doubt doubly necessary to Philby in his present uncomfortable predicament in Moscow where, protest he never so loud, a declared foreign traitor from the days of Stalinist terror can hardly be respected, even by the officials who publicly flatter him. He would have relaxed more comfortably, I think, as well as with greater inward relish, as the crypto-communist head of S.I.S.

* * *

That Philby might have held such a post, that the head of the fabulous British Secret Service might have been, perhaps for twenty years (for once there, who could have exposed him?), a secret Russian spy, is a bizarre possibility. The mind boggles at the thought. No writer of fiction would venture such a fantasy. Fortunately, it remains a fantasy. But it might easily, I believe, have been a fact. Indeed, I am now even more convinced of it than I was at the time; and I do not fear any future revelation. From 1945 to 1950 Philby seemed sure of success. He continued to be, in his own words, 'on the up and up'.

What finally stopped this rise, and turned it into a fatal decline, was not any built-in corrective mechanism in our system, nor any personal suspicion within S.I.S. It was simply an accident: the unexpected bolt to Russia, in 1951, not merely of Donald Maclean,[54] whose imminent arrest might well have incriminated Philby, but of Philby's hitherto unsuspected drinking-companion, Guy Burgess.[55] It was Philby's 'indiscretion' in associating with Burgess, not his crime in secretly directing Maclean, that led to his extrusion from the Secret Service; and he was extruded not as a suspect but as a victim of his own good nature. His honourable refusal to break with an old friend, it was said, had unhappily discredited him, not, of course, with his English colleagues, who understood the variety of human nature, but with the illiberal American McCarthyites of the C.I.A. For it should not be forgotten that the year 1951 saw Senator McCarthy already at the height of his malevolent power, and liberal men might be forgiven for an inclination to err in the other direction.

Philby's boldness in so openly associating with Burgess in America, and thus involving himself in the predictable consequences of Burgess's unpredictable character, has always surprised me. He himself now admits that it may have been an error. That Burgess, by 1950, was of any real use to the Russians seems highly doubtful.[56] However he may have served them in the past, he was now totally irresponsible, and his presence in Philby's house must have been a permanent danger to his host. On the other hand, Philby may well have thought that, by protecting Burgess, he could control him. To a friend who exclaimed in horror at the threatened arrival in Washington of this scandalous character, Philby replied, 'He is my best friend. I will have him to stay with me and he will be all right.' Such protection was, after all, self-protection too, since the unpredictable Burgess knew Philby's dangerous secret, as Philby knew his. Or perhaps here, as elsewhere, Philby enjoyed walking with assurance, even defiance, along the perilous knife-edge of treachery. Just as, afterwards, when first suspected, he did not bolt to safety, but calmly continued on his way – yielding ground here, regaining it there – until the last minute, so now he may have relished the fine flavour of a double danger, confident in his own skill and the steadiness of his nerves. This, after all, is the necessary quality of the high-class spy, the quality on which he piques himself, and to prove which, at least to himself, he enters upon his solitary, outlawed profession.

However that may be, the danger in fact overtook him: but still his nerve did not fail. He fell; but his fall was dignified, and not too painful. A considerate department placed a cushion to receive him, and he was comforted by the sympathy of his liberal friends. Nevertheless, the episode which caused it had been a terrible shock, not only to the department but to the whole of British society. Inevitably, the spectacular flight of two supposedly respectable British diplomats raised far-reaching questions and disturbed the illusions of the last twenty years. Already, in America, the case of Alger Hiss had suggested a possibility which British officialdom had hitherto refused to consider: the possibility that the intellectual communism of the 1930s had thrust deeper roots into wider classes than had once seemed possible. Now the same uneasy thoughts troubled Britain too.[57]

For until 1951 the British establishment had seen communism in two alternative forms. The more conservative, like the rulers of S.I.S., saw it as an appeal to class-war which, by definition, could find no response in the favoured classes of society. This, no doubt, rather than mere snobbism, was the reason for their preference for 'gentlemen', untainted by the solvent force of a university education. (Colonel Dansey, we are told, once declared that 'he would never knowingly recruit a university man' for S.I.S.) The more liberal looked on it indulgently as a romantic liberal deviation which could not survive the chilling experience of Stalinist cynicism. Now at last both these illusions were shattered. If Maclean, the favoured *protégé* of the Foreign Office, could have preserved his secret communism all through those disillusioning years, it was clear that others could have done so too: and if Philby, in spite of his professional respectability, could retain an indiscreet association with his old communist friends, what other dangers might lurk in the obstinate cohesion of that furtive Cambridge fraternity? In the hour of shock, Philby's own communist past was at last remembered, and the question was naturally asked, why had he been so easily admitted into S.I.S. in 1941? Why had a damaging past been so blithely overlooked or ignored. Above all, why had that past[58] not been remembered in 1945 when he had passed the great barrier between amateur and professional status and switched from anti-German to anti-Russian work? These thoughts naturally disturbed S.I.S. And what was perhaps even more disturbing was the fact that any investigation could not be altogether confined to the department.

The checking of British subjects, even if they worked in M.I.6, was bound to involve the old 'enemy', M.I.5.[59]

Moreover, once general suspicion was aroused, a particular cause for it could not be overlooked. Ever since 1945 Philby's 'mishandling' of a certain important case had disquieted all who knew the details of it. This was the now well-known affair of the Russian secret intelligence officer, Konstantin Volkov, which, in Philby's own words, 'nearly put an end to a promising career'. In 1945 Volkov, then Russian vice-consul in Istanbul, had defected to the British and offered, against substantial payment, a complete list of Russian agents working in Britain. Such a list, if genuine, would, of course, have exposed Philby himself. But in fact, it had never been delivered. After strange procrastinations the head of the anti-communist section of the British Secret Service had himself taken over the case, had personally flown to Turkey, and had so handled the business that Volkov was never in a position to complete the bargain. Instead, he was suddenly seized in Istanbul and bundled, unconscious, on to a Russian plane. He has never been heard of since.[60] Philby's handling of this matter – his combination of deliberate personal responsibility and almost criminal *insouciance* – long rankled with those who had hoped, through it, to make a notable contribution to counter-espionage; and after 1951 their voice was heard. The memory of the mysterious Volkov affair then concentrated a suspicion which, otherwise, was diffuse: it formed the central and most persuasive charge[61] in the dossier which was now compiled, in M.I.5, for the interrogation of Philby.

The Way Home

In the autumn of 1951, in consequence of his association with Burgess, Philby was dismissed from the Secret Service. Dismissal was concealed under the polite form of resignation. A few months later he was interrogated by M.I.5 to see if a positive charge could be brought against him. A good deal has been written about this episode. It has been described as a 'scandalous mock trial', and built up, by imagination, into a kind of illegal but amateur inquisition. In fact, Philby was simply questioned by a distinguished but not very subtle lawyer[62] and the results of his interrogation were considered in M.I.5. They were inconclusive, for the victim, it seems, had more self-control than his interrogator. But the circumstantial evidence was persuasive, and at the end of the day the lawyer himself, and others who read the record and whose judgement I respect, were morally convinced of Philby's guilt. Only his old friends in M.I.6 seem to have been unimpressed by it. But even they did not seek to restore him. In their eyes he had paid the price not of treachery but of indiscretion, and they left him in the cold. After that, Sir Stewart Menzies retired from the Service. The dismissal of Philby had been almost the last act of his reign.[63]

Unfortunately, that was not quite the end of the matter. Four years after Philby's dismissal it was revived, in curious circumstances. Primed by an eager journalist, a Labour member of Parliament, Colonel Marcus Lipton, put a point-blank question to the Prime Minister, Sir Anthony Eden, in the House of Commons, naming Philby as 'the third man' who had warned Maclean and Burgess of their danger. The question was deferred for answer to a debate on 7 November 1955, and the answer was then given by the Foreign Secretary, Mr. Harold Macmillan.

Colonel Lipton's question had been precise, and a precise question requires a precise answer. To a question whether a man is innocent or guilty of a particular act the answer can only be 'yes' or 'no'. Unless guilt can be proved, he must be declared innocent: justice does not allow that a minister, covered by the privilege of Parliament, should ruin a man's character or prospect of employment by declaring suspicion or insinuating charges which cannot be proved. The Foreign Minister was therefore, I believe, right to reply that there was no evidence against Philby. This denial was no doubt based, as to fact, on the evidence of the Foreign Office; and the Foreign Office in turn, no doubt, relied on the too-favourable conclusions of S.I.S. But I do not believe that the Minister could have answered otherwise even if he had read all the evidence and had himself been morally convinced of Philby's guilt. Moral conviction required that Philby should be excluded from any position in which he could do further damage. It did not justify public denunciation or interference with private employment. In a recent interview, Philby himself has admitted that Colonel Lipton's question was 'a gift' to him: 'He really could not have done me a better turn if he had wanted to. By naming me he virtually forced Harold Macmillan to clear me.' And in his memoirs he has spelt the matter out with perfect justice: 'No one in the government, and particularly no one in the security service, wanted to make a public statement as early as 1955. The evidence was inconclusive: they could not charge me and did not want to clear me. They were forced to take action by the ill-informed hullabaloo in the popular press and by the silly blunder of Marcus Lipton.'

Mr. Macmillan's enforced clearance of Philby was unfortunate in itself: its consequence was even more unfortunate. The new head of M.I.6, Sir John Sinclair,[64] it seems, had never been convinced of Philby's guilt. In 1952 he had seen an able member of his organisation, on mere suspicion, dismissed from his post and reduced to a life of apparent poverty. Now, after three years, he had seen the victim publicly cleared. Sir John Sinclair evidently considered that some reparation was due. He therefore readmitted Philby to the pay-roll – but not to the centre or the secrets – of S.I.S. and proposed that he should be sent out of harm's way, to Beirut. But before the arrangement could be completed, a new episode occurred which precipitated a new chapter in the history both of Philby and of S.I.S.

This episode was the affair of the frogman, Commander Crabb.[65] In 1956 Messrs. Bulganin and Khrushchev came to Britain on a state visit. They came in the Russian cruiser *Ordzhonikidze*. While the cruiser lay in harbour at Portsmouth, S.I.S. sent Commander Crabb on a secret mission to inspect its hull. The inspection was not a success. The frogman was observed by the Russians and never returned from his mission. How he perished is unknown: all that was known was the reaction of the Russians. In cold, injured tones, they protested against the indignity which they had suffered. The British Government was gravely embarrassed, and the Prime Minister [*Eden*], who knew nothing of this unauthorised espionage against his guests, was naturally furious. His feelings were shared by other members of the Government. Soon they expressed themselves in a remarkable change in the headship of S.I.S.

In 1956 Sir John Sinclair was due shortly to retire. Like his predecessor, he had the misfortune to retire in the wake of a painful incident. For Menzies, the incident had been the flight of Burgess and Maclean; for Sinclair it was the affair of the frogman. But this time the Prime Minister was not prepared to regard the episode as a mere accident. He decided that the Secret Service itself needed a violent change. So, to succeed Sinclair, he did not accept the pre-appointed heir-apparent within the Service. Instead, he broke all its time-honoured rules. First, in defiance of a hitherto unbroken tradition, he appointed a civilian.[66] Secondly, as if to affront the shade of Colonel Dansey, he appointed a university man. And finally, as if to insult the whole mandarinate, he appointed a man whom many of them had regarded as the brain, and who was, in fact, now the head, of the 'enemy' organisation, M.I.5. Good judges[67] had long ago hoped that Sir Dick White would ultimately hold this position, but against the solid opposition of the old mandarinate it had seemed impossible. To the end, the mandarins fought against the proposed appointment. When it was finally made they were aghast. As one of them ruefully observed, 'If Colonel Dansey were not already dead, he would drop dead now.'

For the mandarinate the new appointment was certainly a terrible defeat. It caused deep resentment and at least one resignation.[68] For Philby it was a double disaster. First, this was the moment at which, according to every calculation, he himself should have succeeded to '*C*'s' throne. That hope, admittedly, had now gone: it had been dashed six years ago. But now his position was far worse. For the new '*C*' was not only an able man and an outsider, unentangled in the glutinous web of old internal loyalties: he was also personally convinced of Philby's guilt. In all his recent utterances – and reticences – Philby has shown his personal hatred of the man whom, more than any other, he recognises as the author of his ruin and on whom he would fain be revenged.[69] In his memoirs, which are generally just to persons, he consistently depreciates him as pliant and indecisive, 'the ineffective White'. But sometimes, in his less deliberate moments, the truth has slipped out and he has even paid him a reluctant, unintended tribute. 'Certainly the British Government have great difficulties in finding the right men to run their Intelligence Services,' he told the correspondent of the *Daily Express* between his glasses of Georgian champagne: and he added the significant qualification, 'military men have never really shone in this field.'[70]

The new civilian '*C*', on taking over his position, was perhaps somewhat disconcerted to find that Philby had crept back on to the strength. However, he evidently decided not to disturb his predecessor's arrangement. Philby was already designated to Beirut. In Beirut he would at least be harmless. If he were a Russian spy – and still nothing could be proved – he had already done all the damage that he could. For four years he had been cut off from official secrets. The best course now was to cut him off from his old London contacts. So, by private agreement with the *Observer* (an agreement which seems afterwards to have given rise to some public dissent) he was given journalist 'cover', and was appointed as correspondent of that paper in the Middle East.[71]

* * *

It was in the Middle East that I last met him. In the spring of 1957, after the Suez affair, I decided to make a private visit to Iraq. There, in Baghdad, I found that a small party of journalists was about to travel around the country for 'Development Week', and I applied to join them. On this expedition, I found myself constantly in company with my old friend, the new correspondent of the *Observer*. I was by now satisfied that he had been a Russian spy for over twenty years; but he did not know that I knew this, and I thought it wrong to give any indication of my knowledge. So we mixed again on the old terms; and although I inwardly shrank from him as a traitor, I must admit that I found his company as attractive as ever, his conversation as disengaged, and yet as enjoyable. He had just returned from a visit to his father in puritan Saudi Arabia, and was delighted to be back in an alcoholic country. In our conversation I naturally made no reference to recent history, but I listened carefully for any allusion that he might make. In due course he made it. He wished to date some minor episode, and he chose to date it in an oddly irrelevant way. 'It was about the time,' he said, 'of all that absurd fuss about the "Third Man" ...' I made no comment; but I thought that he did protest a little too much.

Meanwhile, the net was closing around him. Since 1956 suspicion was anyway growing. How, for instance, had Philby financed himself since 1951? His standard of living had always been mysteriously high – as we know, he liked to 'enjoy life to the full'. In America his opulent way of life had already excited comment. Then, with his dismissal, his avowable income had shrunk to £600 a year. In spite of his financial decline, he had not only lived comfortably but had maintained a family of six. How, it was asked, did he do it? We now know, from his third wife, that after his flight to Moscow the Russians paid £4000 a year, untaxable, in sterling, for the maintenance of his family in England. No doubt in the lean years before his flight they discreetly relieved the wants of so faithful an agent who could do them so much damage if he should turn sour.[72]

But it was not only suspicion that was growing. Concrete evidence was growing also as the file on Philby thickened. It was supplied by a swelling number of defectors who now came over to Britain and America from the communist world, and from the K.G.B. itself, and whom now there was no Philby to intercept. Thanks to the evidence supplied to them, another Russian agent in S.I.S., George Blake,[73] was exposed in 1961. Blake had worked for the Russians since his return from North Korean captivity in

1953. Thereafter he had served mainly in Berlin. By 1953 Philby had anyway been extruded from S.I.S. and was under suspicion, so that their paths would seldom have crossed. But it happened that in 1961 Blake was also in Lebanon, learning Arabic at the Middle East Centre of Arabic Studies at Shemlah, near Beirut. He was summoned home, arrested, tried and sentenced. Observing this, Philby must have realised that his turn might well come next.

It duly did. In 1962, in Beirut, he was faced with the evidence.[74] Perhaps it was thought that, in the relative freedom of Lebanon, he might surrender to it. A full confession of facts which only he could reveal might do much to undo past damage. It might also provide useful information for the future. One of the advantages of being a double-agent is that one can defect either way. When the Americans arrested the Russian spy Rudolf Ivanovich Abel in 1957, the F.B.I. thought it worth while to offer him a salary of $10,000 a year if he would co-operate. In fact he did not. Nor did Philby. He was too deeply committed to one side, or too distrustful of the other; and perhaps he reflected on the high death-rate among important defectors. After a period of severe strain, relaxed in violent drinking bouts, which his wife has described, he made his plans. On 23 January 1963 he slipped away from Beirut and, after a period of silence and a mysterious journey, reappeared, like Burgess and Maclean before him and Blake after him, in Moscow.

His flight was certainly, from the British point of view, unfortunate. If there had to be publicity, the publicity of arrest and trial in England would have been preferable to the publicity of escape and emergence in Russia. To that extent, therefore, the negotiations in Beirut may be said to have proved a mistake. But there is something wonderfully unrealistic in the confident, not to say jubilant, denunciations of the professional critics of all our institutions who refuse to allow anyone but themselves to miscalculate and who have come out to make their hay on this occasion.

Prominent among these is Mr. John Le Carré, the novelist, whose rich, flatulent puff[75] opens the way for the more solid offerings of Messrs. Page, Leitch and Knightley. Of course, cries Mr. Le Carré, Philby should have been kidnapped, liquidated, in Beirut. It is perhaps unreasonable to expect Mr. Le Carré to consider the practical, or even the juridical consequences of the course which he so heedlessly advocates. Did the Ben Barka[76] affair redound to anyone's credit? Was the murder of General Delgado satisfactory?[77] But even if he did not think of these questions, Mr. Le Carré might at least, in consistency, have applied his own general philosophy to this particular episode.

It is Mr. Le Carré's general thesis that the Secret Service is a microcosm of society – a rotten microcosm of a rotten society – and that each can thus be used to explain the other. But if this is so, then it must follow that the secret service of a liberal society cannot use the same weapons as the secret service of a totalitarian society. What the K.G.B. could do to Volkov, S.I.S. could not do to Philby; and I know of no evidence for Mr. Le Carré's statement that the Lebanese security service was willing to act as a kidnapping agent – any more than the British were willing to kidnap Gerhard Eisler for the Americans when he jumped his bail and arrived in England *en route* for Russia in 1949.[78] On that occasion, it may be remembered, the British left, in virtuous chorus, demanded that Eisler be allowed to continue his journey: to catch communist spies for other governments, it was then said, is a monstrous invasion of personal liberty. But then it was a question of hitting the American 'establishment'. Now, in order to hit the British 'establishment' the argument is easily put in reverse.

However, on this subject, I think we can leave the last word to Philby. Having read Mr. Le Carré's book *The Spy Who Came in from the Cold*, he wrote to his wife that it was a relief to read a spy-novel that was more sophisticated than 'all that James Bond idiocy', but that 'the whole plot, from beginning to end, is basically implausible – at any rate to anyone who has any real knowledge of the business'. The same can be said of Mr. Le Carré's unhappy deviation from spy-fiction into sociological speculation.[79]

An Imperfect Organisation

With his flight to Moscow in 1963, Philby's long career of duplicity was over and we may now look back on it with detachment and try to judge its significance. He himself has also been looking back on it recently, and with some complacency. He is satisfied, he tells us. He has done his patrons some service; perhaps he may still do them some more. This may be true; but equally it may not. In his present circumstances he would have to say so, whatever the truth. Psychologically, he must now justify his past; politically, he must obey his masters; and having been exposed as a spy he must work for his keep as a propagandist. In order to judge his career more objectively, we must try to see it in its context; and this entails some further questions. We must ask, what is the function of secret intelligence work, and what were the opportunities which Philby found in it?

It seems doubly necessary to pose this question today, because today the case of Philby is being exploited not only in Russia, by the open enemies of the West, but also at home. Our fashionable social nihilists are using it to question not only the efficiency of the Secret Service in which Philby temporarily prospered but also the value of secret intelligence itself. Secret services, they seem to say, are an absurd archaism, a mere relic of the unenlightened past. At best, they are a form of outdoor relief, supplying employment for each other, at public expense. More often, they merely create international friction where none was before. By their irresponsible antics they disturb the natural harmony of the world in which there is no need of vigilance for the lion, unless so irritated, would lie down with the lamb. Unfortunately, this agreeable utopianism is, I believe, utopian. Both in substance and in effect, it reminds me of the Peace Pledge[80] in the days of Hitler's rearmament. For whether directly fostered or not, this fantasy, like that, only serves the enemies of freedom.

Other critics have seen in the Philby case a means of denouncing not only the work of secret intelligence but also the social system, 'the establishment', of which, they pretend, the Secret Service is a microcosm and Philby the natural, or at least the predictable, product. This, as I have remarked, is evidently the view of Mr. Le Carré, who assures us that Philby, 'spiteful, vain and murderous as he was, was the spy and catalyst whom the establishment deserved'; for was not the establishment 'stupid, credulous, smug and torpid'? 'Philby', he tells us, 'is the creature of the post-war depression, the swift snuffing-out of the socialist flame, of the thousand-year sleep of Eden and Macmillan.'[81] Since Philby did all his damage during the socialist rule of Attlee[82] and was destroyed by the reform of the Secret Service under Eden and Macmillan, while Burgess was imposed upon an indignant Foreign Office by the socialist minister Hector McNeil,[83] I find these remarks odd.*

---

* The Attlee Government has a particularly bad record in these matters. Not only did Hector McNeil, by a piece of gross ministerial jobbery, inflict Burgess on the Foreign Office. Herbert Morrison also imposed on M.I.5., as its head, instead of the intelligent Guy Liddell, the self-advertising policeman, Sir Percy Sillitoe. On this appointment, Philby himself has some pertinent observations. 'I am sure that spies, had they but known it', he concludes, 'would have rejoiced at Liddell's discomfiture. One did.'

And in what sense can it be said that 'when the security services and the Press came to suspect him for what he was, Philby was able to rally the establishment to his side'? What 'establishment'? we naturally ask. Are not the security services part of the 'establishment'? Perhaps not, in Mr. Le Carré's shifting vocabulary, for he now refers to the 'plebeians of M.I.5'. (In fact, the directors of M.I.5 came from exactly the same social background as Philby himself.) Or does he mean the social establishment, represented by Mr. Macmillan, speaking in the House of Commons in 1955? Mr. Macmillan was a minister speaking to his brief, and according to the evidence. Even Philby himself has admitted that he could do no other. Does Mr. Le Carré then suppose that in England, as in Stalinist Russia, mere suspicion should be followed by privileged, public official denunciation? Something very like this happened in McCarthyite America; but on the whole that has not been regarded as an edifying precedent.

I do not think that much light comes from mental attitudes like this. Sociological generalisations are not safe in such amateur hands. The Philby affair undoubtedly has its lessons for us; but if we are to deduce them, we must look a little farther, and a little deeper, than our own instant prejudices and fashionable slogans. We must try to see that episode in its context. We must ask questions not merely about individual personalities, and individual responsibility, but about intelligence work in general, and the circumstances of the time.

What, then, is the real function of secret intelligence? I believe that it can be stated quite simply. Secret intelligence is the continuation of open intelligence by other means. So long as governments conceal a part of their activities, other governments, if they wish to base their policy on full and correct information, must seek to penetrate the veil. This inevitably entails varying methods. But however the means may vary, the end must be still the same. It is to complement the results of what, for convenience, we may call 'public' intelligence: that is, the intelligence derived from rational study of public or at least avowable sources. Intelligence, in fact, is indivisible. The greater part of it must always be acquired by open or official methods. Only a relatively small area requires secret penetration, or espionage. Nevertheless, that small area may be vital. Not all official secrets need protection; but some do. The date of a surprise military operation; the details of a vital technical process, the *arcana imperii*[84] of any political system; the identity of an agent who can supply such facts; the list of the secret codes which are read – these all are secrets which are rightly protected by one side, and rightly sought out by the other, in the contests of international power politics, which do not cease because some literary men are virtuous. This struggle for secret intelligence is the central work of any secret service, and to say that it is unnecessary is absurd – provided that its limitations are always recognised. That is, secret intelligence must always be relevant to real political or military purposes; it must always be continuous with 'open' intelligence; and it must always be verifiable – for if it is not verifiable it is, in the strict sense of the word, worthless: it cannot be believed, or used.

These limitations, as it seems to me, are of cardinal importance. All of them emphasise the constant dependence of secret intelligence on public intelligence: in definition, in acquisition, in evaluation. Almost all the errors to which secret services, by their very nature, are liable can be traced to neglect of this essential condition. Instead of continuous pursuit of information from the public into the secret sector, they indulge in sporadic petty larceny within the secret sector only. They prize material because of its secrecy rather than because of its relevance or its inherent value.[85] They test it, if at all, within their own secret world instead of within its general context, which is partly 'public'. A report is regarded as credible because a particular spy has been graded as 'reliable' by his employers, whereas credibility really depends not on the person but on the report: on its demonstrable coherence with its known or knowable context. Finally, this very insularity, to which secret services are naturally prone, tends to lower the intellectual level within them. A secret service which sees itself as a branch of the public service pursuing, though by different means, the same ends will serve a useful purpose. A secret service which, merely because of its secrecy, severs itself from the public service will soon shrink into an irrelevancy.

For ultimately all information, however obtained, is subject to the same tests, nor is there any substitute for understanding and intelligence. In the 1930s the minutes of Hitler's secret conferences would have been invaluable. So, today, would be the central documents of Russian policy. Failing such scoops – the scoops obtained by a Sorge or a Penkovsky – more can be deduced by an intelligent study of public sources than by any number of 'reliable' but unintelligent 'agents' listening at key-holes or swopping drinks at bars.

Moreover, once secret intelligence is thus divorced from public intelligence and becomes irrelevant, it tends – naturally enough – to develop a momentum of its own. Agents pursuing unimportant intelligence run into incidental difficulties. They therefore need protection. In order to protect them, further resources are mobilised, new operations are undertaken, more useless information is sought. In the end, the original purpose of such agents may be forgotten in the maze of secondary developments. Agents become fully occupied in arcane local manoeuvres totally irrelevant to their proper function, and I have known occasions on which real 'hard' intelligence has been suppressed in order to protect agents who have never produced any 'hard' intelligence at all.

* * *

The British Secret Service of the 1930s exhibited many of these defects. It was not a rational extension of an efficient bureaucracy of information. Perhaps it never had been. When it was set up, before the First World War, it had not been intended as such. It had been a piece of machinery designed passively to receive, rather than actively to collect, such intelligence as the friends of Britain, in foreign countries, might wish secretly to impart. For that purpose, its funds were very limited; and although the First World War saw a great temporary expansion of its activities, its basis remained always the same. Novels of clubland heroes may have given it a factitious lustre, but essentially it remained an amateur organisation with a slender budget, dependent often on voluntary assistance. As such, it no doubt performed its limited role well enough. But when it ventured outside those limits, it succumbed too easily to the inherent risks of all secret societies. It became divorced from the 'public' bureaucracy; being recruited by patronage, it acquired some of the character of a coterie; and it preserved, as such coteries easily do, outmoded habits of thought.

Recruitment by patronage is not in itself necessarily bad: it depends on the patrons. Nor are ancient traditions to be despised, provided they can incorporate new ideas. Unfortunately, after 1918, the patronage of S.I.S. was not very intelligent, nor were new ideas very popular in it. Moreover, it seemed to look in one direction only. The main threat to British interests, in those years of unchallenged military victory, seemed to come not from other territorial powers, which were either safely allied or safely defeated, but from the pervasive international movement of revolutionary communism. Therefore the rulers of S.I.S. seem to have concentrated their forces against this enemy – without, however, making much effort to understand its true character and ideological motivation.

The weakness of S.I.S. in the 1920s is well illustrated by what seemed at the time its most spectacular scoop: its acquisition of the famous Zinoviev Letter of 1924. This document is now recognised to have been a forgery handed to a gullible S.I.S. by White Russian *émigrés* in Berlin.* The whole history of this episode painfully illustrates the errors which I have listed above. Particularly pitiful is the letter which Admiral Sir Hugh Sinclair,[86] then 'C', sent to Sir Eyre Crowe reporting his 'check' on the authenticity of the letter.†
It amounts simply to this: our man in Riga (which was not then in the Soviet Union) says that he knows of a conversation between Chicherin and Zinoviev which proves the letter to be genuine. That so contemptible a snippet of unverifiable gossip from an unidentified and distant source – and Riga was notoriously the factory of anti-Soviet propaganda and fiction – should have been sent, as authoritative proof of fact, by the Head of the Secret Service to the Permanent Under-Secretary of the Foreign Office, shows that S.I.S., under Admiral Sinclair, had lost all contact with rational methods. In the one field of activity on which it had concentrated its expertise, and whose importance it regarded as paramount, it was simply the willing dupe of *émigré* forgers.[87]

The Secret Service of 1941, which I knew, seems hardly to have differed from that of 1924, whose character I deduce. It was still, basically, the service of Admiral Sinclair, who had died in 1939, and whose old subordinates now ruled it, in uneasy combination. It was still directed against international communism, which it still misunderstood. It had not yet adjusted itself to a war against fascism, which it also misunderstood. Its permanent officers were drawn largely from two classes of men. There were the metropolitan young gentlemen whose education had been expensive rather than profound and who were recruited at the bars of White's and Boodle's by Colonel Dansey, and there were the ex-Indian policemen who were recruited, through the Central Intelligence Bureau in New Delhi, by Colonel Vivian. The former ran the espionage, the latter the counter-espionage. Neither class had much use for ideas. The former had seldom heard of them (Colonel Dansey, we

---

* See Lewis Chester, Stephen Fay, Hugo Young, *The Zinoviev Letter*, Heinemann (1967).

† This letter, which is in the Foreign Office files, was published in the *Sunday Times*, 31 December 1967.

have seen, did not approve of university men); the latter regarded them as subversive. In view of the rise of the new ideologies in the 1930s this was perhaps unfortunate. I doubt if there was one man among the professionals of S.I.S., at that time, who had read *Mein Kampf*, or more than one who had read any of the works of Karl Marx.

Colonel Dansey and Colonel Vivian, *ACSS* (or was it *VCSS*?) and *DCSS*[88] – what old frustrations they call to mind! All through the war these were the grandees of our Service, the Aaron and Hur who, from right and left (but with eyes steadily averted from each other), held up the labouring hands of our Moses, *CSS* or '*C*', Sir Stewart Menzies. How we used to sympathise with Menzies! He held a most invidious position, responsible to an exacting Prime Minister. And yet where could he lean for support?* At the beginning of the war, Colonel Dansey's 'agents' in Europe were mopped up and swept away, and in a public speech (of which the text was kept secret even within S.I.S.), Himmler named all the chief officers of S.I.S., from '*C*' downwards.[89] As the progress of the war left it further and further behind, '*C*''s whole empire was racked by internal tensions. The Foreign Office sought to sustain him by inserting an adviser from the rational world. The adviser – a grave Wykehamist,[90] now an ambassador – was driven to distraction by what he found and uttered the most un-Wykehamist sentiments. When I looked coolly at the world in which I found myself, I sometimes thought that, if this was our intelligence system, we were doomed to defeat. Sometimes I encouraged myself by saying that such an organisation could not possibly survive, unchanged, the strain of war: it would have to be reformed. In fact I was wrong both times. We won the war; and S.I.S., at the end of it, remained totally unreformed.

The reason, I believe, is simple. S.I.S. in itself, by that time, was unimportant, an irrelevancy. But the Government Code and Cypher School – G.C. & C.S.[91] – which had been founded as an organ of the Admiralty

---

* Since this essay was first published, Sir Stewart Menzies has died, and I would like to take this opportunity to pay a brief tribute to him. No one would claim that he was a brilliant chief of the Secret Service. He was a bad judge of men and drew his personal advisers from a painfully limited social circle, which was quite incapable of giving him the support that he needed. I do not think that he ever really understood the war in which he was engaged. But all who knew him, however critical of the organisation, regarded him with respect. He was personally considerate, patently just, patently honest. These virtues were rare enough, in that world, to excuse any purely intellectual failing, and I remember him with affection.

in the First World War and was now a distinct organisation under the Foreign Office, produced invaluable results which were supplied direct to the intelligence departments of all the services. S.I.S. claimed ultimate sovereignty over this material and, in the sacred name of 'security', Section V made frequent efforts to suppress it or restrict its circulation. These efforts were irritant rather than effective. But in one respect at least the sovereignty of S.I.S. was successfully asserted. It was the head of S.I.S., 'C' himself, who, every day, conveyed a somewhat arbitrary selection of these 'most secret sources' to the Prime Minister.[92] Thanks to the skilful exploitation of this bureaucratic accident, S.I.S. obtained the credit for the most valuable and constant intelligence material of the whole war.

Meanwhile, the other services exploited the same material for more disinterested purposes. The vacuum created by the limitations of S.I.S., as a source of intelligence, was filled by other departments, making use of 'most secret sources', together with all the other sources of evidence – aerial reconnaissance, interrogation of prisoners, etc. etc. – and meeting in interdepartmental committees. Of the great intelligence triumphs of the war not one was directly or exclusively due to the Secret Service proper[93] – i.e. to Colonel Dansey's agents – although almost all of them were made practical by the work of G.C. & C.S. The breaking of the 'enigma' machine was made possible by the Polish Resistance and S.O.E.[94] The highly successful deception programme was largely controlled from M.I.5.[95] The famous episode of 'The Man who Never Was' was conceived by M.I.5 and the Admiralty. Thus the war of secret intelligence was won, and S.I.S., thanks to its accidental property in 'Most Secret Sources', survived, unreformed, to the end.

* * *

Such was the Secret Service in which Philby made his wartime career. It was not a perfect organisation. In many ways it was an archaism, artificially protected against necessary change. But to say that it was a microcosm of the establishment, 'indistinguishable' from the establishment, and that Philby only penetrated it because he, too, was of the establishment, 'was of our blood and hunted with our pack', is quite absurd. S.I.S. was not a microcosm of anything; and the word 'establishment', though a convenient radical term of abuse, is in this case so vague as to be meaningless.

The faults of S.I.S. were the faults of a particular organisation, conditioned by particular circumstances. They were not the faults of the bureaucracy in general, far less of society. They were the effect of secrecy, of insulation, of immunity, of immediate circumstance – and perhaps also of a popular myth. Exactly the same faults were apparent to us at the time in the German Secret Service, which – thanks to the 'most secret sources'[96] – we had totally penetrated, only to find it, sometimes, a mirror-image of our own. No doubt they are to be found in the American and Russian Secret Services too. Certainly, if it is a sign of social decay to harbour traitors in secret recesses, the Russian 'establishment' is as 'rotten' as ours. If we had Philby and Blake, they had Volkov and Petrov, Dolnytsin and Penkovsky. If S.I.S. took ten years to discover Philby's hidden past, the K.G.B. took twenty-three years to discover Penkovsky's suspect origins. If S.I.S. refused too long to believe in the treachery of their own member, Philby, when it was suspected by their own rivals in M.I.5, the G.R.U. in Russia similarly declined to believe in the treachery of their own member, Penkovsky, when it was suspected by their 'neighbours', the K.G.B. If the British Government preferred not to reveal Philby's true position in S.I.S., the Russian Government equally did not reveal Penkovsky's true position in the G.R.U. – the Chief Intelligence Directorate of the Soviet General Staff. A little less of virtuous, radical indignation and a little more of analytical comparative method would save our domestic critics from many errors.

Nor was Philby's career to be explained in terms of his own social status. He did not come from the upper class. He was not one of Colonel Dansey's metropolitan club-men. He came from the middle class and rose by his merits, as others did, and as he would have done elsewhere.[97] Even those of us who were most critical of S.I.S. approved of his appointment; and I do not doubt that if he had been turned down as an ex-communist, and never afterwards exposed, our fashionable left-wingers would have denounced his exclusion, just as they now denounce his appointment, as an infamous example of social and intellectual discrimination. It is true, he was defended, when he came under suspicion, by the 'establishment' of S.I.S. But he was also defended by their enemies. No one has denounced the 'establishment' more radically than that agile nihilist Mr. Malcolm Muggeridge.[98] No man, say the 'Insight' writers, is now a more 'ferocious critic' of the wartime S.I.S. But no man was a more zealous and persistent defender of Philby against the 'McCarthyite' suspicions of his critics.

Philby's appointment as head of anti-communist counter-espionage in 1944 is another matter. Clearly his communist past should then have been re-examined. Equally clearly, it was not. This was an error; but it was not 'shaming'. The facts, by then, were deeply buried in a prewar past which now seemed impossibly remote; 1944 was not a leisurely time for research into that past; and those who appointed him judged him on direct experience, not ancient report. He was appointed to the new post not because his 'pedigree' was superior to his 'intelligence' – it was not – but because his work, in the past four years, had given satisfaction – not only in S.I.S. but to M.I.5 and other departments.[99] He had not yet shown any sign of unreliability. The occasion had not arisen. No Volkov had yet appeared.

For until 1944 I do not believe that Philby had much opportunity, or much need, to do harm. His work was against the Germans, in Spain, where Russia was powerless and, by now, uninterested. He had no access to political secrets. Anyway, the interest of the Russians was, at that time, the same as ours: the defeat of Germany. No doubt he passed on to them whatever he thought of interest to them. No doubt he told them – in so far as he knew – what German ciphers we were reading. But it is improbable that he could tell them much, in secret, that was not anyway told to them through more official channels. Russian instructions to him would be, at that time, to go on with his work against the Germans; to inform the Russians of anything which he might learn touching their vital interests; but, above all, not to compromise himself by unnecessary communication. By hard, apparently loyal work for his British superiors, he must win their confidence and so earn continuation, even after demobilisation, as a professional in S.I.S.

Did any opportunity occur, in those years, to serve the vital interests of Russia? I recollect one incident which, in retrospect, may wear a new colour. Late in 1942 my office had come to certain conclusions – which time proved to be correct – about the struggle between the Nazi Party and the German General Staff, as it was being fought out in the field of secret intelligence. The German Secret Service (the *Abwehr*) and its leader, Admiral Canaris, were suspected by the Party not only of inefficiency but also of disloyalty, and attempts were being made by Himmler to oust the Admiral and to take over his whole organisation. Admiral Canaris himself, at that time, was making repeated journeys to Spain and had indicated a willingness to treat with us: he would even welcome a meeting with his opposite number, 'C'. These conclusions were duly formulated and the final document was submitted for security clearance to Philby.[100] Philby absolutely forbade its circulation, insisting that it was 'mere speculation'. He afterwards similarly suppressed, as 'unreliable', a report from an important German defector, Otto John, who informed us, in Lisbon, that a conspiracy was being hatched against Hitler.[101] This also was perfectly true. The conspiracy was the Plot of 20 July 1944, and Canaris, for his contribution to it, afterwards suffered a traitor's death in Germany.

At the time we were baffled by Philby's intransigence, which would yield to no argument and which no argument was used to defend. From some members of Section V, mere mindless blocking of intelligence was to be expected. But Philby, we said to ourselves, was an intelligent man: how could he behave thus in a matter so important? Had he too yielded to the genius of the place? In retrospect I can see that there may have been another reason. It was not to the Russian interest that the Western Allies should exploit the political division of Germany, or support the conservative enemies of Hitler, while the Red Army was still too far away to intervene. As Philby himself now writes, the Russians would resent our 'dickering with Germans'. But the only rational explanation is not necessarily the right explanation, and I am prepared to leave the matter in doubt. Even if the most sinister interpretation is correct, the effective result may have been negligible. The British government was not, at that time, favourable to alleged German opponents of Hitler. The *Abwehr*'s approach through Dietrich Bonhoeffer and the Bishop of Chichester was ignored. And when 'C' was finally told of Canaris's feeler he replied that he was not interested.[102]

A Palace Revolution

After 1944, of course, the position was different. From 1944 to 1946 Philby was in charge of communist affairs. From 1947 to 1949 he was in Turkey. From 1949 till his fall in 1951 he was in Washington, accredited to the American intelligence service. Those, and those only, were the years of his real activity against the West; and they were important years: the years of the struggle for Central Europe, the Berlin blockade and the Korean War. It seems to me unquestionable that, in that period, Philby could and did serve his foreign masters well. He could watch their interests from a central position. He could pass them such secret documents as came his way. He could warn them of danger. He could tell them what codes were read. Sometimes he could comment on British and American policy and intentions. And above all he could watch over, protect, and if necessary delate other Russian agents in Britain. To have a reliable, intelligent, highly placed agent in the centre of a potentially hostile power, with access to 'hard' evidence, is the dream of every intelligence service. The value of such a man does not depend merely on particular communications. Only rarely does a single revelation make a significant difference of policy, and I cannot ascribe much importance to Philby's alleged frustration of what seems anyway to have been a hare-brained C.I.A. scheme of an Albanian coup.[103] Philby himself has declared that this coup was 'futile from the beginning'. Far more important is the intangible advantage of continuity. A well-placed agent of known fidelity and intelligence who can advise his masters, answer specific questions, comment on the disjointed texts which any Secret Service picks up, correct the illusions to which it is prone, has a value which transcends the occasional questionable scoop.

But such advantages contain their own limitation. As continuity is of such importance, so discontinuity seems disastrous. Once such an agent is removed from his vantage-point, his value quickly shrivels away. This very fact leads to a kind of paralysis in the system. Since every action or communication endangers the agent who makes it, and since his survival is of more value than all but the most exceptional action or communication, action and communication are inhibited in the name of security. This is easily illustrated in Philby's case. By merely sitting in his place as head of British anti-communist counter-espionage, he was able to protect the whole espionage system of his Russian employers. On two occasions that system was suddenly jeopardised. The first was the threatened defection of Volkov. The second was the threatened arrest of Maclean. On both occasions Philby was forced, in his own interest, to act. By his first intervention, he saved the system; by his second, he saved himself, for a time. But on each occasion he took a grave risk; and ultimately this double self-exposure would bring him down.

It happened that in the immediate post-war years Philby's survival was of particular importance to the Russians. Those were the years when Stalin was most confident. He had already occupied eastern Europe; he now believed that he might carry the revolution, through internal subversion, to western Europe too. For such a purpose it was far more important to have reliable creatures already placed in key positions against the hour of action than to receive routine secret information at the risk of losing those agents. And

Philby, in this context, was a particularly important agent; for he was no doubt hoping and expecting to become, before very long, head of the British Secret Service. As he said in 1949, he was on the road to a knighthood. The point was afterwards confirmed by Maclean: 'If they hadn't caught up with Kim,' he told Mrs. Philby in 1964, 'you'd be Lady Philby by now ...' A communist head of the British Secret Service could obviously play a vital part in a communist take-over: had not the head of the Austrian Secret Service been a Nazi agent in 1938, when Hitler took over the country so smoothly? Philby's political conversion had been sealed by the Austrian experience. It is unlikely that he overlooked the parallel, or the lesson.

Nevertheless, with all these qualifications, Philby's service to the Russians in the years 1945–51 must have been great, and it is pointless to under-estimate it. All that we can say is that, fortunately, we were not at war. The contest with the Russians was one in which local battles could be lost without disaster. And ultimately the Philby case led to salutary results. The reform of the Secret Service, which we had vainly hoped from the hidden strains of active war against Germany, was finally achieved by the more public scandal of which Philby was the centre in the cold war against Russia.

Of course, Philby was not the only cause of these changes. There were others. In the immediate post-war decade we all learned a great deal. It was then that we caught up with the experiences of war. During the war the techniques of information had become far more complex and sophisticated. The whole scale of information-gathering operations, too, had been enlarged. Above all, there were the lessons of politics. Hitherto we had reacted immediately, almost instinctively, to the rapid changes of politics. Now at last we were able to take stock of them and to digest their rude lessons. In this complex, chemical change the whole concept of secret intelligence was necessarily adjusted too.

For we should never underestimate the educative experience of that decade which hinges upon the year 1950. To judge the period before 1950 by the hindsight acquired after 1950 is absurdly anachronistic. In the decade 1945–55 a whole series of illusions crumbled: illusions of the left even more than illusions of the right. The illusions of the right – the illusions of the 'appeasers' who thought that fascism might be tamed, that Hitler might prove an ally against communism – had been shattered in March 1939, when Hitler occupied Prague. That disillusion had been final, sealed by a second world war against German aggression. The illusions of the left – of those who thought that Stalin could be a permanent partner in European politics – had been rudely shaken by the Nazi–Soviet Pact of August 1939 and its dreadful aftermath: the murder of the anti-fascists of the left, the Finnish war, the holocaust of Katyn.[104] But this latter disillusion was not final. Within two years, Britain and Russia had become allies against Hitler; the Popular Front had been restored in the Resistance Movements of Europe; and a new generation of British radicals began to behave as if the Nazi–Soviet Pact had never been signed. Then, in February 1948, came another shock. Once again it was an occupation of Prague, this time by a communist coup; and at last even the new radicals saw the light. Stalin's imposition of communism in Poland, Hungary, Rumania had been accepted by the English left without too much discomfort. No socialist tears had been shed for Polish colonels, Magyar landlords, or the Rumanian jackals of Hitler. But the Czechoslovak democracy of Masaryk and Benes was different.[105] The communist seizure of Prague, the death of Jan Masaryk, the elimination of the Czech social democrats, disillusioned the left again.[106] And this time there was no reversal. The true, permanent incompatibility of communism with Western liberal or social democracy was exposed. It takes Mr. Le Carré to regard this second, long-delayed recognition of a permanent fact as 'the greatest historical failure and the greatest historical reversal of all time'.

* * *

Against this larger background of change – change in technique, change in politics, change in philosophy – the operations of one person seem very trivial, and it would be absurd to isolate Philby as the sole cause of the institutional readjustment which was a response to them. It is no less absurd to isolate him from his class: from all the other defectors who, in those unsettled days, operated on either side of the Iron Curtain; or to magnify him at their expense – to say (with Mr. Cookridge) that he 'outdid all such notorious spies as Sorge, Abel, Sobell, Lonsdale and Blake'.[107] When so much of the detail is unrevealed, these comparisons are at best pointless. Sometimes, even on present evidence, they are demonstrably absurd.

How can anyone justify the statement that Philby outdid Sorge? Richard Sorge was a German communist who, until his arrest in 1941, operated as a Russian spy in Tokyo. Thanks to his relations with the German embassy in Tokyo, he was able to forewarn the Russians of the projected German invasion of 1941. Thanks to his relations with the Japanese, he was afterwards able to report that the entire Japanese war effort would be directed southward, against Britain and America, not westward against Russia. Stalin ignored the first warning, as he ignored similar warnings by Churchill. But Sorge's second warning enabled him to denude the Pacific defences of Russia and use his eastern army against the Germans – with portentous results. However he may boast in his memoirs, it is unlikely that Philby can show any service to compare with this.

It would be equally absurd to compare Philby with the most important of post-war spies, the Russian Oleg Penkovsky. In the seventeen months of his activity, from 1961 to 1962, Penkovsky, by Russian admission, gave to the West at least 5,000 separate photographed items of secret military, political and economic intelligence; and he gave them at a time, and in an area, in which they could be politically used – for they included evidence about the real state of Russian rocketry, and the exact position of Russian rockets, at the time when Khrushchev was threatening nuclear adventure over Berlin and Cuba. The difference between the damage done to their own governments by Penkovsky and by Philby may perhaps be gauged by the different consequences of their exposure. In Russia, after Penkovsky's execution, a Chief Marshal of the Soviet Union in command of tactical missile forces was displaced and demoted; the chief of military intelligence – that same Ivan Serov whom British public opinion prevented, as the hangman of eastern Europe, from accompanying Khrushchev and Bulganin to Britain – was deprived of his post and publicly demoted; and some 300 Soviet intelligence officers were suddenly recalled from abroad.* In Britain, after the fall of Philby, the reorganisation was within S.I.S. alone. If the Russian result was a crisis of society, the British was a mere palace revolution.

It was nevertheless important. Whatever its immediate cause, the palace revolution of 1956 ended, in S.I.S., the long period of insulated amateurism, of dissociation of secret from 'public' or 'official' intelligence, which had been the lingering legacy of its original foundation. Admittedly, the process of change had already begun: no institution is entirely static, and the method of recruitment by mere patronage had already been corrected before 1956. But 1956 remains a crucial date. It was then that a new 'C' was imported from outside, then that the privileged enclave was at last rejoined to the 'public'

---

* See *The Penkovsky Papers*, ed. Frank Gibney, Collins (1965), p. 19.

bureaucracy. The change was followed by an internal purge. It was after 1956 that the traitors were exposed and eliminated. Ironically, it was this sudden exposure which caused the Secret Service to be devalued in the eyes of the public. In the days of its inefficiency, while it harboured traitors, it had enjoyed a fabulous reputation. In the days of its reform, when it extruded them, its reputation suddenly fell.[108]

Ideologies and Fossils

It is in this context that the answer to our last question becomes apparent. Why, we ask, are his Russian masters now exploiting the story of Philby in this extraordinary manner? Why did *Izvestia* triumphantly announce his arrival in Moscow? Why is the K.G.B. now producing him in Moscow as its propagandist, celebrating him as its hero, feeding him with praise, awarding him titles and decorations, even pushing his memoirs? Certainly they never did anything like this for Burgess and Maclean.

Burgess and Maclean arrived in Moscow in the summer of 1951 but nothing was said about them by the Russians till February 1956. Then they gave a 'press conference' at the Hotel National in Moscow. But it was a very unusual press conference, for neither Burgess nor Maclean answered a single question. Instead they issued, without comment, a duplicated statement written in Russian, in the third person, together with an English translation which, to judge from the style, cannot have been composed by either of them. According to this document, Burgess and Maclean had never been Russian agents: they were merely honest British officials who had despaired of guiding British policy into peaceful ways. The K.G.B. took no credit for them. After this strange, pointless conference, Burgess and Maclean returned, as far as the Russians were concerned, into their silent obscurity. Very different was the treatment accorded to Philby, whom the K.G.B. openly claims as its lifelong spy and who now boasts that he is only one of many, that the Western intelligence services are full of young Philbies, known to him. This change of Russian policy since 1956 clearly requires some explanation.

Part of the explanation is no doubt personal. The public praise of Philby may be a personal reward. Philby – his third wife has told us – lives for praise from the K.G.B.: he is 'pathetically pleased by the approbation of the

Russians'. The K.G.B. in its turn is grateful to him for his past work: 'We can never repay you for the work you have done for us,' his K.G.B. contact told him in Moscow. Naturally his grateful employers seek to repay him in the coin he so clearly appreciates. No doubt it is also a form of encouragement to other agents. The Russians are clearly determined to show that they look after their own. All recent episodes demonstrate their determination. They arranged the escape of Burgess and Maclean. They ransomed Colonel Abel from his American and Gordon Lonsdale from his English prison. They paid $23,500 so that Gerhard Eisler might jump his bail and escape from America. They rescued Blake from his forty-two-year prison sentence.[109] Today they are making every effort to liberate the two Krogers,[110] now in prison in England. In order to rescue them, they have used both cajolery and threats, offering to withdraw damaging publications and persecuting their unfortunate prisoner Gerald Brooke.[111] Such assurance that Big Brother is watching over them is obviously very useful in maintaining the morale of Russian agents. But these motives, though real enough, do not seem to me sufficient explanation of the public cult of comrade Philby in Moscow. Private flattery, after all, would have sufficed for private vanity. Protection need not entail a personality cult. This public exaltation implies a public purpose: and that purpose, when the episode is placed in its context, seems clear enough.

So long as Philby sat in the British Secret Service, with hopes of promotion to the highest post within it, the Russians had no need to attack or undermine that Service. Why should they? They had their own agent in it, centrally placed, watching their interests, able sometimes to inform, sometimes to control, sometimes to protect. Even when Philby was extruded from the centre, he still had his uses and his hopes. So long as he was not clearly convicted, he might return. So long as he was in London, he had his contacts: no one could forbid him to talk with his old, trusting friends. Besides, from 1953, there was Blake; and with Blake in position and Philby in the wings, other agents also might gradually be inserted. In such circumstances the directors of the K.G.B. had no need to attack S.I.S. They had penetrated it. They were satisfied with the *status quo*.

Then came the change. From 1958 onwards the Russian secret services suffered a series of set-backs. Important officers, like Goleniewski, defected. Important agents, like Blake and Lonsdale in England, Wennerstroem[112] in Sweden, were exposed. In 1962 the K.G.B. discovered, with a shock that reverberated through the entire system, that for the last year a far more important agent than Philby, Oleg Penkovsky, had been sending regular information to the West: information which may well have contributed to the humiliating failure of Khrushchev's brinkmanship in Cuba. In the following year they learned that Philby himself was finally exposed and, in Philby's own words, 'decided to call me to the Soviet Union to ensure my safety'. With Philby and afterwards Blake in Moscow, 'the Centre' must have had some interesting discussions. Perhaps it was in the course of these discussions that the new policy was devised: the policy of open attack, from without, on the Secret Service which they could no longer undermine from within.

Certainly the change of policy in Moscow seems to have been openly applied soon after the arrival of Philby. Philby's arrival was announced in *Izvestia* on 1 July 1963. Next year came the first public sign of change. Hitherto the Russian Government had adopted a policy of complete silence on the subject of its own espionage. But now it reversed its policy. On 5 November 1964, twenty years after his execution in Tokyo, the Russian people were suddenly informed of the hitherto carefully hidden exploits of Richard Sorge. The Soviet Press broke into a unanimous cry of praise. Sorge was declared, posthumously, a hero of the Soviet Union. A street in Moscow was named after him. So was a Russian tanker. A 4-kopek stamp was issued to commemorate him. Hitherto, explained *Pravda*, 'a number of considerations' had made it 'impossible' – we would say 'inopportune' – 'to inform the people of this heroic intelligence officer'. Only now had 'favourable conditions' made it possible. We naturally ask what were these 'favourable conditions'?*

Whatever they were, they were not confined to the case of Sorge – and for this reason I cannot accept, as a complete explanation, the suggestion of his biographers, that Sorge's rehabilitation was intended as a vindication of the Soviet High Command against the military errors of Stalin in 1941. For next year two other spies were similarly given official publicity in Russia. First came the adulatory biography of Colonel Rudolf Ivanovich Abel, the 'resident' or head of the Russian spy-net in America, who had been arrested in 1957 and was exchanged, in 1962[113] for the American U-2 pilot, Francis

---

*   I take all my information about Sorge from F.W. Deakin and G.R. Storry, *The Case of Richard Sorge*, Chatto (1966).

Gary Powers.[114] Then followed the 'memoirs' of Colonel Konon Molody, *alias* Gordon Lonsdale, the 'resident' in England, who had been arrested in 1961 and exchanged, in 1964, for Mr Greville Wynne.[115] It is interesting to note that Lonsdale's *Memoirs* were compiled in Moscow by Philby himself, and that the Russians apparently offered to withdraw Lonsdale's *Memoirs*, like those of Philby two years later, from the English market, in exchange for the release of the two Krogers.* Thus the apotheosis and the memoirs of Philby fall into a pattern. They reflect a Russian policy which was new in 1964, but has been continuous since.

It is continuous in substance too. In 1956 Burgess and Maclean had been made (falsely) to declare that they had never been Soviet agents. But now that is all changed. Philby, we are assured, was always 'an officer of the K.G.B.', performing his 'duties' in England under the instructions of his Russian 'superiors'. But neither he, nor the 'growing' army of other Russian agents whom he claims to know in Western intelligence services, are 'spies'. Since 1964, Russia has had no 'spies'. The point was made firmly in the course of the apotheosis of Sorge. Sorge, it was then said, was not 'like those secret agents whom certain Western authors have created. He did not open safes to steal documents; the documents were shown to him by their owners. He did not fire his pistol to penetrate necessary places: the doors were graciously opened to him by the guardians of the secret.'

This picture of the Olympian K.G.B. agent is perhaps less easy to apply to Abel and Lonsdale, but it has been refurbished for Philby. When he was decorated with the Order of the Red Banner, the Russian Press Agency, Tass, refused to transmit to London an official picture of Philby because the caption described him as a 'spy'. 'The West has spies,' said the Tass official smugly, 'but we don't. Change the caption.'

Philby himself has done his best to build up this myth of the K.G.B. as an international order of chivalry. In an interview with *Izvestia* in December 1967, he paid glowing tribute to Felix Dzerzhinsky, the founder of the *Cheka*, which, after many mutations, has become the K.G.B. Philby described Dzerzhinsky as 'that knight of the revolution and great humanist'. This may seem to most of us an odd description of the Robespierre of 1917 – the fanatical idealist who carried out the Red Terror of 1918–21 and put into

---

* Philby's part in Lonsdale's 'Memoirs' is revealed by Mrs. Philby, *The Spy I Loved*, pp. 155–6.

Stalin's hands the machinery for his great purges. But it is in accordance with the new mythology.

Thus, since 1964 at least, the K.G.B. seems to have adopted a positive new policy. Where it had previously been close and silent, it is now vocal and loud. The Western world, it now declares, is at its mercy. The ubiquitous K.G.B. man, the dedicated servant of an international government, moves like a superior being, irresistible, among the ill-guarded, guilty secrets of the divided West. By their publications the Russians seek both to declare and, if possible, to increase that division. Lonsdale dwells on the feebleness of the British intelligence system, which, however, ended by unmasking him, and seeks to sow dissension between the British and American intelligence services whose co-operation, in the case of Penkovsky, was so inconvenient. Philby utters exactly the same doctrine. The Russian Secret Service, he says, is the best in the world. The Western Intelligence Services are incompetent – he himself penetrated S.I.S. with ease; and he tries to set the British against the Americans by saying that, as an officer of S.I.S. in Washington, 'I was faced with the very delicate task of defending the British security service from the C.I.A., which was constantly displaying the clear intention of swallowing up its ally.'*

Why have the rulers of the K.G.B. switched so emphatically to this new policy? I have already suggested one reason: their own failure in the West, or at least in certain Western countries. But perhaps there is also another, deeper reason. Recent events in Russia have revealed a situation which contrasts strikingly with the situation in the 1930s. Then the young intellectuals of the West, like Burgess, Maclean and Philby, dissatisfied with the social and moral 'contradictions' of their own society, looked east and saw an idealised Russian communism as the hope of the future. Today the situation is exactly reversed. Today the young Russian intellectuals, impatient of the hypocrisy and tyranny of the communist party, look to the West, which they also perhaps idealise. The trial of Sinyavsky and Daniel, and its consequences, clearly show the disillusion of a generation.[116] Perhaps even more telling, in a different way, are the papers of the man who can be described as the Russian Philby, Oleg Penkovsky.

Penkovsky's conversion was not, like Philby's, ideological. Nor was it, like his, juvenile and sudden. It was a long process which began during

---

* *The Times*, 19 December 1967.

World War II and was completed – unlike Philby's – by experience. For whereas Philby was converted as an undergraduate and never set foot in Russia till he had been its agent for thirty years, Penkovsky did not change his allegiance till his judgement was mature, and he had personal knowledge both of the Soviet élite and of the West. Then he made comparisons. He was disgusted by the pretence, the falsity, the blatant corruption of the Party, by the universal spying, and above all by the hypocrisy of 'our rotten two-faced regime': the parade of belief in a philosophy which nobody accepted; the claims of material superiority which every action belied; the hollow pretence of liberty and justice. Penkovsky also believed Khrushchev was gambling irresponsibly with nuclear war. So he decided, at whatever risk to himself, to warn the West and thereby to arm it in defence of international peace. 'To tell the truth about this system', he wrote, 'is the goal of my life, and if I succeed in contributing my little bricks to this great cause, there can be no greater satisfaction.' Like Ewald von Kleist[117] before 1939, he urged the West to stand firm against a lunatic dictator whom it would be folly to appease.

Such disillusion in communist countries is easy to explain. A generation ago, in the 1930s, the primitive squalor of Russian life could be ascribed to the special circumstances of the time. At that time the Revolution still seemed insecure. But today that explanation will not do. Today there is no fascist threat to excuse the tyranny of the Party, no 'great patriotic war' to justify the drab and meagre life of the people; and yet fifty years after the Revolution the Russian people seems little nearer to freedom and its standard of life is infinitely lower than that of the 'despised' bourgeois West, whose 'contradictions', in the 1930s, had seemed so fatal. The élite of the Russian communist party, who themselves delight to visit the golden West (every time he went on an official visit, Penkovsky had to go shopping for the Party bosses at home), may insist, in public, that the West is in decay. The semi-literate masses may be assured that modern England is accurately portrayed in the novels of Charles Dickens. But one cannot deceive all the people all the time, nor is everyone prepared to accept mere power – the impersonal power of the State, the personal power of its chosen agents – as the ultimate human good to which social prosperity and personal freedom must be sacrificed. If western Europe could recover from the devastation of war in a few years, a rational man must ask why Russia cannot; and why a country like Czechoslovakia, which in the 1930s was as prosperous as Switzerland, and which was relatively untouched by the war, has been reduced by twenty years of communism to a shabby central European slum.

Against this background we may well understand that the Russian Government is eager to advertise its waning power of attraction, and to boast of its Western converts. Against the misguided idealists at home, who goggle at the flickering, multi-coloured lights of the West, it points to the uncorrupted idealists of the West, who, having looked more deeply into their own society, find that they prefer the pure, steady, incandescent, eastern light. So the Russian backsliders are buried in silence; the apostles and martyrs in the West are glorified; and the converted high-priests of espionage, who worked secretly for the new gospel while wearing the vestments and authority of the old –the German martyr Richard Sorge, the English fugitive, Kim Philby – are hailed as ideological heroes by men who, themselves, have no ideology left.

Unfortunately, in this comparison, one very important difference is overlooked. It is a difference of generations: that difference which (I submit) provides the real dialectic of historical change. Ideas, ideologies, religions, continue to live in books. Their formulae remain unchanged in the mouths of the priests who chant them and of the heresiarchs who denounce them. But their real strength, and their interpretation, depends not on their formal continuity but on the discontinuous experience of human generations. A sclerotic bureaucracy, even a single personal despot, can prolong obsolete ideas beyond their natural term; but the change of generations must ultimately carry them away. Seen thus, the Russian apotheosis of the Western defectors is anachronistic, irrelevant. For while Petrov and Penkovsky, and all those other Petrovs and Penskovskys who are restrained by walls and wires, visible and invisible, reject communism in the 1950s and 1960s, the newly beatified Russian heroes were attracted to it long ago, Sorge in the 1920s, Philby and his friends in the 1930s. It is now thirty or forty years since these men ceased to think. What, then, can they say to us today?

It is true, history never stops. New experience may yet create new loyalties and disloyalties. The war in Viet Nam may yet prove to be an ideological determinant like the Spanish Civil War, which it so much resembles. Nihilism, love of dogma, love of power are permanent temptations to frustrated or bewildered intellectuals. The convulsions of time sometimes throw up again a long buried figure or give a spurious new relevance to a dead faith or an old idea. But political automata are tied firmly to the wires which once jerked and pulled them. They cannot be separated from their historical context or justified by events which they could not rationally foresee.* Philby, Burgess, Maclean are by now altogether irrelevant. They are fossils of the past.

---

* Thus Philby would have us believe that he really deplored the bloodthirsty tyranny of Stalin, which he served, being inspired by faith in the era of communist liberty, which is still to come. His chief English apologist, Mr. Graham Greene, supports this assertion by an engaging 'historical' fantasy. In his preface to the English edition of Philby's memoirs (MacGibbon and Kee 30s.: an expurgated edition of the American text) he solemnly tells us that the English Catholic conspirators who, in the reign of Queen Elizabeth, worked for a Spanish conquest of their country, were really scandalised by the Inquisition, which their success would have installed, having their eyes fixed on the brief and distant reign of Pope John XXIII. An argument for present policy which depends on telepathic foreknowledge of events 400 years later illustrates the ingenuity of its author. It does not illustrate much else.

4

Deception

From the mid-1960s Trevor-Roper was frequently invited to contribute to the New York Review of Books. *It gave him the space to write with particular freedom and impact, qualities which the authors of the books did not always appreciate. Anthony Cave Brown,[1] who wrote enormous spy histories for a mass market, offered a congenial target. Trevor-Roper always respected Cave Brown's industry, but did not share his unshakeable conviction that Sir Stewart Menzies, the wartime Chief of the Secret Intelligence Service, was responsible for the successes of British intelligence. Cave Brown first expounded this theme in his work* Bodyguard of Lies, *which Trevor-Roper reviewed in early 1976.[2]*

Mr. Cave Brown is a very courageous man. He undertook the difficult task of writing a history of Allied deception during the Second World War at a time when the two essential sources for such a study were officially concealed. These two sources were, first, all material directly relating to deception, and, secondly, all material relating to cryptography and its results. In the course of his research he was able to penetrate these barriers indirectly. Then, while he was still at work, the ban was partially lifted and partially broken. F. W. Winterbotham was allowed to publish *The Ultra Secret*, or at least that part of it – the most jealously protected of all – which concerned the breaking by British intelligence of the German cipher machine called 'Enigma'; and Sir John Masterman, undeterred by the bumble of bureaucracy, published his account of the *Double-Cross System*. The delays caused by the ban, and the labor which it has entailed, are obviously great, and we must respect the energy and industry which have enabled Mr. Cave Brown to produce, in the end, this enormous book.

The book is enormous partly because the subject is large and complex, partly because it has grown in his hands. In fact, it has become something like a general history of Anglo-American – and more especially (since the British were at it longer) British – intelligence in the Second World War. But it is far longer than it need be, first, because it has grown in an uncontrolled manner, so that the essential argument is buried in digressions, and secondly, because the author suffers from a fault (as I conceive it to be) which is only too common among modern historical writers, of 'encyclopedism,' of insisting on telling us everything, whether it is relevant or not. Finally, having inflated an anyway complex subject to a huge and somewhat flabby bulk, he has sought to rearticulate it by inserting into it a novel thesis: a thesis which, in my opinion, is quite wrong.

To the reader, the most obvious characteristic of Mr. Cave Brown's writing is what I have called its encyclopedism. He piles on the illustrative (or irrelevant) detail. He cannot leave anything out. Every person mentioned must have a potted biography. Every place must be equipped with atmosphere, furniture, associations. He cannot use the word 'Jubilee' (code name for the Dieppe raid³) without adding that it was 'the old Jewish word for a time of rejoicing and celebration announced by the sound of a ram's horn,' or refer to the Balkans without adding that the name is 'derived from the Turkish word for "the mountains."' Moreover, these endless illustrative details, which journalists seem to regard as necessary to enliven their stories, are often wrong. Seldom, if ever, have I read a book containing so many unnecessary errors of description. Yugoslavia was not part of the Turkish empire in 1905. The Karel Borromaeus church in Prague is not Greek Orthdox. Etc., etc.

This passion for inessential detail seems to be inseparable from the 'instant history' of which this book is an example. We are never allowed to believe that the author was not himself there. The very first words of the book set the standard: 'General Sir Stewart Menzies, the chief of the British secret intelligence service (MI-6), a pale man – "pale skin, pale eyes, silvery blond hair" – who was known to the Allied high command by the enigmatical cipher "C," walked past the brooding statues of Beaconsfield and Lincoln ...' 'The three men met in Menzies' office, beneath a portrait of his patron, the late King Edward VII, dressed in tweeds and deerstalker, a shotgun in one hand, a brace of grouse in the other, and a gun-dog playing in the heather ...' etc., etc., etc. This fashion of implicitly pretending to have been there is particularly maddening when the details, so lovingly supplied, can be shown, by those who were there, to be wrong, and when the journalist's desire to enliven the attendant circumstances replaces the historian's duty to see the central issue.

However, let us forget these questions of style. Let us turn to the substance; for the book is, after all, very substantial. The history of strategic deception is an important part of the history of Allied intelligence. Such deception was developed from small beginnings. Its development was made possible by some lucky chances and some brilliant coups. On the eve of the invasion of Normandy in June 1944 it became a vital part of strategic planning, contributing, perhaps decisively, to success.

For the invasion of Normandy was a very perilous operation, unparalleled in history. Previous attempts to land on the heavily fortified Atlantic coastline of Hitler's Europe had been ineffective if not, as at Dieppe, disastrous. And yet, if Hitler were to be defeated, it had to be done. In order to do it, it was essential to secure surprise. Ultimately, the whole plan of strategic deception looked forward to the great operation which it was designed to camouflage. Even in the darkest days of 1940 and 1941, the machinery was being developed to protect an adventure which, at that time, seemed remote and scarcely credible.

What was that machinery? My chief objection to Mr. Cave Brown's work is that he does not answer this question clearly and intelligibly. Instead, he involves us in elaborate narratives about strategic ideas and controversies, about personalities and intrigues, ciphers and secret services. His narrative contains a great deal about deception, but it is not a rational or accurate description of the deception program. Instead it is a congeries of stories united only by a thesis which, in my opinion, gravely distorts the truth.

This thesis is that the deception program, and indeed all British intelligence, was ultimately controlled by MI-6; that the intelligence war against Germany was a war between MI-6 and its German equivalent, the Abwehr; and (since he likes to personalize the issues) that this was almost a personal duel – rather a friendly duel – between the head of MI-6, Sir Stewart Menzies, and the head of the Abwehr, Admiral Canaris. In his index, MI-6 and the Abwehr each enjoy nearly a full page. No other organization – not even the London Controlling Section[4] (LCS), the central co-ordinating body for deception – comes near to this. By the end of the book, Menzies has emerged as the hero of the intelligence war: a tragic hero, because the war destroyed the supremacy of his class, the British upper class from which the elite of these able intelligence officers was drawn.

In order to show the absurdity of this thesis, it is only necessary to examine, more closely than Mr. Cave Brown has done, and more briefly than he has done anything, the real structure of British intelligence, and the position of strategic deception within it.

On the British side, the highest organ of intelligence was the Joint Intelligence Committee of the Chiefs of Staff. On this committee, all intelligence bodies were represented. One such body was MI-6. MI-6 was a fact-finding body, whose function it was to secure secret information from abroad and pass it on to other departments for use, under such conditions as might be necessary to protect the source. In wartime, when reliable foreign intelligence became particularly difficult to procure, MI-6 might have to adopt special measures both of penetration and of protection; but, generally speaking, it did not have an active role: it merely sought to obtain, and to supply to other services, information which the enemy sought to protect. These other services of course had other sources of information under their own command.[5] Generally speaking, until the arrival of Ultra, they regarded their own sources as more reliable. Officially, MI-6 was responsible not to the War Office (like most other departments of military intelligence) but to the Foreign Office, and its chief had direct access to the prime minister.

The German Abwehr had a somewhat similar function. Under Hitler, as formerly under the Kaiser, it came under the German General Staff, and was one, but only one, of its intelligence-seeking bodies. Like MI-6 it was divided into sections specializing in distinct service areas, and its chief had a privileged position. However, in the period of the war, the Abwehr was different from MI-6 in two important respects: first, it had an internal rival in the Sicherheitsdienst, or SD, the intelligence and security organization of the SS, whose chief was the notorious Reinhard Heydrich; secondly, its own chief, Admiral Canaris, had political interests of his own: he was anti-Nazi.

This brief statement of facts, which are never set out by Mr. Cave Brown, makes it obvious that neither MI-6 nor the Abwehr determined, or could determine, the intelligence war. And in fact, owing to their structure and personnel, they were very ill fitted to do so. Admiral Canaris was more concerned with politics than efficiency. Sir Stewart Menzies was a man of very limited horizons and his organization, for various reasons, was ill equipped for the times. However, Menzies had, as Kim Philby has remarked, one great asset: 'a sharp eye for cover in the bureaucratic jungle,' and this valuable quality secured him a very important advantage. This advantage was the possession of Ultra.[6]

Ultra, as is now well known, was the name given to intelligence derived from the most secret radio communications of the German Armed Forces. These were in a cipher thought by them to be quite unbreakable. In fact, they were regularly read by the British. So were other 'most secret sources' in similar 'unbreakable' machine ciphers – for instance, the communications of the Abwehr. These precious sources enabled the British not only to follow and foresee German movements, but also to watch German reactions to the intelligence which they received – or which was fed to them. Ultra, in fact, gave to all the activities of high-level British intelligence a sureness of touch which the Germans, having no equivalent source, could not hope to match. Consequently, all intelligence departments competed to exploit the advantages of Ultra information, and MI-6, having obtained bureaucratic control of it, enjoyed an enhanced credit and self-satisfaction. Because of that bureaucratic accident, MI-6 was represented on every body which made use of Ultra.

However, this did not mean that MI-6 had either created Ultra, or was the major user of it, or even understood it. To MI-6, control of Ultra was a fortunate windfall which enabled it to go on as before and remain unreformed throughout the war. It also enabled it, after the war, to claim the credit. Mr. Winterbotham, who first revealed the story in print, was the MI-6 liaison officer for Ultra, and he has seen to that. But the first public version of a story is not necessarily the whole truth. Liaison officers are contact men, not creators or users.

The real creators of Ultra, as a source of Allied intelligence, were the experts of the Code and Cypher School. The real users were the intelligence departments of the [*Armed*] Services. For bureaucratic reasons (and real reasons of security) they had to allow that it was the property of MI-6 and, as it were, pay a royalty of respect in exchange for its use. But that was all.

For practical purposes, Ultra was the property of the intelligence departments of all the Services, which insisted, successfully, on receiving it complete and direct from the cryptographers. And it was inter-Service committees which, using Ultra, carried out the strategy of deception: a strategy which was applied not though British spies abroad (controlled by MI-6) but through German spies in Britain (controlled by MI-5) and by special operations mounted by army, navy and air force intelligence.

From these basic facts of organization, it is clear that although Ultra was central to all intelligence operations, MI-6 was not. In fact, MI-6 was marginal, very marginal. All the deception operations discussed by Mr. Cave Brown were made possible by Ultra, but none of them depended on MI-6. They were all the work of inter-Service bodies. As I have mentioned, these bodies were directed, in a very general way, by the body known as LCS, but in fact even this body – to which Mr. Cave Brown ascribes too great an initiative – was rather a general umbrella for specialist bodies than an originating 'general staff' for deception.

The system, in fact, was constructed upward. The first deception policy was carried out, through captured spies, even before the Abwehr 'Enigma' had been broken. Little by little, thanks to Ultra, the system was expanded and sophisticated, until, in the end, the successes of 1944 were achieved. But even then the most striking successes were not obtained by LCS, with its overambitious 'grand designs,' but by specialists in particular war theaters. Thus it was not the 'grand design' called 'Bodyguard' that was the most effective operation on the eve of D-Day, but the local operation 'Fortitude' (the pretended attack on Norway and the Pas de Calais). Mr. Cave Brown, ascribing the initiative to LCS, is too rational for our empirical world.

The same failure to see the real organization is visible in Mr. Cave Brown's treatment of 'operation Mincemeat,' since known as 'The Man Who Never Was.' In this operation, the corpse of a supposed British staff officer was discharged from a submarine in a position from which it would be washed ashore at Huelva in Spain. The corpse was equipped with a verifiable identity and with spurious papers which indicated that the Allied landings of 1943 would be in the Peloponnese. The papers, as predicted, were handed over to the German Abwehr office in Spain. Thanks to Ultra, we were able to follow the German reactions in detail, and were gratified when German divisions which might have opposed the Allies in Sicily were diverted to the Peloponnese.

Mr. Cave Brown's treatment of 'Mincemeat' is very typical. He begins, somewhat pretentiously, by discovering its origin in the operations of Colonel Meinertzhagen in the Near East in 1917. In fact the origin was not nearly so remote in time or in place. We can stay in Spain and need not go back beyond 1942. Ultra then revealed that the Spanish police had handed over to the local branch of the Abwehr British documents washed ashore from a wreck; and it was decided that what had happened once by accident could happen again, deliberately. MI-6 had nothing to do with the case; nor did the LCS to whom Mr. Cave Brown ascribes it. Its author was Commander Montagu of NID [*Naval Intelligence Department*] 17 M (not F), and the project was worked out, as usual, by an inter-Service committee. Mr Cave Brown's account teems with small errors of name, time, and place – he seems constitutionally unable to get such details right. Some of his details have evidently been taken from the film about this incident, not from historical sources.

There are also errors of biography. Commander Montagu has never been Recorder of London, and as for being 'one of the best fly-fishermen in the realm,' I cannot do better than quote his own comment: 'I was never any good at fly-fishing, but I enjoyed trying until I started sailing. A friend told me that "if you want to get asked to good fly-fishing waters and good shoots, it's worth putting them among your recreations in *Who's Who*." So I did (without getting any invitations), never bothered to take them out – and haven't fly-fished since one week on leave in 1942. That is what I mean by journalists' embellishment for effect.'

Mr. Montagu is not alone in finding himself credited by Mr. Cave Brown with surprising qualities, functions, and distinctions.

Another operation which would have been impossible without Ultra was the continuing Double-Cross work which has been described by Sir John Masterman. As the British, through Ultra, generally knew about German spies before they landed, they were easily picked up and, if cooperative, used to deceive their paymasters. Once in operation, Ultra showed whether they were being successful and gave valuable guidance in playing them. The operation of these agents in support of the general plan of deception was in the hands of Section B1A of MI-5, which Mr. Cave Brown ignores, giving all the credit, as usual, to LCS. (The head of B1A, Colonel T.A. Robertson, who did more than any other man for the deception program, is only mentioned once and then wrongly.)[7] This is in line with his general refusal to master the machinery of intelligence. Those who merely want to read dramatized spy stories will not mind that; but it disqualifies him as a historian.

Thus a study of the organization of deception does not support Mr. Cave Brown's picture of the triumph of MI-6. MI-6 hardly comes into the true story at all. Nevertheless, Mr. Cave Brown consistently represents Sir Stewart Menzies as the genius behind the whole deception program. For Menzies, he maintains, was not only 'the master of Ultra': he also had another secret weapon almost as valuable as Ultra. This was *die Schwarze Kapelle*, or 'black orchestra,' by which he means the *fronde* of anti-Nazi generals to which Canaris certainly belonged. According to Mr. Cave Brown, Menzies and Canaris were bound together by 'long years of peculiar association' and *die Schwarze Kapelle* provided Menzies with usable intelligence. Indeed, in a fine flight of fancy, Mr. Cave Brown even tells us that Menzies organized the murder of Heydrich[8] in 1942 in order to prevent Heydrich from taking over the Abwehr and displacing Canaris, so depriving Menzies of his essential opposite number. 'Heydrich,' he writes, 'had been a marked man ever since he assumed control of the SD. He could not be permitted to live; he was too dangerous to Menzies, to the Allied cause – and to Canaris.'

I am afraid I must say that this picture of a Canaris–Menzies axis, of Canaris as one of Menzies's sources of usable information, and of Menzies ordering the assassination of Heydrich – 'signing his death warrant' – in order to save Canaris, is the purest fantasy. Whatever 'evidence' may be claimed in its support, anyone who understands the structure of MI-6, the limits of its responsibilities, the extent of its knowledge of the internal politics of Germany in 1942, or even the true facts about Germany in 1942, knows in advance that it could not be true.

It is in his account of the alleged relations between Menzies and Canaris that Mr. Cave Brown becomes most irresponsible. Having satisfied himself that such a link existed – having even declared (quite incorrectly) that Menzies employed many men to study the personality of Canaris – he asks himself why that link was not more effective, and answers his question by wheeling out a familiar *diabolus ex machina*, Kim Philby. 'Postwar events would reveal,' he says confidently, that Philby, 'whose desk at MI-6 headquarters was just down the corridor from Menzies,' intervened to block the vital documents. I think I can detect the origin of this firm statement: a speculation by me concerning a possible motive of Philby's action in blocking *one* document, which, for particular reasons, it happened to be in his power to hold up. He could not conceivably have stopped the communications to which Mr. Cave Brown refers – Allied communications from Berne to Washington and Washington to London. And Philby's office, at that time, was not 'just down the corridor from Menzies': it was forty miles away, at St. Albans.

These then are the two main strands of Mr. Cave Brown's thesis. The Allied intelligence achievement, he maintains, was based on two important facts: Ultra and *die Schwarze Kapelle*; and both led to Menzies. Menzies was 'the man behind Ultra'; he also was the sole personal link between the headquarters of MI-6 and *die Schwarze Kapelle*. Menzies was thus 'the chief of MI-6 who commanded much of the Allies' intelligence and counterintelligence with the Germans.' I regret to say that this is pure fantasy. It is a fantasy that could not have been entertained if Mr. Cave Brown instead of adding ever more otiose (and often inaccurate) detail to his spy stories had done his essential homework and learned how the machinery of intelligence worked. For that is the beginning of historical wisdom.

How then, I asked myself as I read his book, did Mr. Cave Brown arrive at this dramatically personal but totally false picture? The answer comes at the end of the book; for as the name 'General Sir Stewart Menzies' begins the work, so it dominates the final epilogue. Here we discover that in 1964, when Menzies was seventy-four years old, retired at his country-house in Wiltshire, he was visited by Mr. Cave Brown, and apparently spoke very freely to him and showed him a complimentary letter from General Eisenhower – not, I need hardly add, about MI-6, but about Ultra. He also seems to have told Mr. Cave Brown some tall stories about Canaris and his own personal contact with him and about the famous German spy 'Cicero,' the Albanian valet of the British ambassador in Ankara.[9] 'Cicero,' it will be remembered, photographed the ambassador's confidential dispatches while the ambassador was playing the piano, and sold them to the Germans for a huge sum which the Germans paid him in forged banknotes. According to Mr. Cave Brown, when he mentioned 'Cicero,' Menzies snapped – and thus confirmed Mr. Cave Brown's own speculations – 'Of course Cicero was under our control.'

It was this last remark which was finally too much for me. I well remember the Cicero affair. How can I forget it? It was a dramatic episode. It is perfectly true, as Mr. Cave Brown says, that we knew that there was a German spy called Cicero in the British embassy, but that was not because we controlled him. Far from it. His existence and his cover-name were revealed by Ultra. It was impossible to warn the ambassador by telegram, because it was precisely such telegrams that Cicero was photographing and selling to the Germans; and that would blow Ultra. We flew a special high-powered messenger – the Marshal of the Diplomatic Corps, no less – to Ankara to warn the ambassador; but by the time he had arrived, new evidence had come in, and, once again, we could not communicate with him without risk to Ultra. Ultimately, the mystery was solved, and Cicero, having been identified, was used to deceive instead of to inform.[10] As the Germans had not believed him anyway, it did not make much difference.

Therefore, when I read, in Mr. Cave Brown's book, that Menzies, in 1964, claimed (implicitly at least) that we had always controlled Cicero, I began to have doubts.[11] Could Menzies really have made so false a statement? My own view was that Menzies was not the man to talk about his work to anyone. However, I reflected, perhaps by 1964, when he was old and distressed by failure – the last straw was the flight to Moscow of Philby, his most trusted officer, whom he had personally designated to be his ultimate successor – perhaps then he broke the habit of a lifetime and spoke to a visiting journalist. I therefore consulted a friend [*Patrick Reilly*] who knew Menzies very well, and asked if he thought this was probable. My friend replied that it was absolutely out of the question: Menzies was the most uncommunicative of men, and after a lifetime of secrecy would *never* have spoken so.

Did Mr. Cave Brown then invent the conversations? That I could not believe. But then the answer came. I discovered, from a close friend [*Dick White*] who was deeply involved in all these events, that in 1964, after the shock of Philby's flight, Menzies decided to write his memoirs in order to show that his life's work had not ended in total failure. The memoirs were typed out, as far as they went, and were described to me as 'self-glorifying rubbish.' It must have been precisely at this time that Mr. Cave Brown called on Menzies; and Menzies no doubt saw an opportunity to unload on this visitor the content of the memoirs which he was writing. From that senile vanity (I do not believe that Menzies was ever very close to the detail), came the strange thesis which runs through Mr. Cave Brown's book.

There is also another thesis, implicit but insistent, in this book. It is that British intelligence was essentially a gentleman's game, even an aristocrat's game. Whenever Mr. Cave Brown can, he dwells on the blue blood, or the wealth, or the expensive hobbies of the officers concerned. He seems to have an interest in presenting intelligence as an extension of country-house life. The Beaufort Hunt, we are told (and not only the Beaufort), 'was as much a political conspiracy as a sport,' and British intelligence was dominated by 'a group of men who represented the aristocratic cream of a caste of blood, land and money.' This thesis, or rather, this insistent suggestion, seems to me worthy of a novelette. There were some rich men in intelligence, and some poor; some nobly, some less nobly born. If any sociological generalizations are to be made, they must be more subtle than this.

There is a great deal in this book which will interest the leisured general reader. There are numerous stories which are well told and amply documented. But alas, there are large errors of emphasis and countless errors of detail, and a grotesquely distorted thesis; and therefore, I am afraid, while it can be enjoyed as narrative, as history it cannot be trusted.

Trevor-Roper's demolition of Cave Brown's argument was welcomed by intelligence experts. Walter L. Pforzheimer of the CIA commented that 'the review is superb. Rarely have I seen a book which deserves the most severe treatment so well destroyed.'[12] John H. Bevan,[13] the wartime head of the London Controlling Section for deception, also wrote to congratulate Trevor-Roper on his article: 'TAR Robertson has kindly sent me a copy of your splendid review of that ghastly book Bodyguard of Lies. *Many congratulations – just what was wanted.'[14] Bevan pointed out that it was Charles Cholmondeley who first suggested the plan to drop a dead body off the Spanish coast as part of the deception to cover the invasion of Sicily, though Ewen Montagu did the detailed planning.[15] The Chiefs of Staff said that the operation required Churchill's approval so Bevan went to see him at 9.30 in the morning: 'He was in bed smoking a large cigar and I showed him (of course on one sheet of foolscap) the* Mincemeat *plans. We discussed it for some time and he was more funny than words can say {…} I hope you will agree that L.C.S. did take a minor part in the operation, though of course I entirely support you in condemning Cave Brown's ridiculous interpretation.'*

Cave Brown clearly caught Trevor-Roper's attention as a particularly strange, indeed almost alarming phenomenon, meriting further inquiry. He learned from F.W. Winterbotham, author of The Ultra Secret, *that Cave Brown was a man with unfortunate idiosyncracies, as Trevor-Roper informed Sir Michael Howard.*[16]

He [*F.W. Winterbotham*] tells me that Cave Brown came to him a few years ago (as he came to me) with a letter of introduction; but now on hearing of Winterbotham's experiences, I marvel at my own good fortune in getting rid of him so soon and so cheaply. For he descended on the unfortunate Winterbothams in rural Devonshire and simply camped on them. On one occasion they returned from church on Sunday and found that he had arrived, had broken into their house, and was helping himself to their whisky. On another, he telephoned (reversed charges) from London, announced that he was ringing from Winterbotham's club, and asked Winterbotham to tell the porter to let Cave Brown stay in the club at Winterbotham's expense. A firm refusal did not discourage Cave Brown who continued to persecute Winterbotham [...]

Undeterred by Trevor-Roper's criticisms of Bodyguard of Lies, *Cave Brown wrote a biography of Menzies of 830 pages which recapitulated some dominant themes of his earlier work. Trevor-Roper reviewed this for the* Spectator:[17]

Stewart Menzies (pronounced in the proper Scotch way[18]) was Chief of the British Secret Service, alias CSS, alias 'C', from 1939 till he retired in 1953. Those who knew him personally and socially were surprised that he should have risen so high. To them he seemed a very ordinary, conventional man of limited upper-class horizons: Eton, the Life Guards, the Beaufort Hunt, White's. Those who worked under him in the war, as I did, saw him as an honourable, fair-minded man in an exacting position made more difficult by inefficiency and intrigue around him and by his own rigid conservatism:

he evidently disliked change, physical movement and new faces, and he was inexplicably loyal to, or intimidated by, some damaging old cronies.[19] However, he knew how to fight his own corner and, as Kim Philby has written, 'had a good eye for cover in the bureaucratic jungle'. Thanks to these gifts, and to favourable circumstances, and to some real achievements, he preserved the organisation which he had inherited, and his own place in it, throughout the testing time of the second world war and (rather less successfully) through much of the Cold War.

In any career there are ups and downs, and in secret intelligence the oscillations can be extreme. Menzies' career as 'C' began and ended in disasters. He was appointed at the very beginning of the war (against the opposition of Churchill, who thought him too limited and class-bound, and wanted the post to go, as always before, to a naval officer), and his appointment was immediately followed by the débâcle of the 'Venlo Incident' – the kidnapping, on Dutch soil, of two of his officers who thought that they were negotiating with German opponents of Hitler but in fact were placing themselves, and the secrets of the SIS, in the hands of the Gestapo. Shortly before his retirement, he was forced to sack Philby, whom he had promoted and had envisaged as his ultimate successor, but who was now compromised by the flight to Moscow of Burgess and Maclean and believed by MI5 (but not by him) to have been a Russian spy. Before he died in 1968 he knew the worst: that Philby, now in Moscow, had been a traitor for 30 years and that his own operations in the Cold War had thereby been ruined.

Against these failures we must place signal wartime successes. Almost all of them were due, directly or indirectly, to our possession of that inestimable treasure, *Ultra*. But for *Ultra* we might well have lost the war. Air Force *Ultra* was vital in the Battle of Britain, naval *Ultra* in the Battle of the Atlantic, in either of which defeat would have been final. Army *Ultra* ensured the victory in North Africa. Abwehr *Ultra* was essential to strategic deception. Neither Menzies nor SIS was responsible for the acquisition of *Ultra*, but since the Chief of the Secret Service was also Director of GC & CS, the cryptographic institution which supplied it, they profited from the association. Deprived by the Venlo Incident of their own agents in Western Europe (which was no great loss), the metropolitan gentlemen of Broadway Buildings, St James's, were able to take credit for the infinitely more reliable sources of intelligence opened by the toiling peasantry on their chief's distant estate at Bletchley. The peasants did not find the connection so useful. When a crisis of manpower threatened production at Bletchley and normal channels brought no remedy, they took the extreme step of by-passing the whole chain of command, including 'C', and appealing direct to the Prime Minister. That did the trick, but did not please 'C'.

Menzies' official monopoly of *Ultra*, whose security he rigorously and rightly protected, was his strongest card in the inevitable inter-departmental battles. Those battles, sometimes fierce, were complicated when the Americans (whom he distrusted) came in. Being armed with *Ultra*, he generally won his battles, but there were some early defeats. He was mortified by Churchill's reliance on Desmond Morton as an independent adviser on intelligence matters, and even more by the creation of SOE as a distinct and rival organisation. Menzies, with some justice, regarded SOE (like the Americans) as amateurs. They were new, enthusiastic, without a proper sense of security. He himself was a professional – he had been in the job since 1915. His critics might reply that his mental attitudes had not changed since then.

The old hands of SIS were indeed deeply influenced by the past, especially by the inter-war years when its establishment had been drastically reduced and its limited funds were directed primarily to the war against Bolshevism. Its recruits, in those years, were not – could not be – of the highest calibre. They were brought in by secret patronage, often nepotism, from a limited field. It was also infected by a romantic, not to say infantile, upper-class myth fostered by popular novelists such as John Buchan (who acted as a recruiter for it in Oxford) or Denis Wheatley (who was brought into MI5 in 1939). One result of this was that the service relied on wealthy, and therefore unpaid, but not highly educated part-timers, 'honourable correspondents', who supplied it with prejudiced gossip from aristocratic houses in Europe. I have known some of these people; they often end by living in a world of fantasy – an occupational hazard. Deciphered material, of course, was different: it was still supplied by the old experts of the first world war; but the vital Russian 'decrypts' were lost when they were cited in Parliament to justify the 'Arcos Raid' of 1927.[20] The Russians then naturally changed their ciphers. In consequence, SIS retained a justified suspicion of all politicians. Like SOE and Americans they were held to be congenitally insecure.

These conditions help to explain the defects of SIS in 1939 – defects which neither Menzies nor any of his colleagues were eager to reform. The pressure came from outside, from the Services and from the Foreign Office.

The Services contrived to insert 'commissars' into SIS as Deputy Directors. They did not achieve much. The Foreign Office seconded one of its members [*Reilly*] as a personal assistant to 'C'. The new assistant was appalled by the disorder and the atmosphere of prejudice and intrigue which he found there. Menzies' overpowering deputy [*Dansey*], he discovered, was 'the most evil and wicked man I had met in public service'. Some rational changes of procedure were introduced, but a real structural change was not to be achieved at that level, or at that time, or with those persons. It had to await a new generation.

Late in his life, shaken by the Philby affair, Menzies wrote his 'recollections'. These have been described to me, by a well-qualified friend [*White*] who read them, as 'self-glorifying fantasy'. They have been used by Mr Cave Brown, who has also had personal information from the Menzies family. His biography, which is written on the American model, bringing in everything, sometimes twice over, dwells with goggle-eyed relish on the Edwardian world of wealth and privilege in which his hero's life was enclosed: but he has also worked industriously, both here and in America. He is particularly interesting on the relations between SIS and the Americans, especially William J. Donovan's OSS. Some of his statements seem to me rash, but the book is documented and full of information: a good, if a very long, read.

My main criticism is that Mr Cave Brown writes as if SIS was the sole source and interpreter of secret intelligence, and credits to 'C' personally decisions and actions for which his responsibility was very limited: he had been a channel of communication, or a member of the approving committee, or had seen the papers. In fact the function of SIS was to collect intelligence by secret means: it neither interpreted it, nor formulated policy, nor (except to obtain it) took action. Mr Cave Brown's references are copious but often fail us when they are most needed. Some of his suggestions seem to me very wild. I know of neither evidence nor probability for the theory that 'C' organised the murder of either Admiral Darlan[21] in Algiers or Reinhard Heydrich in Prague, and the motive which he offers for the latter murder is absurd. So are the arguments by which he would like to persuade himself that 'C' knew all along that Philby was a Russian spy and used him as a double agent, thus deceiving his own colleagues and allies. This would make his hero more of a traitor than his villain.

'C' was not a super-spy or a brilliant 'spy-master'; but if the public mythology needs someone in that role, he is more deserving than the dreadful

Claude Dansey or the egregious William Stephenson, who have already been so honoured; and this biography gives some flesh and a little (off-blue) blood to the sedentary, withdrawn, overworked, unimaginative secret bureaucrat who concealed his work and his personality behind the green light outside his office in Broadway Buildings, the green ink of his laconic official ideogram, and the protective doors of his private citadel, White's.

5

Ultra

Ultra was a term used during World War II to refer to the British decrypts of messages originally encoded by the German Enigma machine. This remarkable feat of code-breaking and its vital importance to the Allied war effort became very widely known after the publication of F.W. Winterbotham's The Ultra Secret *in 1974. Winterbotham's book made Ultra an essential ingredient of any new publication on intelligence in World War II. So it was given a disproportionate role in a deferential biography of the wartime head of British Security Coordination in America which caught Trevor-Roper's attention.*

Review of *A Man Called Intrepid: The Secret War* by William Stevenson[1]

Sir William Stephenson is a man with a very distinguished past. A Canadian of great courage and resourcefulness, he fought gallantly in the First World War. Then he went into business and soon became a millionaire by his own exertions. But he never lost his taste for adventure, or his patriotism, which he showed in various ways. He became a friend and ally of Winston Churchill, and during the Second World War he was the principal agent of the British Secret Service in America. His chosen code name was 'Intrepid,' which he still keeps – see *Who's Who* – as his telegraphic address. We knew him, more impersonally (if I remember aright), as '38,000.'[2]

During the early part of the war, he did invaluable work as liaison officer, in intelligence matters, between Churchill and Roosevelt. His organization in New York was known as British Security Coordination, or BSC, for it coordinated the work of MI-5, MI-6, and SOE. After Pearl Harbor and the entry of America into the war, a separate US secret service, OSS, was set up, and learned some of its early lessons from him. Thereafter, the liaison between the British and American secret services inevitably moved to

Britain; but Stephenson continued to do good work in America, for which he was afterward decorated by both governments. He is now eighty years old and enjoys his retirement in Bermuda.

At the close of his active life, Sir William evidently decided that a little publicity, after so many years of discretion, would do no harm. He therefore commissioned a biography. As its author, he chose Mr. H. Montgomery Hyde, who is well known as an able, scholarly, and prolific historical writer, and had himself worked in BSC. Mr. Hyde has written a number of excellent biographies, and Sir William did well to choose him. The result was a book entitled – since Sir William was known for his modesty – *The Quiet Canadian*. In America its title is *Room 3603*. It was published in 1962, with a preface by Mr. David Bruce, US ambassador to Britain, formerly head of OSS in Britain. Evidently Sir William was pleased with the book, for he cites it in *Who's Who*, as giving further light on his career.[3]

However, with the passage of time, the urge for even greater publicity has overcome this quiet, modest Canadian. This time he has found a different biographer, Mr. William Stevenson, who is also a former colleague and, like himself, Canadian. In order to avoid confusion between these similar names, I propose hereafter to refer to Sir William Stephenson as 'the Hero' and to Mr. William Stevenson as 'the Biographer.' The Biographer is also a prolific writer, but his books are less historical than those of Mr. Hyde. He writes about secret activities, revolutions, romantic escapades, under such titles as *The Yellow Wind, Birds' Nests in Their Beards, The Bushbabies, The Bormann Brotherhood*, etc. I have looked at the last of these books: the less said about it, the better.

Why, we may ask, has the Hero suddenly found himself dissatisfied with the work of Mr. Hyde? Is it because of some error in it? The only error known to me is Mr. Hyde's unfortunate description of M. Henry-Haye, Marshal Petain's ambassador to the US, as a pro-Nazi who ran a 'Gestapo' in the US and kidnapped loyal Frenchmen. That description caused M. Henry-Haye to appeal to the English courts, where he was vindicated. However, it is not to correct this error that the new biography has been written: indeed, the libel (like much else of Mr. Hyde's book, including several of the illustrations) is repeated in full. Presumably M. Henry-Haye is now safely dead.

No, the reason for the new book is not any positive error in the old. Rather, it is its inadequacy. Laudatory though it is, it does not praise the

Hero enough. Whole areas of his activity were apparently overlooked by Mr Hyde: areas in which that activity, we now discover, was particularly glorious. This is made clear in the preface, in which Mr. Hyde's book is cut down to size. That publication, we are now told, was only 'a partial leak,' 'a carefully limited disclosure,' occasioned by the escape to Russia of Kim Philby. Now that the CIA – successor to OSS – is under attack, it is important to make 'a full disclosure' and reveal 'the authentic story.' So the Hero has thrown open his files without reserve; the Biographer has shouldered 'the staggering burdens of investigation and selection from such vast records'; and Mr. David Bruce, who has once again stepped forward to puff the result, describes it as a work of 'profound historical importance,' of 'overwhelming significance.'

Such is the avowed purpose of this egregious publication. The logic, I must admit, escapes me. However, the reader will soon discover a more obvious reason. Since 1962 there have been some important revelations. In particular, Mr. F.W. Winterbotham's book *The Ultra Secret* has made all studies of the intelligence war seem irrelevant unless the authors can show that they knew about Ultra. So now everyone must scramble in on that act. The real purpose of this book is to show that the Hero, in addition to everything else, was the hero of Ultra. He discovered Ultra, and the means of intercepting and deciphering it. That great triumph of the war is really due to him.

Now it is perfectly true that the Hero, like many others, knew about Ultra. Indeed, he was the liaison officer through whom Ultra material was confidentially communicated by Churchill to Roosevelt before Pearl Harbor and the full alliance. But the addition of so modest a postscript to Mr. Hyde's book would hardly justify a complete new work. Therefore the Biographer has gone much further. Stripping away all the veils of secrecy, abandoning all the checks of evidence, or probability, or decency, he has presented the Hero as the universal genius: the Midas who turned all that he touched into gold; the master of economic life; the prescient master-mind who directed all British and American intelligence; the secret manipulator of presidents, prime ministers, and kings.

In a recent review, in these pages, of Mr. Antony Cave Brown's *Bodyguard of Lies*,[4] I ventured to regret that the author of that book had not exerted himself to understand the organization of British intelligence, since such understanding is a necessary precondition of writing sense on the subject.

To make such a charge against this Biographer would be unfair. It would be like urging a jellyfish to grit its teeth and dig in its heels. The poor creature lacks the rudimentary organs for such an operation. Although I cannot now furnish him with an understanding, I can perhaps, by a few illustrations, show why his book, far from having 'overwhelming significance,' is, from start to finish, utterly worthless.

Any historian, before coming down to particular events, or presuming to describe their causes, must know that there are distinctions of responsibility, of function, of machinery, and of evidence, upon which understanding of events must depend. But to our Biographer, leafing mechanically through those disconnected private documents, or listening mindlessly to octogenarian reminiscences, all such distinctions have been merged. Out of the haze there emerges nothing recognizable except the benevolent features of the Hero, no sound except his quiet voice assuring the hero-worshipper that it is he who is responsible for all these events: events which he now condescends to reveal in order (as he tells us in his own foreword) to pay 'tribute to the gallant women and men of many nations' who so faithfully served him, but who somehow seldom get mentioned in this personal apotheosis.

One who does qualify for a mention is King George VI, whose part as an agent of the Hero was, we are told, 'vital.' Any historian knows that the king of Great Britain stands above politics. He may also know that King George VI was not particularly attached to Churchill, preferring Chamberlain and, after him, Halifax. But the Biographer knows better. He tells us that Churchill, as First Lord of the Admiralty, on the instigation of the Hero, persuaded the king to authorize him, behind the back of the prime minister, to convey the secrets of the prime minister's own department to a foreign statesman. This role of the king as 'an active participant in Britain's clandestine warfare,' 'the ultimate authority in secret-intelligence matters,' is, says the Biographer, 'little understood,' and he does not make it more intelligible by saying, on another page, that the king was not allowed to see secret material. But it does not really matter what the Biographer thinks that he understands or that other people do not.

Let us descend from high politics to administration. Anyone who begins to study British wartime intelligence must know that there were several distinct organizations. Among them were SIS (or MI-6) and SOE. The

Hero may have represented both in America, but they themselves were entirely separate in structure, responsibility, and function. SIS was under the Foreign Office and had headquarters off St. James' Park; SOE was under the Ministry of Economic Warfare and had headquarters in Baker Street. Hence Mr. Bickham Sweet-Escott, an officer of SOE, could describe his service as 'Baker Street Irregulars.' But the Biographer, who occasionally appropriates the title, as he sometimes silently appropriates the contents, of a book, never even begins to distinguish these bodies. Indeed, he supposes that the Ministry of Economic Warfare itself was 'a shadow organization' founded by Churchill, as a private citizen, before the war. 'The general term "Baker Street Irregulars,"' he tells us, was applied, 'by those in the know,' to all secret organizations. So he describes Philby (who was in SIS) as one of the 'Baker Street Irregulars' and Sir William Deakin (who was in SOE) as a member of SIS, and Sir Colin Gubbins, the head of SOE, as 'one Baker Street leader.' Whoever else was 'in the know,' clearly our Biographer is not, and never will be.

Least of all in a subject so exact as cryptography. On this subject our Biographer speaks confidently enough. He does not need to refer to Mr. Winterbotham's book, for he already knows everything. He tells us that the Enigma cipher machine, which produced part of the Ultra material, was the property of the Nazi Party, and, particularly, of Reinhard Heydrich. Indeed, he regularly calls it the 'Heydrich-Enigma' and prints a portrait of Heydrich, as its proprietor.

How the name of Heydrich ever got into his head is not clear, but once there, it stuck very firmly. Heydrich, it seems, was almost the inventor of Enigma, just as the Hero, Heydrich's 'opponent in the battle of wits,' was the man who, in the end, mastered it. Heydrich, in fact, is the Antichrist, the Lucifer of this hazy intellectual cosmology. The Hero and his angels are locked in combat with Heydrich and his angels. Heydrich, we are told, was the true author of Stalin's purges; he already dominated 'all branches of German intelligence' in 1941; but he was himself destroyed, in the end, on the orders of the Hero.

It is amusing to note how these authors have Heydrich on the brain. Mr. Cave Brown, it may be recalled, cast Sir Stewart Menzies as Heydrich's dedicated opponent and final exterminator. In fact I do not suppose that either Sir Stewart or Sir William had more than the haziest notion of Heydrich's identity before his assassination. Nor does the Biographer now.

But we shall ignore these secondary fantasies, which are about as true as Hitler's visit to Liverpool in 1913, which the Biographer solemnly accepts from 'BSC documents.' BSC documents, it seems, contain a lot of rubbish, and the Biographer will swallow anything.

In fact, Heydrich had nothing whatever to do with Enigma. His organization, the SS, did not use it,[5] nor did we read its main communications. The Enigma, in different forms, was used by the German Armed Forces, and by the Abwehr, which was an organ of the Armed Forces. The Biographer regularly says that the British deciphered the German Foreign Office communications from the start of the war, and ascribes particular information to these sources. They did not. Here, as elsewhere, the Biographer does not know what he is talking about.

For the rest, this book is one of the tribe. It has the usual 'instant' style. It is peppered with eye-catching names, totally irrelevant to the subject – Lady Astor, Rebecca West, Noel Coward .... What had they to do with secret intelligence? Nothing. Of course the Biographer thinks otherwise. I particularly enjoyed the alleged antics of Noel Coward. We are told how Noel Coward reported for action in secret service after the fall of France; how he was interviewed in suitable secrecy; how he was sent to join the Hero in New York; how he was briefed for a mission to South America and 'shot off into the unknown.'

'Coward's career in secret intelligence,' we are told, 'must have been one of the best-kept secrets' of the war. It must indeed, if even the Biographer cannot be more precise about it. In fact, he need only have looked at Mr. Hyde's 'partial disclosure' to discover the essential facts. There he could have read the telegram in which the Hero informed the Entertainer that he could *not* be employed. He had been turned down by London; and the Hero (though no one would guess it from this book) was under orders from London. But why should the Biographer pay heed to the limited utterances of Mr. Hyde? Mr. Hyde had written that 'at the height of its operations, BSC' employed 'close on a thousand men and women.' A mere thousand? The Biographer knows far better: he raises the number to 'more than 30,000 experts,' all 'linked by invisible threads to BSC in New York.'

Over 30,000 agents .... The imagination boggles. I wonder where the poor fellow got that absurd number? Can it be that he has confused codes with things? All SIS agents were known by their numbers, and those in

America had five-figure numbers beginning with '3.' I have mentioned that the Hero was 38,000. Can it be …? Yes, I fear that it can. The Biographer's howlers are such that I believe him capable of anything.

As for Noel Coward, I happen to remember his attempt to join the Secret Service. I also remember why he was turned down. The Entertainer was very willing to serve, but he insisted on full publicity for all his activities; so it was found difficult to accommodate him. But no doubt, in after years, as two old gentlemen sat together in the luxury of Bermuda (or was it then Jamaica?), their warm imaginations cooked up some more glorious fantasy which then became part of the gospel so eagerly lapped up by this credulous disciple.

There are many other grotesque claims in this book, but I shall not pursue them. I shall content myself with two final observations, one particular, one general.

First, Sir William Stephenson had no direct responsibility in the European theater. He may have known about some intelligence activities there, and been a channel of communication, but his direct responsibility was for British security and propaganda, and the training of agents, in America. This function he performed well; but any claim that he initiated or controlled interception, cryptography, strategic deception, or special operations in Europe is impertinent.

Secondly, I have already observed, in my review of Mr. Cave Brown's book, that Sir Stewart Menzies, the head of SIS, at the end of his life evidently suffered from delusions of grandeur, seeing the war as a dialogue between himself and Canaris. Now it seems that Sir William Stephenson has gone the same way – and been carried further by the greater silliness of his biographer. During my own period in the secret service, I was often astonished by the puerility of some of our grandees, which I ascribed to their insulation from real life, their absorption into a self-contained subculture. I now realize that the same quality, if events are magnified by war, can lead, in old age, to dangerous hallucinations. This is a sad fact, and we should draw the obvious conclusion. We should remember with affection our old club-land heroes but publishers should flee from their approaches and friends should prevail upon them to be silent.

1. Hugh Trevor-Roper: an informal photograph taken in Christ Church, c.1950

2. Lady Alexandra Howard-Johnston in her gown to meet Princess Elizabeth and Prince Philip in May 1948. She married Trevor-Roper in October 1954. (*Xenia Dennen*)

3. Sir Stewart Menzies, Chief of the British Secret Intelligence Service, 1939–52. (*National Portrait Gallery*)

4. Peter Koch de Gooreynd, who kept Menzies company at the bar of White's. (*National Portrait Gallery*)

5. Sir Dick White, the only person to become head successively of both MI5 and SIS, and Trevor-Roper's influential mentor.

6. Charles Stuart: Christ Church historian and Trevor-Roper's first recruit to his wireless intelligence unit. (*Christ Church, Oxford*)

7. (*Above*) Rachel and Patrick Reilly, the diplomat who effectively vetoed Philby's becoming Chief of SIS. (*Bodleian Library, Oxford*)

8. (*Left*) Kim Philby, Soviet spy and British intelligence officer. (*Getty*)

9. (*Opposite*) Broadway Buildings, located opposite St James's Park underground station, provided SIS with headquarters from 1926 to 1964. (*Westminster Council Archives*)

10. (*Above*) Eleanor Philby: the spy's third wife, whom he abandoned in Beirut. She followed him to Moscow where he left her again. (*Getty*)

11. (*Left*) Melinda Maclean: the American wife of the Soviet spy Donald Maclean. Her relationship with Philby contributed to the collapse of his third marriage. (*Getty*)

One of Trevor-Roper's later reviews on intelligence focused on a wide-ranging collection of essays about Ultra by those who had produced it.

Review of *Codebreakers: The Inside Story of Bletchley Park* edited by F.H. Hinsley and Alan Stripp[6]

The wartime achievements of Bletchley Park, alias BP, alias Station X, alias GC & CS, are now generally known. Throughout the war, and for nearly 30 years after it, they were a wonderfully kept secret. Churchill, in his war memoirs, never mentioned them, although those already in the know could interpret his arcane allusions to 'our spies in Germany'. Then suddenly, in 1974, the story was revealed by Group-Captain Winterbotham, a former member of MI6, whose official function during the war had been to enforce the rule of absolute secrecy. Indeed, he once told me that he threatened any officer who should break that rule with instant execution. So his own pioneering breach of it has always struck me as paradoxical. To the former members of BP it was a shock; indeed, it shocks them still.

No doubt this long preserved silence was partly psychological. Those engaged in this delicate work were so conscious of its importance, so careful of its security, and so bound together in loyalty that secrecy became second nature to them and its maintenance a point of honour. Besides, the details of their work were so complicated that it is hard to explain them, or make them interesting, to the uninitiated, as some readers of this book may find. But the book is an important record, for it is essentially their book: a series of essays and reminiscences describing life and work at the institution which, in the course of a single year, uniformly disastrous in the field, 'raised secret intelligence to a position in the directing of war which it had never held before', and so contributed, perhaps decisively, to final victory.

I first knew BP in January 1940. It was then in its infancy and seemed informal, even amateur, in its organisation. The few officers worked mainly in the hideous Victorian mansion which had been taken over by the late head of MI6, Admiral Sinclair. But these officers were, or included, the survivors from Admiral 'Blinker' Hall's famous 'Room 40' at the Admiralty in the war of 1914 and the institution still retained a certain naval flavour. Its head, Alistair Denniston, had the rank of Commander and had acquired, while teaching French at Osborne [*Naval College*], a very convincing nautical roll. Other professionals were Colonel Tiltman, Nigel de Grey, Dillwyn Knox – a classical scholar who had translated an unbelievably boring Greek writer into indescribably mannered English,[7] and Oliver Strachey, the elder brother of Lytton, an Epicurean pillar of the Oriental Club. These men not only provided continuity with the first war: they also brought in, mainly from Cambridge, the mathematicians, linguists, papyrologists, Egyptologists, chess-players, etc, who would continue their work in the second. Denniston had asked for 'professor-type' men. Since no one knew that the place existed, there could be no applications to enter it, no open competition. Recruitment was by patronage only: an excellent system, provided that the patrons are sound.

Such were the apparently amateur beginnings of an organisation which, by 1942, was a highly professional factory employing thousands of persons turning out some 4,000 German signals a day (as well as Italian and Japanese) and communicating vital intelligence extracted from them direct to high commands in the field. The Germans, of course, deciphered some of our secret codes, but they had nothing like this.

The material sent out from BP was known generally as 'MSS' (Most Secret Sources), then, once the Americans came in, 'Top Secret (U)', or simply 'Ultra'. The most spectacular and valuable category of it was the regular communications of the German armed forces (including the Abwehr or Secret Service[8]), which used varying forms of the famous 'Enigma' machine. The Germans believed the Enigma cipher to be quite unbreakable. Again and again, faced by evidence that their plans and dispositions were known to the enemy, they asked themselves whether perhaps Enigma was being read, but always they ended by excluding such a possibility. The machine, they thought, was invulnerable – as indeed, in theory, it was; but there are also facts of life, including especially 'the indiscipline of the German operators' which, as Peter Twinn writes, led to this 'catastrophe for German intelligence'.

The cryptographical problem was solved in the end by a combination of luck, daring and genius. The Poles – brilliant cryptographers – had reconstructed the Enigma machine before the war, which gave us a good start, though the design was changed later; the Channel gave us time, which was denied to the Poles and French; the capture of Enigma machines on trawlers and submarines helped. The genius, the hero of Enigma, was Alan Turing. Knox, who worked on it first, was (I now learn) defeatist about it, but

Gordon Welchman was convinced that success was possible and persevered.[9] He is the second hero of Enigma. At a critical moment, when an increase of manpower had been refused, he, with Turing and some others, appealed directly, over the heads of their compliant superiors, to Churchill, and won. After the war he was 'ridiculously persecuted' by the secret establishment for revealing what had already been published by Winterbotham. The scholars of BP were not a privileged class like the clubmen of Broadway.

Of the four sections of this book, the first deals with the production of Ultra – the organisation of the factory, the distribution of the work between its units – Huts 6 and 8 assigned to cryptography, 3 and 4 to analysis and intelligence – and the changes brought about by events, including the arrival of the Americans. The second section is devoted to the actual machinery: the Enigma variations (for they varied in type and time), the mechanics of decipherment, the construction of the *bombes*[10] which unravelled the wheel-settings of the machines and yielded the daily changing key. The third section deals with an altogether different kind of material: the non-Morse teleprinter impulses transmitted at high speed by radio and used by the German armed forces at the highest level. It was known as 'Fish' and served to supplement Enigma, or to replace it when that traffic was unobtainable, being passed by land-line, as in occupied Europe. Fish was invaluable after the invasion of Europe in 1944, for it revealed the information passed between Berlin and Field-Marshal von Rundstedt, the Commander-in-Chief, West. The fourth section deals with 'Ultra's poor relations' – field ciphers and tactical codes. Finally there is a section on the codes used by the Japanese armed forces. But the greatest cryptographical triumph against Japan was not British but American: the breaking of 'Magic', the Japanese diplomatic code, which incidentally turned the Japanese ambassador in Berlin into an invaluable, if involuntary, spy for us in the heart of the Reich.

Much of this is inevitably highly technical and does not make easy reading, and some of the recollections are on a trivial level, for the regular work was monotonous and continuous, in eight-hour shifts, and the discipline strict. As one of the humbler workers puts it, the triumphs of cryptography and interpretation depended on 'the unremitting toil and endurance of almost 2,000 Wrens' who kept the machinery going – 500 of them tending the *bombes* – but had no direct part in the thrills of the chase: they were members of a chain-gang. Their 'long chain began with the Y service which intercepted the cipher radio messages and finished with the SLUs (Winterbotham's threatened officers) which distributed the information to the Allied Commanders, who, in the final reckoning, either used or misused it.'

Or perhaps could not use it. For battles are not won by intelligence alone. The best intelligence in the world is helpless against overwhelming force. Ultra revealed dispositions during the Norwegian and Greek campaigns, but to no avail. It gave the complete German plan for the capture of Crete but could not save the island. Though valuable against the Italians in the African desert, it was not till 1942 that it could turn the scale against Rommel, who replaced them. Then it was vital. Analysis of its use, says Sir Harry Hinsley, 'fully bears out the view which Auchinleck expressed at the time, that but for Ultra "Rommel would certainly have got through to Cairo".'

And it ensured the final victory there. After El Alamein the analysts of Hut 3 were impatient of Montgomery's excessive caution. Why did he not press on? He had 270 tanks while Ultra showed that Rommel had only 11 left: his supply ships, again thanks to Ultra, had been regularly sunk. Now he could surely be 'annihilated'. Above all, Ultra was invaluable at sea: it not only deprived the Afrika Korps of supplies; by locating and so defeating the U-boats in the Atlantic it also saved us from starvation. To say that BP won the war would be untrue and unfair. But it certainly tipped the scales, shortened the war, and preserved us from defeat. Where would we be – what would the world now be like – without it?

————————

Always aware of the importance of code-breaking, Trevor-Roper discussed other technical contributions to wartime British intelligence in the following review, during which he also reiterated some of his own principles of intelligence.

Review of *Most Secret War: British Scientific Intelligence, 1939–1945* by R. V. Jones[11]

'The formidable Dr Jones', as Kim Philby described him, was the wartime head of the scientific section of the Secret Intelligence Service, and deputy director of scientific intelligence on the Air Staff, which alone of the three armed services had such a department. He played an important personal part in some very critical moments of the war, both in the defence of Britain in its darkest days, and in the protection of British aerial attacks on Germany. His story is a success story, which excuses a certain amount of self-congratulation.

Most wartime careers owed a good deal to chance. At Oxford, Dr Jones had come into the orbit of Professor F.A. Lindemann, afterwards Lord Cherwell. He also did some work for Sir Henry Tizard,[12] who presided over the prewar Committee for Scientific Survey of Air Defence, and for Robert Watson-Watt[13] of Radio Research. As is well-known, Lindemann and Tizard did not agree, and the experience of the Tizard committee inflamed their mutual antipathy. Lindemann, whom Churchill had imposed on the committee in 1935, so enraged his colleagues by his political short cuts that he was pushed off it again in 1936, meditating revenge. He was still in revengeful mood in 1938 when Dr Jones, thinking himself 'a pawn in a distinctly unpleasant game', resolved to get away. He had, he thought, wasted his time and lost his chance of an academic post. In his frustration, he almost decided to join the Grenadier Guards, in which his father had been an efficient and devoted sergeant. In the end, he went to the Admiralty Research Laboratory: 'a rotten reward', he thought, for three wasted years; but 'I wanted never again to be involved with Lindemann, Tizard or Watson Watt.'

The war ended that hope. Soon he was back with his old masters, and involved once again in their rivalries, at the highest level, and in the most critical times. His first task was to discover whether SIS had any means of identifying the secret weapon of which Hitler had ominously boasted. He found no evidence either of the weapon in Germany or of scientific intelligence in SIS. 'The average SIS agent,' he observes, 'was a scientific analphabet'; and he wrote a report urging the formation of a Scientific Intelligence Service for war. Tizard supported it, but the Admiralty did not, and it foundered. At the end of the war, from a much stronger position, he would make a comparable report recommending a similar service for peacetime. It, too, would founder, this time against the 'disastrous' policy of the Joint Intelligence Committee and its favoured scientist, P.M.S. Blackett.[14] But by that time the war had been won – thanks largely to scientific intelligence and to its appreciation by Churchill, who 'alone among politicians valued science and technology at something approaching their true worth'.

Dr Jones had first seen Churchill in 1936, when he came to support the unsuccessful parliamentary candidature of his protégé, Lindemann. 'I remember well the impression that he created upon all of us. He looked so tired and florid that our general verdict was "Poor old Winston – he can't last much longer!"' I remember it, too: the impression was general. However, the challenge of 1940 soon changed all that. With Churchill, Lindemann also rose, and Tizard, of course, declined. On one occasion, Tizard suggested to Jones that, in the interest of the war, he might effect a reconciliation and end 'this ridiculous quarrel' between them. The olive branch was offered, but not accepted. Lindemann's only response was 'to give a mild snort and say "Now that I am in a position of power, a lot of my old friends have come sniffing around."' 'So that,' says Dr Jones, 'was that.'

The crucial moment in Dr Jones's wartime career came on 21 June 1940. The question was, did the Germans possess radio beams for navigation of bombers or not? Jones believed that they did, but Tizard doubted it. Lindemann caused Jones to be summoned to a meeting in the cabinet room, and there he found himself speaking on the subject 'for some 20 minutes, which is quite a time to have the prime minister listening at the height of the greatest crisis that had ever confronted the country.' Churchill never forgot that moment, for Jones, having depressed him by saying that the Germans had a system of beams whereby they could now bomb accurately by night, went on to show how they could still be defeated by 'bending the beam'; which was effectively done. The episode was fatal to Tizard. Two years later, Churchill remarked, 'if we had listened to Sir Henry Tizard in 1940, we should not have known about the beams. As it was, it was left to that young Dr Jones, who spoke so well at our meeting.' From that moment, Jones was made. 'Your name,' Churchill once said to him, 'will open all doors.'

It also opened windows. 'Window' was the cover-name given to the method of disconcerting enemy anti-aircraft radar by creating spurious signals. The air authorities were at first reluctant to use this device; for obviously this was a game at which two could play. Lindemann, originally a supporter of Window, was converted to this view. Jones countered this 'squeamishness' on the ground that the Germans must anyway know the principle, and in October 1942 he drew support from the report of a Danish agent. But Lindemann was adamant, dismissing this report as merely 'something two WAAFs [*members of the Women's Auxiliary Air Force*] had said to one another in a train. When I told him that I would have to oppose him at the meeting, he said: "If you do that, you will find Tizard and me united against you." I could not help replying: "If I've achieved that, by God, I've achieved something."'

In the end, this matter, too, was argued before the prime minister, and Leigh Mallory, the head of Fighter Command, pronounced for Window. 'That concluded the argument and Churchill said: "Very well, let us open the Window."' It afterwards transpired that the Germans had been as squeamish as the British, and for the same reason. They had carried out trials which had shown Window to be disastrously effective; whereupon Goering had all the reports destroyed, and imposed complete silence in case the British might acquire the idea. 'So for more that a year both we and the Germans had hesitated to use Window against one another in the fear of losing on the exchange.'

However, Dr Jones did not always have it his own way. In 1943, he was mortified when investigation into German rocket weapons was entrusted to a committee under Duncan Sandys. To Dr Jones, this seemed almost an impertinence. 'How had the chiefs of staff overlooked us, when we had already proved ourselves in the beams, the Bruneval raid, the Gibraltar barrage, radar, Window, heavy water, and the German night-fighters?' Here is a summary of the achievements of his team, all of which are described in detail in this book. As a 'scientific analphabet', I shall not attempt to follow him on such difficult terrain. Some of his stories are complex, some exciting, and they are seasoned with some light (and some heavy) relief. The Bruneval raid was a brilliant commando raid on the French coast in February 1942 which captured German radar equipment for the guidance of fighter planes. The Gibraltar barrage was a system of ship-reporting in the straits of Gibraltar mounted by the *Abwehr*, or German Secret Service, in order to inform the Germans of allied naval build-up in the Mediterranean in 1942. The Spaniards, who had connived at the whole operation, were ultimately obliged, by diplomatic pressure, to dismantle it.

The Sandys committee did not, in the end, monopolise the study of the German rocket weapons. Lindemann saw to that. Lindemann was himself wrong about the rockets – both V2, which he dismissed as a blind, perhaps for hypothetical flying-bombs, and V1, the real flying-bombs, which he dismissed, when they were reported, as 'a mare's nest.' But he saw to it that Sandys knew of Jones's work, brought them together, and ensured that the prime minister heard both sides of the argument. Once again, the prime minister was convinced by Jones, and Lindemann had to retreat. 'Had it been Tizard, as it was in 1940,' says Dr Jones, 'it might have been the end of him, but fortunately Churchill's confidence in Lindemann was far too firm to be shaken.'

This is a long book and, for an amateur, sometimes difficult reading; but its content is fascinating – in casual detail as well as in its main argument. Dr Jones remarks that 'the Germans, at the beginning of the war, had not thought nearly so much about the use of radar as we had ourselves, in contrast to navigational beams, where they had obviously thought a great deal further than we had.' They had, of course, been planning aggression, we defence. He disposes (as others have done) of the story that Churchill deliberately sacrificed Coventry to save the secret of Ultra. He makes the interesting observation that (as revealed by postwar inquiry) there was no German photographic reconnaissance of London from 10 January 1941 to 10 September 1944, while our photo-reconnaissance pilots were flying over 500 miles of German occupied territory. The Germans, we might add, were then concentrating on their Eastern front. He believes that area-bombing might have ended the war if it had been kept up on the same scale after the great raids on Hamburg. Lindemann agreed; so did Milch on the German side. Tizard did not; 'but it was on the grounds of probable effectiveness and not of morality that the battle was fought.'

On the use of intelligence sources, Dr Jones has much to say. Like everyone else, he pays tribute to Ultra, the single consistently valuable and unquestionable source of 'hard' evidence. But he remarks on the danger of over-reliance on that great accidental benefit which could so easily have been withdrawn from us, leaving us naked. In fact, many other sources contributed to the most successful operations. The 'Oslo report' from a Norwegian source in 1939, though at first doubted, proved remarkably accurate.[15] Aerial photography and the work of the French Resistance were essential at Bruneval. The identification of the rocket work at Peenemünde owed nothing to Ultra.[16] There are no absolute rules in intelligence – except that intelligence officers must be intelligent. The nearest to a rule which Dr Jones offers is his conviction that the collection and the collation of intelligence must be under the same authority.[17] This was the strongest conclusion which I carried away from my own wartime experience: both the British SIS and the German *Abwehr* made, in my opinion, avoidable errors by separating the two functions.

Dr Jones introduces many personalities. He had some enjoyable buccaneers as collaborators, and there are heroic figures in the European Resistance. Of the great, only two men stand out. There is Lindemann, who is vivid to me perhaps because I knew him well: a man of great ambition and great personal courage, uncompromising and demanding, he positively courted unpopularity, and yet was fundamentally considerate and always open to reason. Then there is Churchill who, in those years, cast his spell over all, especially if they were young. 'Whenever we met in the war,' writes Dr Jones, 'I had the feeling of being re-charged by contact with a source of living power. Here was strength, resolution, humour, readiness to listen, to ask the searching questions and, when convinced, to act.' Besides, in him, 'we had a prime minister with a genuine and strong interest in the possibilities opened up by science, such as none of his successors has had. Even his controversial dependence on Lindemann was evidence of this interest which, for example, made him anxious to be flown – even at some discomfort – in experimental aircraft to see for himself the state of airborne radar.' Beside him, all the other politicians fade into insignificance. They do not take decisions. After the great debate on bombing the rocket-sites at Peenemünde, 'Herbert Morrison, for some reason or other, wanted to know whether the evidence from German personnel had come from officers or other ranks … Anthony Eden thought that the arguments were nicely balanced.' On another occasion, Herbert Morrison took the chair in Churchill's absence. The issue was whether to mislead the Germans about the accuracy of their V- weapons. The acting chairman 'finally ruled that it would be an interference with Providence' to do so. Churchill did not mind grasping the initiative from Providence.

6

Percy Sillitoe and Dick White

While Trevor-Roper was often at odds with his superiors during his wartime years in the Secret Intelligence Service (MI6), his relations with the Security Service (MI5) had been easier. His old tutor, J.C. Masterman, served in MI5, as did Dick White, who became such an influential friend. During the war Trevor-Roper was also on good terms with other MI5 officers, including Herbert Hart and 'Tar' Robertson, the ingenious and energetic mainspring of the 'Double Cross' system which turned German spies and deployed them as agents of deception. Trevor-Roper understood the purpose and achievements of MI5 very well and so was particularly suited to review the memoirs of its postwar director general, Sir Percy Sillitoe.[1]

Sillitoe was conspicuously inept as director general. Clement Attlee, Churchill's successor as prime minister, appointed the former policeman Sillitoe to manage the intelligence officers of MI5, even though there was a strong internal candidate in the form of Guy Liddell. The slight to Liddell alienated the senior officers from Sillitoe. His schooling had been incomplete and on one occasion he felt the MI5 directors were deliberately quoting Latin tags he could not understand in order to humiliate him. Sillitoe stormed out of the building and complained to his son about the 'bastards'. He also alienated the junior staff, who gave him cheek and complained he spent too much time playing golf. His attempts at clandestine behaviour were particularly inappropriate. He sought to avoid attention by methods which attracted amazed scrutiny, such as leaving a plane backwards.[2] *On retirement in August 1953 Sillitoe opened a sweet shop in Eastbourne which folded within two days. This left him free to work on his memoirs. Among senior Whitehall officials there was dismay at his literary ambitions. He was made to submit a text to the Home Office and later complained that the government had ripped the guts out of his book.*

Review of *Cloak without Dagger*
by Sir Percy Sillitoe[3]

M.I.5 was (until 1946) and is (since 1953) a secret service. As Sir Percy Sillitoe writes, 'Since its earliest beginnings it has alternately intrigued and infuriated the public by the aura of hush-hush with which it has seemed to be surrounded.' His own sympathies, it is clear, are with the public in this matter, and he is the only Director-General of M.I.5 who has ever blown aside this infuriating aura. Who could name any of his predecessors, or his successor? They are not even named in this book. But between 1946 and 1953 things were very different. Whenever some vital atomic secret was found to have leaked out, or diplomats to have fled beyond the Iron Curtain, the press loudly announced that 'Sir Percy Sillitoe, head of M.I.5,' was on the way belatedly to bolt the flapping stable-door, and Sir Percy himself contrived often to be photographed, skilfully failing in an ostentatious attempt to elude the camera. It is perhaps unfortunate that the only personal reign known to the public should have included all the major failures of our intelligence service; but Sir Percy is not abashed at this unfortunate coincidence. On the contrary, thanks to his self-advertisement, he says, 'the public were inspired with confidence in me.' This may be so, although it is arguable that their confidence would have been more rational if the secrets and the diplomats had not escaped, even though the head of M.I.5 had been anonymous.

To enjoy still more of the public confidence, Sir Percy has now produced his memoirs, but anyone who hopes to learn from them about M.I.5 will be disappointed. On this subject he is merely trivial: the greater part of the book is simply an account of a particularly energetic and useful chief constable in two great industrial towns, centres of mob-violence. I found this fascinating. The account of gang organisation in Sheffield and Glasgow is as interesting as the methods by which Sir Percy broke it. In Sheffield there were 'The Mooney Boys' and 'The Garvin Boys,' named after their leaders, and in Glasgow the Roman Catholic 'Norman Conks' and the Orangist 'Billy Boys.' These gangs fought each other, intimidated and robbed shop-keepers and publicans, and held parts of the city at their mercy. The Irish element is obvious in both cities, as in American gangsterism; and side by side with this social fact of modern great cities is another, which also has its American parallel. Glasgow was not only, like Chicago, terrorised by gangs;

it was also, like Old New York, ruled by a municipal oligarchy of corrupt and demagogic Tammany bosses. Sir Percy's account of these cities is a useful chapter of social history.

How did he in fact break up both the gangs and the corruption? His answer is clear: by organisation, by determination, by raising the standards and morale of the police – and by self-advertisement. Sir Percy made it clear that the police would act and he would always take responsibility. Earlier in his career, as chief constable of the placid town of Beverley, he had shown this by prosecuting a prominent local landlord for swearing at a local bobby. The only evidence was the unsupported statement of the bobby, and the Bench quickly dismissed the charge; which still seems to Sir Percy a strange miscarriage of justice, evidently due to the social composition of the Bench. However, the incident clearly showed that he would support the police, and his promotion to Sheffield, where the police needed support not against hot-tempered landlords but against armed urban criminals, was appreciated both in Sheffield and in Beverley. In Sheffield, too, he always put himself forward 'to take the weight of responsibility from the magistrate and let it fall upon my own shoulders. The results,' he says with satisfaction, 'were good.'

No doubt. But were the results equally good in a 'secret service'? On the whole, I doubt it. A secret service is secret and it deals with, and should employ, clever people. Now Sir Percy, it is clear, not only dislikes secrecy: he also dislikes clever people, at least in the police ('indeed, I once argued with some passion on this point with Lord Trenchard'); and he found the 'highly intelligent but somewhat introspective' – i.e. I suppose, thoughtful – members of M.I.5 too complex for his philosophy. When he retired – naturally in a blaze of publicity – his successor's name was announced in banner-headlines in that confident paper, the *Daily Express*. It was the name of another provincial chief constable. But although the *Daily Express* never acknowledged error (it seldom does), I believe that on this occasion it was wrong. After the reign of Sir Percy, the Prime Minister believed in leaving useful chief constables in the scene of their usefulness.

When Sillitoe's term as director general was nearing its end, the officers of MI5 began to fear he might indeed be succeeded by another chief constable. So they mobilised their influential alumni, in particular the previous director general, Sir David Petrie, and J.C. Masterman, who had become provost of Worcester College Oxford. Petrie thought that his successor had been a disaster and encouraged Masterman's efforts to secure the appointment of an internal candidate to succeed Sillitoe. Masterman's decisive intervention was to mobilise an influential Conservative minister, Lord Swinton, who button-holed the Home Secretary, David Maxwell Fyfe, and alerted him to the troubles in MI5, of which he was quite unaware. Masterman wanted Guy Liddell to follow Sillitoe and then for his old pupil Dick White to succeed Liddell. But Liddell made a diffident impression and White was given the job straight away.

White was fortunate to follow the bungling Sillitoe, whom he considered 'vapid and shallow and frequently wrong'.[4] Sillitoe's successor was bound to make a good impression by contrast alone, and White made the most of his opportunity. But he only stayed as director general until 1956, when Anthony Eden insisted on his taking over as chief of SIS. White served as chief until 1968, when he became security coordinator in the Cabinet Office. Dick White's remarkable career meant that for nearly two decades one of Trevor-Roper's closest friends was amongst the most influential figures in the British secret community. After White's death in 1993 Trevor-Roper wrote an affectionate memoir.

Sir Dick White 1906–1993: A Personal Memoir[5]

Dick Goldsmith White was the only person to have been head of both MI5 and MI6 and the first civilian to be head of either: hitherto these posts had always gone to admirals, generals or policemen. He was also the first university graduate to be head of MI6: he had read Modern History at Christ Church, a pupil, like myself later, of J.C. Masterman. No doubt it was Masterman, that great fixer, who launched him on his first career, as a schoolmaster. Then, in 1936, he was recruited by MI5. Five years later he turned the tables, recruiting his former tutor to be a wartime member (and afterwards the unauthorised historian) of the famous Double-Cross system, which so completely misled the German Secret Service.

I came to know him in 1940, when I was working closely with, though not in, MI5. Our offices were then in the cells of Wormwood Scrubs prison.

Soon afterwards I was transferred to MI6, but we remained both officially and personally close. After I had (on Masterman's recommendation) recruited another of his pupils, Charles Stuart, and then the ex-Censor of Christ Church, Gilbert Ryle, while my former classical tutor, Denys Page, was our official contact at Bletchley, there was a sub-audible grumble about a Christ Church *mafia* in the secret world. Dick would touch lightly on this many years later in his speech as guest of honour at the Censors' Dinner. We were regarded with some suspicion by our superiors – unlike the Cambridge *mafia* (Philby, Blunt, etc.) who won golden opinions. We were all involved in the same general task: counter-espionage, deception, and the collection, interpretation and exploitation, for that purpose, of 'Ultra' material. Dick White, the professional among us, was our main contact in MI5.

He was a true professional in his methods, but what we most admired was his intellectual lucidity, his equanimity, his unfailing sense of proportion and humour. Secret services contain, or create, some curious human types. The secrecy of their operations can generate paranoia and limit understanding. Dick was a rational man at ease in the real world and proof against these failings; he believed that all problems are soluble by reason; and he never lost his balance. He was also very good company. Uninhibited conversation with him was a great relaxation, in the stress of war.

In 1944 the intelligence war had been won and it was time to think of mopping up the enemy. An inter-departmental 'War Room' was created to direct the operation once Germany was invaded. After a farcical attempt by the head of MI6 ('CSS') to impose his (quite incapable) nominee,[6] we ignored orders and elected Dick as our chairman. From that position he moved naturally on to be head of British counter-intelligence in Germany. For this purpose he was seconded from MI5 to SHAEF (Supreme Headquarters, Allied Expeditionary Force), as I was from MI6; so I was effectively under his command, and our association was closer than ever.

In Germany, in 1945, I saw much of him. There he had, at weekends, the use of an elegant rural *Schloss*, requisitioned from a German baron who, to judge from the photographs in it, had spent much time obsequiously kowtowing to the dreadful Ribbentrop.[7] I greatly enjoyed those Arcadian weekends. We had congenial company, long walks in the Teutoberger Wald, and wide-ranging conversation, oblivious, for the time being, of the war, the Germans, and our own bureaucracy. Dick there revealed his love of music, literature and ideas; which perhaps is what preserved his stability in dark days and in his devious profession.

He also had a sense of history, and a dislike of the oppressive secrecy so devoutly cultivated and resolutely enforced by some of our colleagues. Hence, I suppose, his instruction to me in September 1945, to find out what had happened to Hitler, who had disappeared without trace nearly five months ago. Afterwards he urged me to write the story as a book. I objected that I would never be allowed to publish it, but Dick said he would take care of that in the Joint Intelligence Committee, of which he was a member; as indeed he did, leaving CSS, who continued to veto it, in a minority of one.[8] Two years ago [1991] he told my wife that he had entrusted this task to me on the strength of a paper I had submitted, during the war, on the German Secret Service. By that time I was not at all sure whether it was I who had written that paper. It may well have been Charles Stuart.[9]

Later, when he was himself CSS, Dick told me that if I were to write about the Philby affair there would be no objection, provided that I neither asked his permission nor showed him the text. I never knew whether he approved of the result: perhaps not; I may have gone too far even for him.

Philby, of course, was a subject often discussed between us. Dick had suspected that he was a Russian spy well before 1951. In 1951 he was sure of it. So were others in MI5. But not in MI6. There the establishment stood firm in defence of their man. Though they were obliged to 'release' him (with a golden handshake), they afterwards secretly re-engaged him in Beirut. When Dick became himself head of MI6 and discovered that Philby was back on the pay-roll, he was naturally shocked. Seeing that the game was up, Philby absconded from Beirut to Moscow. There he has never missed an opportunity to present Dick as 'ineffective', 'nondescript', etc. He even wrote to me from Moscow to press this view. But then he would, wouldn't he?

Dick was put in charge of MI6 in 1956, after being head of MI5 for three years. He was appointed to clear up the mess after yet another disaster: the bungled affair of the frog-man Commander Crabb. After that disaster an infuriated Prime Minister sacked the whole directorate. The survivors were not pleased at the new appointment: to them MI5 was the ancient enemy. 'If Colonel Dansey were alive now', they said, 'this would kill him'. Colonel Dansey, former Acting CSS, who had retired with a knighthood after the war, was the peppery hero of the old gung-ho brigade who recruited in the bars of Boodle's and White's. Luckily, he was now dead: *felix opportunitate mortis*.[10]

After retiring from MI6 Dick became Security Co-ordinator in the Cabinet Office. He had won the personal trust of successive Prime Ministers and their advisers and changed both the character and the image of both security services. Foreigners who dealt with him were astonished to find that the head of British Secret Intelligence was a man of wide culture, civilised tastes and open, easy conversation: that is unusual in any such organisation: I suspect that, in the end, he was not really in love with so constricting a profession, but he took everything with such genial good humour that one never knew. Every year hitherto, the dwindling veterans of the secret war against Germany have met for a celebratory luncheon. I greatly enjoyed those meetings. This summer we shall hold the last of them. They could not now be the same.

7

Anthony Blunt

Long after the initial wave of books about Kim Philby, the treachery of the Cambridge spies continued to fascinate the British public. Industrious authors such as Andrew Boyle[1] sought to satisfy the voracious demand for books on Soviet secret agents. Trevor-Roper thought that Boyle and other writers about Russian moles supplied too much detail and too little explanation, as the following review shows.

Review of *The Climate of Treason* by Andrew Boyle[2]

Maclean, Burgess, Philby – here they are again, that squalid trio. Over 40 years ago they sold their miserable souls to one of the nastiest tyrants in history. Nearly 30 years ago the net began to close and they had to bolt for safety. For 15 years they had lived double lives, betraying their country, their professions, their friends. For what? With what result? Why?

After the lapse of a generation, the mechanics of petty treachery become unimportant, of antiquarian interest only. Mr Boyle has gone over the whole ground in great detail, and we must respect his industry. He has read everything, consulted the persons involved, obtained access to the files of the CIA and FBI. And he has added to our knowledge. 'Unless I had succeeded in breaking fresh ground, and producing some startling new evidence', he writes, 'I would not have written this book'; and he duly produces such evidence, exposing, but not naming, two accomplices, whom he describes as the Fourth and Fifth Man, or by their cover-names 'Maurice' and 'Basil'. By now we all know their names. But, with his leave, I do not think this 'startling new evidence' is important. It reveals nothing that was not known – perhaps more accurately known – to authority and merely gives occasion for belated public persecution. Mr Boyle's insatiable thirst for detail – illustrative but often irrelevant – is, in my opinion, excessive. It overcharges his anyway heavily padded sentences and makes him tedious to read. The only real value of such a book, in my opinion, lies not in such factual detail but in the answers which it may give to general questions. Here I think that it is less satisfactory.

Why did the infamous trio become communist spies in the 1930s? Mr Boyle dwells heavily, and recurrently, on the decline of the British Empire at that time: a decline which, he says, was visible in spite of apparent strength. This, he suggests, created the psychological condition for the transfer of loyalty. I do not follow his reasoning. I do not recollect that those of my contemporaries who became communist in the 1930s were much exercised by, or even conscious of, such decline. Their motives were perfectly clear. First, capitalism, in those years of depression and unemployment, seemed not to be working, and communism – a magic nostrum whose actual operation could not be checked – claimed to have the answer. Secondly, those were the years of Fascism, which threatened a new World War, and of the Popular Front[3] against it. The communists then presented themselves as the strongest enemies of Fascism, perhaps – since the 'Appeasers' in the West could not be relied upon – its only resolute enemies. These were sufficient reasons, so long as they lasted, for undergraduates to listen to communist propaganda; and many did.

There was also another reason, less reputable but not, I think, less real. Intellectuals often pretend that, as a class, they are advocates of liberty. This is seldom true. Intellectuals like the beauty of mathematical order. They like tidiness, symmetry. Liberty is untidy, asymmetrical. Consequently young intellectuals, even when they speak of liberty, really worship power. They generally grow out of this when they realise that they are less likely to exercise power themselves than to be the victims of it. But for a time they think that they respect it. Communism, as intellectually justified system of total power, has a fatal fascination for young intellectuals seeking short cuts to total solutions.

All these causes, in my opinion, led many of my contemporaries in the 1930s to look sympathetically on communism, and some of them to join the Communist Party of Great Britain. But they did not become spies or sell themselves to be the blind creatures of a foreign government. They did not surrender their freedom to change their minds. And later, most of them used that freedom. For very soon, all the arguments which had at first converted them were proved false. Stalin's tyranny could not long be regarded as a humane solution to social problems. The Popular Front was shown to be a fraud. The Russian government did not prevent World War or resist Nazism: by its cynical pact with Hitler it precipitated a war which might otherwise have been avoided. And the young men grew up. Anyone who watched the events of those years with any intelligence could see this process of re-education, and therefore, in 1939, it seemed absurd to persecute, simply on that account, those who had been communist in the previous years. To do so would have been to play into the hands of stupid reaction.

The difference between the unholy trinity and the communist contemporaries whose motives I have described is that the former were not idealists who preserved their independence. They were spies. They sold themselves unconditionally, irreversibly, not even to the British Communist Party but to a foreign traitor. This makes them contemptible. Of course, being intellectuals, they offer intellectual justifications, but their justifications are worthless. Philby, the most articulate of them, protests that, but for communist Russia, 'the world would now be ruled by Hitler and Hirohito'. In fact, it was Great Britain, not Russia, which resisted Hitler. If Stalin had got his way Hitler and Hirohito really would have won. The Russians only came into the war two years later, when they were directly attacked. Maclean similarly tried to argue that it was only Russian strength which stood in the way of atomic war in the 1950s. But the argument is just as flimsy, and anyway he had already sold himself in the 1930s, when that argument could not have applied; so it too is a mere rationalisation. Whatever the motives which caused others to support Russia or communism for a time in the 1930s, those motives cannot be invoked to explain the permanent and secret transfer of loyalty by Philby, Burgess and Maclean. The difference between an idealist supporter and a blind, dependent tool is absolute.

For these reasons I cannot greatly blame 'the Establishment', or their colleagues for overlooking the communist past of Philby, Burgess and Maclean in the circumstances of the later 1930s. Where they can be blamed is for overlooking their misdemeanours in office, after they had been accepted. The Foreign Office was incredibly tolerant of Maclean, after his various excesses,[4] which were no doubt caused by the tensions of his double life. The extraordinary survival of Burgess (whom the [*Foreign*] Office generally detested) can only partly be explained by the personal patronage of the Minister, Hector McNeil. Philby was protected by SIS against the justified suspicions of MI5. Here I believe that social factors did operate, with lamentable effect. But I do not think that these factors were peculiar to that time (the Protection of Employment Act gives an even greater security now.)

At all times, professional corporations are indulgent to erring members, and particularly such corporations as impose on their members an artificial way of life which must create, in intelligent persons, unnatural tensions. The history of monastic orders, and of university colleges is a record of such tolerance. Life in SIS, *experto crede*[5] is very unnatural.

In saying this, I am not seeking to justify the tolerance of these organisations. I am merely saying that since such tolerance is a natural phenomenon in a corporation, external tests are necessary. A corporation should not be the only judge of its own members.

Finally, how much harm did the trio do? I am unrepentant in my view that in fact they did very little. This is partly because I am sceptical about the value of secret intelligence. Most secrets are in print if one knows where to find them or how to deduce them. Of course there are exceptions, especially in wartime. If Philby had been a German agent, he could have done us great harm. He could have told the Germans about 'Ultra'. In fact he may have told the Russians[6] (as we tried to do, in sterilised form) – but if so, they kept the secret and no harm was done. I think that Philby did try to block intelligence which might have given opportunity for a separate peace between Germany and the West; but the British government was opposed to a separate peace anyway. Philby's main function, I believe, was to protect himself, not to supply vital information to the Russians who were never sure how far they could trust him.

Maclean is credited with the conveyance of vital atomic secrets. But even scientific secrets are generally in print somewhere, and anyway, the capacity to exploit them is not supplied by mere knowledge. Information about nuclear fission is of no use to a power which has not the necessary industrial base and the necessary scientific education; and a power which has those assets will very soon get the information anyway. According to the experts, Maclean gave nothing to the Russians that the Russians were not able do deduce themselves. For all these reasons I believe that the importance of this unholy trio has been exaggerated. In themselves they are unimportant, contemptible.

> The earth hath bubbles as the water hath
> And these are of them

said Banquo of the three witches on the blasted heath, and the same can be said of these three bubbles who have long ago burst. The 'climate' which incidentally generated them is of some interest, but Mr Boyle, who has so patiently reconstructed the iridescent rotation of those malodorous bubbles while they floated in the air of Whitehall, seems to me to have got their chemistry wrong.

The identity of the person Boyle had described as the 'Fourth Man' and 'Maurice' was soon revealed. He was the distinguished art historian and wartime MI5 officer Anthony Blunt. Blunt (1907–83) had been educated at Marlborough and Trinity College Cambridge, of which he was elected a fellow in 1932. In 1937 he was recruited as a talent-spotter by the NKVD and in 1940 he was brought into MI5 on the recommendation of his old Cambridge friend Victor Rothschild. Blunt inserted British agents amongst the domestic staff of foreign embassies and opened their diplomatic bags. He also provided the KGB with over a thousand secret documents. He enjoyed the complete confidence of Guy Liddell, who on 14 August 1941 recorded his suggestion that 'Blunt should go down periodically to G.C. & C.S. and make notes. That would save everyone a great deal of trouble and avoid filing a large amount of this material in our office.'[7] In 1945 Blunt was made surveyor of the king's pictures. Further appointments as director of the Courtauld Gallery and professor of the history of art at London University meant that Blunt enjoyed the most successful professional career of the five principal Cambridge spies. On 15 November 1979 Margaret Thatcher identified him as a Soviet spy to the House of Commons. In the aftermath his knighthood was cancelled and he resigned from the British Academy.

'Blunt Censured, Nothing Gained'[8]

The exposure of Anthony Blunt has followed a certain classical pattern. In 1956 a Labour MP, prompted by journalists, asked in Parliament about the 'third man' and named Kim Philby. Philby was then under suspicion; but since there was no firm evidence, the Minister, thus forced, was obliged to clear him; which gave him a new lease of life. This was unfortunate. Now, other Labour MPs, prompted by the investigative work of Mr Andrew Boyle, have asked in Parliament about the 'fourth man' and named Anthony Blunt. The Minister, in her reply, has been bound by the evidence to state the facts and thereby expose the manner in which Blunt has been neutralised. This I believe is equally unfortunate in its implications.

I do not say this out of personal concern for Blunt. Although I have known him since the war, when we were in related departments, I have never known him well. From the start I was put off by that cold, aloof manner, that slightly supercilious drawl. The Cambridge aesthete seemed to look down, from an apostolic height, on us outsiders. No doubt I misjudged a mere mannerism. By 1951 I realised that his life was far less olympian than I had thought. I then knew that he had been dangerously close to Guy Burgess and his world, and I made certain deductions. These deductions were not invalidated, in my eyes, by the fact that he was a distinguished art-scholar, for history shows that that profession has always been compatible with extra-curricular activities.

Holding these views, and knowing something about the security services, I took it for granted that Blunt, in 1951, would be (like Philby) carefully grilled, and that although (again like Philby) he might survive, he would, thereafter, be closely watched. That being so, I reckoned that, between fear for his skin and care for his now honourable career, he would – assuming that he had been a Russian agent – retreat into cautious inactivity, modified only by the occasional imperative of self-protection. I also assumed that he would now anyway be harmless, for since 1945 he had nothing to tell the Russians that was worth the risk of conveyance or could safely be believed by them. I still believe that this is true.

We met occasionally in recent years, but awkwardly. I always felt that he avoided me. However, at our last meeting he assured me, spontaneously, that this was due to short sight. As a victim of the same disability, and consequent embarrassment, I sympathised with him. In those years I felt somewhat contemptuous of his apparent timidity. Now that I know how deeply he had been involved, I am more impressed by the strength of his nerves in carrying, for so long, such a burden of fear.

His main fear, after 1951, must have been of Burgess, that *homme fatal* whom no one knew with impunity. It was Burgess whose indiscretions to Goronwy Rees in 1937 could have blown both himself and Blunt; it was

Burgess who, by planting himself on Philby in Washington, jeopardised both Philby and Maclean; and it was Burgess who, by bolting with Maclean to Moscow, brought about Philby's extrusion from SIS.[9] Once in Moscow, Burgess threatened to expose Blunt too. Wishing to return to England, he sought to negotiate a guarantee of immunity from prosecution there. Such a guarantee could only have been obtained against an undertaking to reveal all that he knew, which of course would have been fatal to Blunt. I suspect it was this fear which prompted Blunt to make his confession – a confession which in fact may have been unnecessary, since Burgess then died in Moscow, having revealed nothing.[10]

It has now been revealed that the immunity which was denied to Burgess was granted to Blunt in return for his co-operation. This is the revelation which the Prime Minister has been obliged to make in answer to a parliamentary question. Predictably, it has provoked a storm. Was this not a most improper concession? Was it not given solely to save established faces? Was not indecent indulgence shown to an 'establishment' mole? Why was Blunt not prosecuted, like smaller fry, to make a popular holiday? I believe that this clamour is misguided and unfortunate, and demonstrates the need not for more but for less freedom of information – or for less co-operation with the Americans whose legislation makes secrecy and confidentiality alike impossible.

I regard with contempt anyone who sells himself as a mere tool to a foreign tyranny. I have no great love for secret services. But if spies exist, as they do, and if secret services are necessary, as I admit that they are, then we must accept the consequences; and one of those consequences is that secrecy must be met with secrecy. In the war, if we caught a German spy, we did not cry havoc and stage a public trial. We gave him the alternative: either he must work for us against his German employers or he must face the consequences. Those who did not co-operate were shot. Those who did were protected. This policy produced valuable dividends: through it we controlled a large part of the German secret service. In peacetime the penalty is less severe but the system, and the potential dividends, are the same. The Surveyor of the Queen's Pictures was not given an exclusive privilege: he was simply 'turned round' like any vulgar agent who preferred to survive. He was worth turning round because he had much to give, which a public prosecution would have lost. Many a worthless spy has been handsomely paid because he has given vital information. The rewards and penalties of espionage are not measured by natural justice but by results. To clamour against such a bargain is merely stupid: it is to clamour against the facts of life.

Of course this does not answer the quite distinct question, why were the facts not told to the Prime Minister or the Home Secretary of the time? This seems to me a strange omission. Admittedly, the security services always regard politicians with suspicion, as being leaky vessels, and perhaps there are some matters which Ministers prefer not to know. But in this case such an omission seems, to say the least, imprudent. Only eight years before, the Chief of the Secret Service and his deputy and preselected successor[11] had both been retired in disgrace through precisely such an omission. If the voice of protest concentrates on this imprudence, it is, in my opinion, entirely justified. But all other complaints seem to me irrational. It is absurd to subordinate a secret service to egalitarian morality, or to demand that it operate in public; and it is positively damaging to go back, in effect, on a promise of immunity. For who will offer valuable evidence in return for an immunity which can be practically overturned by a parliamentary question?

If the clamour, then, is largely absurd, what (we may ask) lies behind it? The voice of protest, we may note, is indistinct and discordant, changing from day to day. The *New Statesmen* led off by attacking those who persecuted the innocent Blunt. That looks rather silly now, so the charge has been changed – indeed reversed. Now Messrs Dennis Skinner and William Hamilton belabour the Establishment and MI5 not for persecuting an innocent Marxist scholar but for being too indulgent to a guilty spy. In other words, the stick has been changed, but the buttocks remain the same. They are those of MI5.[12] So do the whackers. They are the prefects of the Left – men, it may be added, not normally noted for their hatred of communism. But any stick – as Sir Harold Wilson has shown – will serve them to beat MI5.

Why this hatred of MI5? It seems that our Labour vigilantes want to destroy the institution by denying it the means to operate, and that an imprudence by MI5 15 years ago has given them an ideal opportunity to do so. On such a matter, the support of the press and the public can be enlisted, for spy-scandals always make headlines, especially if royalty is thrown in too. But we should keep our heads and ask, *cui bono?* What have we gained from the exposure of Blunt? Apart from the pleasure of a public scandal, and the evacuation of tribal resentments, precisely nothing. What would we have lost if Blunt had remained unexposed, with his dead past sunk in secret memory? Equally, nothing. What will we gain if, like the Americans, we effectively dismantle our security service? Less than nothing.

The real reason for left-wing hatred of MI5 can hardly be in doubt. It is the function of MI5 to keep an eye on suspect contacts, and who can say exactly where, in the amorphous Labour party, the eastern frontiers are now drawn? The tribunes of the Left attack MI5 openly for being dangerously soft on communist agents in what Mr Hamilton calls 'the black holes of Buckingham Palace and Whitehall'. This is a good excuse for destroying an institution which may be dangerously vigilant against Soviet agents, if such exist, in the black holes of Westminster or Transport House.

We know of no spectacle so ridiculous, wrote Macaulay, as that of the British people in one of its periodic fits of morality. At the moment we are witnessing such a spectacle: a peculiarly bizarre spectacle, since the particular issue is of no immediate relevance. It is purely historical, about the fossils of a past age. When the fit is over, this will be clear. The flight of Burgess and Maclean was a shock because it took the security services themselves by surprise and revealed Russian spies in vital positions. But Blunt has not suddenly been identified as a working spy in a critical place. He was finally identified 15 years ago when he had been inactive and useless for at least 13 further years. We have merely learned a piece of history. If the rumpus is used to destroy the security service, the only gainers will be the moles who may be lurking undetected, or may afterwards be inserted among us.

Eight years later Trevor-Roper wrote, but did not send, a letter to Noel Annan admitting that his own dislike of Blunt may have predisposed him against Cambridge.

I must admit that I did not like Blunt, and perhaps that faint symptom of anti-Cambridge bias which you say, or imply, that you detect in me springs from an improper generalisation from my contacts with him during the war. I thought him insufferably superior, condescending, disdainful. No doubt he had good grounds for disliking me, and no doubt it is not easy for a man who is a spy and a traitor to be uninhibited and jolly in conversation with those he is spying on and betraying.[13]

8

Michael Straight

In 1980 Hugh Trevor-Roper was elected master of Peterhouse, Cambridge. This gave him the opportunity to observe Cambridge University in sharper focus, and he was not impressed. He told Dick White:

Cambridge is really an extraordinary place, totally cut off from the known world: a sort of fossil society in which are preserved (but in a lifeless form) the habits of a lost world. Sometimes I see it as an untouched, still-unravished relic of the early nineteenth century: an image of unreformed Oxford, Oxford before 1850. Its immunity to reform is remarkable. All kinds of abuses which were corrected in Oxford from 1850– onwards are still taken for granted in Cambridge: plurality, non-residence, life-fellowships, fellowships regarded as sinecures, non-teaching dons, non-functioning heads, etc. etc. Macaulay, in the period 1830–50, always saw Cambridge as the progressive, modern university, the university of Bacon and Newton, and Oxford as the conservative, obscurantist, antediluvian, reactionary university, the university of Keble and Pusey; and he (quite wrongly) extrapolated this antithesis and applied it throughout history. But I suppose it must have been true in his time. And yet now Oxford seems modern, lively, active, extrovert, penetrating the world and, to some extent, driving it intellectually; while Cambridge is an enclosed society, provincial and sanctimonious.[1]

Trevor-Roper still contemplated with particular interest the careers of the Cambridge spies and their associates. One of the most eloquent of these was the affluent American Michael Straight, whose prospect of a senior public appointment was blighted by his Cambridge friendships with Blunt and Burgess. Impressed by Straight's irony in adversity, Trevor-Roper judged his memoirs very favourably.

Review of *After Long Silence*
by Michael Straight[2]

To Europeans, the 1930s are an unforgettable decade. Those who were young then were marked by it for life, and still, in their old age, live under its shadow: not till they are dead will it sink into its historical context and become objectively comparable with other periods. For those were very special years, different from the decades that had preceded and would follow them. Society was divided not only by class or nation but also, more sharply than is usual, by generation.

The shift came about the time that Hitler took power in Germany. I was myself an undergraduate at that time and could observe the change. The problems of the 1930s loomed before us all: economic, political, ideological; but young and old faced them from radically different positions. The old hated war and feared Bolshevism: they remembered 1914–1918 and the revolution in Russia. The young, who remembered neither of these events, were more tolerant of both. They were prepared to regard communism and even war as preferable to the new and visible horrors of economic chaos and fascism. The period of crisis began with the Spanish Civil War in 1936; it culminated in 1938, at the time of the Munich surrender – the last victory of those who, through fear of war, believed in unconditional 'appeasement.' Munich, in particular, divided generation against generation within families. The division was healed next year, but only by the palpable failure of appeasement and the sheer necessity of a new, defensive war.

I have said that the shift came about the time when Hitler came to power. That was January 1933. Next month, the Oxford Union debated the famous motion 'That this House will in no circumstances fight for king and country.' I well remember the furor which followed the passing of that motion. Afterward it was said that Hitler and Mussolini were much encouraged by it. But in fact the event was insignificant. Hitler was not then a dictator, nor did he yet have an army: his public utterances were professions of peace. The motion was therefore unrelated to any real threat. It was an expression of the pacifism, and the unreality, still surviving from the 1920s; and its author was the London philosopher C.E.M. Joad,[3] an elderly pacifist whose opinions had been formed long ago. In the following years, as the menace of Nazism[4] grew, the attitude of the young would change. Under the impact of events, pacifism would dissolve and in a period of political and ideological bewilderment the propagandists of a new faith would see their chance: the Communist International would move in.

Omne ignotum pro magnifico.[5] To the young of 1933 Soviet Russia was unknown except through its propagandists, and as the bugbear of their elders and of the bourgeoisie in general. Ever since the revolution it had been sealed off from the West. Only a few privileged visitors had visited it, and they, of course, had only seen what they had been shown. Therefore, when the Western, capitalist world was in confusion and it seemed that capitalism could be saved only by the 'fascist' methods adopted first in Italy, then in Germany, the bewildered young turned toward communism – to the smiling face of communism that was presented to them – and saw it, if they wished, as the magic talisman that might yet save the world. It happened that, precisely at this time, the Bolshevik government was adopting a new policy that greatly helped this process.

In the early years of their power, the Russian Bolsheviks had preached world revolution. Only by being spread to the rest of Europe, Lenin believed, could communism be perpetuated at home. But by 1923 that policy had failed: Mussolini's victory in Italy, as Hitler recognized, had been the turning of the tide, and Stalin fell back on the policy of 'socialism in one country.' In order to consolidate his own dictatorship over Russia, he was prepared to accept the legitimacy of the non-communist world and to seek conventional relations with it. But acceptance did not mean trust, and the old aims were not renounced, only suspended. So the revolutionary Comintern went, effectively, underground and operated at the new level. The idealistic young, in capitalist countries, were now to become not open propagandists of the communist cause but secret agents of Stalin's machine.

This change in itself put a premium on a particular class of recruit. What Stalin now needed was not proletarian agitators but young men who, in the normal course of events, might hope to prosper within capitalist society: the intelligent products of good families, good schools, good universities; young men who, through their social status or their education, would have, or could be expected to acquire, contacts within the governing elite of their countries. Of course, such men would not prosper, or acquire such contacts, unless they kept their communist allegiance strictly secret. That in itself imposed a further condition. Since any active espionage entailed the risk of exposure, such a risk could not be justified except by the gravest necessity.

Therefore, short of such necessity, these young men must lie low. Ultimately, when they had arrived, they might be used. Meanwhile, they were 'moles.'[6]

As is well known, the most prolific breeding ground for such moles was at Cambridge University. Why was this? On the face of it, Oxford would have seemed more promising. Oxford was the scene of that famous Union debate. Just before that, the Oxford University Communist Society – the 'October Club' – had been dissolved by authority: an invitation to its members to go underground. Oxford is traditionally more political than Cambridge. But Oxford, as far as we know, produced no Russian spies,[7] whereas Cambridge can glory in the names of Burgess, Maclean, Philby, Blunt, not to speak of smaller fry. How are we to account for this? Was it a mere accident: the presence of a particularly expert angler at that well-stocked pool? Or was it the consequence of some particular quality of the place?

The two ancient universities of England, as Macaulay wrote, have always had distinct characters. Oxford, in this century, has been gayer, more sophisticated, more cosmopolitan: ideas there overflow, collide and mingle with other ideas, and are diluted or complicated in the process. Cambridge is more esoteric and intense, even solipsistic: its ideas (where they exist) gather steam and build up pressure in the sealed test tubes of introverted coteries. It is difficult to imagine the philosophy of G.E. Moore,[8] with its complacent cult of 'good states of mind,' or the sanctimonious teaching of E.M. Forster, with its subordination of public virtue to private relations, being received in Oxford. And what is one to say of the 'Apostles,' the egregious secret society of self-perpetuating, self-admiring narcissi to which Moore and Forster, Burgess and Blunt, belonged? Could it have existed at Oxford? Would it not there have been blown up from within, or laughed out of existence?

However that may be, the fact is that Cambridge was the pool in which Stalin's anglers fished, and in which they made their greatest catch. Hitherto we have had no account of the pool except from the outside; for Philby's memoirs – a work of propaganda written in Russia – gave nothing away, and Blunt's promised memoirs, for which British publishers were outbidding each other a few years ago, have suddenly disappeared from the horizon.[9] Now at last we have a view of the pool from inside, from one of the fish who, having taken the fly, broke away, escaped – with the hook still in his jaw – to his home waters, and now, after many adventures, tells his tale: Michael Straight.

* * *

Michael Straight is an American brought up in England. His father, Willard Straight, became familiar to me when I was studying the strange career, in China, of Sir Edmund Backhouse; for as a young man he had worked in China for an American finance house, raising loans for China as afterward, during the war, for the Allies. In China, Willard Straight met Dorothy Whitney, whom he later married. She was heiress to a great American fortune. The Straights were a cultivated, high-minded, public-spirited couple, devoted to liberal causes. They founded *The New Republic*, of which Michael Straight would later be editor. After the early death of Willard Straight in 1918, his widow married an Englishman, 'Jerry' Elmhirst, and they made their home in England, at Dartington Hall, in Devonshire.

There they established a 'progressive' school and a cultural centre which still survives under other auspices. The two Straight sons received an unconventional early education at the school, and afterward went to Cambridge. The elder, Whitney, became a British subject. Conservative and conventional, 'more British than the British,' he went in for motor racing, fought in the RAF during the war, and died in England in 1979. He does not feature much in this book. Michael, the younger son, was very different. Like his parents, he was liberal and unconventional, with cultivated interests, and after some hesitation he would decide to remain American. Nevertheless, it was his English education that determined his life and gives form and interest to his book.

Before going to Cambridge (to Trinity College, of course), he spent a year at the London School of Economics, then dominated de jure by Sir William Beveridge,[10] de facto by that self-important *fantasiste*, Harold Laski.[11] There are agreeable portraits of both Beveridge and Laski in this book, as also of the rabid fanatic V.K. Krishna Menon,[12] 'a perpetual student, in a perpetual rage.' The school was a hot-bed, or oven, of half-baked radicalism. That was a good start. But more important were the years at Cambridge. There Mr. Straight quickly gravitated toward the radical-chic Marxist world. His teacher was at first Maurice Dobb,[13] the economist, who was a member of the Communist Party, then the classical economist Denis Robertson,[14] whom he deserted in order to seek tuition from Keynes's maverick disciple Joan Robinson.[15]

The lectures of Maynard Keynes were, to some extent, a corrective. But how could any lectures prevail against the current of events and the pressure of contemporaries? For Straight's years at Cambridge were 1934 to 1937, the years in which Hitler was establishing his dictatorship in Germany and Stalin, in Russia, while destroying his own rivals in show trials and monstrous purges, was presenting himself to his gullible admirers in the West as the champion of liberal democracy, the leader of the united 'Popular Front' against Nazism, the only hope of preserving peace in the world. The influence and friendship of Keynes provided Mr. Straight with his long-term stability; but immediately he found himself carried along by the communist enthusiasm of his time and place.

Why did Mr. Straight, with his cultured, privileged, liberal background, slide so easily into the Cambridge communist world? Perhaps it was because of such a background, which, in a time of crisis, can be a source of weakness, not of strength. He refers to his sense of guilt because of his inherited wealth, and of rootlessness because of his cosmopolitan upbringing: he 'lacked a sense of loyalty to British or American institutions.' However, that cannot be the whole story, for others who had less wealth to inspire guilt and whose roots lay in solid English earth slid as easily as he: a friend of mine, who was at the same college at the same time, has assured me (perhaps with some exaggeration) that he was the only scholar of his year who was not a communist. Nor did such wealth, or such rootlessness, draw others (like his brother Whitney) in the same direction. We are forced to conclude that these factors merely lubricated the slide, or are invoked as later rationalizations: that the real motive was the fashion of the time, similarly rationalized. Undergraduates are gregarious. Easily carried away by apparently idealist slogans, they move in shoals, following some luminous, charismatic pilot fish. The young in Germany did the same thing at the same time. The direction was different but the reflex action was the same.

Who was the pilot fish? Early in his Cambridge career, Mr. Straight fell under the influence of two young men who are always named in the story of the Cambridge communists, and whom he still mentions only with respect and affection: John Cornford and James Klugman.[16] Cornford, idealist and poet, was the son of a distinguished Cambridge classicist; he would be killed in the Spanish Civil War. Klugman was the devotee of the Party: he would be writing its official history in Britain when he died in 1978. These two were the communist leaders in Cambridge: they controlled the communist core of the University Socialist Society,[17] and they were responsible to the head office of the British Communist Party in King Street, London. From the moment when they called on him in his lodgings in Trumpington Road, Klugman and Cornford – 'James and John' – were the directors of Mr. Straight's conscience. They politicized him, making him join the Cambridge Union and compete for office in it; they also brought him into the center of the communist cell in Cambridge; and from there it was a short step to the inner citadel ruled by Burgess and Blunt.

Guy Burgess is the most elusive of the Cambridge traitors. Some will say or hear no good of him: he was, they assure us, dirty in his habits, aggressive in his homosexuality, obsessive in his conversation. He behaved outrageously when – as so often – he was drunk. Others found his company enchanting. Clearly all were right. A diplomat friend of mine who met him at luncheon during the war was so charmed by his conversation that he invited him to fill a place at a dinner party that evening. The result was disastrous: at dinner he behaved so grossly that his host refused ever to see him again. I met him only once and found his company delightful. In any case, it is clear that he had a powerful personality, able to seduce highly intelligent men.

He also had extraordinary self-confidence. Just before reading this book, I happened to read Martin Gilbert's latest volume of Winston Churchill's papers. There I found that in 1938, after Munich, Burgess, having visited Churchill on behalf of the BBC and evidently been well received by him, sent to him a long lecture on the correct foreign policy to be adopted by Britain.* Since Churchill had been in politics for over forty years and in the cabinet, on and off, for thirty, this shows an almost sublime assurance in one whose only experience of politics was in homosexual brothels and as a Russian spy. Such confidence gives the habit of command; and Burgess clearly commanded his little Cambridge world.

One member of it whom he commanded was Blunt. Burgess recruited Blunt, who was older than himself and already a fellow of his college, in November 1935. He then directed him to recruit others. Mr. Straight had already met Blunt on a visit to Russia, sponsored by a communist student, earlier in that year, and soon he was friendly with both him and Burgess. Next year, he found himself co-opted into the secret society of the Apostles and could be scrutinized closely by them. Burgess had by then publicly broken with the Communist Party and, as a blind, was moving in reactionary, not

---

* Martin Gilbert, *Winston S. Churchill, Companion Volume V, Part 3: The Coming of War, 1936–1939* (London: Heinemann, 1982), p. 1193.

to say Nazi, circles. Philby and Maclean, we may note, were not Apostles. Consequently they did not come his way. Apostles were hardly expected to know anyone outside the society. As one of them once said, when asked a question about other undergraduates, 'There are no other undergraduates.'

Mr. Straight has a delicate sense of irony and I particularly enjoyed his account of this absurd secret society. Like most university societies, it had originally been founded (in the early nineteenth century) with a serious purpose (the laicization of the university), and had not been secret at all.* But – again like most university societies – it had quickly become purely social. It had also become secret and complacently exclusive. One of the silliest members in Mr. Straight's time was the then provost of King's, J.T. Sheppard, a third-rate classical scholar.[18] According to Sheppard, in order to be an Apostle, one had to be *very* brilliant and *extremely* nice.' There was an initiation ceremony and a fearful oath: the initiate prayed that his soul might writhe in unendurable pain for the rest of eternity if he so much as breathed a word about the society to anyone who was not a member. When Mr. Straight remarked that this seemed a bit harsh, Provost Sheppard reassured him: 'You see,' he explained, 'our oath was written at a time when it was thought to be most unlikely that a member of the society would speak to anyone who was not Apostolic.' Such was the self-constituted elite which, by now, had become the envelope for an even more secret cell: the crypto-communist recruiters of Russian spies.

The critical moment came in February 1937, soon after the death in Spain of John Cornford. Blunt then summoned Straight to his rooms in Trinity, and a grave dialogue ensued. Blunt began by asking what Straight intended to do after graduation. Straight replied that he had various ideas, all assuming that he would stay in England and, like his brother, become a British subject. Blunt listened, and then said portentously, 'Some of your friends have other ideas for you.' In fact, Straight was told, he was to be an international banker in New York. Straight demurred. He had no intention of becoming a banker, he said. But Blunt was not to be put off. 'Our friends,' he said, 'have given a great deal of thought to it. They have instructed me to tell you that that is what you must do.' 'Our friends,' it emerged, were the Communist International. The orders came from a particular friend who 'knows you and

---

* See Hugh Sykes Davies, 'Apostolic Letter,' in *Cambridge Review*, May 7, 1982 and June 4, 1982.

respects you' but 'regrets very much that he is not permitted to identify himself to you.' In other words, Burgess.

Straight was to pretend a nervous breakdown caused by the death of Cornford, break openly with the Communist Party, and then, like Burgess and Blunt, become a mole, operating in Wall Street. When Straight still protested, Blunt told him that his 'plea' would be conveyed to his 'friends' and 'their decision' would be reported to him within a week. Then 'he laid a hand on my shoulder as I left his rooms.' In due course the decision of 'the friends' was reported. His plea, Straight was told, had been considered 'in the highest circles in the Kremlin,' but it had been rejected; he must do as he was told, and go underground: the proper place for a mole.

If we can forget the tragic character of the predicament, the scene is pure farce. Here was a young art historian, whose life, after leaving the family vicarage, had been spent in the pampered security of Trinity College and the complacent elitism of a secret society, assuming the role of priest, and ordering his penitent, in the name of a hidden, distant high priest, to sacrifice himself for the divinity which they were privileged to represent. It is a perfect example of the self-importance of young dons – perhaps especially young Cambridge dons, at least in the 1930s; for of course they are quite different now.

To our surprise – but he knows how to rationalize his indecisions – Mr. Straight did not (like an undergraduate friend similarly instructed) reject the outrageous proposal out of hand. Imprisoned by his past surrender, he did what he was told. Overtly, he broke with the Party which retained his sympathy; but he still sought to avoid the next step of becoming a 'mole.' He hoped, no doubt, that his 'friends' would give up the effort and let him go. He was wrong. Returning from a visit to America, he was summoned once again by Blunt. His 'plea to be released,' he was told, 'had been reviewed by Stalin,' but had been rejected, and so he was still considered to be under orders. To confirm this, Blunt summoned him to London to meet his future manager: 'a stocky, dark-haired Russian' who gave him some very low-level general advice and 'was more like the agent of a small-time smuggling operation than the representative of a new international order.' This, presumably, was the 'friend' who spoke with the voice of Stalin. On parting, Blunt asked Straight for 'some highly personal document,' and on being given a drawing, tore it in half. One half he returned to Straight; the other half, he explained, would be used as an identity card by 'the man who, some day in the future, would approach me in New York.'

For the remaining years of peace, and throughout the war, Straight remained based in America, moving easily in the high political circles to which his own background and the magic name of Keynes opened the door. He became an 'unpaid volunteer' on the fringe of Roosevelt's administration, electioneered for the New Deal, wrote speeches for the president, promoted, by action and in writing, the cause of liberalism at home and Britain in the war. He kept in touch with some old Cambridge communist friends, and he humored the promised emissary of Blunt by giving him some unimportant documents from his own pen. But in 1942 he broke away. Thereafter he had some difficult passages – Henry Wallace, as editor of *The New Republic* after the war, proved a liability through his communist allies, and the McCarthy period could have been more dangerous to Straight than it was – but in general, his American career was successful and honorable. It was his English past which in the end caught up with him and caused him, in explanation, to write this book: a beautifully written, occasionally discursive, but always fascinating and sometimes moving *apologia pro vita sua*.[19]

In 1949, at an Apostles dinner in London, Straight again met Burgess and Blunt, and next day a crucial conversation took place. Burgess was eager to ensure that Straight would not betray them, and Straight, having been assured that both were now inactive – that Blunt had returned to art history and Burgess was about to leave the Foreign Service – gave or implied such an assurance. In fact Burgess did not leave the Foreign Service and Blunt did not cease to act as his accomplice. But Straight did not betray them – at least not yet. On three occasions between 1949 and 1951, he tells us, he drove to the British embassy to do so; but like Hamlet he could never quite bring himself to act, and each time he drove away again. Of course, we must remember the date: it was the time of Senator McCarthy. If he had told all at such a time, 'my story,' he writes, 'would result in a trial in England; it would be leaked to a congressional committee in America; I was certain of that. Within a few months, I would be facing Anthony Blunt in an English court-room, or else I would find myself in a witness chair facing Senator McCarthy.' Even in 1951, when Burgess bolted to Russia with Donald Maclean, Straight did not speak up. Once again there were good reasons for silence: 'I told myself that Guy was gone forever, and that Anthony had been rendered harmless.' Hamlet too always found good reasons for inaction.

Why then, in 1963, did Straight decide to tell all? The occasion was comparatively trivial. John F. Kennedy had proposed to make him chairman of the National Endowment for the Arts. It then turned out that the appointment entailed the formality of FBI clearance. That clinched the matter. Alarmed at the thought of exposure, Straight refused the post and then, feeling that the old objections no longer applied, he told all, first to the FBI in Washington, then in London to MI5. Finally, in the presence of MI5, he confronted Blunt in person. That effectively ended the story. Blunt had long been suspected, but he had denied everything and no hard evidence had been found against him (or indeed against Burgess). Now he confessed all, against a promise of immunity from prosecution. Blunt afterward said that he felt free to confess because something that had happened in 1964 'freed him from loyalties to his friends.' That phrase, which recalls the sanctimony of the Cambridge guru E.M. Forster, is now clearly shown to be untrue. He confessed because denial was no longer possible: he had been caught out.

For fifteen years Blunt's secret was protected by MI5 and the FBI. Then, in 1979, the investigative writers smelled it out and protection became impossible. When the prime minister, in answer to a parliamentary question, stated the facts, there was a public outcry. Blunt was stripped of his knighthood, forced to resign his honorary fellowship of Trinity College, squeezed out of the British Academy. Still, he had had a long run. He had fared better than his friends, whose lives he had ruined. He could not complain.

When I look back on this history, and reflect on the ideological commitments of the 1930s which destroyed or distorted the lives of so many of my contemporaries, I am often struck by the irony of it. In the spring of 1933 we followed the course of the Reichstag trial[20] and admired, above all, Georgi Dimitrov, the accused Bulgarian who stood up to the bullying of Hermann Goering. We supported the London 'antitrial' which we supposed to be 'objective' in opposition to the 'political' justice of the Leipzig court. After the war we were disillusioned: we saw Dimitrov installed in Sofia as the ruthless tyrant of Bulgaria, and we discovered that the Leipzig court had been fairer than the London trial, which was rigged by Willi Münzenberg, with forged documents, on behalf of the Comintern. To all of us, communist and noncommunist alike, the great crisis, before Munich, was the civil war in Spain. The survival of liberalism, of democracy, even – if we preferred – of the British empire, seemed to hang on the defeat of General Franco, and we were prepared to support the communist International Brigade, if not for love of communism, or Spanish 'democracy,' or legality, then in order to prevent our own defeat in the coming war.

In fact, though nobody could have predicted it, precisely the reverse was true. If a left-wing government had prevailed in Spain, Hitler, in 1940, would not have stopped at the Pyrenees. He would have sent his army into Spain to overturn it and would have taken Gibraltar by force. Thereby he would have closed the Mediterranean, transformed the position in the Near East, and won the war. The self-sufficient Cambridge communists were convinced that they alone knew how to save the world. If they had prevailed, they would have handed it over to Hitler – which, of course, Stalin himself would have done in 1939.

For this reason, although I can forgive their error and even, at a pinch, their treachery, I cannot forgive their arrogance. The picture of the priestly Blunt, with his thin precise voice, ordering the lives of others at the behest of 'our friends' in the Kremlin and laying a paternal hand on their shoulders as they leave his presence, will remain with me as the perfect icon of a Cambridge Apostle in 1937. So might St. Paul have sent Timothy to the Christian cells of Greece, or the Jesuit general sped a doomed missionary to the secret priest holes of Elizabethan England.

9

Peter Wright

After Philby's defection in 1963, British mole-hunters wondered if another Soviet secret agent had made it to the top and so gained the power to cover his tracks. This would mean that the worst traitor was still to be discovered. Suspicion of a mole in MI5 was crystallised by the statements of the KGB defector Anatoli Golitsyn, who visited Britain during the first half of 1963. Golitsyn could only offer theories and coincidences, not hard evidence. Nevertheless, he convinced Arthur Martin,[1] the head of MI5's Soviet counter-espionage section. Golitsyn's time in Britain saw the beginning of Martin's collaboration with Peter Wright,[2] who had been recruited in 1955 to advise MI5 on how to use electronic and other technical devices in operations. Wright had particular success with improving eavesdropping equipment and later claimed with some justification to have 'bugged and burgled' his way across London 'at the state's behest'.[3]

Martin's suspicions initially focused on Graham Mitchell,[4] the deputy director general of the Security Service. In March 1963 Martin told the director general, Roger Hollis,[5] of his concerns, and was authorised to begin inquiries into Mitchell. In May Martin compared notes with Wright, who had fallen under Golitsyn's spell and also thought that MI5 had been penetrated and that Mitchell was the probable culprit. Mitchell's telephones were bugged and a small hole bored through his office wall so that he could be kept under continuous CCTV surveillance; the film showed that Mitchell muttered very suspiciously when quite alone in his office. He retired in September 1963 before final proof could be discovered.[6]

The failure of the Mitchell investigation undermined Martin, who now regarded the director general himself as the principal suspect. Hollis peevishly resented the accusation that he was a Soviet spy and even suspended his senior mole-hunter. Martin turned to Dick White, who recruited him for SIS in late 1964. In November SIS and MI5 established a joint working party codenamed Fluency. Under the chairmanship of

Peter Wright it was to investigate penetration of both services. In May 1965 the working party reported that both MI5 and SIS had been, and remained, penetrated. The following month Wright accused Hollis to his face of being a Soviet spy. Hollis authorised the continuance of the Fluency *investigation even though he was now the main suspect. In November Hollis protested to Wright: 'Well, Peter, you have got the manacles on me, haven't you?' Hollis retired in January 1966 but the suspicion against him persisted. Indeed, the very difficulty of finding evidence about Soviet penetration of MI5 only proved to the mole-hunters how deep and insidious that penetration was.*[7]

Peter Wright himself retired from MI5 in 1976. On joining MI5 more than 20 years earlier, he had fretted about losing 15 years' of Admiralty pension from his previous job, only to be reassured that something would be arranged 'when the time comes'.[8] *But the officer who had made the promise was long gone, and no one else seemed to remember it. Wright lacked the capital to make a success of his retirement farm in Tasmania and decided to write his memoirs. He was encouraged by Victor Rothschild,*[9] *who had endured false rumours that he was a Soviet spy and hoped Wright would scotch them in his book. Rothschild introduced Wright to the prolific espionage writer Chapman Pincher, who included revelations from Wright in* Their Trade is Treachery, *published in 1981.*[10]

As public interest in moles became more intense, Trevor-Roper received an informative letter from Dick White, who was well acquainted with both the mole-hunters and their evidence, or rather, lack of it. White told Trevor-Roper that under Hollis MI5 had enjoyed one of its most successful periods. White felt the case against Hollis was quite devoid of credibility. Hollis had no motive for espionage and there was not a jot of direct evidence against him. Indeed White assured Trevor-Roper that the MI5 officers who had tried to destroy Hollis's reputation, and that of the Security Service with him, had very little evidence at their disposal beyond that in the public domain.[11]

On 16 July 1984 Wright took part in a World in Action *television documentary on MI5 and for the first time claimed in public that Hollis had been a Soviet spy. It was revealed that with the help of his* World in Action *producer, Paul Greengrass, Wright was preparing a book. MI5's legal adviser, Bernard Sheldon, planned to stop publication by warning off potential publishers, and two did indeed back out under pressure. But Heinemann decided to go outside British jurisdiction and publish Wright's book, entitled* Spycatcher, *in Australia. Thereupon the attorney general sought an injunction to prevent publication of the book in Australia by claiming that Wright was breaking his duty of confidentiality to the Crown.[12] The* Spycatcher *trial began in Sydney in November 1986 and made the British government look very foolish. The choice of Cabinet Secretary Sir Robert Armstrong as the principal witness against Wright was unwise. Armstrong appeared stiff and out of touch. Under cross-examination he conceded that he had been 'economical with the truth', a reluctant admission which quickly became a catchphrase. The British government lost the case and gave* Spycatcher *so much publicity it became a best-seller, bringing Wright considerable wealth. Trevor-Roper published his first article on Wright during the* Spycatcher *trial.*

'The Great Mole-Hunt Must Come to an End'[13]

What a long shadow is cast by the 1930s! Hitler has been dead for 42 years, Stalin for 33; their world has been changed out of recognition; threatened by atomic destruction, it has enjoyed the longest period of peace between the great powers in modern history; and yet we are still haunted by the spectres of that disastrous decade.

In the last few weeks, the spooks have had a high old time. They have drawn the Cabinet Secretary to the Antipodes to resist the publication of a book stating that Sir Roger Hollis, who has been dead for 12 years, was a Russian spy, and they have forced Lord Rothschild, after a long and distinguished public career, to appeal publicly for an authoritative statement that he was not.

No one that I know has ever suspected Lord Rothschild of spying, though many are mystified by his involvement with Peter Wright. Surely anyone whom a Conservative Prime Minister put in charge of his Think Tank was by then above suspicion.

As for Hollis, I have never seen anything to suggest that he was anything but a loyal public servant. The attacks on his memory seem to me as implausible as those on other men whom I have known: some, like Hollis, now dead, others alive and, like Lord Rothschild, able to feel them.

How do such myths grow up? What keeps them going so long? They seem an echo – a weak, belated echo – of the McCarthyism of the early 1950s in America. Here, as there, it is the nemesis of the complacent liberal establishment which did so much harm in the 1930s. But the time-scale has been different. In America, the disease was evacuated in a sudden hysterical explosion. In Britain, it was at first contained and apparently absorbed, but its residue has lingered long and is with us still. Its continuity has been visible in the great English mole-hunt which has now lasted 35 years.

The history of this great hunt falls into three stages. In the first stage, from 1951 to 1964 – from Burgess and Maclean to Philby, Blake and Blunt – it was a desultory affair. The digging out of the moles was then left to the professionals. But, after 1964, it became popular.

Dissatisfied, perhaps, with the pace of the operation, or excited by the prospect of sport, the amateurs joined in. Equipped with spades and poles, snapping terriers and resonant convoluted horns, the 'investigative journalists' poured into the field and, whenever anything moved, hollered 'Mole!'. The third stage is a reaction against that phase of the hunt: the attempt of the present government to return to professional standards, professional methods.

'About time too!' we may say. For what has been the result of the noisy popular period? A number of phantom moles have been sighted, only to vanish again. Mr Andrew Boyle piqued himself on discovering Blunt, and was able to hold him up to public execration, which was no doubt very satisfying, but, in fact, Blunt had been dug up by the professionals long ago and was in a cage. Of the others cited, most were safely dead – Pigou, Beves, Liddell, Hollis, Gow.[14] One, who was thought to be dead, turned up alive and well. That was very inconvenient: damages had to be paid and the whole edition of the book denouncing him was pulped. After that, the innuendos against the living were more cautious. Meanwhile, naturally enough, the morale of the security services suffered. It is that morale, I feel sure, which Mrs Thatcher is now trying to restore.

What caused this unfortunate second stage which has done so much damage? I believe it was a combination of two factors. The first is general. In all enclosed societies and especially in secret services, there is an inherent tendency to fantasy, even paranoia. It is the occupational disease against which such services must always be on guard. I have seen many instances of this and have a fine collection of case-histories to support my thesis, if necessary.

Secondly, in Britain in the late 1960s and the 1970s, there was the selective, unavowed erosion of the ban on publication by members of the services.

Both factors were set in motion by the shock of Philby's defection in 1963.[15] It was this shock which generated the furious search for other moles, culminating in the attack on Hollis. That search was, at first, internal. But it also had external effects. It put the security services on the defensive and caused them to relax their own rules about publication. After all, they could say, if the public was to feast on damaging stories about their present failures, why should it not also read about their past successes? So, in the 1970s, the triumphs of war-time cryptography and interception became known. Inside information started to creep out. Official histories were commissioned. Other books, which appeared to be by freelance authors, in fact rested on unacknowledged inside drafts, secretly released. The supposed writers were sometimes little more than ghosts.

This was all very well while the system was under control. Unfortunately, it soon got into the wrong hands. Rules once broken are hard to mend, and now the paranoia pours through the licenced and ever widening leaks.

The Prime Minister, it seems to me, is aware of the damage and is determined, here as elsewhere, to end the laxity of the permissive years. Five years ago she stopped the publication of official histories of war-time intelligence, and Sir Michael Howard's commissioned work on strategic deception, already written, was suddenly suppressed. That seems to me rather drastic.

Now, Mr Wright has been called to heel. Having published his views once under cover of Mr Pincher's name, he thought he could go a little further and publish another [*book*], under his own. He has found that is not so easy. The government has decided that, at whatever cost, internal discipline, the necessary basis of morale, must be restored.

Of course, it is charged with inconsistency. But why should it be consistent in error? The rules are still there: if they have not always been enforced, that does not make them invalid. Mr Wright has sworn a great oath. Morally, he has no leg to stand upon: what right has he to speak of treachery? Legally, there may be difficulties of enforcement: Australia is another country.

Tactical errors may have been made: I can think of some. But the purpose of the exercise is clear. Whatever we may think of secret services, we cannot dispense with them, and, before they can be reformed, they must be shown to obey their own rules.

Having said that, I believe that there is a price to pay. If a secret service is to be an effective organ of state, it must not only mend its leaks: it must also mend its ways. Protective secrecy in a free society is an anomaly which needs rational defence. The whole affair of Peter Wright has illustrated a surprising lack of control and responsibility.

If it is true that the victims of occupational paranoia have conducted a witch hunt against their own head and undermined an elected prime minister, it is time that steps were taken to neutralise the paranoia, to restore internal control, and to ensure a system of responsibility, not to a party but to the state. I also believe, as an historian, that the secret service should come to terms with its own history.

As the price of protecting its present, it should yield up the records of its past. Then, perhaps, it will free itself from a past that has imprisoned it for fifty years.

The first two decades following the end of the Cold War did indeed see for the first time very extensive releases of records from British intelligence to The National Archives, where they could be consulted by the public. The newly available files included documents from the Special Operations Executive, the Government Code and Cypher School, MI5 and the Radio Security Service. Although the Secret Intelligence Service did not release its records, considerable amounts of SIS material had found their way into the files of other secret departments.

Trevor-Roper returned to the problem of Peter Wright with a review of Spycatcher *which identified many flaws in the book.*

Review of *Spycatcher*
by Peter Wright[16]

Poor Mr Wright, what frustration he has suffered, at least since 1964! Till then, all went well. He was the first scientist in MI5, the man who modernised its techniques of bugging and burgling, the expert mole-catcher who dug up the creatures and skinned them alive. But then things went wrong. At the height of his success, he found himself denounced by his colleagues as 'that bloody man Wright', a 'McCarthyite' who had set up 'a privileged Gestapo' within the service, and was 'poisoning us all'. His last campaign, the inquisition which was intended to destroy his own chief, Sir Roger Hollis, was a flop. This embittered him. The interrogator, he thought, had let him down: why had he not got close enough to Hollis 'to street-fight, to grapple and gouge him, and make him confess'? For of course Wright *knew* that Hollis was guilty. In that defeat he saw all his own achievements 'frittered away'. It was the end of an era: 'the age of heroes was being replaced by the age of mediocrity'. So the rejected hero retired to Tasmania, there to brood on the failure of his crusade, the exiguity of his pension, and the means of revenge.

Yes, revenge. For ten years he has pursued it, as he once pursued his moles, methodically, scientifically, and, at first, secretly. That is, at first he hid behind Mr Chapman Pincher. Wright provided the matter, Pincher wrote the book, and they shared the profits. Then, his appetite whetted and his thirst for revenge unslaked, he moved forward to make a second killing, this time in his own name. The British government, which had mysteriously allowed the first book to pass, pounced on the second, and, by banning it, have made it a best-seller. But is Mr Wright grateful? Not at all. Today, as the tide of dollars rolls in, he rants at 'those bastards' who, like himself, 'will never give up'. He rants also at his critics and commentators who do not credit him with sufficient virtue. Do they not realise, he asks, why he has done what he has done?

Why has he done it? Not for money, he insists, but as a public duty. Some Labour MPs have swallowed this: they would honour him for exposing the privileged illegalities of the hated Security Service. But that has never been Mr Wright's intention – far from it. In spite of occasional implausible hypocrisies, he never regrets such illegalities. Rather, he glories in them: in his bugging, his burgling, his proposals (turned down by his timid superiors) to murder. He advocates the 'independence' of the Security Services, their right to be a law to themselves. His avowed models are Lenin and Dzerzhinsky,[17] the Founding Father of the KGB. So he is impatient of the politicians and civil servants who interfere with such 'independence'. How he despises their 'residual upper middle-class' prejudices, their traditional decencies, even their 'public-school vowels'! What he wanted was not more control of the Security Services but less. Then perhaps the heroes could have caught and skinned the King Mole whom the mediocrities had protected.

For this is the heart and substance of his book. The bugging and burgling give it incidental colour; the alleged 'conspiracy' against Harold Wilson – a conspiracy initiated by Wright's disastrous American ally James Angleton[18] and blocked by the MI5 establishment – is a mere epilogue. It is Hollis who gives to the book, and to Wright's whole career since 1964, their unity and purpose: Hollis, whom he has hunted so single-mindedly, first by night in the dark covert of MI5, then vicariously, hidden behind Chapman Pincher, now in broad daylight in the open field.

And what is the sum of it? Mr Wright sets out his argument, but in the end, he has to admit, it is insufficient. Intuition – his intuition – must replace evidence. Hollis's guilt is a 'hypothesis' which, to him, has 'become an article of faith'. The 'evidence', such as it is, is circumstantial, and its presentation is advocacy: advocacy coloured by personal prejudice – 'I must confess I never liked him' – and distorted by reckless inaccuracy.

The errors are everywhere. Many have already been exposed. I can add more. For instance, there is the case of Sir Stuart Hampshire, who, having been denounced by the disreputable Goronwy Rees, was questioned for almost a year by Wright and others. Wright describes Hampshire dogmatically as 'a brilliant war-time code-breaker … one of the elite team who broke the ISOS Abwehr codes' (he means cyphers). In fact Hampshire was an officer of mine. I know exactly what he did, and not a word of this is true. Mr Cyril Mills, the circus-owner, is also mentioned in the book, in a dramatic context which makes a good story. Unfortunately, as Mr Mills assures me, every detail is pure fantasy. Such errors may be dismissed as circumstantial, but since all the essential 'evidence' is agreed to be circumstantial, they are damaging. How can we have confidence in his interpretation of other circumstances which rest on his authority alone? In justice we have to allow that the experienced and more objective men who saw all his evidence and rejected his conclusions are as likely as he to have been right.

Of course Mr Wright does not speak to us direct. His voice is filtered by his unnamed script-writer, a fluent and persuasive journalist. But even so, his own character appears, and it is clear that, in the course of his work, he became, like Angleton in America, somewhat paranoid. This is an occupational hazard in secret work, especially after retirement. I have observed many cases of it – it is enough to mention the bizarre fantasies of the Man called (by himself) Intrepid.[19] It happens to defectors too (defection is itself a kind of retirement). Wright and Angleton were both inspired to hunt for the missing mole in MI5, the last of an alleged 'Ring of Five', by a highly rated KGB defector, Anatoli Golitsyn, who also became paranoid. Another defector, who began well, the Pole Michael Goleniewski, also became dotty and had illusions that he was descended from the Tsar.

The result of these activities was wholly disastrous. They led to a mini-witch-hunt which drove some innocent persons to suicide or the mental hospital and undermined the morale of the Security Service. We can sympathise with Hollis who, on one occasion, retorted to Wright (who had high hopes of thus trapping another supposed mole) that he 'had no intention of approaching the Home Secretary for permission to bug or burgle his own deputy's house', and with Hollis's successor, Sir Martin Furnival Jones, who protested to Wright, 'Where is this going to end? You've sent me a paper which says that my predecessor and my most likely successor are both spies!' It is hardly surprising that, by this time, Wright was hated by his colleagues – 'like Angleton I could sense my enemies multiplying' – and was cut in the MI5 canteen.

Ironically, Wright himself admits that, by this time, MI5 was proved to be mole-free. It was all past history that he was seeking to dig up and reinterpret. But nothing would stop him. In 1974, nine years after Hollis's retirement and four years after his final acquittal, Wright and his fanatical friends were still seeking to revive the case against him. Wright himself, he tells us, travelled 370,000 kilometres looking for evidence 30 years old. When the heads of the service refused to reopen the case – what was the point, they asked, of this retrospective inquisition, so damaging to morale? – the fanatics were very depressed. They had enjoyed the excitement of the chase. But now, they said sadly to each other, 'the fun has gone'. They thought it all great fun.

Wright's book raises many questions. How was it written? He claims total recall of every detail, every conversation. There is even a verbatim conversation between President Nixon and J. Edgar Hoover. Perhaps it was bugged by Wright. More probably it is simply invented. No statement can be wholly believed. No doubt Wright kept diaries and always intended to use them. If so, his statement on page two that, on retirement, he obediently shredded his diaries, is economical of the truth. More important are the general problems. How is a Secret Service to face the possibility of its own penetration? Hollis may have been innocent but, after all, there was Philby. Even an elected Prime Minister could be suborned. Secret Services must exist, and they must face these possibilities. But they must also be controlled. Perhaps we control ours better than the Americans control theirs. After all, the fanatics were stopped. But we have not yet found a means of controlling egregious traitors from within like Peter Wright.

10

Otto John and Reinhard Gehlen

Otto John (1909–97) was a German anti-Nazi conspirator who managed to escape in the aftermath of the July Plot and was eventually brought to England. With British support he became the first head of the Federal Office for the Protection of the Constitution, the West German equivalent of MI5. Then on 20 July 1954, exactly ten years after the unsuccessful attempt to assassinate Hitler, John vanished after an anniversary ceremony in West Berlin. In the company of an old acquaintance, Dr Wolfgang Wohlgemuth, he drove into East Berlin. Although John later claimed that he been drugged before this journey, a West Berlin customs official who stopped the car later reported that both men seemed normal. When the official warned them that they were about to enter the Eastern Sector, John and Wohlgemuth both said they wanted to go there. The very next day the West German government stopped paying John's salary.[1]

Former KGB officers claimed plausibly in their memoirs that John was lured to East Berlin. John was concerned that Chancellor Konrad Adenauer was destroying any prospect of German reunification by his pro-Western policies, compounded by his willingness to employ former Nazis. Through Wohlgemuth, John was promised a meeting with an important figure to discuss the politics of a united Germany. To the KGB's surprise, John agreed to come and suggested the discussion of joint measures against the Nazis in West Germany. John was self-important and naively saw himself as an independent figure who could exert significant influence on Germany's future. John did not go East to change sides, but to unite them. When he arrived at a secret villa in East Berlin, he found not an important politician but the KGB, who wanted to recruit him as a spy. John refused, lost his temper and was subdued with drugs. John had come East of his own free will, but was kept there by force.[2]

Once he realised the true weakness of his position, John decided to play along, as he later admitted. On 11 August 1954 he gave a big press conference in which he claimed that Western policy was damaging the prospects of reunification. John did not use the press conference to protest that he was being held against his will; rather he made the most of the opportunity to vent his political frustrations. He explained that his decision to come East arose from a realisation that it was the best place to work for the reunification of Germany and against the danger of a new war; and that this was not possible in West Germany, where the political elite was infested with Nazis. As well as the big event on 11 August, John took part in many other press conferences and meetings with East German organisations.[3]

In addition to propaganda, John was also spilling the secret beans. It seems the twenty-four volumes of Stasi documents about John suggest that he revealed far more than he admitted to in his memoirs.[4] He was extensively questioned by the Stasi (East German state security and intelligence service) and KGB. Certainly he was initially reluctant to talk about his secret work, but as early as 27 July repeated interrogation on the same themes was yielding more and more specific detail. John gave information about the Gehlen[5] Organisation, the forerunner of the Federal Intelligence Service. He also clarified the identities and work of his own representatives with the Allied High Commissions. In September 1954 John was taken to the Soviet Union, where the persistent questioning continued and he revealed even more. On 15 September he admitted that his office controlled an agent at a senior level in the West German Communist Party who provided photocopies of its working documents. The following month his information included the identities of West Germans who were suspected of working with the Soviet secret service, the location of the Allied training schools for agents and detail about his cooperation with the American Counter-Intelligence Corps. John also provided the names and other details of his 11 agents in right-wing organisations in West Germany and revealed the personal weaknesses, such as money problems, which made these agents vulnerable. In many cases John's revelations about agents not only made it easy to find them but showed how they could be approached to best effect.[6] All in all, John provided a very considerable amount of secret material to the hostile service he had been appointed to counter.

In his later memoirs John claimed that the focus of his questioning in the Soviet Union was on his relations with the British Secret Service and his contact role between the German Resistance and the Western powers. John clutched at the sinister potency of Philby's name to provide support for his account. John wrote that after reading My Silent War *and* The Philby Affair *he realised that he had been kidnapped so the Soviets could check whether Philby was reliable or a double agent: 'Philby could only be verified against me, his only surviving adversary from the German Resistance.'[7] While the Soviets were long suspicious of Philby, and no doubt took this opportunity to check up on him, by the time of John's interrogations Philby was no longer a major spy: he had been on ice for three years. When questioning John, the KGB was surely more interested in the secrets of 1954 than those of 1944. With or without the enigma of Philby, they would have aimed at such a vulnerable and promising target as a West German security chief. It would seem that John brought in Philby as the* deus ex machina *of the disaster which had befallen him in a maladroit attempt to conceal his own substantial betrayal of national secrets.*

In Soviet hands John had become so melancholy that he was on the verge of suicide. He realised that the cooperation he was offering could only lead to his becoming a Soviet stooge; his hopes of political influence were chimerical. To universal surprise, he returned to West Berlin on 12 December 1955 and less surprisingly was arrested ten days later. He was charged with 'treasonous relations', in particular the spreading of false or grossly distorted factual statements with the intention of helping the efforts of a foreign regime to undermine the Federal Republic. On 22 December 1956 John was sentenced to four years' hard labour.[8] After his release he fought against this sentence for the rest of his life.

Trevor-Roper exchanged letters with the despondent former anti-Nazi. Their correspondence focused on Kim Philby, but Trevor-Roper later noted that he could no longer find these letters among his papers. He also wrote the introduction to the English edition of Otto John's memoirs. In this essay Trevor-Roper described the reasons John gave for his kidnapping as 'interesting speculations' *which* 'may well be true.'[9] *It was a less than ringing endorsement of John's theory about Philby. In the following piece published soon after John's death, Trevor-Roper provided an appraisal of the troubled conspirator's story.*

'Why Otto John Defected Thrice'[10]

To cross the lines once in a time of ideological war is common enough, indeed part of the necessary lubrication of the secret service industry. To cross them twice looks like carelessness. To do so three times suggests a serious problem. In the 11 years from 1944 to 1955, the late Otto John defected, or seemed to defect, first from Nazi Germany to Britain, then from post-Nazi Germany to Russia, and finally back again. He was imprisoned in three countries – Portugal, Britain and Germany – and spent most of his last 40 years in a fourth, the guest of another distinguished exile, his old friend Prince Louis Ferdinand, heir to the phantom throne of Prussia. There he wrote two books explaining his actions which, however, remain a mystery.

The central mystery is his second 'defection', to Moscow in 1954, but if a solution is to be found, it must be sought in the first, to Britain in 1944, which at least is well documented.

Otto John was a cultivated and agreeable man, with a gift for making influential friends. In 1937 he began to study law in Berlin and soon found himself one of a group of young men, most of them lawyers in official posts, who were united by a determination to preserve or restore the *Rechtsstaat* [*rule of law*] which Hitler was systematically undermining. This group, which included Fabian von Schlabrendorff, the Bonhoeffer brothers and Hans von Dohnanyi, was a consistent intellectual nucleus of opposition, but in order to achieve anything they needed an alliance with the military leaders who, though they had helped Hitler to establish his dictatorship, were now frightened by his policy and alone had the power to frustrate it.

With them, though similarly ambiguous, were some members of the Abwehr, the German secret service, under the enigmatic Admiral Canaris, who enjoyed a safe haven for conspiracy in Franco's Spain. During the war, John was employed in the legal department of the Lufthansa airline, whose head was Klaus Bonhoeffer. This gave him a pass to travel freely on any Lufthansa flight, which would prove very useful. He became the emissary of the group to the British secret service in Spain.

When the conspiracy drew to its climax after the Allied landings in Normandy, John was sent to Spain by Colonel Hansen, the more resolute successor of Canaris (who had been sacked by Hitler). His mission was to offer to Britain, on behalf of a post-Nazi government, a separate – and conditional – surrender on the Western front. He was told that only unconditional surrender on all fronts would be accepted. On 19 July, Hansen recalled him to Berlin, and the next day he was in the War Office in the Bendlerstrasse, where the conspirators awaited the return of Stauffenberg from his feat of tyrannicide. When Hitler was found to have survived, John escaped the general carnage thanks to his Lufthansa pass. He flew to Spain and the British secret service brought him from Lisbon to England.

The long agony of the conspiracy, its dismal end, the terrible fate of all his friends, were a profound shock to John. What, he asked himself, was the fundamental cause of that failure? He found it in the moral weakness, the lack of principle, the opportunism of its essential agents, the generals. In England, he was employed largely in propaganda, advising the BBC and lecturing to German prisoners. He spent some time in a special camp in South Wales where some of the highest German officers were held, including Manstein, Brauchitsch and Rundstedt. Many of them had been his friends, but now he despised them, and perhaps they him. The German high command, he now believed, had been morally rotten, without civil courage or honour.

How different were Stauffenberg and his friends! Hitler was quite right when he described them, contemptuously, as a small aristocratic clique. Yes, they were very few, an elite, 'an aristocracy in the best sense'; they did not represent the General Staff – or indeed the German people. Afterwards, in 1948, John would assist the prosecution of Manstein and Brauchitsch for war crimes, and thereby make more enemies in Germany.

Among German generals in South Wales, with new English friends in London, John agonised over 'the burning question' of the moral decay of the German military leaders, how they had obeyed Hitler 'to the bitter end', although they had known, since the wholesale murders of 30 June 1934 'at the latest', that he was 'a criminal'. The closest of his new friends was the historian Sir John Wheeler-Bennett,[11] with whom he discussed the problem at length. It would be the subject of Wheeler-Bennett's next book, *The Nemesis of Power* (1953), in which he would acknowledge the documentary and oral evidence supplied by John.

Influential British support soon bore fruit for John. In 1950 he was appointed head of the new West German Federal Office for the Protection of the Constitution – protection, that is, against extremists of Right or Left, a German equivalent of MI5. In fact, he had been imposed by the British government, which vetoed all the other candidates. And why not, for surely his credentials were good? But alas, it turned out badly. For by now the war-time Grand Alliance was dissolving and being replaced by the new alignments of the Cold War; Dr Adenauer did not like the purist Dr John and was quite willing to employ the opportunists of the past; and if the British had imposed their candidate as head of his new MI5, he would use the Americans to impose his candidate on his new MI6, the BND.

Even in Britain, MI5 and MI6 are sometimes at odds over jurisdiction and policy. In Germany it was far worse, for the head of the new BND was General Reinhard Gehlen, an unrepentant Nazi whose chief, indeed only, merit was that he had been Hitler's intelligence officer against Russia. He also had a particular hatred of Otto John as the persecutor of his hero, Field-Marshal Manstein.

For over three years, John and Gehlen faced each other in unequal contest. Then, on 20 July 1954, the tenth anniversary of the attempted putsch against Hitler was celebrated in Berlin. As one of the few survivors, John was there. After the celebrations he withdrew to his hotel. Then he disappeared altogether. What had happened to him? Had he been kidnapped (for such things happened at that time)? Or – worse still – had he defected? Had the head of Germany's MI5 been a Russian spy all along? In Bonn and London embarrassed lips were sealed. Then the silence was broken by the voice of Dr John himself, broadcasting from somewhere in the Communist bloc, denouncing the rule of Dr Adenauer, his employment of former National Socialists in government, his policy of rearmament. To one man at least the news was welcome. 'Once a traitor, always a traitor,' was the comment of General Gehlen. To him, opposition to Hitler was still treason.

But the story did not end there. Eighteen months later, Dr John was able to give his own explanation. Suddenly, without warning, heavily disguised, he returned to West Germany in the car of a Danish journalist. He was arrested and put on trial. The prosecution demanded imprisonment for only two years. The court raised it to four, which he served in full.[12] When he emerged he withdrew to the Austrian Tyrol. There he would write books and appeal, constantly but in vain, against his condemnation.

John maintained that after the celebration on 20 July he had called on an old friend in East Berlin (the Wall was not yet built), Dr Wohlgemuth.[13] Dr Wohlgemuth, a versatile man, was not only a gynaecologist but also a jazz trumpeter, and he had recently widened his interests (though Dr John did not know this) by becoming a communist – jazz artists seem particularly susceptible to such temptations – an agent of the Stalinist dictator Walter Ulbricht. In Dr Wohlgemuth's flat, John had been drugged and had woken up to find himself a prisoner of the KGB. He had been taken to Moscow and there had decided that his only chance of escape was to play along with the KGB and in the meantime work out a plan of deliverance – which he had ultimately achieved.

A likely story indeed! we may exclaim. But what are the alternative explanations? That he was a long-term communist secretly inserted, like Philby, into a vital position? This is hard to believe. In 1942–4 he had worked for a separate peace with the West. That was quite contrary to Soviet policy. Perhaps he had changed since then, but no evidence has been produced. The archives of the KGB and the Stasi have yielded nothing,[14] and KGB officers have explicitly denied that he came willingly to Moscow. Dr Wohlgemuth has not, as far as I know, denied his story. There must be files on John in London and Berlin, but unless they yield clear evidence we can only say that his story has not been disproved. He had plenty of enemies, but apart from his broadcast they have failed to demonstrate any culpable collusion.

Must we then believe his story? Bizarre though it is, it seems, on the available evidence, the least improbable answer to the problem. But perhaps it is less simple than he suggests. John was clearly a man of courage and conviction. He was disgusted by the lack of such qualities in the German establishment which he had trusted to overthrow Hitler and, being a passionate man, he reacted violently against them. His experiences in Adenauer's Germany, like the old agony of conspiracy, must have been frustrating. And then, on that evocative anniversary, what thoughts must have run through that intense mind! The communist leaders had joined in celebrating the martyrs whom Gehlen would still describe as traitors. Since the generals had betrayed their trust and the 'aristocracy in the best sense' had been slaughtered, may he perhaps have conceded too much in conversation as he drank, perhaps too deeply, with Dr Wohlgemuth and unconsciously put ideas into his head? After all, his brother Hans, who had been among those murdered as a fellow conspirator, had been a communist.

So, for Otto John, in 1954 as in 1944, 20 July ended in anticlimax, flight and disillusion. History, at first tragedy, had been repeated as something like farce. For of course in Moscow any illusions would be swept away – on both sides. The Russians got nothing further out of him[15] and sent him back to East Germany. Now that he is dead, perhaps new evidence will emerge which will confound me, but until then I shall see him as an example of Aristotle's tragic hero: a courageous and honourable man ruined by a damaging mistake, a fatal obsession.

In private letters[16] *Trevor-Roper provided a more specific and more favourable explanation of John's baffling defection.*

Otto John's case is indeed mysterious. The main reason for believing that he did not deliberately defect – apart from any estimation of his character which may be subjective – is that it poses an even more difficult question: why then did he return? Having been a Western agent, to return in such circumstances would seem ruinous, unless he was confident that he would prove himself innocent of any treasonable intent; which he did to the satisfaction of the court. His explanation is that he went to Berlin to take part in the celebration of the 20 July Plot, with which he was genuinely connected (I remember the secret rescue of John from Lisbon after Jebsen *alias* 'Artist',[17] his associate, had been sent back, as a corpse, in a trunk, to Berlin – as we knew from intercepted German Secret Service signals); that he was invited, by his former friend Professor Wohlgemuth, to come to his flat [...]; that he was there drugged and kidnapped and taken to Moscow; and that his only hope of escape seemed to him to be to play along till he could find some means of returning.

This of course raises further questions. Why did he visit Professor Wohlgemuth? Why did he broadcast against Adenauer? His answer would be that he was genuinely alarmed at Adenauer's policy of using former Nazis; that he visited Wohlgemuth because he regarded him as a like-minded friend with whom he could discuss the problem, never suspecting that Wohlgemuth was a Soviet agent; and that he was, after this experience, in a disturbed psychological state when he broadcast and expressed ideas and emotions which he genuinely held and felt (about the Adenauer regime), and no doubt uttered among his friends, but should not – and, if he were in a rational state, would not – have uttered as Soviet propaganda.

This does not seem to me unplausible, for the following reasons.

(1) The Adenauer government <u>did</u> recruit ex-Nazis, some of them pretty scandalous characters. The one most shocking to John, or to anyone who had been in the world of secret intelligence, was Reinhard Gehlen, who had been high in Hitler's secret service and was made, with American support, head of Adenauer's secret service. To anyone who (perhaps naively) objected to the Cold War and looked, for German reunification, to a continuation of the alliance with Russia, this was a shocking appointment; and Gehlen, who of course knew about John's history in Intelligence, and regarded him as a traitor to Hitler, detested John as John detested him. This seems enough to make someone in John's position at that time very unhappy.

(2) The drugging and kidnapping of West Germans (and others) in Berlin was quite common at the time. Nuclear physicists and other wanted or needed persons were periodically kidnapped, and anyone who was thought to be in danger of such a fate was provided with a bodyguard by the Anglo-Americans if he went to Berlin. (I remember that my colleague Dimitri Obolensky,[18] who went to a Byzantine conference in Berlin, had such a guard: as a White Russian prince who, at that time, had only a Nansen passport,[19] he was thought vulnerable).

(3) John was a person who fell into the kidnappable class. He had been connected with the German Secret Service, had defected to England, was no doubt supposed by the Russians to have been in the British Secret Service, and had then been in the post-war 'Anti-Russian' Adenauer secret service. He could therefore – it would be supposed – give valuable information, apart from any propaganda value he might have. And his known views about the Adenauer regime, which would have been reported to them by Wohlgemuth and others, would suggest to the Russians that he could be used. In addition to this there is a further reason, which is suggested by John himself, and though speculative, may be true. The Russians had, at that time, a long-serving 'mole' in Gehlen's secret service, <u>viz</u> Heinz Felfe,[20] whom they greatly valued. He was recruited in 1950 and not exposed till 1961. They were naturally anxious to find an alternative source from which they could be thought to have derived the kind of material that Felfe gave them. John could fulfil that role. I don't suppose John was kidnapped for that purpose, but it could have been an added reason.

For all these reasons I consider that John's version is not unplausible, and is indeed more plausible than the alternative theory which raises the, to me, insoluble question, why then did he risk return, the certainty of a trial for treason, etc.; and why did the German court, which must have gone into the matter closely, accept his version? Can you imagine Philby coming back? (And Philby is a tougher nut than John!) [...] Maurice Oldfield[21] and, I think, Harold Caccia[22] accepted John's story [...] Caccia was Deputy Under-Secretary of State of the Foreign Office at the time. Maurice Oldfield was in S.I.S. Surely they had opportunities of knowing; and if they knew, would not gratuitously have declared belief in a story that they knew to be false?[23]

Trevor-Roper was not only intrigued by John but also took considerable interest in the latter's formidable antagonist, Reinhard Gehlen. In the following essay[24] Trevor-Roper recalls follies he first had detected in Percy Sillitoe and also return to some of his wider concerns about the challenges facing secret intelligence which he had explored in The Philby Affair *four years previously.*

Reinhard Gehlen, founder and head of the Bundesnachrichtendienst or BND, the Federal intelligence service in the days of the cold war, has enjoyed a publicity remarkable for one who, ostensibly (not to say ostentatiously), has fled the limelight. For in the days of his power he always moved in the shadows. He invariably wore dark glasses and a low hat that concealed his face. He approached and left his office by the back door. He allowed false photographs of himself to circulate. And yet, in spite of all these precautions, he has evidently failed in his ambition of anonymity. In his own account of his work, he dwells with apparent envy on the methods of the British secret service, whose reigning head is never known to the public or named in the press. Could this, he asks, happen with us in Germany? Perhaps not, we may reply, if the head of the German secret service makes himself so conspicuous by his secretiveness; if he boasts of his contact with the media; if he seeks to use the press as an ally, or a weapon, in the internal politics of his department; if he allows his organisation to be known by his name; and if, in the end, he publishes his memoirs.

Gehlen himself would say that this publicity has been forced upon him. It was Sefton Delmer's[25] article in the *Daily Express* of 17 March 1952, he says, which, by unleashing a 'flood of further publications', dragged him into the daylight. The public loves a spy-story; it also loves a mystery-man; and in a period of ideological war there are many who love to have someone to hate. Moreover, Gehlen himself has doubled the intensity of feeling about him by being active in two different, if overlapping, ideological struggles. Once the hunt was up, he could be attacked alike from the West as an old Nazi, employing other old Nazis, and thereby discrediting the 'democratic' West German government, and from the East as an agent of American imperialism, using that government, and the old Nazis in it, to continue Hitler's aims. The former argument is implicit in the article by Sefton Delmer; the latter has been repeated, with fanatical iteration, in the copious writings of Gehlen's most persistent East German persecutor, Julius Mader.[26] The climax of the publicity came when Hermann Zolling and Heinz Hoehne published in the German periodical *Der Spiegel* a series of articles about Gehlen. It was those articles, Gehlen now says, which provoked him into writing, in his retirement, his own memoirs. It is those articles which have now been expanded into this book.

Gehlen is certainly a very controversial man; but he is also, it must be admitted, a remarkable man. Apart from anything else, he is remarkable for his power to survive. When his name first came to my notice during the war, he was head of Fremde Heere Ost (FHO), the section of the German General Staff which, through the Abwehr or secret service of the Armed Forces, collected military intelligence about the countries of Eastern Europe. He had held this position since the spring of 1942: the failure of the first offensive against Russia had been fatal to his predecessor, whose intelligence reports had been almost invariably wrong. Two years later it looked as if it would be Gehlen's turn to go. Hitler then decided that the whole Abwehr had failed. He dismissed its chief, Admiral Canaris, and ordered Himmler to create a new unified service under the control of the SS. In the following months, heads rolled throughout the old Abwehr and the SS took over the amputated fragments of its body. But Gehlen somehow survived. His own Eastern organisation remained intact within the new system, and he himself became the trusted ally of the SS. This was the first of his survivals. It was a pattern that was to be repeated again and again.

It is true that Gehlen was once dismissed; but that dismissal proved a great asset to him. It came three weeks before the end of the war, the outcome of one of Hitler's rages. It had no practical effect except to provide Gehlen with a small drop of anti-Nazi virtue, which he afterwards greatly increased and used to lubricate his next, and most difficult, act of survival: his transformation from Hitler's and Himmler's chief intelligence officer in the East into the Central European expert of the American CIA and, afterwards, the head of the secret service of the Federal Republic of Germany.

The key, of course, lay in the East. If Gehlen had been an intelligence officer on the Western front, we would probably never have heard of him again. But in the East it was different. Circumstances there were special. For when the halcyon days of the Grand Alliance ended and the Iron Curtain dropped, cutting off half of Germany and all of Eastern Europe, the Western Allies had almost no sources of intelligence behind it. During the war, inevitably, they had left military intelligence there, like military operations, to their Eastern ally. So, when the Eastern ally became, potentially, the Eastern enemy, they were at a great disadvantage. Their disadvantage was Gehlen's opportunity. The Germans alone had had an intelligence system which had worked continuously in the vast area now dominated by Russia. Gehlen had controlled that system. He had controlled and used it effectively. The very fact of his dismissal by Hitler was proof of his efficiency, for Hitler had resented the discouraging accuracy of his reports. And finally the very fact of German division strengthened his hand. For intelligence purposes, a divided country is a natural bridgehead. East Germany was a natural recruiting ground for West German agents, which only a system controlled by Germans could fully exploit. The formula could also, of course, be reversed: as Gehlen was to find.

With the visible imminence of the Cold War, the opportunity was clear, and Gehlen's tactical skill lay in his seizure of it. This book shows, in detail, how he seized it and how, through every crisis, he contrived to preserve his position: how he persuaded first the Americans, then the Federal Government of Dr Adenauer, that he alone could provide intelligence from the East; and to what extent he provided it. It also shows the price at which these Western governments bought that provision, and the internal manoeuvres by which Gehlen ensured the continuation, and expansion, of his personal power.

Part of the price was, of course, that Gehlen was, or had been, a Nazi and was believed to continue into the Adenauer era not only the methods but also the contacts which he had discovered and used when he had served Hitler. Naturally the Russians would seize on this fact, in order to exploit the doubts of Western moralists – although, being themselves realists, they do not apply this severe morality to their own political actions. Allen Dulles and Adenauer would no doubt have had an answer to this objection. Gehlen was certainly a Nazi in his mental structure, and it is clear from his memoirs that even today his only objection to Hitler is that he lost the war. However, most German professionals of his time had this mentality, and it could be argued that what was needed in 1946 was, above all, a professional. The British did not like Gehlen, and preferred to back a more virtuous *amateur.* The result was not a success. The ruthless Gehlen soon destroyed (with his own aid) the more sympathetic Otto John.

More serious was the objection that Gehlen recruited into his service other Nazis who perhaps, as they were less professional, were more objectionable than himself, and that, as it grew in power, the organisation used Nazi methods to protect itself against internal enemies. One of the most interesting parts of this book describes how Gehlen, having at first kept his distance from the ex-SS men, gradually recovered confidence and brought them into his organisation – and how, after the disastrous Felfe trial, he was obliged, in order to avoid damaging publicity, quickly to pay them off.

Why did Gehlen's power so grow? This book makes the answer quite clear. Whatever extensions he added to it, with his excursions into Asia, Africa, South America, and the Near East, the centre of Gehlen's system was always, after as during the war, espionage against Russia in Eastern Europe. He lived on the Cold War and on the favour of those American and German governments which believed in the primacy of the Cold War. This need not be held against him, or them. The Cold War was a historical fact, perhaps a historical necessity. If Western governments had not hardened their postures in the decade after the Second World War, Germany, and with it Western Europe, might well have been subverted and conquered by Stalin. This being so, no Western government is to be blamed for taking what may have been the only means of filling a vital gap. It is legitimate to use Beelzebub to drive out Satan. What can be deplored, and what those Germans who were determined to clear German politics of the Nazi taint did both deplore and oppose, was the large measure of irresponsible power which these governments, in their anxiety, allowed to Gehlen: a man whose philosophy – as shown by his own book – was narrow, whose past was tainted, and whose methods reflected that past. This book shows how Gehlen, by his personal courtship of Adenauer, gained a central position, responsible, through the State Secretary Hans Globke, to the Chancellor alone. Since Globke himself was widely distrusted for his past services to the Nazi Party, this made Gehlen's privileged and secret activities even more suspect.

However, the proof of the pudding is always in the eating. Ultimately, any secret service justifies itself by results. How well did Gehlen in fact serve his Western masters? How fully did he justify the huge budget which he obtained, the power and the privilege which he exercised? Gehlen himself, of course, makes large claims; but they are curiously vague and undocumented. Those who read his memoirs* will also find that they leave much out. There is, in that book, a curious lack of proportion. Two-thirds of it is spent in describing the author's history, and that of his organisation, up to 1955 – i.e. up to the year in which the Gehlen organisation at last achieved its long-pursued aim and became the official secret service of the Federal Republic. The events of the next twelve years, the period when it acted as such, are squeezed into one chapter; and the rest of the book consists of not very profound generalities. Those who seek a reason for this falling-off in the memoirs will find it, amply documented, in Messrs Höhne and Zolling's book. The falling-off in the detail of the memoirs is directly related to the falling-off of the efficiency of the BND.

In its early days the Gehlen organisation certainly enjoyed some successes, which are here recorded; but from 1958 the decline in its efficiency is clear. There was a series of small failures. Then, in 1962–3, came the great failures. First came the '*Spiegel* affair' of 1962 – Gehlen's attempt, in an alliance of convenience with the periodical *Der Spiegel*, to ruin Adenauer's Defence Minister, Franz Josef Strauss.[27] This led to a public scandal. Those who enlist the media in their private battles must expect publicity, and although Strauss was destroyed, so was the old alliance between Adenauer and Gehlen. Then, in 1963, came the trial of Heinz Felfe, which showed that Gehlen's whole organisation in East Germany had been penetrated by the 'enemy'. Finally, in 1963, Adenauer retired and was replaced as Chancellor by the unsympathetic Ludwig Erhard, who loved neither Gehlen nor espionage. Erhard even evicted the BND's liaison staff from the Chancellery attics: he

---

* All my comments on Gehlen's memoirs are based on the German text, *Der Dienst* (von Hase & Koehler, Mainz & Wiesbaden 1971). H.R. T-R.

refused 'to live under the same roof with these people'. With the heart of his empire rotten and his external patron gone, Gehlen's days were numbered. He was allowed to serve out his time, but the legend had been destroyed and, after he had gone in 1968, a government enquiry revealed the nepotism, the scandal and the ineptitude that had thrived in a privileged private empire sustained and protected from criticism by the political conjuncture of the Cold War.

There is a certain momentum in the history of secret services which, I believe, is accentuated by their secrecy and compounded by their privilege. Espionage is always at a disadvantage compared with counter-espionage, for the former depends on individual skill in hostile surroundings, while the latter operates on home ground, supported by the ample resources of the state. Successful espionage therefore requires continual regeneration: fresh thought, constant vigilance, continuous adaptation to changing circumstances. Only thus can it keep the advantage which it may have gained by initial enterprise. But the privileged secrecy of a secret service, which can protect its members from the strain, or the stimulus, of regular criticism, operates in the opposite direction. The chief of a secret service, who knows that he has this additional protection, is inevitably tempted to exploit it. He is the priest of a mystery, guarded by ritual formulae and sacred taboos, which it becomes second nature to invoke when success is lacking or small failures need to be attenuated or covered up. Only a great failure, which cannot be so concealed, can finally break through the protective wall which successive uncorrected small defects may already have silently rotted.

Appendix 1

Correspondence with Patrick Reilly

Much of Trevor-Roper's information about Philby came from friends he had made during his wartime service, and in particular Charles Stuart, Dick White and Patrick Reilly. Charles Stuart was valuable because he had a better memory for wartime detail than his old chief; Dick White and Patrick Reilly had enjoyed access to material of particular secrecy. White and Reilly trusted Trevor-Roper completely and told him secrets which were not meant for wider publication, confident that he would not abuse their friendship. While he was writing about Philby, this constraint put Trevor-Roper in an awkward position, as he was naturally concerned to enhance the value of his essay by including important new evidence.

Trevor-Roper's dilemma emerges with particular clarity from his correspondence with Patrick Reilly during 1967–8. In 1942 Reilly had been seconded from the Foreign Office to work as personal assistant to the Chief of the Secret Service. His recollections of that period provide the most objective individual account of SIS headquarters during World War II. After the war Reilly enjoyed an outstanding career in British diplomacy. He became ambassador to the Soviet Union in 1957 and to France in 1965. The following extracts from the correspondence between Reilly and Trevor-Roper concentrate on intelligence material.

Hugh Trevor-Roper to Patrick Reilly, Chiefswood, 28 December 1967[1]

My dear Patrick,

[...] May I ask you a question? You will no doubt have observed that our old friend Kim Philby has been in the news recently. The articles which were published in the *Sunday Times* are now to appear, multiplied fourfold, in a book, published by André Deutsch, with a foreword by one David Cornwell,[2] who writes under the name of Le Carré. (Cornwell was in

SIS [...] [*where he had served as an intelligence officer*].) In view of all the fuss, culminating in the surfacing and spouting of Philby in Moscow, I have decided to write a long article, to appear topically when the [*Sunday Times*] book is published, in which I shall totally ignore the book but will try to put the Philby affair in its context. (I realise that my view of its context may not be that of some others.) However, rest assured: I do not propose to quote your grave comparison of Dansey and Vivian with 'fleas in the folds of a diseased dog's ear' – much though I would like to do so, out of admiration for so fine and exact a literary metaphor. My question is very harmless. It is this.

Am I rightly informed that you, when you were F.O. adviser to C, left it on record that Dick White ought to be the next (or next but one) head of SIS? If so, may I allude to this (without mentioning either your or his name)? [...]

Yours ever,
  Hugh

Patrick Reilly to Hugh Trevor-Roper, British Embassy, Paris, 2 January 1968[3]

My dear Hugh,
  Very many thanks for your as always most entertaining letter of 28th Dec, which I was delighted to get [...]
  I am naturally much interested in hearing of your proposed article & can't wait to see the whole affair put in its context & proper perspective. Naturally I read the *Sunday Times* articles with extreme interest. There were a few things wrong (eg Peter K[och] de G[ooreynd] wasn't a stockbroker?, but not many, were there? – at least up to mid 1953, when all knowledge stops for me. I also thought the wife's[4] articles of very great interest – at any rate for anyone who has lived in Moscow.
  On the question you put to me – the facts – for your very personal information, please are as follows. Some time in 1950 (or possibly early 1951 – but I think 1950) when our wartime boss [*Menzies*] was about to retire, he & his successor [*Sinclair*] were proposing to bring the chap in question [*Philby*] back to London as No 3. I was asked to meet him when he came

over for a visit. I believe that I am intermittently – certainly not always, I fear! – & less and less, I suspect – capable of exceptional perception & I have no doubt that on this occasion I was. I had of course known him in 1942–43 as a blue-eyed boy: & I had seen him once or twice in Athens on leave around 1946/47. The change since then was startling. I had a very strong impression – from the face & the eyes – of something fundamentally wrong. I went back to the F.O. & said that I was convinced that this appointment must not be made. It wasn't: & I have often thought this was one of the best things I have done in my service!

At the same time I recommended that our mutual friend [*Dick White*] should be brought in as No 3, with a view to eventual succession. This was turned down flat by the then management of the firm [*SIS*]. I had of course left for other things when he later came in as No 1: and the curtain having come down for me on all this as it always does, I have no idea whether by then anyone remembered my earlier recommendation or whether it had anything to do with the decision taken. I wd guess almost certainly not!

Now did I tell you about this or someone else, I wonder? As regards use of the story in your article, I fear I am bound to ask you not to, however wrapped up. The first part – about the proposal for the other fellow [*Philby*] – I may publish one day if I ever publish anything about the whole affair: but at present it cd only add to the troubles of the two old gentlemen, [*Menzies and Sinclair*] which must be bad enough & I owe too much kindness to the first & am too sorry for the second (who of course refused to contemplate the chap's guilt when we all were convinced of it) to want to do this in their lifetimes.

As regards my proposal for our mutual friend [*Dick White*], will it really add anything to your setting of the story in its context? Anyhow, to my great regret, in the light of the line being taken about all this on high in London, I must ask you not to use the story. I am so sorry. I don't think it will wreck the article! Cd you say something like 'Good judges already recognised that etc.? … !⁵

With love to you both & very best wishes for 1968
Yours ever
Patrick.

Hugh Trevor-Roper to Patrick Reilly,
Chiefswood, 5 January 1968[6]

My dear Patrick,

Thank you very much for your letter, and for taking so much trouble to write at length in your own hand, when you might have been reading Johnson's *Journey to the Western Isles*![7] I am most grateful. The information you give me will remain firmly at the <u>back</u> of my mind.

It was <u>not</u> you who told me of your recommendation, and I can't say, from the circumstances in which I heard it, whether your recommendation was an operative factor in Dick White's appointment in 1956 or whether it has since turned up on the files; but I suspect that it was an operative factor. Harold Macmillan would know. If I get a chance I will ask him – on the basis of what I knew <u>before</u> writing to you![8]

I shall not, of course, quote anything you say; but to cover myself in what I will or may say, I should tell you that, long before you wrote to me, I had always been convinced that Philby[9] was being groomed for the succession to C. I based my conviction on three grounds, <u>viz</u>: (1) his ability; (2) the lack, inside the organisation, of any other competent person; (3) the succession of posts to which he was appointed, which seemed positively designed to lead to that end. I once put this reasoning to Dick, and he – rather to my surprise, because he, naturally enough, would like to play down the importance of Philby – positively agreed. So I was already quite convinced myself on this point before hearing from you, and had in fact already written that part of my article.

It is a devilish difficult article. I don't want to make any trouble, but if I am to say what I think, and if my opposition to the social nihilists is to be plausible, I cannot possibly defend the wartime S.I.S. Like you, I have a weak spot for the then No.1; but V and D [*Vivian and Dansey*] ...

I assure you that I have quoted you <u>ipsissima verba</u>[10] about those two old frauds. You added, to give substance to your metaphor, 'I have seen it in Persia.' I had not then been in Persia and <u>couldn't</u> have thought of the metaphor! I remember also that, on that occasion, Rachel [*Reilly's wife*] added that you used to wake up in the small hours uttering the names of D and V! [...]

Yours ever,
Hugh

P.S. Your story about Philby sheds an interesting light on Sir SM's [*Stewart Menzies*] statement that Philby was a very unimportant person in the Old Firm and never had any prospect of rising to the top! What a narrow squeak we had! I now realise that – next to Burgess – we owe it to you. I will now (but would I not always) trust your judgement on <u>anything</u>!

PPS. I too noticed the error about P.K. de G. being a stockbroker; but then I discovered that this error only appeared in the provincial + overseas edition (we in Scotland get it): it was corrected in the London edition. I fear that P.K. de G. is now in a sad way: an undischarged bankrupt, obliged to resign from White's, maundering about his past glory in S.I.S.

Trevor-Roper was intrigued by Reilly's letters. On 8 February he invited Dick White to lunch at the Savile Club and afterwards noted that White 'told me that in 1950 one air commodore James Alfred Easton was nominated no. 3. in SIS {i.e. with right of succession} {…} In other words, when PR {Reilly} vetoed Philby, & SM {Stewart Menzies} & JS {John Sinclair} vetoed DGW {White}, Easton was the <u>tertius gaudens</u>'.[11]
  Once Trevor-Roper had decided to give his Encounter *essay more substantial form as a book, Reilly's secrets became an even more important source to him. Trevor-Roper knew that the inside story of Philby's nomination by SIS to become its chief would much enhance his new publication if he could include it. In March 1968 Hugh and Lady Alexandra Trevor-Roper had gone to stay with Reilly at the British Embassy in Paris, but pressure of work denied the Ambassador any opportunity to discuss Philby. So while still at the embassy Trevor-Roper wrote a letter instead.*[12]

My dear Patrick,
  I want to persuade you, if I can, to let me mention in print, in the final version of my article on Philby (which is to be published in book form, together with an old article on Canaris, now a collector's piece), your minute to the F.O. of 1950 advising that Philby should <u>not</u> be made no 3 and that Dick White should be appointed instead.

My main reason for this request is as follows.

Philby, in his memoirs, has consistently sought to represent Dick as insignificant. He refers to him as 'the ineffective White'. If I could refer to the 1950 minute, it would show two facts, <u>viz</u>: that Philby's upward career in SIS was checked <u>before</u> the Burgess and Maclean episode; (2) that Dick was recommended as early as 1950, and by a good judge, whose good judgement is proved by his correct appreciation of Philby's character. This in turn – since it <u>must</u> have been reported to Philby – accounts for Philby's personal animosity against Dick, which he revealed by sending a message to Dick from Moscow in 1963 promising revenge. The memoirs are no doubt part of the revenge.

I don't ask you to answer this request till you have read my article in <u>Encounter,</u> which I hope will strike you as grave, temperate and judicious. I admit that when I read it in proof I was, like Clive [*of India*] astounded at my own moderation.

You will remember that when I wrote to you first about this subject, I showed that I already knew the facts, in a certain form, from another source. I wrote to you to check them. So I could publish the version that I had before writing to you. But I would naturally prefer to publish the authentic version as confirmed from the horse's mouth – if you will let me.

Your sagacious minute[13] on Cowgill's draft letter from C to Hoover is recorded (Philby p. 85). May not this equally sagacious minute also be mentioned, which is so creditable to the angels of light?

Yours ever,
  Hugh

———

Patrick Reilly did not reply properly for some time. He was preoccupied by the irascible and bibulous Foreign Secretary George Brown.[14] In July 1966, during a dinner at the French Embassy in London, an intoxicated Brown had told Rachel Reilly in front of other guests that she was not fit to be an ambassadress. It was an untrue and appalling remark. Despite this affront to his wife, Reilly himself had given Brown energetic support during the British bid to join the EEC in 1967. Reilly had also predicted correctly that de Gaulle would veto the attempt. Yet the Foreign Secretary claimed that the embassy was completely out of touch and Anglo-French official relations were frigid. Brown truncated the Ambassador's period in France and pushed through his replacement by a political appointment from outside the Diplomatic Service. Reilly's treatment was much resented by his fellow ambassadors, who knew he was an extremely able British diplomat.[15] He served in Paris until September 1968 and was succeeded by the former Conservative cabinet minister Christopher Soames. Trevor-Roper wrote again from the Savile Club on 27 March 1968.[16]

My dear Patrick

We loved seeing you – although I never, alas, see much of you when you are <u>en poste</u> – and we greatly enjoyed our visit. Thank you both very much for having us. We are very sad to think that your stay in Paris is being curtailed by that Old Wretch [*Brown*], to whose damnation every preliminary libation of every bottle that I open shall now be offered: but you must take an exquisite revenge, if not practical, then at least literary: remember the sage remarks of Colonel Vivian about the unfair advantage of 'the All Souls style', and take as your motto, as I take for mine, the aphorism of Logan Pearsall Smith: 'how I would like to distill my disesteem of my contemporaries into prose so perfect that they would all of them have to read it!' [...]

Thank you for forwarding the telegram, and for your own marginal note. I won't take no for an answer – at least until you have read my article and seen how innocent it is. Dick White has found it so innocent that he has asked me to appear on T/V on the subject, as a corrective force, a bulwark of orthodoxy, a prop and shield of the Old Firm. I now think he will let me quote him, so perhaps I can prevail on you too!

I dare say you noticed Kim's remark on the F.O. advisers in S.I.S. 'of whom only Patrick Reilly left a mark'. I now think that I know what that mark was; and so, I am sure, does he! (In fact, I could almost attribute the story to him, on the sound old Cowgillesque principle of protecting the source!).

Come and visit us, and drink damnation to G.B. in a bottle of Krug which I reserve for that purpose.

Yours ever,
Hugh

Patrick Reilly to Hugh Trevor-Roper, 14 April 1968[17]

My dear Hugh

[...] I have of course given much thought to the question of your referring to my successful opposition to Philby's promotion in 1950 (or possibly early 1951) & to my unsuccessful proposal that Dick W. shd fill the vacancy. First of all, let me say how greatly I have admired your *Encounter* article. It is brilliant & everybody I know who has read it says the same. It is a real joy to read something so completely in the highest possible class & so right [...]

I am really terribly sorry but I must beg you not to press me more to agree to your recounting my 1950 or 1951 intervention in the book version of your article. I have several reasons for doing so.

1. Since it wd surely be regarded as coming from me, it wd – I am afraid – inevitably be treated as a breach of the Official Secrets Act: particularly as quite recently – feeling in recent circumstances what was no doubt a rather pitiful need to blow my own trumpet - I told those in authority in the F.O. about this incident, of which they were unaware.

2. I doubt very much whether your assumption that Philby will have been told of my intervention is valid. I have myself no reason to believe that he was told at the time that he was being considered for promotion to ACSS [*Assistant Chief of the Secret Service*] (Does his book suggest anywhere that he was?) or that he wd have known that I had proposed Dick for the job.[18] I did not interpret his reference to my 'leaving a mark' as applying to this period or incident. He is surely referring to the time 8 years earlier when I was working in Broadway.

Now it may well seem to you pusillanimous, but the truth is that I am not at all anxious in present circumstances for any unnecessary trouble or worry. We have had a tiresome & upsetting blow in the early ending of our time in Paris & more especially in the highly disagreeable way in which it was done. I want to look ahead & start anew. A row about a breach of the Official Secrets Act would be a great bore: and one never knows what Philby might be able to do that cd be extremely tiresome for us. The mere fact that he mentions me twice, even tho' favourably, has resulted in a highly disagreeable reference to my departure in the *Canard Enchaîné*.[19] Of course this doesn't matter.

But an ex-Ambassador at Moscow can remain vulnerable all his life – it is one of the wretched consequences of having that post. Philby – or the Russians – cd eg say falsely (or indeed perhaps truly) that we had our Vassall[20] too. In fact we had the narrowest possible escape from having one (if indeed it <u>was</u> an escape.) In say 5 years time such an allegation or revelation cd matter no more to us than the Vassall story did to William Hayter[21]: but now or in the next year or two it cd be a real bore.

3. My third reason is quite different but I wd like to think it is really my strongest one. I do not see how the story cd fail to be very hurting for Menzies & Sinclair. I have no particular obligation to Sinclair, tho' I respect him as an honourable if limited & misguided man. But I do have strong personal obligations to Menzies, whose wartime kindness to me meant a great deal to me at a very difficult time. I really cdn't bear to think of him reproaching me for revealing something for which he wd surely be strongly criticised.

I have tried to find a form of words which wd give the essential facts without mentioning my name: but I do not see how the facts can be stated without revealing that MI6 <u>did</u> propose to appoint P [*Philby*] no 3 & were prevented from doing so & that they refused to appoint DW [*Dick White*].

So, my dear Hugh, I must beg you to forgive me – but I really do not feel able to agree to what you ask of me. I am so sorry to be disobliging to you – particularly as I so much admire & applaud what you have written about Philby. I wonder, however, whether the information in question would really add all that much to your very powerful argument.

[…] Much love to you both
Yours ever
 Patrick

———

Reilly's strongest reason for reticence was removed when Stewart Menzies died on 29 May 1968. Yet Trevor-Roper did not reopen the question of using Reilly's special information. Instead he acceded to his friend's wishes.

> *He did not publish the details in question and merely recorded his dissent in an undated note.*[22]

The following are facts which I would like to have included in my article on Philby, but am precluded from including:

(1) In 1950 C & Sinclair proposed to promote Philby[23] to no. 3 (presumably with a view to succession). Patrick Reilly interviewed Philby and was so shocked by the change in him since he had last known him that he insisted to the F.O. that this appointment must not be made. Instead he urged the apptmt of DGW [*Dick White*]. This was absolutely vetoed by C & Sinclair. This shows (a) that the SIS establishment intended Philby to succeed; (b) that they were solid against DGW; that Philby & DGW were in a sense, at that time, personal rivals. See PR's letter to me of Dec 1967.

(2) On arrival in Moscow, Philby sent a personal message to DGW saying 'You have won this round, but I will win the next'. This again shows that Philby regarded the struggle as a personal duel with DGW.

———————

> *Despite the refusal from Reilly, Trevor-Roper offered to dedicate* The Philby Affair *to his wartime friend. No doubt he wished to give Reilly a boost after the disappointing end to the ambassador's Paris appointment.*

Hugh Trevor-Roper to Patrick Reilly, 8 St Aldate's Oxford, 24 June 1968[24]

My dear Patrick,

[…] My essay on Philby, together with an older essay on Canaris, is to be published as a little volume, and I would like – thinking of those days of shared frustration, and also of your unique but (alas) secret distinction [*of blocking the SIS nomination of Philby to become its eventual Chief*], to dedicate it to you, under the protective colouring of initials, D.P.R. [*D'Arcy Patrick Reilly*], if you prefer. Will you allow me to do this? To whom can I dedicate it more appropriately. I hope you will allow me to do so.

I enclose a copy of the draft forward, so you will see how innocent it is!

Yours ever,
Hugh

On 30 June 1968 Reilly replied: 'I am greatly touched by your thought of dedicating your Philby/Canaris book to me & by the language of the last two sentences of your preface. I have never dreamed of ever having a book dedicated to me & I am proud & delighted to accept. It means a lot to me. Thank you very much indeed. Pusillanimous to the end, I think perhaps I would opt for "D.P.R.": but I feel rather ashamed of myself.'

Hugh Trevor-Roper to Patrick Reilly, Chiefswood, 9 September 1968[25]

My dear Patrick,

It is sad to think that, about this time, you will be leaving the Foreign Office. Like many other people, I shall not forgive G. Brown for the manner of your retirement; and I am glad to see how widely this feeling is shared. However, no such passing episode can alter the facts of your career, and I shall always regard it as a happy accident that the fortunes of war (intestine as well as external) brought us together. I value your friendship enormously – and show this, I hope, by often using it. I hope we shall see much of you both now that you will probably be more often at Ramsden.[26]

A small (but perhaps not entirely de-fused) token of my friendship and admiration will soon be ready, in the form of a specially prepared copy of my little book on the Philby affair which, with your permission, is dedicated to you. The publisher (Wm. Kimber) says that it will be ready at the same time as the public edition, <u>viz</u>. on 23 September. Where will you be then, so that I may place it – personally or indirectly – in your hands? Of course I should like to do it personally, as befits an author offering his tribute to his patron; and the proper course would no doubt be to alight – if you are still in

Paris – on my (probable) way to Venice on the actual date of publication. But binders' dates are not always exactly forecast, and if you are in Paris you are presumably preoccupied with moving. So would you tell me where you will be and how and where you would most conveniently accept it?

I hope you will appreciate the quotation from Pindar, which I deliberately left in Greek, with no translation and no reference, so that the profane may not intrude upon those arcane mysteries.[27]

Xandra sends her love to you both. So do I.

Yours ever,
  Hugh

The level of personal trust between Trevor-Roper and Reilly was shown again in a letter Trevor-Roper wrote nearly 30 years after the Philby controversy. In this letter Trevor-Roper described graphically the false accusations of betraying Ultra made against him during World War II. He began by discussing a new biography of Philby by Anthony Cave Brown.[28]

Hugh Trevor-Roper to Sir Patrick Reilly, 12 December 1994[29]

Dear Patrick,

Your copy of Cave Brown's book has just reached me. I think (but I cannot be sure of the date in your letter) that it may have been nestling in the Porter's Lodge for some time; in which case I apologise for this delayed acknowledgement. Like all CB's books it is long, turgid and full of error, but there are interesting bits in it. Your patience in rectifying its errors is exemplary: I shall not imitate you; one might as well count the pebbles of the sea-shore, or try to overtake a Bandersnatch.[30]

One detail fascinated me. Dealing with my 'trial' (at which I am interested to read that you were present as advocate or prisoner's friend[31]) CB, who draws his information from 'two interviews with Cowgill in April 1983' – who also was not there – says that I was accused of having had 'unauthorised contact with the enemy in Ireland – a grave offence in time of total war'; so naturally 'Cowgill and Vivian both demanded that T-R be dismissed from the service'.[32] I should have thought that dismissal was insufficient penalty for so grave an offence. It amuses me that Cowgill should solemnly state this 40 years later: amusing, but also instructive, for it provides a piece of evidence hitherto missing.

Some months <u>after</u> the alleged 'trial', R.L. Hughes, who was MI5's liaison officer with RSS, invited me to call on him; which I did, and he showed me a document which he thought would interest me; as indeed it did: my eyes popped as I read it. It was by Vivian, in that inimitable Babu style, and it suggested that I had spent my leave in Ireland not, as I alleged, for the innocent purpose of fox-hunting, but in order to leak the secret of <u>Ultra</u> to the German Legation in Dublin. The argument by which Vivian reached this interesting conclusion was this: (1) Colonel Worlledge, the head of RSS before it was taken over by MI6, lived in Ireland. (2) Having been kicked out by MI6 and replaced by Col. Maltby, Colonel Worlledge might perhaps feel some resentment. (3) T-R probably visited Col. Worlledge in Ireland. (4) Col. Worlledge was no doubt an entirely loyal British subject, <u>but</u> there was also Major Gill, who might suppose that he had grounds for greater resentment and who was T-R's immediate superior; <u>so</u> (5) it is likely that T-R, perhaps in collusion with Major Gill, or through loyalty to him, was seeking to take revenge on MI6 by leaking the <u>Ultra</u> secret to the Germans. QED. MI5 please take note.

Hughes assured me that MI5 was paying no attention to this ridiculous document: it was shown to me for interest only: I could forget it. But of course I did not. Reflecting on it, I decided that Vivian, in despair, having failed to have me sacked by C, was trying to get me declared a traitor by MI5 and so achieve the same purpose. However, I now realise, since Cowgill repeated the charge, apparently quite seriously, 40 years later, and declared that it was formally made at my 'trial', that it had been cooked up between Cowgill and Vivian much earlier, and was designed to persuade Menzies. In fact the charge was never laid at my trial, or indeed ever to me, so it merely circulated in the background and was finally passed underhand to MI5.

What a *galère*! The passage of time had softened my heart towards poor old Cowgill, who was so scurvily treated by the unholy alliance of Vivian and Philby; but the process has been arrested by this discovery. Even the passage of forty years cannot soften me towards Vivian [...].

Appendix 2

Charles Stuart on Kim Philby

Some of the most perceptive comment on The Philby Affair *came from a former member of Trevor-Roper's Radio Intelligence Service, Charles Stuart. Until Trevor-Roper was elected Regius Professor of Modern History in 1957, he and Stuart were both tutors in Modern History at Christ Church. Like Trevor-Roper, Stuart was extremely tenacious and penetrating. He became exceptionally dedicated to teaching his undergraduate pupils and fostering their careers. Although he could not match his mentor's eloquence or the range of his intellectual interests, Stuart was more pragmatic and a better judge of character. The two friends cooperated closely in college politics and corresponded frequently. Stuart spent the long vacation of 1947 with his family in Surrey, where Vivian was amongst his neighbours, as he reported to Trevor-Roper: 'the polite hum of S.I.S Packards is now a regular accompaniment to our lives. So far, my only contact with Viv has been at a meeting with the other residents when he persuaded everyone to pay £50 to repair the road opposite to his house {...} I contrived to give him an uncomfortable moment, as he warmly shook my hand, by assuring him that we had met before when I worked at Barnet for you. His wall eye cavorted around the room at the syllables Trevor-Roper and several of his hair-pins fell out.'[1]*

Although Trevor-Roper relied on Stuart's exceptional memory for detail of their shared experiences in wartime SIS, the recollections of the two men differed about the methods by which SIS had been recruited. The subject of SIS recruitment was broached by Trevor-Roper in a letter about the Philby biography by a team of Sunday Times *journalists.[2] Trevor-Roper told Stuart that Colonel Vivian,*

in his cosy retirement, has been drawing balances and striking conclusions (if that is the phrase) to some tune: and he has contrived to sell his conclusions to the naïve young men who have boldly tackled this subject. In brief, he has persuaded them that he was the far-sighted, honourable, but unfortunate reformer who sought, against the opposition of Colonel Dansey *et al.*, to raise the intellectual level of SIS, by bringing in dons, and particularly Fellows of All Souls, and other university-educated men, into the Old Firm. It was in this general context, he explains, that he made the mistake of introducing Philby; who, however, was only one of the 'intellectuals' through whom he, and he alone, contrived to regenerate the Service [...]

I have cast my mind back to see if I can recall any 'intellectual' except Philby, who was personally recruited by Vivian, or even known by him; but although I recall that the Colonel did once offer himself as a patron to Gilbert [*Ryle*], and dangled before that unresponsive creature the carrot of a major's rank 'with all that that implies' I do not remember any other evidence for this new and retrospective theory. However he seems to have got away with it. Such are the advantages of survival, and of what Gilbert once described as 'promotion recollected in senility.' [...] I happened to mention this new theory which that plausible old hypocrite [*Vivian*] has evolved (but of course, after forty years in the public service, one cannot help having a persuasive style) to Dick White. He laughed aloud.[3]

During 1968 Stuart published two essays of his own about Philby. He was prompted to do so by SIS. While the Chief of SIS was encouraging Trevor-Roper to write The Philby Affair, *one of his officers was urging Stuart to write for the* Spectator. *Stuart's primary SIS contact was a counter-intelligence officer who had confronted the Soviet spy George Blake and discovered the extent of his treachery. This officer now belonged to the joint MI5–SIS working party codenamed* Fluency *on the hostile penetration of British intelligence. On 21 February he wrote to Stuart:*

We are now busily engaged in watching preparations for the publication of the [*Philby*] 'Memoirs'. Their first appearance in this country seems likely to be in the *Sunday Express* of 17th March. We have been able to sight a copy of the manuscript, in which you and your wartime colleagues rate an honourable mention! If you think that you might have an opportunity to write an article in connection with this, I should be most grateful if you would let me know. You can always drop me a line at the above address or communicate through *[the SIS recruitment officer who had been at Harrow with Stuart]* and I would be very happy to come to Oxford again to discuss the matter with you and to let you have a preview of the manuscript *[Philby's]*.[4]

On 26 March Stuart's SIS contact wrote again.

You will, I imagine, now have seen Hugh's piece on the subject in ENCOUNTER, which revives all his previous criticism of Section V. No doubt you will have seen that he has once again pirated your recollections of P*[hilby]*'s reactions to Stuart Hampshire's paper and to the Otto JOHN affair. But there is really nothing one can do about that.[5] Now we must concentrate on the Memoirs and I should be very glad to avail myself of your kind offer to review them. If you can organise this in advance with the *Spectator* this would be most helpful. Although nothing much about the wartime years appeared in the *Sunday Express* serialisation, this period is fully covered in the manuscript, which we hold, and references to Vivian and Cowgill have appeared in serialised versions abroad. So it will probably not be until the summer that the full version will appear in book form in this country. If in the meantime you would like to browse through the full text, I would be most happy to let you have a copy of the manuscript.[6]

Stuart did not wait for Philby's book to be published before writing his first piece for the Spectator *on Philby. On 12 April Trevor-Roper urged him on: 'I hope you are writing – perhaps you have written – your article for the* Spectator. *I think it is important that the point you propose to make be made' – that is, that British intelligence triumphed in the secret war against German spies. Stuart replied to Trevor-Roper: 'Egged on by Nigel Lawson {then editor of the* Spectator} *over a splendid lunch at the Garrick*

Club I have sharpened up my nationalistic views and added – with proper notes of respect to your article – my disapproving doubts of your view of the nature of MI6's recruitment. After all, Section V, by the time it got to Ryder Street, had become as much a dons' & schoolmasters' preserve as any.'

On 23 April Trevor-Roper replied, insisting 'that the <u>Broadway professionals</u> came from Brooks's & Boodle's etc., just as the Section V. professionals came from the Indian police (via the East India & Sports Club, no doubt): the amateurs of course snowballed – they recruited each other, just as I recruited Gilbert, you & Stuart {Hampshire} (none of whom, I suspect, would have been found for me by Cowgill or Vivian).'[7] Nevertheless, in his article of personal testimony for the Spectator, *Stuart expressed a more positive view of SIS recruitment than his former head's.*

Personal Column[8]

The Philby Phenomenon

The recent eruption of works on Philby and by Philby has thrown open to public discussion the subject of the secret intelligence of the recent past, and in the course of this discussion ill-founded allegations and prejudiced conclusions have been confidently disseminated. It therefore seems a suitable moment to try to set the record straight and to speak out as one of those with experience of this work in the war. And it is time enough. For, if it is generally true in life that 'the soft answer turneth away bunkum,' this whole affair has proved a painful exception. Dignified silence has achieved nothing. It is time to try some sharper medicine to cure this growing irritation.

One of the allegations against both of the permanent British intelligence services, MI5 and MI6, and particularly the latter, is that they were recruited exclusively from the upper class without regard to efficiency. It is further suggested that whereas MI5 in the course of the war turned away from this policy to recruit more liberally from the world of the law and letters, MI6 remained wedded to its old ways, adding to its numbers from clubland to preserve its identity as a narrow self-perpetuating clique. Even my friend and wartime section commander, Hugh Trevor-Roper, whose brilliant essay published in *Encounter* is a shining exception to the general run of ignorant commentary, implicitly supports this thesis when he writes of the members of MI6 as 'agreeable epicureans from the bars of White's and Boodle's' and describes Philby as 'the one amateur who was appreciated by the professionals.'

Yet this is surely a caricature of the truth. The section of MI6 that he and I knew well for four years contained a large element which could not possibly be so categorised. They were dons and schoolmasters – future professors, heads of colleges and headmasters – besides others from the museum and art world. That they returned to their chosen professions when the war ended seems to me perfectly natural. I do not believe that they did this because they were rejected for permanent employment by the professional directorate of MI6. Certainly I was not so rejected. Too young in 1945 to have chosen a profession to which to return, I was given every encouragement to apply to stay in MI6 if I wanted, but I preferred to go my own way. So, in my view, Philby was not so much the one amateur to be appreciated by the professionals as the one wartime recruit to take advantage of his opportunity to stay, albeit for ignoble and treacherous motives.[9]

So much for the illusion of narrow recruitment, narrowly maintained. But a second point deserves greater emphasis because it has been widely ignored. This is that British intelligence in the war achieved overwhelming success against Germany. Between them, MI5 and MI6 penetrated completely all German intelligence activity, whether by the army (Abwehr), party (SD) or the unhappy service which evolved in 1944 from the swallowing of the first by the second. This important truth has been submerged under the copious flood of trivial personalities and sociological claptrap which has flowed from many pens. And worse may yet follow. Past defeats are easily forgotten and past triumphs easily imagined. Just recently old Abwehr officers have begun to boast of the imagined successes of their notional agents and there are, no doubt, some innocents who will take them at their word. But in the last months of the war when a procession of disillusioned German intelligence officers, including their last chief, Walter Schellenberg, was captured and interrogated, there were few such boasts. The full extent of our success was then clear. It was not they who could tell us about their plans, their movements, their organisation and their reorganisation, but we who had to prompt them. It was as if they needed the comforting presence of our interrogators to give meaning to the chaos of their lives. But to read any of the recent work on Philby it could hardly be inferred that we won the war as decisively on this front as on the battlefield.

It is the old story of not seeing the wood for the trees. Instead of viewing the large forest of this remarkable achievement, the new generation of self-appointed intelligence experts prefers to concentrate its jaundiced and myopic gaze upon such diseased and misshapen trees as it can find within it, and in particular upon the parasitic growths around them – the poison-ivy Philby and the toadstool Burgess. It is this approach which explains the morbid exaggeration of internal office feuds. Now, of course, the rivalry of MI5 and MI6 was a prominent feature of the wartime intelligence scene and it often hindered and delayed efficient action. This rivalry was not the creation of individuals within the two organisations but the consequence of their different functions. MI5 was a security organisation concerned with catching spies and with locking them up. For this purpose it needed information for action. MI6 was an intelligence-collecting organisation concerned with recruiting agents and extracting information from them. Above all, it was determined to guard its sources in order to preserve them for further use.

For MI5 the emphasis had to be on finding and closing any leak of information, even if this involved the risk of 'blowing' a source; for MI6 the reverse was the case – the preservation of a source was worth the price of a leak. The opposition of function was exacerbated by the mutual mistrust and suspicion which existed between certain of the career officers. Many of the wartime recruits in each department deplored this rivalry and did their best to get round it. For them, the immediate needs of war came first. This tended to place them, whatever their department, on MI5's side of the fence favouring 'free trade' in information and accepting the risks of action upon it. The counter-espionage section of MI6 (Section V) was in the middle of all this. Its directors naturally took an intelligence, as opposed to a security, view of its function. They favoured 'protectionism' in respect of information and feared the risks of using it. And because they adopted this defensive and negative position, they were probably the more to blame for inter-departmental friction.

What was needed in this situation, and what has since been long achieved, was a supervising authority to balance these two essential functions. Yet, although this need was not filled during the war, great successes were achieved by the joint, if sometimes competing, labours of both services. It is as pointless as it is vain to look back now after a quarter of a century and to dig up old rivalries with the purpose of giving marks to one section or another in this victory. The Zoroastrian complex which casts MI6 as Ahriman, the force of evil, and MI5 as Ahura-Mazda, the shining light of good, is historically unjust and politically unwise. Why play this game for Philby and his Russian employers? The important point is that in the war against Germany British counter-espionage was completely successful.

If, in this success, MI6 and Section V in particular, received more credit than was their due; if MI5 was denied proper recognition; if intelligence officers exploited the work of cryptographers, and cryptographers that of their wireless technicians; if all of these deviations from ideal justice can be substantiated, of what possible significance are they today? It is natural for Philby to want to revive these stale quarrels as part of the Russian attempt to discredit our present intelligence service. But it makes no sense for us; and but for the present fashion of denigration of ourselves and our achievements, to which the world of half-letters enthusiastically panders, it would have no market among us. Mr Brown may have been unmannerly when he rebuked Lord Thomson, but in substance he was right. *In vino, veritas*.[10]

Still, it is not enough to emphasise the successes of British intelligence in the war, or the hostile motives of Philby in trying to discredit these, or even the folly of those who use the story of his career to argue his case for him. It is also important to see the consequences of Philby's treachery in their true proportions. First as to time. It is my belief that, whatever he may say now, Philby was not[11] *active* as a Russian agent until early in 1945 when he became head of MI6's newly created anti-Russian section. Before that he was surely working under general Russian direction to insert himself permanently inside MI6, in which task he succeeded; but this task was the consequence of his able and efficient work at a comparatively junior level as head of the sub-section dealing with Spain and Portugal in the war against Germany. During 1944, it is true, he received that transitional promotion which was to lead to the fall of his immediate superior at the end of the year.[12] But only in 1945 did he rest his viper's head where it could strike with deadly effect. However great the evil that he was able to do in the six years that followed, this does not justify the creation for ourselves of insubstantial bogies about his achievements in his earlier years. This is equally true of the years following his dismissal as an officer of MI6 in 1951, even though he was restored to the payroll in 1955 as an agent and slipped into a soft job in Beirut where his boozy philandering kept him busy.

It seems unlikely, then, that Philby can have done much harm as a half-pay agent in Beirut. But what of the war years? Here the nature of his duties and his knowledge, which concerned the activities of the Germans in an area of marginal interest to Russia, meant that he was in no position to do positive harm. His influence on behalf of our Russian allies, if exerted at all, would of necessity have been negative. I recall two possible occasions when this may have been the case, when it would appear, looking back, that he was trying to suppress information in the interests of Russia. Both incidents have been touched on by Hugh Trevor-Roper, but as each depends ultimately upon my recollection it is worth stating them as I remember them.

The first concerned a paper written towards the end of 1942 (not 1943)[13] by a close colleague [*Stuart Hampshire*]. It was based on information about the activities of the Nazi intelligence service (SD) in Italy. Skilfully untangled, this material was used to illustrate the growing rivalry and mistrust in the intelligence field between the army and the party and, far more important, to suggest the wider political significance of this division. This was within a month or two of the dismissal of Halder and of the first signs of dissension between Hitler and his generals over Stalingrad.[14] The circulation of the paper required the approval of the head of Section V. He delegated the decision to Philby, not as Spanish expert – it had nothing to do with Spain – but as the officer thought to be expert in the kind of material on which it was based. My colleague and I presented ourselves and sat at Philby's desk while he went through the text. I had gone as Abwehr expert to back up my colleague whose territory was the SD.

But I was not needed. Philby was not interested in the evidence (he did not know it as we did), but only in its suppression. I sat back while my colleague argued. It was like that early scene in *Erewhon* where the narrator argues with the native Chowbok ... 'For more than two hours he had tried to put me off with lies, but carried no conviction; during the whole time we had been morally wrestling and neither of us apparently gained the least advantage.'[15] But, alas, whereas Chowbok finally yielded to the lure of grog, Philby was adamant. Perhaps we should have taken a bottle of whisky. The paper was not circulated until May 1943, when our section was detached from Section V, and then in a watered-down version.[16]

The second incident came nearly two years later. Early in July 1944 the MI6 station in Lisbon learned from the subsequently notorious Otto John that an attempt to assassinate Hitler was impending. I doubt if he had any special mission from Canaris, who, dismissed as head of the Abwehr in the previous February, had nothing to offer. His report was nevertheless of interest and importance. But Philby, as practically his last act of Iberian specialism, dismissed it as unreliable. These incidents are of interest now simply as early and unrecognised indications of Philby's treachery. At the time, however, it seemed as if he was adjusting his judgements to the opinions of those in command of MI6. In the first, he appeared to be following the departmental line of suppressing the circulation of information to protect its source. In the second, he seemed to be taking the position of 'professional' caution. That he was also acting in Russia's interests by suppressing indications of divisions within Germany did not occur to any of us.

It remains to ask whether either of these actions had any serious consequence in the deflection of high policy. I am sure they did not. It is true that the first incident came early enough in the war to have made possible, in theory, a reconsideration of the doctrine later enunciated as 'unconditional surrender.' But this would have required the point to be taken at Cabinet level and at that time we had no route to such high quarters. Six months earlier, while Lord Swinton was still in charge of security, this might have happened. Lord Swinton had shown a remarkable insight into the nature of our work and what was significant in it. He spoke with junior officers; he listened; he understood. It is a pleasure to be able to pay tribute to him even at this long interval of time. But by the end of 1942 Lord Swinton was in West Africa; his security tasks had been entrusted to Duff Cooper. Where Lord Swinton saw much and understood all, Duff Cooper was bored by the subject and disapproved its existence. No application to him would have made any impression. By 1944, when the second incident occurred, the possibility of Otto John's report – even if vouched for – making much impression in high quarters scarcely arose.

What conclusions can be drawn from peering into this muddy backwater of the past? First, that the British intelligence services of the war defeated their German counterparts completely. Secondly, that Philby's power for evil was concentrated in the six years that followed the defeat of Germany; before and after those years the practical results of his treachery were small whatever the scandalous enormity of its fact. The British public should therefore be careful not to follow him and his naïve journalistic troubadours into giving to the trivia of secret intelligence a significance they do not possess. It is time to say, as Campbell-Bannerman once said to Balfour, 'enough of this foolery.'

Finally, let us not forget the old truth that eternal vigilance is the price of liberty. The scandals of the past do not remove the needs of the future. The Government's decision to cut the secret service vote by nearly 10 per cent in the coming year is a bad one. We should, then, look to the future and stop puddling in the past. As Miss Millicent Martin was accustomed to wail when keening over the events of the preceding week – 'It is over – let it go.'

Trevor-Roper told Stuart:'I enjoyed your piece in the Spectator *– although of course I insist that I am right about Boodle's & White's. It is the* <u>Broadway professionals</u> *who came from those jolly bars, and they held the top positions. C himself, P{eter} K{och} de G{ooreynd}, Guy Westmacott,[17] Mark Johnson {or Johnston} from White's; rather less grand people like George Pinney … from Boodle's {…}Aeneas was also found in Boodle's, but he let the side down by being efficient. I have just had a letter from his widow {Charlotte}, who says, "Goodness, those Indian policemen, Felix Cowgill (how Aeneas hated him)."'[18]*

Who was right, Stuart or Trevor-Roper? There appears to be truth in both accounts, depending on which part of SIS is under consideration. The number of officers grew from 42 in 1939 to 750 including the Radio Security Service in 1944, an expansion which took SIS well beyond the resources of clubland. On the other hand, when in August 1943 Brigadier Edward Beddington, Deputy Director, Army within MI6, was looking for someone to head SIS in India, he ran into his old friend 'Bogey' {Brigadier Philip Bowden-Smith} at Boodle's and brought him to see Menzies. 'Bogey' got the job. This recruitment was 'in classic SIS fashion', according to the historian of MI6.[19]

SIS naturally turned both to former officers of the armed services, whose experience had taught them what to look for, and to businessmen, journalists and other professional people familiar with foreign countries and the challenges of finding information abroad. Intelligence officers were chosen with a relative informality based on personal acquaintance which reflected wartime urgency and was often vindicated. Philby was the most obvious failure, but as Trevor-Roper emphasised, the error was more culpable at the time of Philby's promotion as victory approached in late 1944 than during the fight for survival of 1941. Trevor-Roper filled his own unit from personal knowledge or recommendation and by these informal methods assembled a group who worked highly effectively both as individuals and as a team.

In 1968 SIS was well aware that the Philby story might damage future recruitment. Its recruitment officer was delighted by Stuart's entry into the Philby controversy and wrote: 'Congratulations on a very telling and welcome piece of prose: it should certainly shake some of the backbiters and get the record looking a bit straighter. It will also, I'm sure, be a help in my own particular job – because inevitably a lot of younger men have been conditioned by their Sunday reading. I happened to run into Dick W this morning, and he was off to read his copy. More power to your pen.'[20]

Stuart's SIS contact wrote to him:

I was most interested to read your piece for the *Spectator*, which I think gives a very fair assessment of the wartime work, even if it is not entirely uncritical of our side of the house! [...] I am taking advantage of [*the recruitment officer's*] visit to Oxford to-day to send you a copy of the [*Philby*] 'Memoirs'. When you have had a chance to read them, I would very much like to call on you again to discuss whether there is any further action you think you could take in this field on our behalf.'

In reply Stuart reassured his SIS contact, 'I did not really mean to be critical of Section V in toto. My dart was aimed at poor Felix Cowgill who, for whatever worthy motives, certainly seemed, and still seems to me, to have made rivalries worse.'[21]

Pleased by Stuart's first article, SIS was eager to influence his review of Philby's memoirs, My Silent War. On 10 September Stuart's SIS contact wrote: 'I am very glad to hear that you have been approached again by the Spectator – your previous piece was clearly well received, as it deserved to be. I should be very pleased to have an opportunity to read your review and to discuss it with you.'[22] The SIS officer duly came up to Oxford to meet Stuart on 18 September. Charles Stuart alerted Trevor-

Roper to his impending review: 'I am trying to compress my thoughts on Philby etc. in the next few days. I agree that his pen-portraits of Vivian and Cowgill are good. But he only rarely deviates into thinking about the problems of intelligence. Graham Greene is AWFUL and I shall certainly have a crack at him. On the whole my advice to readers of the Spectator *will be to buy Trevor-Roper and to borrow Philby from the public library if they must.'*[23]

Charles Stuart, 'Trade Secrets', Reviews of *My Silent War* by Kim Philby and *The Philby Affair* by Hugh Trevor-Roper[24]

The welcome peace of the summer on the Philby front has now been broken by two further publications, one by the protagonist himself. Those who feel that they have had a surfeit of the subject already may now be inclined to shun it. But they would be mistaken to do so. Both these books are of a far higher quality and interest than the ephemeral journalising of the spring. Of course, Philby's own story is partial and spiteful, concerned to obscure the truth on larger issues by a parade of accurate detail on smaller matters. It is, as Professor Trevor-Roper says of it, 'a work of careful and skilful propaganda.' Nevertheless, it is founded on personal experience and has the authenticity that this brings.

Professor Trevor-Roper's book is substantially a reissue of his article published in *Encounter* earlier this year, together with a brilliant essay on Admiral Canaris first published as long ago as 1950. What makes his work one of outstanding interest is the fact that he is concerned with just those larger questions which Philby avoids – the problem of the real function of secret intelligence (which Mr Donald McLachlan has also illuminated in his recent book, *Room 39*), and the objectives of the Soviet government in launching Philby as a weapon of propaganda. On both these points he writes with admirable penetration and in this way he lifts the whole topic out of the sterile bog of spy-story personalia.

It is through this bog that Philby moves with delicate tread, uttering from time to time insincere bleats of comradely affection for his former colleagues. Only very occasionally does he venture out of it, once to outline the organisation of SIS at the beginning of the war, and later to discuss the battle between the vertical and horizontal systems for the postwar reorganisation of the service. Both these discussions, however, are subordinated to his personal story. This emphasis is intentional; his book, he says, is only 'an introductory sketch' and there is more to follow 'in due course.'

In the meantime, his self-satisfied egotism fits him splendidly for the present instalment. His theme is one of self-congratulation on his skilful treachery. His bravery in standing firm to face inquiry after the flight of Maclean and Burgess in 1951 is implicitly contrasted with the cowardice of Krivitsky or Kravchenko,[25] who would not 'risk their necks' by staying in position. But while he acknowledges the civilised limitations of law and convention in the West which made it possible for him to remain there, though long suspected, he does not draw the contrast with the conditions of barbarous tyranny in Russia where suspicion passes for evidence and suspects swiftly disappear. This odious touch of complacent cruelty makes his story distasteful reading, although his character-sketches contain much clever observation. In short, he illuminates the scene, like the moon, with cold reflected light, and, like the moon, he conceals far more of himself than he shows.

The personal kindness which Philby denies to others is granted him in full measure by Professor Trevor-Roper, who, though merciless in his analysis of Philby's intellectual position, speaks of him generously as personally charming and good company. I did not know Philby outside the office and it is possible that my present distaste for him clouds my memory, but in my recollection he exercised no powerful personal charm. The stammer which Professor Trevor-Roper found engaging was for me a source of awkwardness, making our exchanges stilted. It is true that he was normally cooperative and helpful; his desk was not defended against the passing caller, as was Mr Graham Greene's, by rebarbative silence and repulsive demeanour; but his general attitude was too cool and detached to produce any marked attraction. Promotion accentuated this detachment and my last recollection of him is in the Athenaeum in November 1945 when, to borrow one of his own wounding phrases, he was 'running self-importantly to fat.'

If Professor Trevor-Roper is perhaps overgenerous to Philby personally, he is sometimes less than generous to SIS. I do not believe, for example, that even Colonel Vivian considered Philby to have been in touch with the Germans. The situation which I believe he had in mind was a great deal more Irish than that.[26] Nor do I think that Colonel Cowgill's departure was solely the consequence of Philby's intrigues. Cowgill sincerely resisted the reorganisation of intelligence against the Germans in connection with the war; it was this that built up feeling against him inside and outside SIS and which made his removal probable, Philby or no Philby, intrigue or no intrigue.

But these differences of emphasis are of small account. The fascination which Professor Trevor-Roper's book exercises arises from its search for the truth on things that matter, from the characteristic elegance and balance of its construction and from its convincing answers. His analysis of Russian objectives has been amply confirmed by the recent engulfing of Czechoslovakia; his summary of the real function of secret intelligence is lapidary; and his demolition of Mr Le Carré's sociological clap-trap leaves, as Gladstone observed of Purcell's *Life of Manning*, 'nothing for the Day of Judgement.'

Sadly, he has been unable to take similar judicial notice of Mr Graham Greene's strange introduction to Philby's book apart from one sardonic footnote. For this, though shorter than Mr Le Carré's effort, is no more convincing. Mr Greene's verdict, for example, on the statement that Philby betrayed his country is – 'yes, *perhaps* he did.' His gloss on this extraordinary judgement is no less astonishing; 'who among us,' he asks, 'has not committed treason to something or someone more important than a country?' The inconsequence of this is worthy of Mr Wilson at Question Time. At least there is no 'perhaps' about it for Philby. He is a self-confessed traitor and he is proud of it. So Mr Greene's intriguing comparison of his perjury with some seedy individual infidelity will hardly gratify him.

The details of Philby's career are now, as Professor Trevor-Roper concludes, irrelevant. But the Soviet Intelligence Service remains powerful and baleful, as the Czechs are learning.[27] We should not assume that it is any less active among us now than it was thirty or forty years ago. When Philby writes: 'I felt that I knew the *enemy* well,' he means us and he speaks for the Soviet Intelligence Service. Let us be on our guard.

Editor's Notes

Editor's Preface

1 SOC.Dacre 1/2/43, George Kennan to Hugh Trevor-Roper, 5 May 1968.
2 SOC.Dacre 10/54, Walter L. Pforzheimer to Hugh Trevor-Roper, 15 February 1976.
3 SOC.Dacre 6/4, Sir John Masterman to Hugh Trevor-Roper, 11 June 1976.
4 SOC.Dacre 10/48, Dick White to Hugh Trevor-Roper, 10 February 1980.

Editor's Introduction

1 See also Adam Sisman's fascinating study, *Hugh Trevor-Roper: The Biography* (London: Weidenfeld & Nicolson, 2010) and the informative monograph article by P.R.J. Winter, 'A Higher Form of Intelligence: Hugh Trevor-Roper and Wartime British Secret Service', *Intelligence and National Security* 22/6 (2007).
2 F.H. Hinsley and C.A.G. Simkins, *British Intelligence in the Second World War. Vol. 4: Security and Counter-Intelligence* (London: HMSO, 1990), p. 13; Philip H.J. Davies, *MI6 and the Machinery of Spying* (London: Frank Cass, 2004), p. 144; John Court Curry, *The Security Service, 1908–1945: The Official History* (Kew: Public Record Office, 1999), pp. 143–4.
3 Maurice P.A. Hankey (1877–1963) was educated at Rugby and the Royal Naval College, created the Cabinet secretariat in 1916. He served as secretary to the Cabinet and to the Committee of Imperial Defence from 1923 to 1938 and was raised to the peerage in 1936.
4 The National Archives United Kingdom (henceforth TNA) WO 208/5096, 'Leakage of Information about Military and Other Movements in this Country': Report by the Minister without Portfolio, 28 September 1939.
5 Ernest Walter Brudenell Gill (b. 1883) was educated at Bristol Grammar School and Christ Church Oxford; his recreations were 'riding', 'rebuking sin' and 'wireless research' (*Who's Who 1941* (London: Adam and Charles Black, 1941).
6 SOC.Dacre 6/34 and 13/29; TNA KV 4/170, 'Introduction to Organisation and Method for C.E. Work' [by Dick White, 1942].

7   Dacre, 'Sideways into SIS', see below.

8   Guy Maynard Liddell (1892–1958) won the MC in World War I and joined Special Branch in 1919. In 1931 he moved to MI5 and earned a reputation as one of its most accomplished officers. In 1940 he was appointed as director of MI5's B Division. Under his guidance, B Division was remarkably successful against Nazi spies. Some of Liddell's staffing decisions were less fortunate: he recruited Anthony Blunt into his own division and unsuccessfully recommended Guy Burgess to another MI5 division (Christopher Andrew, *The Defence of the Realm: The Authorized History of MI5* (London: Allen Lane, 2009), pp. 269 and 272).

9   Thomas Argyll 'Tar' Robertson (1909–94) was educated at Charterhouse and Sandhurst. After serving in the Seaforth Highlanders, he joined MI5. As head of Division B's 1a sub-section he built up the system of double agents which made possible the implementation and monitoring of the deception which covered the invasion of Normandy in 1944. After the war he controlled security at Government Communications Headquarters (GCHQ). Trevor-Roper remembered him as 'affable, genial, charming [...] totally modest and unassuming' (SOC.Dacre 6/34/3).

10 Dick Goldsmith White (1906–93) was educated at Bishop's Stortford College and Christ Church. Recruited by MI5 in January 1936, he specialised in counter-espionage against German intelligence. He was appointed director general of MI5 in 1953 and in 1956 moved sideways to become the first civilian head of MI6. He remains the only person ever to have been head of both services. In 1968 he was appointed the first intelligence coordinator in the Cabinet Office, where he stayed until his retirement in 1972.

11 Dacre, 'Sideways into S.I.S.', see pp. 36–7; F.H. Hinsley, with E.E. Thomas, C.A.G. Simkins and C.F.G. Ransom, *British Intelligence in the Second World War: Its Influence on Strategy and Operations. Vol. 1* (London: HMSO, 1979), p. 120; Hinsley and Simkins, *British Intelligence. Vol. 4*, p. 44 and Appendix 3, 'Technical Problems Affecting Radio Communications by the Double-Cross Agents: Notes Written by a Former MI5 Officer ['Tar' Robertson] from his Personal Experience', pp. 311–12.

12 TNA WO 208/5097, Interception Work of R.S.S., 19 November 1940 [by E.W.B. Gill]; KV4/170, 'Introduction to Organisation' and 'Mr Dick White' (1944). Dick White wrote that the first German Secret Service cipher was 'actually cracked by amateurs', i.e. not by Bletchley Park, a statement which supports Trevor-Roper's account. There remains uncertainty over the date for the first breach of the Abwehr hand-cipher. Dick White gave it as 29 January 1940. Hinsley and Simkins (*British Intelligence, Vol. 4*, p. 44) state the cipher had been broken by March 1940.

13 Oliver Strachey (1874–1960), brother of the writer Lytton and a concert pianist manqué, joined the code-breaking unit of the War Office in 1915, transferring to the GC & CS on its establishment in 1919.

14 TNA KV 4/170, R.S.S. and M.I.6, 15 September 1942; Hinsley and Simkins, *British Intelligence. Vol. 4*, p. 44; Curry, *The Security Service*, p. 178.

15 Sisman, *Trevor-Roper*, p. 86.

16 Hinsley and Simkins, *British Intelligence. Vol. 4*, pp. 88–9; TNA KV 4/120, B.1.B. to DGSS, 27 July 1942.

17 Nigel West and Oleg Tsarev, *The Crown Jewels: The British Secrets at the Heart of the KGB Archive* (London: HarperCollins, 1998), pp. 146–7.

18 John Felix Cowgill had joined Section V of SIS in 1939 from the Indian Police, where he was serving as a deputy commissioner in charge of the Calcutta Special Branch. He had previously carried out counter-terrorist work in Bengal and served in the Intelligence Bureau of the government of India, gaining an OBE in 1935.

19 Hinsley and Simkins, *British Intelligence. Vol. 4*, pp. 72–3; TNA KV 4/170, R.S.S. and M.I.6., 15 September 1942.

20 Philip Cunliffe-Lister, first Earl of Swinton (1884–1972), was a senior Conservative politician who took particular interest in security and intelligence matters.

21 Sir David Petrie (1879–1961) gained an MA at Aberdeen University and joined the Indian Police in 1900, rising to become director of the Intelligence Bureau of the government of India in 1924. He was particularly successful in preventing the formation of communist cells and was knighted in 1929.

22 Hinsley and Simkins, *British Intelligence. Vol. 4*, p. 53; Curry, *The Security Service*, p. 182.

23 Richard 'Pop' Gambier-Parry (1894–1965) was educated at Eton and served with distinction in the Royal Welch Fusiliers and in the Royal Flying Corps during World War I. More a radio expert than an intelligence officer, he was promoted brigadier in 1942. Trevor-Roper recalled Gambier-Parry as 'a robust and genial extrovert [...] with some of the qualities more often associated with Harrow than with Eton: he was jovial, flamboyant, and somewhat loud in voice and tastes' (SOC.Dacre 6/34/4).

24 Curry, *The Security Service*, p. 43; Hinsley and Simkins, *British Intelligence. Vol. 4*, p. 9; Geoffrey Pidgeon, *The Secret Wireless War: The Story of MI6 Communications, 1939–1945* (London: UPSO, 2003), pp. 16–17.

25 TNA WO 208/5095, D. Petrie to Lord Swinton, 30 January 1941; Swinton to Major-General F.H.N. Davidson, no date [early February 1941].

26 Davies, *MI6*, pp. 146–7; King's College London, Liddell Hart Centre for Military Archives (hereafter LHCMA) Davidson Papers 4/1 entry for 13 March 1941.

27 Charles Stuart Papers; SOC.Dacre 6/34.

28 'Hence those tears'; TNA KV 4/170, R.S.S. and M.I.6., 15 September 1942.

29 SOC.Dacre 6/34. Trevor-Roper knew Gambier-Parry through fox-hunting.

30 SOC.Dacre 6/34/4.

31 The German armed forces, police and railways used the Enigma machine to generate codes which they believed were unbreakable despite much evidence to the contrary.

32 Alfred Dillwyn 'Dilly' Knox (1884–1943) was a classical scholar and fellow of King's College Cambridge until World War I, when he took up codebreaking. When puzzling over a cipher he was known to stuff his pipe with sandwiches.

33 The Sicherheitsdienst or SD.

34 TNA ADM 223/298, NID 12, Selections from History 1940–1945.

35 TNA, KV 4/188, entry for 12 June 1941.

36 SOC.Dacre 6/34/2; 10/54, Hugh Trevor-Roper to Dick White, 21 July 1983. Christ Church was a men's college during Trevor-Roper's time as an undergraduate and tutor. It accepted women undergraduates from 1980.

37 John Cecil 'JC' Masterman (1891–1977) was educated as a naval cadet but won a scholarship to Oxford, where he taught modern history at Christ Church from 1919, was elected provost of Worcester College in 1946 and served as vice-chancellor in 1957–8. During the war he worked in MI5 as chairman of the Twenty Committee which supervised the information provided to double agents controlled in the United Kingdom. Masterman was knighted in 1959. In the teeth of bitter opposition from official circles, he later published a book about his wartime service, *The Double Cross System in the War of 1939 to 1945* (New Haven, CT and London: Yale University Press, 1972).

38 Charles Harborne Stuart (1920–91) was educated at Harrow and Christ Church, where in 1948 he was appointed student (tutorial fellow) in modern history. Stuart's incisive approach made him an exemplary tutor as well as an authority on eighteenth-century British history, which he taught with memorable enthusiasm.

39 Colin Matthew, 'Charles Harborne Stuart', *Christ Church Report* (1991) p. 39.

40 Sisman, *Hugh Trevor-Roper*, pp. 56–7 and 64–7; SOC.Dacre 6/34/4. Gilbert Ryle (1900–76), author of *The Concept of Mind* (1949), was particularly interested in the meaning of concepts.

41 TNA KV 4/191, 5 January 1943.

42 Stuart Newton 'the gazelle' Hampshire (1914–2004) was educated at Repton and Balliol College Oxford. He enlisted in the army at the outbreak of war, but transferred to intelligence because he had difficulty assembling a gun. After 1945 Hampshire acquired great distinction as a moral philosopher and taught at London, Oxford and Princeton universities before his election as

warden of Wadham College in 1970. He was knighted in 1979 and moved to Stanford University in 1984.

43 Sisman, *Hugh Trevor-Roper*, p. 96; SOC.Dacre 6/34/4.

44 (D'Arcy) Patrick Reilly (1909–99) was educated at Winchester and New College Oxford and elected a fellow of All Souls in 1932. He joined the Foreign Office the following year and was seconded to the Ministry of Economic Warfare in 1939 and to SIS in May 1942. After his particularly demanding spell with Menzies, Reilly was posted to Algiers in October 1943 to assist the British minister resident, Harold Macmillan.

45 Charles Stuart Papers; Bodleian Library MS Eng c. 6918, fol. 232.

46 TNA HW 19/331.

47 Valentine 'VV' or 'Val' Vivian (1886–1969) was educated at St Paul's School and served as a criminal intelligence officer in the Punjab until 1914. He joined SIS in 1923 and two years later became head of its counter-espionage section. By 1941 he was deputy chief of the Secret Intelligence Service (DCSS) as well as director of security. According to Trevor-Roper, Vivian was 'a gelatinous but serpentine character, with affectations of culture, he reminded me of Uriah Heep' (SOC.Dacre 6/34/4). For his part, Vivian considered Trevor-Roper 'a rather undesirable channel' for information (TNA KV 4/195, entry for 18 November 1944).

48 Davies, *MI6*, p. 148.

49 TNA KV 4/97, W.1 [Frost] to 'B' [Liddell] 19 May 1941; 'First Meeting of Joint S.I.S. & S.S. Wireless Committee', 20 May 1941.

50 Herbert L.A. Hart (1907–92) was educated at Bradford Grammar School and New College Oxford. After his wartime service in MI5, Hart returned to Oxford to teach philosophy. His distinction as a legal philosopher brought him election to the chair of jurisprudence in 1952, though he refused a knighthood in 1966. In 1973 he became principal of Brasenose College. In 1983 Hart suffered a nervous breakdown after both his wife's pre-war Communism and his own service in MI5 drew press attention.

51 TNA KV 4/188, entry for 5 July 1941.

52 TNA KV 4/188, entry for 25 August 1941.

53 TNA KV 4/188, entry for 1 September 1941.

54 TNA KV 4/188, entry for 9 September 1941.

55 TNA ADM 223/298, NID 12, Selections from History 1940–1945.

56 H.A.R. 'Kim' Philby (1912–88) was educated at Westminster School and Trinity College Cambridge. Philby was a Soviet spy from 1934. In autumn 1941 he was appointed head of the Iberian sub-section of Cowgill's Section V.

57 TNA KV 4/217, A.D.B.1 [White] to D.B. [Liddell], 4 April 1942.

58 TNA KV 4/217, [Liddell] to Vivian, 22 April 1942.

59 Sisman, *Hugh Trevor-Roper*, p. 90.

60 SOC.Dacre 10/44, Hugh Trevor-Roper to Ralph Erskine, 9 December 1996. 'C' or 'CSS' denoted the Chief of the Secret [Intelligence] Service, namely Sir Stewart Menzies (1890–1968), old Etonian and decorated Guards officer. Reputed to be an illegitimate son of Edward VII, Menzies headed the military intelligence section of SIS until autumn 1939, when he won the contest to become chief, with support from the Foreign Office.

61 SOC.Dacre 6/4, Hugh Trevor-Roper to Ronald Lewin, 8 December 1977.

62 Sisman, *Hugh Trevor-Roper*, p. 104.

63 Frederick Alexander 'the Prof' Lindemann (1866–1957), student (senior member) of Christ Church and head of Oxford's Clarendon Laboratory; from 1941 he was Baron Cherwell.

64 Nuffield College Oxford, Cherwell Papers K 295/1–5, Hugh Trevor-Roper to 'My dear Prof', 22 February 1942. The comment about gramophone salesmen is a reference to Gambier-Parry's former calling.

65 Nuffield College Oxford, Cherwell Papers, K 295/6, Hugh Trevor-Roper to 'Dear Prof', 15 April 1942.

66 Nuffield College Oxford, Cherwell Papers K295/7–8, Hugh Trevor-Roper to 'My dear Prof', 10 May 1942 and 'Interception and Intercepted Intelligence'.

67 Sir Edward W.H. 'Jumbo' Travis (1888–1956) was made de facto head of Bletchley Park by Menzies in February 1942 and its formal director in March 1944. Travis wrote in brown ink known as 'the director's blood'.

68 Nigel Arthur 'the dormouse' de Grey (1886–1951) had distinguished himself in 1917 by decoding a telegram from the German Foreign Minister Arthur Zimmermann which led to America's entry into the war. In 1939 he joined Bletchley to work on Enigma traffic.

69 TNA HW 14/35, V.w.21/30/3/42, 'An Italian Network'; [Travis] to CSS, 21 April 1942; H.R. Trevor-Roper to CSS, 27 April 1942; Trevor-Roper's liason with Hut 4 [by Nigel de Grey] 28 April and Trevor-Roper's Research into Italian Naval Messages, 29 April 1942.

70 TNA HW 14/36, P.F.G. Twinn to Commander Travis, 4 May 1942.

71 Peter Koch de Gooreynd was from a Belgian banking family. After Eton he became a music entrepreneur. As principal staff officer to the Chief of the Secret Service (PSO/CSS) he dealt with issues concerning the armed services, wireless and cryptography. After the war he returned to business but eventually went bankrupt and had to resign from White's, a prominent gentlemen's club in London.

72 Charles Stuart Papers.

73 TNA KV 4/97, 'S.S. & S.I.S. Wireless Committee Minutes', 5 December 1942 and Annexe, 9 December 1942.

74 KV 4/97, Guy Liddell minute of 21 December 1942.

75 TNA KV 4/191, entry for 11 December 1942.

76 TNA KV 4/97, V. Vivan to G.M. Liddell, 24 December 1942; 4/98, DB [Liddell] to Colonel Vivian, SIS, 8 and 15 January 1943; V. Vivian to Captain G.M. Liddell, 23 January 1943.

77 Charles Stuart Papers, 1943 pocket diary, entry for Wednesday 3 February.

78 KV 4/98, Draft Letter from C.S.S. to Mr Duff Cooper; GML to Colonel V. Vivian, 19 February 1943.

79 Probably Stuart and Hampshire: Ryle was equally congenial, but idiosyncratic. He was left behind when the other three were seconded in 1945: see page 24.

80 Sir Denys Lionel Page (1908–78) was student (tutorial fellow) in Greek from 1932 at Christ Church, where he taught Trevor-Roper; he spent the war years at Bletchley Park. In 1950 he was elected Regius Professor of Greek at Cambridge University, where he later became master of Jesus College. In a draft for a memoir (which he did not complete) Trevor-Roper described Page as 'a true scholar', 'a lifelong friend, and an ally and colleague in secret intelligence during the war' (SOC.Dacre 6/34/2).

81 Nuffield College Oxford, Cherwell Papers K 295/11, Hugh Trevor-Roper to 'Dear Prof', 17 December 1942.

82 Nuffield College Oxford, Cherwell Papers K 295/12, Cherwell to Trevor-Roper, 24 December 1942.

83 TNA ADM 223/298, 'German Appreciation of Allied Intentions', NID 12, 20 July 1945.

84 E.D.R. Harrison, 'On Secret Service for the Duce: Umberto Campini in Portuguese East Africa, 1941–1943', *English Historical Review* 122/499 (2007), pp. 1137–8.

85 TNA HW 34/5.

86 TNA KV 4/217, A.D.B.1. [White] to D.B. [Liddell], 14 March 1943.

87 TNA KV 4/217, DB [Liddell] to C [Menzies], 22 March 1943; Sisman, *Hugh Trevor-Roper*, p. 118.

88 Curry, *The Security Service*, p. 212; Sir Patrick Reilly to E.D.R. Harrison, 15 April 1993; Charles Stuart Papers.

89 Keith Jeffery, *MI6: The History of the Secret Intelligence Service, 1909–1949* (London: Bloomsbury, 2011), p. 565; F.H. Hinsley with E.E.Thomas, C.F.G. Ransom and R.C. Knight, *British Intelligence in the Second World War: Its Influence on Strategy and Operations. Vol. 2* (London: HMSO, 1981), p. 66.

90 HW 34/23, Telegram to Moscow, CXG 49, 31 August 1943.

91 HW 34/23, Ted [Maltby] to 'Dear Felix', 11 September 1943; V [Cowgill] to Lt Col Maltby. During a discussion about providing other material to the Soviet Union, Liddell noted that Cowgill's 'contribution has been that since the Russians are only in part our allies, not having declared war on Japan, we are not under any obligation to give them anything. It is difficult to imagine a narrower or more stupid point of view [...] Some people think

that Felix is going off his rocker' (TNA KV 4/192, entries for 29 and 30 August 1943).

92 HW 34/23, KdG PSO/CSS to Lt Col Maltby [no date], EFM [Maltby] to Lt Col Cowgill, 20 September 1943, [Cowgill] note to Col M.

93 Hinsley et al., *British Intelligence. Vol. 2*, p. 66; Jeffery, *MI6*, pp. 565–6.

94 TNA HW 19/347, R.I.S. 1, 5 June 1943.

95 TNA HW 19/347, R.I.S. 1, 5 June 1943.

96 Leonard Robert Palmer (1906–84) was educated at Trinity College Cambridge and taught classics at Manchester University until 1941. An expert on Mycenaean texts and post-Ptolemaic papyri, after the war Palmer was successively Professor of Greek at King's College London and Professor of Comparative Philology at Oxford.

97 TNA HW 19/347, PIN 11/L.R.P., 8 June 1943.

98 TNA HW 19/347, HRT-R to [Patrick] Reilly, 11 June 1943.

99 KV 4/191, entry for 19 June 1943. Stuart Hampshire was the author of the document in question.

100 Michael Wildt, *Generation des Unbedingten. Das Führungskorps des Reichssicherheitshauptamtes* (Hamburg: Hamburger Edition, 2003), pp. 702–4.

101 TNA HW 19/333, No. 4325, 'Germany. Decline of the Abwehr', 24 March 1944.

102 TNA HW 19/347, R.I.S. 33, 2 September 1944 [by Stuart Hampshire and Charles Stuart].

103 TNA KV 4/100, Note of a Meeting Held in the Director-General's Room at 5 p.m. on 23 November, 1944, to Consider the SHAEF Proposals for the Creation of a German War Room in London; Tim Milne, *Kim Philby* (London: Biteback Publishing, 2014), pp. 145–6.

104 Ian Innes 'Tim' Milne (1912–2010) was educated at Westminster School with Philby, who recommended him to SIS. He joined Section V in 1941 and became its head in 1945. Milne stayed in SIS until 1969, when he began a new career as a senior clerk in the House of Commons.

105 Supreme Headquarters Allied Expeditionary Force.

106 TNA KV 4/195, entries for 13, 22 and 30 November 1944, 4/196, entries for 8 and 15 January 1945.

107 TNA WO 208/4701, 'History of the Counter Intelligence War Room'.

108 TNA KV 4/196, entry for 5 February 1945.

109 SOC.Dacre 10/45, draft reply to Cowgill's letter.

110 TNA WO 208/4701, 'History of the Counter Intelligence War Room'.

111 SOC.Dacre 9/13, 'The German Intelligence Service and the War'.

112 SOC.Dacre 10/44, 'The German Intelligence Service and the War'.

113 SOC.Dacre 9/13, 'The German Intelligence Service and the War'.

114 Ibid.; in RIS 27 of 31 March 1944 Stuart Hampshire emphasised the personnel continuity of Department 3 (TNA HW 19/347).

115 SOC.Dacre 9/13, 'The German Intelligence Service and the War'.

116 Ibid.

117 Ibid.

118 Ibid. This paragraph partly foreshadows both in content and phrasing p. 2 of *The Last Days of Hitler* (London: Macmillan, 1947).

119 SOC.Dacre 9/13, 'The German Intelligence Service and the War'.

120 SOC.Dacre 10/44, 'The German Intelligence Service and the War'.

121 SOC.Dacre 10/20, Sir Dick White to Lord Dacre, June 1985; Hugh Trevor-Roper, *The Wartime Journals*, edited by Richard Davenport-Hines (London: I.B.Tauris, 2012), p. 263.

122 TNA WO 208/3787, C.I.B. [Dick White] to Lt Col T.A. Robertson, 10 September 1945, Counter Intelligence War Room [T.A. Robertson] to Brigadier D.G. White, 14 and 19 September 1945.

123 SOC.Dacre 10/49, Hugh Trevor-Roper to Peter Strafford, 6 August 1985.

124 SOC.Dacre 13/29: 338-9; H.R. Trevor-Roper, 'Introduction to the Third Edition', in *The Last Days of Hitler* (London: Macmillan 2002), pp. xxvii and xxxvi.

125 Trevor-Roper, 'Introduction', pp. xxvi–xxvii; SOC.Dacre 10/20, Trevor-Roper to Leslie Randall, 6 February 1946.

126 SOC.Dacre 10/28, 'The Death of Hitler'.

127 SOC.Dacre 10/20, 'The Enquiry into Hitler's End'.

128 SOC.Dacre 10/7, Willi Johannmeier HRT-R, 17 December 1945.

129 SOC.Dacre 13/58, entries in Trevor-Roper's pocket diaries for December 1945 and January 1946; SOC.Dacre 10/7, Willi Johannmeier HRT-R, 17 December 1945 and CSDIC (WEA) to IB, 21 December 1945; SOC.Dacre 10/7, Wilhelm Zander H.R. Trevor-Roper, Major. Int. Corps, 1 January 1946; SOC.Dacre 13/29.

130 SOC.Dacre 10/20, 'The Enquiry into Hitler's End'; SOC.Dacre 10/7, Fortnightly Notes: The Discovery of Hitler's Wills and Third Interrogation of Willi Johannmeier; Sisman, *Hugh Trevor-Roper*, p. 349.

131 The Hon. Peter Ramsbotham (1919–2010) was educated at Eton and Magdalen College Oxford. He joined the Foreign Office in 1948, was awarded a KCMG in 1972 and appointed ambassador to Washington in 1974.

132 SOC.Dacre 10/7, Major P.E. Ramsbotham to Trevor-Roper, 7 January 1946.

133 SOC.Dacre 13/29, 367–8; Hugh Trevor-Roper, 'Recherchen der ersten Stunde. Hugh Trevor-Roper ueber "Hitlers Letzte Tage"', in Henning Ritter (ed.), *Werksbesichtigung Geisteswissenschaften. Fuenfundzwanzig Buecher von ihren Autoren gelesen* (Frankfurt am Main: Insel Verlag, 1990), p. 44.

134 SOC.Dacre 10/31 and 10/30, Hugh Trevor-Roper to Macmillan, 22 May 1946.

135 SOC.Dacre 10/30, 'Extract from Minutes of the Meeting held on 14th June 1946'.

136 SOC.Dacre 1/2/1, Patrick Reilly to Hugh Trevor-Roper, 27 November 1950.

1 Sideways into SIS

1 First published in Hayden B. Peake and Samuel Halpern (ed.), *In the Name of Intelligence: Essays in Honor of Walter Pforzheimer* (Washington, DC: NIBC Press, 1994), pp. 251–7.

2 The office which developed into MI5 only dated back to 1909.

3 A combination of two slightly different high radio frequencies producing an audible lower frequency.

4 Jeffery, *MI6*, pp. 307 and 805.

5 Ibid., p. 486.

6 SOC.Dacre 6/4.

7 According to a report Philby sent to Moscow dated 30 October 1941, by then Section V had a regional department, VB1, consisting of two officers working on Scandinavia and Germany (West and Tsarev, *The Crown Jewels*, p. 310). Later in the war a Berlin station-in-waiting, P.6, was established (Jeffery, *MI6*, p. 546). Only in 1944 did Cowgill belatedly establish a well-staffed new sub-section (Vf) for Germany: Milne, *Kim Philby*, p. 128.

8 Stewart Menzies, chief of the secret service.

9 SOC.Dacre 6/34.

10 Ewen E.S. Montagu (1901–85) was educated at Westminster, Harvard and Trinity College Cambridge. A barrister by profession, from 1941 he worked in the Naval Intelligence Division of the Admiralty, where he played a leading part in Operation *Mincemeat*, a deception to cover the landings in Sicily. In 1953 Montagu published an account of this operation entitled *The Man who Never Was*. His book was written over a weekend; it sold more than 2 million copies.

11 Brian Trevor-Roper Melland's mother was Trevor-Roper's paternal aunt. After the war Melland worked in the Historical Section of the Cabinet Office.

12 Sir John Pope-Hennessy (1913–94) was a historian of Renaissance art. Bernard Berenson caustically observed that Pope-Hennessy 'has many gifts as a scholar, is good, helpful, and yet his dull aspect, his voice, his old maidish, rather surly, camel-like look, puts me off' (Hugh Trevor-Roper, *Letters from Oxford: Hugh Trevor-Roper to Bernard Berenson*, edited by Richard Davenport-Hines (London: Weidenfeld & Nicolson, 2006), p. 241).

13 Trevor-Roper recalled elsewhere in his unpublished memoirs that Hampshire and Stuart had returned 'frustrated and furious. Philby had refused to argue, or to listen to argument: he simply vetoed. At one point, as they were describing their conversation, Charles Stuart hit the table with his fist and exploded, "There is something <u>wrong</u> with Philby!" There was indeed, but we did not then know, or guess, what it was' (SOC.Dacre 6/34/3). There was another source on Abwehr/SD conflict beyond Philby's control. By the end of 1942 this power struggle was also being reported by the SIS agent *Outcast* run from Stockholm (Jeffery, *MI6*, p. 516).

14 This is an unlikely date for such a confrontation, as by May 1943 Trevor-Roper was already highly regarded by MI5 and appreciated by Menzies, who realised his young wireless expert was an asset in relations with the Security Service. Retrospectively Trevor-Roper appears to have conflated the circumstances of two vivid but separate events: the most dramatic confrontation of his service in intelligence, and the achievement of autonomy by his unit. The uncertainty of his memory is revealed by his statement that 'at a date of which I have no record (but I think it must have been in April 1943) I was summoned by C' (SOC.Dacre 10/46, letter to Patrick Reilly, 26 January 1981). The only available record of such a meeting points to the date 14 April 1942.

2 Admiral Canaris

1 Wilhelm Canaris, 'Politik und Wehrmacht', in Richard Donnevert (ed.), *Wehrmacht und Partei* (Leipzig: Verlag von Johann Ambrosius Barth, 1938), pp. 49–51.

2 Adam Sisman, 'Letter to the Editor', *Journal of Military History* 75/3 (2011), pp. 1003–4.

3 Ibid.

4 This foreword is an abbreviation of the original foreword to the William Kimber edition of *The Philby Affair*.

5 The phrase 'penetrated from afar' refers to Britain's ability to decipher German secret service codes.

6 Broadway Buildings, opposite St James's Park underground station, provided the London headquarters for the British Secret Intelligence Service (SIS), which Trevor-Roper usually refers to as the secret service; Whaddon Hall was the home of the SIS wireless section. The Abwehr's headquarters occupied an old block of flats at 47–9 Tirpitz-Ufer, from where Canaris could slip into Wehrmacht HQ in the Bendlerstrasse without crossing the street.

7   The particular attraction of Spain was that it could provide observation points to watch Allied ships moving in and out of the Mediterranean, and intelligence about this traffic was of great interest to the German Armed Forces whom Canaris served. In 1942 Canaris visited Spain under a false name and accompanied by three senior officers no fewer than five times in six months. The British ambassador complained to the Spanish dictator Francisco Franco, who merely laughed.

8   Ulrich von Hassell (1881–1944) was a career diplomat who had served as German ambassador in Rome until February 1938. During the following years he strongly influenced the foreign policy ideas of the German Resistance and became its foreign minister designate. After the failure of the July Plot, Hassell was tried by the Nazi People's Court and executed. He left behind a remarkable personal record of his daily activities during the years of resistance. Trevor-Roper was sent the first edition of von Hassell's diaries in December 1946 from Switzerland by a German acquaintance. Entitled *Vom Andern Deutschland* (Zurich: Atlantis Verlag, 1946), this early edition comprised two-thirds of the diaries. There is now an almost complete edition: Ulrich von Hassell, *Die Hassell-Tagebücher 1938–1944 Aufzeichnungen vom anderen Deutschland*, edited by Friedrich Freiherr Hiller von Gaertringen (Berlin: Siedler Verlag, 1988). In reading the original edition Trevor-Roper followed his usual practice of making frequent pencil markings in the margins and, on the endpapers, of summarising the book with the page numbers of points which specially interested him. He told the war correspondent Chester Wilmot that 'the light shed on the whole group, & particularly on Goerdeler, by v. Hassell, is extraordinarily interesting – & depressing [...] [They] were politically very inferior people, mumping conservatives with no ideas at all, and not even aware of the Plot of 20 July; also extremely divided, defeatist, and indiscreet' (LHCMA 15/15/162, Hugh Trevor-Roper to Chester Wilmot, 29 December 1946 and 4 January 1947).

9   The Röhm Putsch of June 1934 during which many Nazi stormtroop leaders were murdered by the SS to appease the army and its supreme commander Reich President von Hindenburg.

10 The Reich Security Head Office (RSHA) directed the activities of the Gestapo and the Nazi Security Service, or SD. The RSHA combined Nazi Party and traditional state functions to carry out the security mission entrusted to Himmler by Hitler as Führer.

11 Erwin Lahousen Edler von Vivremont (1897–1955) was a much-decorated Austrian veteran of World War I who by 1935 headed the information service in the Ministry of Defence. Following Hitler's annexation of Austria, Lahousen was recruited for the Abwehr. In March 1943 he took part in an unsuccessful but fortunately unnoticed attempt to assassinate Hitler. In

August the same year he was transferred from intelligence duties to the command of troops, but came to the Gestapo's attention in the aftermath of the July Plot.

12　Colonel-General Ludwig Beck (1880–1945) was Chief of Army General Staff from 1935 to 1938, when he resigned in protest over Hitler's willingness to risk war with the Western powers. Designated by the military resisters as head of state for the new Germany, Beck was executed late on 20 July 1944 by order of Colonel-General Friedrich Fromm. Fromm was marginally involved in the conspiracy, and may have acted so swiftly either to save other conspirators or himself, or because he felt dishonoured when the plotters tied him up, as his biographer has suggested.

13　Carl Goerdeler (1884–1945) served as mayor of Leipzig until he resigned in protest when the Nazis removed a statue of Felix Mendelssohn. Although Goerdeler consistently rejected Hitler's regime, he lost influence within the resistance due to his reluctance to contemplate the tyrant's assassination, and saw the failure of Stauffenberg's bomb plot against Hitler as 'God's judgement' on such methods. Goerdeler's scruples did not save him from execution on 2 February 1945.

14　This paragraph was added in the Kimber edition.

15　Gustav Noske (1868–1946) was an exceptionally eloquent Social Democrat politician who belonged to the pragmatic wing of the party. He served as minister for the armed forces from February 1919, but he failed to anticipate the Kapp Putsch of March 1920 during which military elements made an unsuccessful attempt to seize power.

16　Karl Liebknecht (1871–1919) was the only Social Democrat Reichstag member who voted against providing money for war in 1914. After the war Liebknecht insisted on the formation of a separate Communist Party. In early January 1919 the Communists tried and failed to seize power in Berlin. In the aftermath Liebknecht was murdered.

17　Rosa Luxemburg (1871–1919) was a Socialist theoretician and revolutionary of remarkable charisma. Initially a Social Democrat, she denounced revisionism, imperialism and militarism with impartial vigour. At the end of 1918 she was an influential force in the establishment of the German Communist Party. The following month she was murdered with Liebknecht and their bodies thrown into a canal.

18　Grand Admiral Erich Raeder (1876–1960), Commander in Chief of the German Navy and Chief of Naval Warfare from 1935, deployed his surface forces in bold but costly operations after the outbreak of war, particularly the successful invasion of Norway in April 1940. After violent disagreements with Hitler, who wished to conserve the remaining German heavy warships, Raeder resigned as Commander in Chief in January 1943.

19 In an earlier draft of the review Trevor-Roper explained this point in more depth: 'Secret Services, like any other highly organised monopolies, are bureaucracies [...]. They have the same basic rules and weaknesses, and require the same qualities in their highest executives. This is a fact which anyone experienced in administration must know. But Hitler and the Nazi leaders were not experienced in administration. They were adventurers who had never held a regular job but passed straight from the streets to the summit of power. Moreover, Hitler personally had the mind of a reader of novelettes. He liked thrills and stunts, intuitive results, miraculous achievements, and everything of a colossal size. The patient workings of exact science and efficient routine were foreign to his mind. Just as he surrounded himself with quack miracle-doctors instead of scrupulous experts, so, in intelligence work, he required sudden, mysterious and gigantic results. All the Nazis seem to have been hypnotised by their conception – an absurdly romantic conception – of the British Secret Service. In the headquarters of the Gestapo in Berlin I discovered, in 1945, quantities of official, secret, numbered books about the British Secret Service: they describe British intelligence about as accurately as Tarzan of the Apes describes life in Africa' (SOC.Dacre 9/15/1).

20 'Babu-ji' was widely used in India as a term of respect meaning 'sir'; without the suffix it had the pejorative connotation of someone with an inadequate veneer of European letters.

21 Baroness Emma 'Emmuska' Orczy de Orczi (1865–1947) was a British writer born in Hungary to a noble family which fled into exile. She was famous for her novels about 'the Scarlet Pimpernel', who rescued French aristocrats from the guillotine. Edward Phillips Oppenheim (1866–1946) was a prolific and extremely popular author of novels about intrigue in high society, the German menace and international espionage.

22 Three of the books Trevor-Roper found in Gestapo Headquarters were included in the posthumous sale of his working library. A copy of the *Informationsheft G.B.* (Berlin, 1940) was on offer for £2,500.

23 In 1938 Canaris had written, 'One cannot try to do two things simultaneously, both of which require total commitment' (Canaris, 'Politik und Wehrmacht', p. 51).

24 In the *Cornhill* edition Trevor-Roper had written 'the dictatorship of the German proletariat'.

25 All but three sentences of this paragraph were added for the Kimber edition.

26 In this paragraph, most of which he added for the Kimber edition, Trevor-Roper mentions that the Germans were misinformed via the Abwehr about the Normandy invasion. This was not widely known in 1968, though the deception before the invasion of Sicily was already common knowledge.

27 The part of this sentence revealing British success against Abwehr hand- and machine-ciphers was added for the Kimber addition. Trevor-Roper himself broke an Abwehr hand-cipher in early 1940 (see above), the first time this had been done within British intelligence, but the principal Abwehr hand-cipher was only decrypted later in the year.

28 Colonel (General Staff) Hans 'Piecki' Piekenbrock enjoyed the complete confidence of Canaris. Michael Howard characterises him as 'an anti-Nazi officer of the old school who not only tolerated but appeared to encourage extreme inefficiency in his subordinates. Under his genial and relaxed regime posts were left unfilled, officers were encouraged to take extended leave, files got lost, reports, if made, were seldom read and even more seldom checked' (Michael Howard, *British Intelligence in the Second World War. Vol. 5: Strategic Deception* (London: HMSO, 1990), p. 48).

29 Colonel (General Staff) Egbert 'Benti' von Bentivegni was a professional soldier from a family of Prussian officers. He invariably wore a monocle, through which he contemplated without enthusiasm Canaris's opposition to Hitler. Piekenbrock, Lahousen and Bentivegni were sent on active service in 1943 as a matter of routine so they could qualify for promotion.

30 Non-belligerency meant ostensible neutrality during which Franco in practice favoured one side, namely the Axis. In 1940 Franco declared that Britain had lost the war and his policy became one of 'malignant neutrality', as it was termed by the British official historian Sir Llewellyn Woodward.

31 *Bodden* was an attempt to deploy infra-red instruments to monitor Allied convoys; it took its name from the Greifswalder Bodden, the stretch of water at the eastern entrance to the straits separating the island of Rügen from the north German coast. The Greifswalder Bodden resembles the eastern approaches to the Straits of Gibraltar.

32 The Vermehrens were added for the 1968 edition. Dr Erich Vermehren had worked since October 1942 as deputy to Paul Leverkuehn, the head of the Abwehr in Turkey. Frau Elisabeth Vermehren was related to the German ambassador to Turkey, which compounded the embarrassment of their defection. Leverkuehn later claimed that British propaganda inflated Erich Vermehren's importance to such proportions that Himmler was able to exploit the crisis to get rid of Canaris, and Leverkuehn himself was recalled from Turkey.

33 The second half of this paragraph, more indulgent to Canaris than much of the essay, was added for the 1968 edition. Canaris did not always oppose Nazi killings. He certainly expressed grave doubts about Keitel's decree of 8 September 1941, which stipulated that Bolshevik soldiers had forfeited any claim to be treated honourably in keeping with the Geneva Convention and that those taken prisoner who tried to escape would be shot without warning

(Helmut Krausnick, Hans Buchheim, Martin Broszat and Hans-Adolf Jacobsen (eds), *The Anatomy of the SS State* (London: Collins, 1968), pp. 524–6). On the other hand, Canaris agreed with Heydrich on 1 March 1942 that intelligence from the Russian front 'which could result in execution activities' would be passed immediately to the relevant SS agency (Bernd Wegner, 'The War against the Soviet Union, 1942–1943', in Militaergeschichtliches Forschungsamt (ed.), *Germany and the Second World War. Vol. 6: The Global War* (Oxford: Clarendon Press, 2001), p. 1019).

34 Major-General Hans Oster (1887–1945) was a highly decorated but unconventional veteran of World War I whose later military service was brought to a temporary end in 1932 after a liaison during Carnival. The following year he joined the Abwehr in which his career progressed rapidly while taking an influential part in every major military plot against Hitler until he was dismissed from his secret service post in April 1944. Hans von Dohnanyi (1902–45) worked in the Abwehr as Oster's deputy from 1939. He recruited his brother-in-law Dietrich Bonhoeffer as an Abwehr confidential agent to prevent him being called up. In April 1943 Dohnanyi was arrested for breaching currency regulations, in the Gestapo's fashion of making an arrest for a minor infraction when they suspected something more serious for which they lacked evidence.

35 Dietrich Bonhoeffer (1906–45), an influential Protestant theologian, met the bishop of Chichester in Sweden during May 1942 in a vain attempt to modify the Allied policy of unconditional German surrender. Bonhoeffer was arrested in April 1943.

36 Colonel Georg Hansen had previously been head of Department 1 (Secret Intelligence) of the Abwehr. Abwehr defector Erich Vermehren described Hansen as 'certainly the most efficient officer in the Abwehr [...] honest, cultivated, energetic and determined to get results' (TNA HW 19/333, 'Vermehren on Abwehr and SD').

37 Field Marshal Erwin Rommel (1891–44), who held Germany's highest military decoration, was a professional soldier who enthusiastically described the Wehrmacht as 'the sword of the new German ideology'. Nazi propaganda boasted of Germany's 'Desert Fox', but Rommel's ingenuity was baffled by Hitler's erratic military interventions. Trevor-Roper viewed Rommel as a renegade who had finally turned against the regime not because of its Nazism but because of its failure. He described Rommel's opposition as 'vague and unpractical' and criticised 'the attribution to Rommel of exceptional public virtue simply because he was an able general' (*Picture Post*, 29 April 1950).

38 H.G. Hjalmar Schacht (1877–1970) was president of the Reichsbank from 1923 to 1930 and 1933 to 1939, and Reich minister of economics from

1934 until 1937. He arranged the funding of Nazi rearmament but finally left the Reichsbank after disagreeing with Hitler over the dangers of inflation.

39 Walter Schellenberg (1910–52) trained as a lawyer before joining the SD, the Nazi Security Service staffed by members of the SS. In 1949 an American military court sentenced him to six years' imprisonment in connection with the murder of Soviet prisoners of war.

40 Captain Sigismund Payne Best (1885–1978), the representative in Holland of Dansey's Z Organisation, and Major Richard Stevens, SIS head of station at The Hague. All but the last two sentences of this paragraph were added for the Kimber edition.

41 Count Marogna-Redwitz, a Catholic aristocrat from Bavaria, shared Canaris's political stance. While head of the Abwehr office in Munich, the Count had served as liaison officer to Austria for the exchange of intelligence about Czechoslovakia and formed a high opinion of his Austrian counterpart Lahousen, whom he recommended to Canaris. Marogna-Redwitz participated in the July Plot, was tried in the aftermath by the Nazi People's Court and executed on 12 October 1944.

42 In 1943 Colonel Wessel Freiherr von Freytag-Loringhoven had succeeded Lahousen as head of the Abwehr's Department 2 (Sabotage and Subversion).

43 Most of the second half of this paragraph, showing that Canaris's friends did not betray him, was added for the Kimber edition.

3 The Philby Affair

1 SOC.Dacre 10/45, Dick White to Hugh Trevor-Roper, 14 January 1968.

2 Sisman, *Hugh Trevor-Roper*, p. 93.

3 The *Sunday Times* paid Trevor-Roper a retainer.

4 Melvin Jonah Lasky (1920–2004) was educated at the University of Michigan. After a flirtation with Trotskyism, Lasky became a vigorous anti-Communist and cultural Cold Warrior. He established *Der Monat* in 1948 and edited *Encounter* from 1958 until its demise in 1991.

5 SOC.Dacre 1/2/11, Melvin Lasky to Hugh Trevor-Roper, 10 October 1967; 1/2/12, Leonard Russell to Hugh Trevor-Roper, 18 January 1968, Trevor-Roper to Russell, 20 January 1968; Sisman, *Hugh Trevor-Roper*, pp. 196–200 and 393.

6 Frances Stonor Saunders, *Who Paid the Piper? The CIA and the Cultural Cold War* (London: Granta Books, 1999).

7 Goronwy Rees (1909–79) was a controversial contributor to *Encounter*. The First Prize Fellow of All Souls College from Wales, Rees was strongly

influenced by his close friend Guy Burgess in the direction of Communism, but changed his allegiance after the Nazi–Soviet Pact of 1939. In 1953 Rees was appointed principal of the University College of Wales at Aberystwyth. He named his dog Burgess. In 1956 the *People* newspaper published lurid articles about Burgess by Rees and the ensuing rumpus forced the principal to resign from Aberystwyth. By the 1960s he was an eager Cold Warrior and, as if to compensate for past heresies, his monthly column for *Encounter* struck a vigorously anti-communist note. Rees gave a vivid account of his relationship with Burgess in his remarkable autobiography, *A Chapter of Accidents* (London: Chatto & Windus, 1972).

8   SOC.Dacre 1/2/12, Goronwy Rees to Trevor-Roper, 25 February 1968.

9   SOC.Dacre 1/2/12, Noel Annan to Trevor-Roper, 29 March 1968 and 1/2/23, 18 December 1979; 1/2/12, Louis de Jong to Trevor-Roper, 1 April 1968; Alan Clark to Trevor-Roper, 27 April 1968; Geoffrey Grigson to Trevor-Roper, 9 June 1968. Grigson (1905–85) was a poet and prolific essayist.

10 SOC.Dacre 1/2/12, Dick White to Hugh Trevor-Roper, 27 March 1968.

11 Andrew, *The Defence of the Realm*, pp. 374–5. Thistlethwaite was educated at the Queen's College Oxford. After his return from Washington, he became head of an anti-Communist section in MI5. On 3 July 1968 he wrote to Trevor-Roper: 'My dear Hugh, May I return to the theme of Ladislas Farago? We should very much like to know when his book on the Abwehr is likely to be published and by whom. Can you possibly help?' (SOC.Dacre 1/1/F, Richard Thistlethwaite to Hugh Trevor-Roper, 3 July 1968). It is unlikely that Trevor-Roper could assist, as even Farago did not know when his book would appear. His work on the Abwehr, *The Game of the Foxes*, was eventually published in 1971. Trevor-Roper told Patrick Reilly it was '(like everything he wrote) quite worthless' (SOC.Dacre 10/46, letter of 26 March 1981).

12 Alysoun Sanders, archivist of Macmillan Publishers Ltd, to E.D.R. Harrison, 25 September 2013.

13 Nigel West, *The Friends: Britain's Post-War Secret Intelligence Operations* (London: Weidenfeld & Nicolson, 1988), p. 2.

14 SOC.Dacre 10/48, Hugh Trevor-Roper to Ewen Montagu, 11 February 1980.

15 SOC.Dacre 13/59, Oxford University Pocket Diary 1967–1968, entries for Tuesday 6 August.

16 SOC.Dacre 10/44, Hugh Trevor-Roper to Isaiah Berlin, 9 October 1981.

17 SOC.Dacre 1/2/12, Dick White to Hugh Trevor-Roper, 23 September 1968.

18 This is an abbreviation of the original foreword.

19 The Kimber edition published only the Greek original. This translation of a controversial passage is from the poet Ernest Myers (1844–1921), Ernest Myers (ed.), *The Extant Odes of Pindar* (London: Macmillan, 1904), pp. 9–10, Olympian Odes II, 84–5. Pindar composed the ode in honour of the Sicilian

tyrant Theron of Akragas, who won the four-horse chariot race during the Olympic competition of 476 BC.

20 Philby's secret communism began on 2 May 1934. The previous day he had openly attended a May Day demonstration. His communism was well known to his family and friends: his mother complained vociferously about it.

21 New testimony convinced Philby's remaining supporters in SIS that he was guilty. Angered by articles he had written criticising Israel, his friend Flora Solomon told MI5 Philby was a Communist and had asked her to join him in 'important work for peace' (Flora Solomon, *Baku to Baker Street: The Memoirs of Flora Solomon by Herself and Barnet Litvinoff* (London: Collins, 1984), p. 226.

22 Philby was initially puzzled by the Nazi–Soviet Pact of 1939, but soon came round with a surge of enthusiasm for the Soviet occupation of the eastern half of Poland.

23 Philby's heavy consumption of alcohol was perhaps a sign of strain: Patrick Seale and Maureen McConville vividly describe an occasion on which Philby lapped up the bathroom eau de cologne in *Philby: The Long Road to Moscow* (London: Hamish Hamilton, 1973), p. 186.

24 This paragraph and the two which follow vary considerably from the original *Encounter* version, in which Trevor-Roper wrote, inter alia, that 'the "Insight" writers, though generally accurate in detail, isolate Philby and his friends too completely from their background. Who would think, reading the "Insight" book, that Philby was but one passenger in a two-way traffic, and that while he was working for the Russians in Britain, some thirty Russian employees of the K.G.B. defected, with their secrets, to the West?' This figure of 30 presumably came from Dick White or Richard Thistlethwaite.

25 The foreign correspondent G.E.R. Gedye vigorously challenged the detail about himself in Cookridge's Austrian testimony. In the *Encounter* edition Trevor-Roper noted that 'Mr. Cookridge's knowledge is very uneven although his confidence in stating facts is uniform.'

26 Philby and Mrs Melinda Maclean met in the Soviet Union. The Macleans had a long history of marital problems, and Philby consoled the distraught Melinda. He then abandoned his own wife Eleanor, who had loyally followed him to the Soviet Union.

27 Seale and McConville, *Philby*.

28 Vladimir Petrov (1907–91) was a KGB colonel who directed Soviet espionage in Australia from 1951 under cover as a third secretary at the embassy in Canberra. His assistant Kislitsyn knew about Burgess and Maclean from previous intelligence work in London and Moscow. In 1954 Petrov became fearful of recall in disgrace to the Soviet Union. Not only had he fallen out of favour in Moscow, his fashionable wife Evdokia Alexneyeva (1914–2002), also a KGB officer, was outshining the spouse of the Russian ambassador.

Following clandestine meetings with the Australian Security and Intelligence Organisation, on 2 April Petrov defected in Canberra without telling Mrs Petrov, who was forced onto a plane back to the Soviet Union. This resulted in such public outcry that her aircraft was halted at Darwin and she was rescued from her armed Soviet guards by Australian police. Mrs Petrov's observations to her husband during their unexpected reunion are not recorded, but she had much to tell the Western authorities about Soviet ciphers.

29   Michael Goleniewski (1922–93) was a Polish intelligence officer who first betrayed Polish secrets to the Soviet Union and subsequently Polish and Soviet secrets to the CIA. His material led to the arrests of George Blake, Harry Houghton, who was a clerk in the British Underwater Weapons Establishment at Portland, and Stig Wennerstroem. But it seems that Goleniewski had nothing to reveal about Philby. After his defection to the United States in 1961, Goleniewski became convinced that he was the haemophiliac son of Tsar Nicholas II, even though he had been born nearly two decades after the Tsarevich. Goleniewski's claim was only supported by an equally doubtful Grand Duchess Anastasia.

30   Dolnytsin was an alias of Anatoliy Mikhaylovich Golitsyn, CBE (born 1926), a major in the KGB until his defection to the United States in December 1961. Golitsyn brought with him a toxic mix of solid information, vague intelligence and fanciful claims, which included the allegation that the KGB had assassinated Labour Party leader Hugh Gaitskell to bring about the succession of Harold Wilson, whom Golitsyn claimed was a Russian secret agent. Later he declared that the Sino-Soviet split was a charade to fool the gullible West while the Communist superpowers concerted their secret plans for world domination. His alias Dolnytsin was coined by the British Defence, Press and Broadcasting Committee, which used 'D' notices to alert the press that they might be in danger of breaking the Official Secrets Act. While Golitsyn was in Britain in July 1963, the committee issued a notice telling the press not to mention his defection, but changed his name to Dolnytsin in case any journalists flouted their warning. Golitsyn did not clinch the case against Philby – in fact he unintentionally misled MI5 by insisting that 'the ring of five' Cambridge spies had all been at the university at the same time, which seemed to exclude Blunt and Cairncross and suggest the existence of two further undiscovered but important Soviet agents. Golitsyn admitted that he had not seen the KGB files of any of the five, and the value of his evidence in their regard remains uncertain. For example, the authorised historian of MI5 claims both that 'Golitsyn had little precise intelligence on the so-called "Ring of Five"' and that his defection had provided 'significant new intelligence on the Five' (Andrew, *Defence of the Realm*, pp. 380 and 435).

31 It was indeed a third person who clinched the case against Philby, namely Flora Solomon, as mentioned above.

32 Philby knew the Turkish–Soviet frontier well from his time as SIS head of station in Istanbul, when he had organised Operation *Spyglass*, a survey of the border region. But it was a long way from Beirut, and would have been an awkward, even dangerous journey. The route across the Lebanese border and by air from Syria was also problematic. A merchant vessel in Beirut harbour offered a relatively safe and inconspicuous exit, and naturally this was the one the KGB chose: Genrikh Borovik, *The Philby Files: The Secret Life of the Master Spy – KGB Archives Revealed*, edited and with an introduction by Phillip Knightley (London: Little, Brown, 1994), pp. 348–9.

33 This paragraph was newly written for the Kimber edition. Subsequent research has established many inaccuracies in Philby's memoirs, some no doubt deliberate, others perhaps the result of faulty memory compounded by chronic alcohol abuse.

34 The friend Trevor-Roper and Philby had in common was 'Tim' Milne. Trevor-Roper wrote to me (5 September 1995) that 'It was Milne, whom I cite, but do not name, in my book on Philby, who told me, in our undergraduate days, that Philby [...] was a communist.' Although Milne did not contest using the word, he later wrote that he had not meant to indicate that Philby was a communist in the thoroughgoing sense understood by Trevor-Roper (SOC.Dacre 6/4, Andrew Boyle to Hugh Trevor-Roper, 26 July 1977). Trevor-Roper wrote, 'I met him [*Milne*] once at a Christ Church dinner, and after dinner did ask him whether he ever suspected Philby. He replied that although he was intimate with him for so long he had never entertained any suspicion' (5 September 1995). Dick White was perplexed that Milne had failed to rumble Philby: 'It is one thing to have been wholly unaware of Philby's spying prior to the time when B[*urgess*] & M[*aclean*] ran away but much less easy to explain why you continued to be trustful after that event. Why should it have been so difficult to make the connection between what he knew of P's Communist past & the circumstances of the great escape. After all I always found him the most intelligent member of wartime Section V' (SOC.Dacre 6/4, Dick White to Hugh Trevor-Roper, 11 July 1983). Milne joined V after Philby: Milne, *Kim Philby*, p. 54.

35 Trevor-Roper's account of Cowgill in this paragraph reflected his recent reading of *My Silent War*.

36 Sir Claude Dansey (1876–1947) had briefly served with Winston Churchill in the Boer War before transferring to intelligence duties. During a varied career with much intelligence work, Dansey's most noteworthy initiative before World War II was to establish the 'Z' network of agents operating under business cover in parallel to the usual SIS cover of passport control officer.

Menzies entrusted Dansey with control of all SIS offensive espionage, and he was knighted in 1943.

37 Vivian did indeed know some of the less damning facts. He discussed Kim's recruitment over lunch with the latter's father, St John Philby, whom he had known in India. When Vivian raised the issue of Kim's communism at Cambridge, St John insisted that his son had reformed and put aside such schoolboy nonsense. Vivian then supported Kim's recruitment by telling SIS that he knew Kim's family.

38 Dick White was struck by this passage and later wrote to Trevor-Roper that secret service employers usually did not know about the prior communism of wartime recruits. White added with some satisfaction, 'On balance it was not such a bad bet to fight the war as a united front. The cost was to have had Blunt in 5, Philby in 6 & B[*urgess*] & M[*aclean*] in the F.O. On the other side of the equation a massive intake of brains and abilities from the Universities which set entirely new standards of intellectual achievement' (SOC.Dacre 10/48, Dick White to Hugh Trevor-Roper, 10 February 1980).

39 Regulation 18B of the Emergency Powers (Defence) Act stated, 'If the Secretary of State has reasonable cause to believe any person to be of hostile origin or associations or to have been recently concerned in acts prejudicial to the public safety of the defence of the realm in the preparation or instigation of such acts and that by reason thereof it is necessary to exercise control over him, he may make an order against that person directing that he be detained' (A.W. Brian Simpson, *In the Highest Degree Odious: Detention without Trial in Wartime Britain* (Oxford: Oxford University Press, 1994), pp. 50 and 65).

40 'Anglo-German Society' in original.

41 The final sentence of the paragraph is not in the *Encounter* edition. The records of the Security Service in 1940 contained at least two negative references to Kim Philby. Their file on the pro-Nazi Anglo-German Fellowship showed Kim Philby as a member. More to the point, the trace inquiry from SIS to MI5 brought to light the fact that Kim had been mentioned by the Communist *Labour Monthly* in 1933. This was edited by Rajani Palme Dutt (1896–1974), whose contributions epitomised the party line on current events.

42 This is a reference to career intelligence officers such as Menzies, Dansey and Vivian.

43 Graham Greene also compared Philby and sixteenth-century Catholics, though Greene's purpose was to praise the self-sacrifice of both: foreword to Kim Philby, *My Silent War* (London: MacGibbon & Kee; New York: Grove Press Inc, 1968). See p. 119 for Trevor-Roper's discussion of Greene's comparison.

44 This paragraph and its equally vigorous predecessor, both discussing Philby's egotism, were added for the Kimber edition after Trevor-Roper's reading of *My Silent War*.

45 Philby was two years older than Trevor-Roper. Both headed sub-sections in SIS counter-espionage, and so might have been considered for the same appointments. Their temporary rivalry ended when Trevor-Roper returned to Oxford in late 1945.

46 Philby was awarded an OBE, as was his friend Tim Milne.

47 Documents from the KGB archives published during the 1990s showed the ambiguity of Soviet intelligence towards Philby and the other Cambridge spies. In particular, for much of the war some Soviet intelligence officers suspected that it was not they who had chosen Philby, but rather that he was a British double agent slyly inserted into their network. See E.D.R. Harrison, *The Young Kim Philby: Soviet Spy and British Intelligence Officer* (Liverpool: Liverpool University Press, 2012), chapter 9.

48 This overestimates Vivian's role in Cowgill's demise: Cowgill too was a protégé of the Colonel, though less appealing than the charming Philby.

49 Philby's account of his intrigue is an ingenious blend of truth and lies: see Harrison, *The Young Kim Philby*.

50 MI5 did not detect a general improvement, not least because the problems were structural as well as personal. Counter-espionage remained divided between MI5 and SIS at the three-mile limit of British sovereignty. MI5 was responsible for British territory, SIS for counter-intelligence overseas. Unaware of this demarcation, enemy agents often worked on both sides of it. This led to some friction between the British security services, though there was also much effective cooperation.

51 Trevor-Roper's conviction that Philby was the man of the future predated the Soviet spy's promotion to head the anti-Communist section of SIS. In August 1943 he commented in his notebook, 'As each area becomes really important, it will have to be given to Philby, and thus, in the end, he will control all, and Cowgill and Vivian and the rest will drop uselessly from the tree, like over-ripe plums' (Trevor-Roper, *Wartime Journals*, p. 170).

52 A bucket-shop is an unauthorised office for market speculation or gambling.

53 An American official who knew Philby in Washington recalled that 'Luxury *chez* Philby was a full martini pitcher and several bottles of whisky' (Seale and McConville, *Philby*, p. 208). According to Tim Milne, Philby's existence in Turkey was far from luxurious: Milne, *Kim Philby*, p. 246.

54 Donald Duart Maclean (1913–83), was educated at Gresham's School in Norfolk and Trinity Hall Cambridge. He was recruited by the NKVD in 1934 and the Foreign Office in 1935. From 1936 he provided the Soviets with intelligence of great quantity and quality. While Maclean was serving in the United States in 1944, a mistake by a Soviet cipher clerk was exploited by American code-breakers. By 1951 Anglo-American cryptanalysts and counter-espionage officers had painstakingly identified Maclean.

55 Guy Francis de Moncy Burgess (1911–63) was educated at Eton and Trinity College Cambridge. He was recruited by the NKVD in 1934 and by the BBC in 1936. From 1944 he served in the Foreign Office. In August 1950 he was posted as a second secretary to the large British Embassy in Washington, where it was hoped his idiosyncracies would pass unnoticed. To the despair of Mrs Philby, Burgess moved in with his old friend. After the ambassador decided to send Burgess home, Philby told his fellow agent to warn Maclean that the net was closing in. Burgess promised Philby not to defect himself and he accompanied Maclean reluctantly under pressure from the Soviet secret service, which realised that Maclean was too agitated to travel alone. Maclean was the only one of the Cambridge spies the KGB had never really doubted, his material had been the most valuable, and to save him the Soviets were willing to jeopardise the others.

56 Burgess acted as a courier taking Philby's material to the KGB spy-master Valeri Makayev in New York.

57 Alger Hiss (1904–96) worked in the US State Department until he was denounced as a secret Communist to the House of Representatives Committee on Un-American Activities in August 1948. Although Hiss protested his innocence, he was vilified by the young congressman Richard Nixon and eventually jailed for perjury.

58 In the *Encounter* version Trevor-Roper had written, 'Why had a damaging trace' and 'why had that trace'. In the Kimber edition the vague word 'past' was substituted for the specific word 'trace' in both phrases. It seems Trevor-Roper was originally told correctly that MI5's trace, namely their check on Philby against their list of suspects in 1940, had revealed a Communist link, *viz.* his being mentioned in Palme Dutt's *Labour Monthly*. After the *Encounter* publication Trevor-Roper was told instead that, as he now wrote, 'the truth […] had altogether eluded the Registry of MI5.' Perhaps Thistlethwaite proposed this amendment at his meeting with Trevor-Roper prior to the delivery of the book to Kimber.

59 MI5 maintained extensive records on British subversives and could request further inquiries.

60 Unfortunately Konstantin Volkov, a KGB operative working under consular cover in Istanbul, had not actually defected, merely offered to defect. Betrayed by Philby, he was forcibly returned to the Soviet Union, interrogated and executed. After Philby fled to Moscow, Nicholas Elliott of SIS asked his former colleague to put some flowers on Volkov's grave.

61 Both the *Encounter* and Kimber versions of this essay mention 'the most central and persuasive change'.

62 Philby was questioned by Helenus J.P. 'Buster' Milmo (1908–88). Educated at Downside and Trinity College Cambridge, Milmo trained as a barrister

before serving in MI5 during World War II. Milmo interviewed Philby using a brief prepared by Arthur Martin of MI5, who was also present during the interrogation. Philby's lame answers convinced both Milmo and Martin that the SIS officer had indeed tipped off Maclean. Afterwards Philby complained bitterly to his friend Nicholas Elliott that MI5 had enticed him to London and put him through a formal inquiry during which he was not even allowed to smoke.

63 Menzies outlasted Philby in SIS by about 18 months.

64 Sir John Alexander 'Sinbad' Sinclair (1897–1977) had made a career as a staff officer and military planner until he was appointed director of military intelligence at the War Office in 1944. He only stayed a year in this post before moving to SIS as vice chief. Philby resigned in late 1951.

65 Lionel 'Buster' or 'Crabby' Crabb (1909–56), naval frogman, won the George Medal and OBE for his great bravery on diving missions. But a training regime of Scotch whisky and heavy smoking was less than ideal. On behalf of the Royal Navy, SIS asked Crabb to measure the *Ordzhonikidze*'s propellers. He went into the water at Portsmouth harbour on 18 April 1956: his headless body was washed up more than a year later. Nicholas Elliott attributed Crabb's death to respiratory trouble or faulty equipment but malignant Soviet action may have been responsible.

66 The first two chiefs of SIS had served in the Royal Navy; Menzies and 'Sinbad' Sinclair had been army officers. RAF Air Commmodore James Easton (1908–90) was the internal candidate to succeed Sinclair. His obvious ability made it paradoxical that an outsider who did not even want the post was imposed on SIS.

67 The 'good judges' included William Hayter and Patrick Reilly, senior members of the Foreign Office who had recommended the appointment of White to succeed Menzies. Reilly suggested Trevor-Roper use the wording 'good judges' in a letter of 2 January 1968: see Appendix 1.

68 Easton left two years after White's appointment. He became consul-general in Detroit and lived amid the splendour of its Grosse Pointe suburb.

69 The author of Philby's ruin was surely KGB headquarters, which had insisted that Burgess accompany Maclean when the latter defected. This brought suspicion on Philby, as Burgess had lived with him in Washington. In 1941 White had passed Philby's name to Cowgill for employment in SIS. As the new Chief of SIS had played a small part in Philby's recruitment, by 1956 White had good reason to be set against a traitor whose devastation he had unwittingly made possible.

70 Trevor-Roper had published an article in the French newspaper *Le Figaro* on 1 April 1968 in which he emphasised Philby's depiction of White as an ineffective mediocrity and asserted that the Soviet spy had sworn to be

revenged on White as the author of his ruin. On 30 April Philby wrote to 'My dear T-R' in protest: 'This passage frankly astonishes me, and I can assure you that it is quite wrong to say that "Philby s'etait depuis longtemps juré de se venger de lui" [*Philby had long since sworn to be revenged upon him*]. The fact is that from late 1951 I was quite sure that a whole string of security officers thought me deeply, if not wholly, suspect. The list would include Liddell, White, Milmo, Skardon, Martin, Marriott, Mackenzie. I have never had reason to single out White as any more dangerous than the others. I have described him as ineffective, etc. because I really thought he was. My judgement may have been wrong, but it was not insincere. Surely you yourself would agree that White was pretty nondescript beside such colleagues as Liddell, Hart, Blunt, Rothschild, Masterman and others? Or perhaps not?' (SOC.Dacre 1/3/10, Kim Philby to Hugh Trevor-Roper, 30 April 1968).

71 Intelligence officers have an ostensible profession as cover for secret service.

72 Disgruntled agents might reveal tradecraft details such as how they were recruited, tasked and contacted by their spy-masters. MI5's monitoring of Philby after his 'resignation' from SIS suggested he was still receiving money from his late employer.

73 Blake had been born in Rotterdam; he was named George in honour of King George V. After wartime service in the Dutch resistance and the Royal Navy, he joined SIS in 1944. Working under consular cover in Seoul, he was captured during the Korean War and volunteered to work for the KGB. He betrayed not only the elaborate spy tunnel by which Western intelligence tapped Soviet secret messages in East Berlin, but also numerous British agents, many of whom were executed. In 1961 he was sentenced to 42 years' imprisonment, the Lord Chief Justice deciding he should serve a year for each death he had caused.

74 Philby was confronted in Beirut by Nicholas Elliott, one of his most loyal defenders during the long years of suspicion. Eliott's appearance made it clear to Philby that there was no point in continuing his charade of wronged innocence.

75 Le Carré told his friend A.D. Peters, the literary agent, that this piece had given him more trouble than anything else he had ever written (SOC.Dacre 1/2/12, A.D. Peters to Hugh Trevor-Roper, 5 January 1968).

76 Mehdi Ben Barka (1920–65?) a Moroccan teacher of mathematics and revolutionary opponent of King Hassan II, had fled into exile. In October 1965 he was kidnapped in Paris and vanished without trace, to the considerable embarrassment of President Charles de Gaulle.

77 Humberto 'General Fearless' da Silva Delgado (1906–65), the youngest general in Portuguese history, stood in the 1958 presidential elections. He threatened to sack the Portuguese prime minister and dictator Antonio

Salazar if he won, so the secret police ensured the victory of a rival candidate for the presidency by forging votes. After some years in exile, Delgado tried to return to Portugal but was ambushed and shot near the Spanish border.

78 Gerhard Eisler (1897–1968), a Marxist journalist, was elected to the central committee of the Communist Party of Germany in 1929. In 1933 he went to New York to encourage American communists to follow the policy of the Communist International, the organisation which coordinated the activities of national Communist Parties with the interests of the Soviet Union. In October 1946 he was accused of being 'the major Moscow agent in the USA', an allegation repeated by his own sister. Arrested repeatedly, Eisler escaped from America on a Polish vessel in 1949. Although he was detained when his ship docked in Southampton, he was later released by a London court and he travelled on to the German Democratic Republic, where he was rewarded with membership of the executive committee of the ruling party.

79 Graham Greene tartly commented in his review of Page, Leitch and Knightley's book: 'It is true that the introduction is written by someone who calls himself John Le Carré, but there is no copyright in pen names, and I can hardly believe that these wild Philips Oppenheim speculations and the vulgar and untrue portrait of Philby at the end are by the distinguished author of *The Spy Who Came in From the Cold*' (*Observer*, 18 February 1968).

80 The peace pledge, to renounce war and work for the removal of its causes, is a commitment made by those joining the Peace Pledge Union (PPU), an organisation of British pacifists. The PPU was founded in 1934 by Dick Sheppard, a canon of St Paul's Cathedral, who published a letter in the press asking men to send him postcards promising never to support war. He received 135,000 replies. During the 1930s the PPU supported appeasement and opposed conscription.

81 Anthony Eden, first Earl of Avon, was prime minister from 1955 to 1957. Harold 'Supermac' Macmillan (1894–1986), first Earl of Stockton, succeeded Eden as prime minister and leader of the Conservative Party.

82 Clement Richard Attlee, first Earl Attlee (1883–1967), was Labour prime minister from 1945 to 1951.

83 Hector McNeil (1907–55) served as parliamentary under-secretary of state at the Foreign Office from August 1945 until October 1946, when he was promoted to minister of state for foreign affairs. He stayed in this post until February 1950. McNeil was very pro-American and hostile to the Soviet Union. The sudden and mysterious disappearance of his protégé Burgess must have troubled McNeil more than anyone, except of course Philby.

84 State secrets.

85 In April 1943 Trevor-Roper noted in his journal: 'Stuart Hampshire observed that S.I.S. values information in proportion to its secrecy, not to

its accuracy. They would attach more value, he said, to a scrap of third-rate and tendentious misinformation smuggled out of Sofia in the fly-buttons of a vagabond Rumanian pimp than to any intelligence deduced from a prudent reading of the foreign press. And of course he's quite right' (Trevor-Roper, *Wartime Journals*, p. 149).

86 Sir Hugh F.P. 'Quex' Sinclair (1873–1939) was director of naval intelligence from 1919 to 1921 and appointed Chief of the Secret Service and non-operational director of GC & CS in 1923. During the international crisis of the late 1930s, Sinclair championed appeasement and advised against a Soviet alliance.

87 For the Zinoviev letter affair, see Gill Bennett, *'A Most Extraordinary and Mysterious Business': The Zinoviev Letter of 1924* (London: Foreign & Commonwealth Office, History Notes 14, 1999).

88 Dansey was ACSS (Assistant Chief of the Secret Service) until October 1942, when he was promoted to VCSS (Vice Chief of the Secret Service). At the end of March 1943 Vivian was reduced from DCSS (Deputy Chief of the Secret Service) to Deputy Director/SP. There were three other deputy directors besides Vivian; Jeffery, *MI6*, pp. 476–7.

89 Menzies' particular friends in SIS were F.W. Winterbotham, David 'Creeping Jesus' or 'Creeping Christ' Boyle and Peter Koch de Gooreynd, who kept Menzies company at the bar of White's. Reilly thought that 'Winterbotham was certainly closer to Menzies than any of his other pre-war SIS officers, I wd say – except perhaps David Boyle. I can [sic] see his full figure in RAF uniform frequently in the passage waiting to see Menzies' (SOC.Dacre 10/46, letter of 23 February 1981). Winterbotham (1897–1990) was educated at Charterhouse and Christ Church and became head of the new RAF section of SIS in 1930. By 1939 he had pioneered high-altitude photo-reconnaissance. Menzies used Winterbotham as one of the conduits for sending Ultra, the product of decrypting and translating signals enciphered by the German Enigma machine, to the prime minister, Winston Churchill. Menzies also entrusted Winterbotham with the secure distribution of Ultra to military planners and field commanders through a system of special liaison units. Menzies used the former colonial officer Boyle for particularly sensitive tasks such as passing Ultra to William Stephenson, the SIS representative in North America. Boyle was also responsible for office security. He acquired his sobriquet by popping his head round the door of colleagues' rooms to check the identity of visitors. Another of his roles was to act as a go-between for Vivian and Dansey, who were not on speaking terms. Finally Boyle was responsible for the secret scrutiny of documents from diplomatic bags passing through Bermuda; SOC.Dacre 6/4, F.W. Winterbotham to Hugh Trevor-Roper, 5 April 1976, and notes for Lord 'Daker', 1980.

90 A Wykehamist is a pupil of the public school Winchester College, endowed by William of Wykeham, Bishop of Winchester, who also founded New College Oxford in 1379. Former pupils are 'Old Wykehamists', though in practice the 'Old' prefix is usually dropped when referring to alumni. The 'grave Wykehamist' was Patrick Reilly.

91 'General Code and Cypher School' in the Kimber edition.

92 'Most secret sources' was a cover term for Ultra. *The Philby Affair* was one of a number of publications at this time which mentioned British code-breaking successes in World War II. *Spiegel* magazine published an article on Philby in January 1968 which referred to the British capture of an Enigma machine, the breaking of its naval codes and the successful concealment of this achievement from the Germans. Bruce Page, David Leitch and Phillip Knightley, *Philby: The Spy who Betrayed a Generation* (London: Andre Deutsch, 1968), p. 159, not only mentioned Bletchley's success with naval codes, but also pointed out that it had extended to most German machine-codes. Philby himself wrote that Dilly Knox 'had succeeded in penetrating the secrets of the cypher machine used by the Abwehr'. He emphasised that much GC & CS work was 'brilliantly successful' so Section V largely filled gaps in 'the extraordinarily comprehensive picture' from signals intelligence; Philby, *My Silent War*, pp. 54–5 and 65. When F. W. Winterbotham published *The Ultra Secret* in 1974, Ultra was no longer much of a secret. See also Sisman, 'Letter to the Editor'.

93 SIS did gather valuable Humint (intellegence from human sources) on the V1 pilotless jet and the V2 rocket, which facilitated a bombing raid in August 1943 on the Peenemünde rocket installations, forcing the Germans into dispersal and a substantial delay in deployment.

94 Patrick Reilly queried this phrase in a letter of 9 February 1981: SOC.Dacre 10/46. It was indeed not the Polish Resistance but the prewar cryptographers of the Polish General Staff who explained to British code-breakers in July 1939 their successes against the Enigma machine. In August they sent a reconstruction of the machine to their British allies. This was brought to London by the chief French code-breaker, accompanied by an SIS officer. They were welcomed at Victoria Station by Menzies in full evening dress. The Polish assistance was a vital catalyst for British code-breaking and saved up to a year on aspects of the work: F.H. Hinsley with E.E. Thomas, C.A.G. Simkins and C.F.G. Ransom, *British Intelligence in the Second World War: Its Influence on Strategy and Operations. Vol. 3, Part II* (London: HMSO, 1988), p. 957.

95 Trevor-Roper is referring here to the deception practised through the use of double agents controlled by the Twenty (XX) Committee. MI5 was certainly well represented on this committee, and provided its chair in the form of

Trevor-Roper's old history tutor, J.C. Masterman, though 'Tar' Robertson himself was not a member. Masterman always stressed the importance of cooperation between MI5 and SIS. When Cowgill proved an obstructive committee member, Menzies sent Frank Foley to represent SIS instead. In 1945 Masterman emphasised the importance of Foley's contribution to Menzies: E.D.R. Harrison, 'J.C. Masterman and the Security Service, 1940–1972', *Intelligence and National Security* 24/6 (2009), p. 777.

96 'most Secret Services' in the Kimber edition.

97 Philby was able to make a rapid career not least because privilege was a catalyst for his merit. He won a special entrance award at Cambridge for which only pupils of Westminster School could apply, and his *Times* appointment was approved by its deputy editor, Robin Barrington-Ward, the former chairman of the Westminster School Appeal, who cheerfully noticed that Philby was a former pupil of Westminster like himself. The *Times* appointment, the result of merit and the Westminster connection acting together, laid the basis for Philby's later penetration of SIS counter-espionage. It both enabled him to acquire a specialist knowledge of Spanish affairs and gave him a status and respectability which made him appear something of a catch to Vivian, who considered Philby both 'able and charming'.

98 Malcolm Muggeridge (1903–90) had been posted in 1942 as SIS head of station to Lourenco Marques, the capital of Portuguese East Africa. Muggeridge showed a particular flair for bribing Portuguese officials and organised successful kidnappings of enemy agents. Trevor-Roper's *Wartime Journals* show that by 1945 he was on friendly terms with Muggeridge, who provided hospitality and the opportunity of a lively argument. A journalist by profession, Muggeridge wrote a superb autobiography, *Chronicles of Wasted Time*, and a much commended study of Mother Theresa of Calcutta.

99 The other departments included the Foreign Office, which effectively vetoed Philby's return to *The Times* as a war correspondent in 1944.

100 In *Encounter* Trevor-Roper mentioned that the conclusions were submitted to Philby 'in view of the Spanish interest'.

101 Trevor-Roper added in a private letter, 'It was through Otto John that Canaris made his approaches to us and indicated his willingness to meet "C"' (SOC. Dacre 6/4, Hugh Trevor-Roper to Geoffrey Hudson, 27 March 1969). Otto John had done some work for the Abwehr while representing Lufthansa in Madrid. In addition to British contacts, from November 1943 John was in touch with Colonel William Hohenthal, the American military attaché. John dreamed of a Hohenzollern restoration and sought to establish contact between Prince Louis Ferdinand, a grandson of Kaiser Wilhelm II, and United States President F.D. Roosevelt; Winfried Heinemann, 'Der militaerische Widerstand und der Krieg', in Militaergeschichtliches

Forschungsamt, *Das Deutsche Reich und der Zweite Weltkrieg* 9/1 (Munich: Deutsche Verlags-Anstalt, 2004), p. 857. See also Milne, *Kim Philby*, pp. 130–1.

102 Trevor-Roper later stressed that Philby was seldom in a position to suppress intelligence. Even when he could, it was not likely to be effective, for 'a Foreign Office does not base policy on the narrow trickle of evidence which a single counterespionage officer can occasionally block' ('Blunt and Philby, Letter to the Editor from Dacre of Glanton', the *Listener*, 3 December 1981, © Immediate Media Company London Limited).

103 Philby represented SIS on an Anglo-American committee in Washington which sought to topple the communist regime in Albania. The Albanian exiles sent back to subvert their country's new government were usually caught and sometimes executed. Yet even after Philby's resignation, the West's agents were still captured, which suggested that he was not the only one betraying the brave but unfortunate exiles.

104 When the Soviet Union attacked the Republic of Poland in 1939, many Polish officers fell into Russian hands and went missing. In 1943 the Germans announced they had found thousands of bodies in the forest of Katyn, where the Poles had been murdered by the Soviet secret police.

105 Tomas Masaryk (1850–1937), first president of the Republic of Czechoslovakia from 1918, resigned this office in 1935 and was succeeded by Edvard Benes (1884–1948).

106 Jan Masaryk (1886–1948), the son of Tomas, became Czech foreign minister in the postwar government. Trevor-Roper called on him in Prague on 7 January 1948. Masaryk fell from a window to his death later the same year, when the Communists sought to consolidate their grip on power.

107 In the Kimber edition 'Tokyo' in the next paragraph is followed by a comma. The Sobolevicius brothers from Lithuania, later known as Jack Soble and Dr Richard Soblen, had infiltrated Trotsky's circle on behalf of Soviet intelligence by 1929. Trotsky entrusted the brothers with much of his secret correspondence to followers in the Soviet Union whom they betrayed to the secret police. Rudolf Ivanovich Abel (1902–71), an officer of the GRU (Soviet Military Intelligence), used a forged Canadian passport to enter the United States, where the Communist Party gave him the birth certificate of a dead child so he could obtain American documentation. After an interval spent murdering Russian exiles in Finland, Abel returned to the United States, where he was denounced to the FBI by another GRU operative. He was sentenced to 30 years in prison, but after five years was exchanged for the American spy-plane pilot Gary Powers in 1962. Gordon Lonsdale's real name was Konon Trofimovich Molody (1923–70). Having spent his childhood in North America, Molody returned to the Soviet Union in 1938

and was trained in intelligence by Rudolf Abel during World War II. In 1955 he was sent on an espionage mission to Britain under the false identity of Gordon Lonsdale. His unusual but effective cover included selling bubblegum machines. Lonsdale's espionage focused on NATO bases and proved of great help to the Soviet navy in the development of less audible submarines. In 1961 he was arrested and sentenced to 25 years in prison, but was exchanged three years later for Greville Wynne.

108 White's reforms included recruiting officers from a wider range of universities, greater emphasis on their career development, bolstering SIS security and counter-intelligence, and creating new targeting sections to recruit agents who could operate in the Soviet bloc and China; Davies, *MI6*, pp. 251–8.

109 Blake was sprung, after their release, by friends he had made in prison.

110 The American KGB agents Morris and Lona Cohen had fled their own country when Philby reported that they might be exposed by the efforts of Western code-breakers. They came to Britain, where they assumed the names of Peter and Helen Kroger and cover as antiquarian booksellers. The Krogers provided Lonsdale with wireless and other technical support. In March 1961 they were each sentenced to 20 years in prison.

111 Gerald Brooke (born 1937), a British teacher of Russian, visited the Soviet Union with his wife Barbara in 1965. Both were arrested for smuggling anti-Soviet leaflets. Brooke later admitted he had been carrying concealed documents. Although his wife was eventually allowed to return to Britain, Brooke himself was sentenced to five years' incarceration. His case was raised in the House of Commons by his local MP, Margaret Thatcher, and he was finally exchanged for the Krogers in July 1969. His captors no doubt had this swap in mind all along, as Trevor-Roper implies. The espionage crimes of the Krogers were far more serious than Brooke's smuggling.

112 Colonel Stig Eric Wennerstroem of the Swedish air force spied for Soviet military intelligence from 1948 until a lead from Golienewski led to his exposure. Wennerstroem had enjoyed almost perfect cover as a Swedish officer posted in turn to Moscow, Washington and Stockholm. He passed on perhaps 30,000 documents in official meetings with Soviet representatives, providing technical information on American missiles and fighter aircraft and even a film roll of the type used by the U-2 spy plane. In 1964 he was sentenced to life imprisonment.

113 1961 in the Kimber edition.

114 Francis Gary Powers (1929–77), was a bomber pilot recruited by the CIA in 1956 and given cover as a civilian employee of the Lockheed Aircraft Corporation. Powers flew U-2 spy planes at high altitude from Pakistan across the Soviet Union to Norway. On 1 May 1960 his plane was shot down and he was eventually convicted of espionage. He served two years in prison

before he was exchanged for Rudolf Abel at Glienicke Bridge near Berlin on 10 February 1962.

115 Greville Maynard Wynne (1909–90) served in Britain's field security police during World War II before developing a small business assisting exports to Eastern Europe. After an approach by Oleg Penkovsky of Soviet military intelligence, he became one of the channels by which the disaffected GRU colonel passed secret information to the West. Wynne was eventually arrested and subjected to a show trial together with Penkovsky in May 1963 before being exchanged for Molody the following year.

116 Andrei Donatovich Siniavskii (1925–) and Iulii Markovich Daniel (1925–88) worked together on satirical writings which were published abroad. Both men were prosecuted for slandering the Soviet Union in 1965 and eventually received sentences of seven and five years' incarceration, respectively. Their trial not only provoked international outrage, it also marked the birth of the dissident movement in the Soviet Union.

117 Ewald von Kleist-Schmenzin (1890–1945), a monarchist landowner, vociferously opposed Hitler's rise to power, denouncing him as a warmonger. At the end of August 1938 he travelled to London on behalf of General Beck to urge England to stand firm against Hitler, but his mission was to no avail. Kleist-Schmenzin was executed shortly before the end of the war.

4 Deception

1 Anthony Cave Brown (1929–2006) was educated at Luton Grammar School. As a correspondent for the *Daily Mail* he interviewed the Soviet writer Boris Pasternak but during a night on the town in Berlin lost one of the two poems he was given to smuggle to the West. Cave Brown later worked in the Middle East, where he would meet Philby for martinis. After abandoning the *Daily Mail* and his wife in 1962, Cave Brown eventually became a successful author thanks to his formidable energy and the substantial resources of his affluent American companion. In later life he drew attention by berating loudly the unfortunate staff of the Public Record Office because so few documents were then available on British intelligence.

2 'The Ultra Ultra Secret', review of *Bodyguard of Lies* by Anthony Cave Brown, first published in *New York Review of Books*, 19 February 1976.

3 The Dieppe Raid was a seaborne landing between dawn and 2 p.m. on 19 August 1942 of about 6,000 troops, mostly Canadians, to assault a French port strongly defended by the Germans. The attackers suffered heavy losses, only partly offset by damage inflicted on the enemy.

4 'Station' in original.

5 The Admiralty, Air Ministry and War Office had their own intelligence staffs which collated information received from the Royal Navy, Air Force and Army respectively.

6 Menzies inherited general authority over the GC & CS from his predecessor, Rear Admiral Hugh 'Quex' Sinclair, who was made its non-operational director in 1923 because he was acceptable both to the armed services and the Foreign Office. GC & CS produced Ultra at Bletchley Park. Menzies ensured Bletchley's work was included in the close relations which developed between British and American intelligence; Jeffery, *MI6*, pp. 209–11 and 443–5.

7 J.C. Masterman had written to Trevor-Roper on 28 October 1975 that 'TAR, in my opinion, did more for Double Cross than any other two men, and I have not yet forgiven the Government for preventing me from mentioning him by name in my book' (SOC.Dacre 10/42).

8 Reinhard Heydrich (1904–43) was chief of the Gestapo and Reich Protector for Bohemia and Moravia until his assassination at the hands of Czech agents trained by SOE.

9 Trevor-Roper corrected 'Istanbul' to 'Ankara' on his copy of the published review. Nicholas Elliott, who served as Section V representative in Istanbul from spring 1942, considered that 'the Cicero case was probably the most serious diplomatic security leak in British history prior to the defection of Burgess and Maclean' (Nicholas Elliott, *Never Judge a Man by his Umbrella* (Salisbury: Michael Russell, 1991), p. 133). *Cicero*'s name was Elyesa Bazna. The British ambassador was Sir Hughe 'Snatch' Knatchbull-Hugessen (1886–1971), who had been educated at Eton and Balliol College Oxford. Despite the *Cicero* episode, in which Sir Hughe had blithely disregarded specific instructions concerning the safe-keeping of documents, his career proceeded smoothly with appointment in 1944 as ambassador to Belgium.

10 *Cicero* did not contribute to British deception.

11 The previous year Trevor-Roper had written to Masterman, 'Of course Menzies [...] may well have forgotten who Cicero was, and mixed him up, in his own mind, with [*the double-agent*] Brutus – one classical name was probably, to him, the same as another' (SOC.Dacre 10/42, Trevor-Roper to Masterman, 23 August 1975).

12 SOC.Dacre 10/54, Walter L. Pforzheimer to Hugh Trevor-Roper, 15 February 1976.

13 John Henry Bevan (1894–1978), intelligence officer and stockbroker, was educated at Eton and Christ Church. He was appointed controlling officer for deception by the Chiefs of Staff on 21 May 1942. Under their supervision, Bevan's London Controlling Section coordinated deception between different theatres of operation and defined overall deception policy.

14 SOC.Dacre 10/46, John H. Bevan to Hugh Trevor-Roper, 1 March 1976

15 Flight-Lieutenant Charles Cholmondeley was serving in section B1A of MI5. He remained in the Security Service after the war, and consequently is mentioned only as 'George' in *The Man who Never Was*, Ewen Montagu's account of *Mincemeat*.

16 SOC.Dacre 10/54, Hugh Trevor-Roper to Michael Howard, 19 May 1976.

17 Hugh Trevor-Roper, review of 'The Secret Servant: The Life of Sir Stewart Menzies, Churchill's Spymaster' by Anthony Cave Brown, first published in the *Spectator*, 2 April 1988.

18 i.e. 'Mingiz'. Menzies was appointed 'C' after the 'Venlo Incident'.

19 Menzies was reputedly intimidated by Dansey, an old rival rather than crony.

20 Arcos (All-Russian Co-operative Society) ostensibly promoted Anglo-Russian trade from its London premises but covertly assisted Soviet espionage. In May 1927 the British Prime Minister Stanley Baldwin approved a raid on Arcos by British police and intelligence officers in search of evidence that the Official Secrets Act had been broken. But no significant espionage was discovered. The government had hoped to find material which would justify breaking off diplomatic relations with Moscow. As the Arcos raid had failed to deliver, Baldwin read out in the House of Commons telegrams between the Soviet legation in London and its Foreign Ministry which had been deciphered by the GC & CS. Although the revelation of these decrypts proved Soviet meddling in British politics and so justified the subsequent breach in relations, it also showed the Soviet Union that its communications were vulnerable. So Moscow closed the window by adopting virtually impenetrable codes from encrypting pads used only once for its intelligence and diplomatic traffic; Andrew, *Defence of the Realm*, pp. 154–6.

21 J.L.X. Francois Darlan (1881–1942) was Commander in Chief of the Vichy armed forces when the Anglo-Americans invaded French North Africa in November 1942. By chance on a visit to Algiers, Darlan signed an armistice with the invaders and agreed to change sides. His defection prompted Hitler to invade the unoccupied zone of France. Churchill considered Darlan 'A bad man with a narrow outlook and a shifty eye'; the Foreign Office regarded him as the antithesis of international decency. Darlan was assassinated on Christmas Eve by a French monarchist trained by SOE but acting independently; Michael Howard, *Grand Strategy. Vol. IV: August 1942– September 1943*, in J.R. M. Butler (ed.), *History of the Second World War United Kingdom Military Series* (London: HMSO, 1972), pp. 151 and 176.

5 Ultra

1 First published in *New York Review of Books*, 13 May 1976.

2 SIS field officers were designated by a number referring to their host country, and 38,000 was indeed Stephenson's. There is nothing in the SIS archives to prove that Stephenson was ever code-named *Intrepid*. Indeed, MI6 files apparently suggest that after his remarkable successes during the early war years, Stephenson's subsequent conduct of secret business did not go unquestioned. By April 1942 Dansey complained that Stephenson was urging American intelligence down the 'noisy paths' of SOE operations. In January 1943 Menzies demanded that Stephenson reduce his staff by a quarter, though he later relented. In mid-1944 Vivian complained that Stephenson's weekly intelligence bulletin was not SIS work and did not give value for money; Jeffery, *MI6*, pp. 449–53 and 785.

3 About 85 per cent of Hyde's text was either lifted verbatim or summarised closely from a history of British Security Coordination compiled on Stephenson's instructions at the end of the war. Then he had ordered the destruction of the organisation's documents. The original history commissioned by Stephenson, *British Security Co-ordination*, was published in 1998.

4 See Chapter 4.

5 The Security Service (SD) of the SS did make slight use of the Enigma machine, but relatively little SD Ultra was circulated. Most of the 13,000 SD decrypts were from hand-ciphers: Hinsley and Simkins, *British Intelligence. Vol. 4*, p. 182.

6 First published in the *Spectator*, 18 September 1993.

7 Knox had translated the indecent mimes of Herodas, a writer of the third century BC, including passages assembled from papyrus fragments.

8 'Secret Sources' in the original publication.

9 Gordon Welchman, *The Hut Six Story. Breaking the Enigma Codes* (Harmondsworth: Penguin Books, 1982).

10 The bombes were code-breaking machines which quickly tested possible solutions for the daily key setting of a particular form of Enigma.

11 First published in the *Listener*, 9 March 1978, © Immediate Media Company London Limited; Reginald Victor Jones (1911–97) was educated at Alleyn's School, Dulwich and Wadham College Oxford. As a postgraduate he did research on infra-red rays at the Clarendon Laboratory and after the war he became professor of natural philosophy at Aberdeen University.

12 Sir Henry Thomas Tizard (1885–1959) was educated at Westminster School and Magdalen College Oxford. Tizard's Air Defence Committee successfully fostered radar, but he resigned in 1940 when Lindemann became the dominant figure in Whitehall science. Although the two men had become

close friends while studying in Berlin during the autumn of 1908, their association clouded when Tizard demonstrated his superiority at boxing. In 1942 Tizard challenged the area bombing of Germany championed by his rival.

13 Sir Robert A. Watson-Watt (1892–1973) was educated at Brechin High School and University College, Dundee. His interest in radio waves led him into a pioneering role in the development of radar for aerial defence on behalf of Tizard's committee.

14 Patrick M.S. Blackett (1897–1974) was educated at Osborne Naval College and Magdalene College Cambridge. His success as a research physicist brought a series of professorial appointments and membership of the Tizard Committee. From 1942 he was chief adviser on operational research to the Admiralty and strongly influenced anti-submarine warfare. He was awarded the Nobel Prize for Physics in 1948 and given a life peerage in 1969.

15 The Oslo report was sent anonymously to the British naval attaché in the Norwegian capital in the autumn of 1939. Its astonishing detail included the German use of acoustic torpedos and electric bomb fuses; the development of remote-controlled rocket shells for the army; and the testing at Peenemünde of a remote-controlled aircraft with an explosive charge; F.H. Hinsley with E.E.Thomas, C.F.G. Ransom and R.C. Knight, *British Intelligence in the Second World War: Its Influence on Strategy and Operations. Vol. 1* (London: HMSO, 1979), p. 100 and appendix 5.

16 Valuable intelligence on Peenemünde came from SIS, whose Danish agent *Elgar* provided a photograph of a rocket which had landed on the Baltic island of Bornholm; Jeffery, *MI6*, p. 513.

17 The SIS head of station in Singapore, Major J.H. Green, claimed that he had received excellent advance warning from Indo-China about the Japanese plans to invade Thailand and Malaya, but that the absence of scientific collation contributed to much intelligence being disregarded: it was filed and forgotten; Jeffery, *MI6*, pp. 574–6.

6 Percy Sillitoe and Dick White

1 Sir Percy Joseph Sillitoe (1888–1962) was educated at St Paul's Choir School until the age of 14 and then had some private tuition at home. He served in various police forces in southern Africa and then held a succession of chief constable posts in Britain before his unexpected appointment to head MI5 from 1 May 1946.

2 Andrew, *The Defence of the Realm*, pp. 322 and 327.

3 First published in the *Spectator*, 29 April 1955.

4 Andrew, *Defence of the Realm*, p. 325.

5 First published in *Christ Church Report*, 1993.

6 Trevor-Roper identified the nominee in a letter to Charles Stuart of 10 April 1972: 'one Mark Johnston [...] a stockbroker from White's Club. Mark Johnston only attended twice. Each time he had to be fetched from White's and arrived incoherent from the bar; then he faded away' (Charles Stuart Papers). As 'Tar' Robertson was the undisputed head of the War Room, Trevor-Roper mistook these occasions of Johnston's inebriation.

7 Joachim von Ribbentrop (1893–1946) was a champagne salesman elevated by Hitler to Reich foreign minister. He negotiated the Nazi–Soviet Non-Aggression Treaty of 1939 which proved a catalyst for the outbreak of World War II. After Germany's defeat Ribbentrop was tried as a war criminal and hanged in 1946.

8 CSS (Menzies) did not veto the book. His representative 'Tim' Milne, who had been on the same staircase as Trevor-Roper when an undergraduate at Christ Church, in fact equivocated about the proposal in a way which was tantamount to approval: see the Editor's Introduction, p. 34.

9 See the Editor's Introduction concerning the authorship of the paper in question, 'The German Intelligence Service and the War'.

10 'Happy in the timing of his death'.

7 Anthony Blunt

1 Andrew P.M. Boyle (1919–91) was educated at Blairs (Aberdeen) and Paris University. He served in military intelligence during World War II before joining the BBC, where in 1965 he became the first editor of the *World at One*. A successful biographer, his subjects included Brendan Bracken and Erskine Childers.

2 First published in the *Spectator*, 17 November 1979.

3 The Popular Front was a Communist stratagem to bring together those on the left and centre of politics to combat the danger from Fascism; it did not survive the Nazi–Soviet Pact of 1939.

4 For example, on one occasion in Cairo a drunken Maclean broke into the flat of two American female secretaries and tried to smash a giant mirror on their bath tub. This threatened Britain's special relationship with the United States so he was sent home.

5 'Believe one who knows from experience'.

6 Philby passed Ultra to the Russians, as did Anthony Blunt.

7 TNA KV 4/188.

8 First published in the *Spectator*, 24 November 1979.

9 Burgess can be cleared on two counts: a mistake by a Soviet cipher clerk had been exploited by American code-breakers to prompt the investigation which led to Maclean's downfall, and it was Soviet intelligence which insisted that Burgess accompany Maclean, reckless of the spotlight this would throw on Philby.

10 Blunt's secret past was revealed by the American Michael Straight, who told the FBI that Blunt had recruited him as a Communist agent at Cambridge: see Chapter 8. Straight's confession gave MI5 the upper hand in dealing with Blunt.

11 Sir John 'Sinbad' Sinclair and Jack Easton lost credibility due to 'Buster' Crabb's ill-fated investigation of a Soviet cruiser in Portsmouth harbour. The ensuing Soviet protests made Prime Minister Anthony Eden furious with SIS.

12 This phrase was originally published in brackets, but these were crossed out by Trevor-Roper in his copy.

13 SOC.Dacre 6/4, Hugh Trevor-Roper to Noel Annan, 11 October 1987. Trevor-Roper told Blunt's biographer Miranda Carter, 'I had a clear impression that he disliked me – that he looked down his nose at me and did not think me worth talking to: he was, after all, a Fellow of Trinity, and I was a nobody' (SOC.Dacre 10/46, answers to Miranda Carter's questions concerning Blunt).

8 Michael Straight

1 SOC.Dacre 6/4, Hugh Trevor-Roper to Dick White, 21 July 1983.

2 First published in *New York Review of Books*, 31 March 1983.

3 Cyril E.M. Joad (1891–1953) was educated at Blundell's and Balliol College Oxford. He was head of the philosophy department at Birkbeck College London from 1930 until his death and a prominent member of the first 'Brains Trust'.

4 'Marxism' was printed by mistake in the original publication, which Trevor-Roper corrected to 'Nazism' on his own copy.

5 'Everything unknown is splendid'.

6 Here Trevor-Roper assumes that Soviet intelligence operated in a calculating and shrewd manner, which often it did not. From an early stage in his espionage, Philby was instructed to collect material of doubtful significance and exposed to considerable risks.

7 In 1937 Guy Burgess asked Stuart Hampshire 'to work for peace', but nothing came of it. It is very likely that Burgess also approached Goronwy Rees, whose degree of involvement in secret work for Communism remains mysterious.

8 George Edward Moore (1873–1958) was educated at Dulwich and Trinity College Cambridge, where he was elected fellow in 1908. An eminent philosopher, he taught at Cambridge until 1939, urging that philosophy should stick to common sense.

9 Blunt's memoirs are now held in the British Library.

10 William Henry Beveridge (1879–1963) was educated at Charterhouse and Balliol College Oxford and from 1919 to 1937 served as director of the London School of Economics. The architect of the welfare state, he was made a peer in 1946.

11 Harold Joseph Laski (1893–1950) was educated at Manchester Grammar School and New College Oxford. He taught politics at the London School of Economics from 1920 until his death.

12 Vengalil Krishnan Kunji-Krishna Menon (1896–1974) was educated at Madras Presidency College and the London School of Economics. A cofounder of Penguin Books, he became India's first high commissioner in London after independence. In 1962 he served as minister of defence during India's disastrous war with China.

13 Maurice Henry Dobb (1900–76) was educated at Charterhouse and Pembroke College Cambridge and joined the Communist Party in 1922. A lecturer at Cambridge from 1924, he taught Philby economics and provided the international contacts which led to his pupil's eventual recruitment as a Soviet agent.

14 Dennis Holme Robertson (1890–1963) was educated at Eton and Trinity College Cambridge. He taught economics at Cambridge from 1924 until 1957, lastly as professor of political economy. In 1934 he declined to write Philby a civil service reference. A vigorous opponent of Keynes's theories, he was knighted in 1953.

15 Joan Violet Robinson (1903–83) was educated at St Paul's Girls' School and Girton College Cambridge. She taught economics at Cambridge from 1931 until 1971, for the last six years as professor of economics.

16 N.J. 'James' Klugmann (1912–77) was educated at Gresham's School and Trinity College Cambridge. An active communist from 1934, he led a student delegation to visit Mao. During the war he served in SOE and after 1945 became a prolific writer about communism, serving as editor of *Marxism Today* from 1963 until his death.

17 'Party' in original.

18 John Tressider Sheppard (1881–1968) was elected provost unanimously in 1933. A remarkable lecturer, his fondness for reminiscing considerably extended college meetings. He was knighted for services to Greek scholarship in 1950.

19 'Vindication of his life'.

20 The Reichstag was badly damaged by fire in February 1933; the trial of those presumed responsible took place in the autumn of the same year at Leipzig in Germany.

9 Peter Wright

1 Arthur S. Martin (1914–96) joined MI5 in 1946 after six years in RSS. He prepared the brief for Philby's questioning by the Security Service. Head of MI5's Soviet section from 1960, he led the inquiries which resulted in the arrests of Gordon Lonsdale and John Vassall. In November 1964 he transferred to SIS, where he served until 1969. After his retirement from British intelligence, Martin worked as an assistant clerk in the House of Lords.

2 Peter Maurice Wright (1916–95) was educated at Bishop's Stortford and became an Admiralty scientist during World War II. Proficient with machines, Wright was out of his depth as an intelligence officer, and easily deluded by conspiracy theories.

3 Andrew, *The Defence of the Realm*, pp. 337–8 and 503.

4 Graham Russell Mitchell (1905–84) was educated at Winchester and Magdalen College Oxford and joined MI5 in 1939 from the research department of Conservative Central Office. In 1952 he became head of MI5's counter-espionage branch and was appointed deputy director general four years later.

5 Roger Hollis (1905–73), director general of MI5 from 1956 to 1965, was educated at Leeds Grammar School, Clifton College and Worcester College Oxford, where he was known as 'a good bottle man' due to his conviviality. He later worked for eight years with the British American Tobacco Company in China before joining the Security Service in 1938. He developed particular expertise in the struggle against international communism, and was appointed deputy director general three years before taking over the top job. He was created KBE in 1966.

6 Andrew, *Defence of the Realm*, pp. 505–8.

7 Ibid., pp. 510–15; Peter Wright with Paul Greengrass, *Spycatcher: The Candid Autobiography of a Senior Intelligence Officer* (New York: Viking Penguin, 1987), p. 290.

8 Ibid., p. 26.

9 N.M. Victor Rothschild (1910–90), third Baron Rothschild, was a Cambridge zoologist who later served in MI5, where he won the George Medal for bravery in defusing a German bomb. In 1971 the prime minister, Edward Heath, appointed Rothschild as the first head of the Central Policy Review Staff, or Think Tank.

10 Andrew, *Defence of the Realm*, pp. 760–1.

11 SOC.Dacre 6/4, Dick White to Hugh Trevor-Roper, 25 April 1984.

12 Andrew, *Defence of the Realm*, pp. 761–5.

13 First published in the *Independent*, 12 December 1986.

14 Arthur Cecil Pigou (1877–1959), professor of political economy at Cambridge from 1908, influenced the study of welfare economics and unemployment despite sharp attacks by Keynes. Donald Howard Beves (1896–1961) taught modern languages at King's College Cambridge, where he became vice-provost. Andrew S.F. 'Granny' Gow (1886–1978) taught classics at Trinity College Cambridge from 1925. He edited the works of Nicander, a Greek writer who composed poems on snake-bites, poisons and their cures.

15 1964 in original.

16 First published in the *Spectator*, 10 October 1987.

17 Feliks Edmundovich Dzerzhinskii (1877–1926) was the son of a Polish landowner who took part in the Bolshevik Revolution of October 1917. In December Dzerzhinskii was appointed first head of the Cheka, a precursor of the KGB. Although he led a murderous campaign of terror, Dzerzhinskii claimed that the secret policeman should have a 'warm heart, cool head and clean hands'.

18 James Jesus 'the Gray Ghost' Angleton (1917–87) was educated at Yale and Harvard Law School. After wartime experience in American counter-espionage, which brought him in contact with Philby, in 1954 Angleton was appointed first chief of the Counterintelligence Staff of the CIA. Golitsyn convinced Angleton that the KGB had planted numerous moles in the CIA but the most intensive investigations failed to unearth any of them. Angleton was forced to retire in 1974 after the *New York Times* revealed he had illegally organised operations inside the United States.

19 Sir William Stephenson, head of British Security Coordination in the western hemisphere during World War II. See Chapter 5 above.

10 Otto John and Reinhard Gehlen

1 Bernd Stöver, 'Der Fall Otto John: Neue Dokumente zu den Aussagen des deutschen Geheimdienstchefs gegenueber MfS und KGB', *Vierteljahrshefte fuer Zeitgeschichte* 47/1 (1999), pp. 107–8.

2 Ibid., pp. 108–9.

3 Ibid., pp. 103 and 111–12.

4 Otto John, *Zweimal kam ich heim: Vom Verschwörer zum Schützer der Verfassung* (Düsseldorf: Econ Verlag, 1969).

5 Reinhard Gehlen (1902–79) headed from 1942 Fremde Heere Ost, which gathered intelligence on the Soviet armed forces for the German army. After the war he was recruited by the American army, and his ring of agents became known as the Gehlen Organisation. Although many of his spies were captured, in divided Germany it was easy for Gehlen to find new agents, whose reports included military movements on the railway which linked East Germany with the Soviet Union: Paul Maddrell, 'Einfallstor in die Sowjetunion. Die Besatzung Deutschlands und die Ausspähung der UdSSR durch den britischen Nachrichtendienst', *Vierteljahrshefte fuer Zeitgeschichte* 51/2 (2003), pp. 202–3.

6 Stöver, 'Der Fall Otto John', pp. 113–16.

7 John, *Zweimal kam ich heim*, pp. 302 and 354.

8 Stöver, 'Der Fall Otto John', pp. 116–18.

9 *Twice Through the Lines: The Autobiography of Otto John*, introduction by H.R. Trevor-Roper (London: Macmillan, 1972), p. xii.

10 First published in the *Spectator*, 12 April 1997.

11 John Wheeler-Bennett (1902–75) was educated at Malvern College. Although illness prevented his entering Christ Church, his name was later added to the college books. He made a special study of the international history of Germany, publishing a series of pioneering works. A founding fellow of St Antony's College Oxford, he served as historical adviser to the Royal Archives and was created GCVO (Knight Grand Cross of the Royal Victorian Order) in 1974.

12 He was pardoned and released 16 months early, as one-third of his sentence was remitted for good behaviour, the usual practice with first offenders.

13 In fact John met up with Wohlgemuth in West Berlin.

14 i.e. nothing to suggest that John was a Soviet penetration agent.

15 But see the introduction to this chapter.

16 SOC.Dacre 10/49, Hugh Trevor-Roper to Peter Strafford, 6 and 13 August 1985.

17 Johannes Jebsen, the Abwehr case officer running the double agent *Tricycle*, was himself recruited as a British double agent code-named *Artist* in September 1943. By the following April he realised that yet another double agent, code-name *Garbo*, was also working in Britain's interest. *Garbo* was to play a central part in the the the deception to cover the D-Day landings. Although the Gestapo arrested *Artist* in May 1944, this was for embezzlement not treason. He survived his transportation in a trunk from Lisbon to German territory, where he endured brutal interrogation and eventually died. But because of his courage and the complexity of his case, D-Day arrived, and the deception took place before the Gestapo could make sense of it all; Andrew, *Defence of the Realm*, pp. 297–8 and 304–5;

Thomas Hennessey and Claire Thomas, *Spooks: The Unofficial History of MI5* (Stroud: Amberley, 2009), pp. 463–5.

18 Prince Dimitri Obolensky (1918–2001), who claimed descent from Ryurik, traditionally regarded as founder of the Russian state, was rescued by the Royal Navy from the Crimea as an infant and educated at the Lycée Pasteur in Paris and Trinity College Cambridge. He was elected student (tutorial fellow) of Christ Church in 1950 and held the Oxford Chair of Russian and Balkan History from 1961 until 1985.

19 The Nansen passport, an identity card for international travellers without state citizenship, was introduced by the Norwegian explorer and humanitarian Fridtjof Nansen (1861–1930) in 1922, the year he won the Nobel Peace Prize in recognition of his work for the casualties of war.

20 Heinz Felfe (1918–) was a former SS officer whose wartime service included a spell in the Reich Security Head Office. After the war he trained as a lawyer and was recruited by Soviet intelligence in 1949. Two years later Felfe joined the Gehlen Organisation, which became the Federal Intelligence Service in 1956. Felfe was appointed head of anti-Soviet counter-espionage. Exposed by a defector in 1961, he was sentenced to 15 years in prison, but was swapped in 1969 for 21 people who wanted to leave East Germany. Felfe then began a new career as a lecturer in criminology at the Humboldt University in East Berlin.

21 Sir Maurice Oldfield (1915–81) was educated at Lady Manners School, Bakewell and Manchester University. He served as Chief of SIS from 1973 to 1978 and as security coordinator in Northern Ireland from 1979 to 1980.

22 Harold Anthony Caccia (1905–90), educated at Eton and Trinity College Oxford, was deputy under-secretary of state at the Foreign Office from 1954 to 1956, head of HM Diplomatic Service from 1964 to 1965 and created a life peer in 1965.

23 The discussion of Caccia and Oldfield is from Trevor-Roper's letter of 13 August 1985, SOC.Dacre 10/49. The evidence from the Stasi files also supports Trevor-Roper's thesis that John did not deliberately defect.

24 First published as the introduction to *Network: The Truth about General Gehlen and his Spy Ring*, by Heinz Höhne and Hermann Zolling (London: Secker and Warburg, 1972). A brief last paragraph has been omitted from this piece and the sequence of the final two remaining paragraphs exchanged.

25 Denis Sefton Delmer (1904–79) was educated at St Paul's School and Lincoln College Oxford. Hired by Lord Beaverbrook to work on the *Daily Express*, he was the first British journalist to interview Hitler. He worked for the Political Warfare Executive during the war, and after it returned to the *Daily Express*, achieving a succession of scoops, such as his 'exposure' of Gehlen, until he was sacked in 1959.

26 Julius Mader (1928–2000) joined the Socialist Unity Party which ruled East Germany in 1958; his protracted university studies culminated with a PhD in politics. Mader became a professional writer with a particular interest in espionage and the Third Reich; more than 3 million copies of his books were printed.

27 Franz-Josef Strauss (1915–88) authorised a raid on the offices of *Der Spiegel* and in the aftermath lost his post as minister of defence. For many years the dominant figure amongst the Bavarian Christian Socialists, Strauss was a determined opponent of rapprochement with the German Democratic Republic. A controversial figure, his attempt to be elected federal chancellor in 1980 was a flop.

Appendix 1

1 Bodleian Library MS. Eng. c. 6888, folios 97–8.
2 'Cornwall' in original.
3 SOC.Dacre 1/2/43.
4 Eleanor Philby. Her articles in the *Observer* were later published as *The Spy Who Loved Me*, and reviewed in *The Philby Affair*; see above, pp. 75–6.
5 Trevor-Roper did indeed use the words 'Good judges': see above, p. 94.
6 Bodleian Library MS. Eng. c. 6888, folios 99–100.
7 Trevor-Roper had recommended the book to Reilly.
8 It is unlikely that Macmillan would have explained White's appointment, as he held the traditional view that secret services worked best in secret.
9 Trevor-Roper referred to Philby as 'P' throughout the original letter.
10 'In your very own words'.
11 'The successful third-placed candidate'. SOC.Dacre 13/59, Oxford University Pocket Diary 1967–8, entry for 8 February 1968 and separate note on the same date.
12 Bodleian Library, MS. Eng. c. 6888, folio 101, British Embassy, Paris, Hugh Trevor-Roper to Patrick Reilly, 19 March 1968.
13 This was a complete fabrication by Philby: Reilly never wrote such a minute.
14 George Alfred Brown (1914–85) had considerable ministerial experience by the time he was appointed foreign secretary in 1966. A politician of exceptional but flawed talent, he resigned from the Cabinet in March 1968 and became a peer in 1970.
15 Bodleian Library, MS. Eng. c. 6882 and c. 6925.
16 Bodleian Library, MS. Eng. c. 6888, folios 102–3.
17 SOC.Dacre 1/2/43.
18 Philby may well have realised he was being considered for significant

promotion. Why else would Reilly have interviewed him? On the other hand, Philby's reference to Reilly's 'leaving a mark' did not refer to this interview, but to his service in 1942–3, as the ambassador pointed out.

19 A French satirical magazine.

20 John Vassall was an Admiralty clerk who served for a time in the Moscow Embassy. In 1955 the KGB photographed his homosexual activities and blackmailed him into working as a Russian agent. After information from the Soviet defector Golitsyn had prompted an investigation, in 1962 incriminating film of espionage material was discovered in Vassall's London flat. He was arrested and later sentenced to 18 years' imprisonment.

21 Sir William Goodenough Hayter (1906–95) was ambassador to the Soviet Union from 1953 to 1957 and warden of New College Oxford from 1958 until 1976. So he had left the Diplomatic Service four years before Vassall's arrest.

22 SOC.Dacre 10/45.

23 Trevor-Roper used 'Phi' for Philby here and elsewhere in this and the following paragraph.

24 Bodleian Library, MS. Eng. c. 6888, folio 104.

25 Bodleian Library, MS. Eng. c. 6888, folio 108.

26 The Reillys' home in England. 'Intestine' refers to conflict within SIS.

27 The quotation in Greek beneath the dedication to D.P.R. at the beginning of the Kimber edition was supplied to Trevor-Roper by the late Hugh Lloyd-Jones, Regius Professor of Greek and a frequent correspondent.

28 Anthony Cave Brown, *Treason in the Blood: H. St. John Philby, Kim Philby, and the Spy Case of the Century* (Boston: Houghton Mifflin, 1994).

29 SOC.Dacre 6/4.

30 The bandersnatch, a creature of astonishing speed and ferocity, appears repeatedly in the writing of Lewis Carroll.

31 This was meant ironically, as Reilly was not present.

32 Cave Brown, *Treason in the Blood*, p. 311.

Appendix 2

1 SOC.Dacre 1/2/1, Charles Stuart to Hugh Trevor-Roper, 11 September 1947.

2 Page, Leitch and Knightley, *Philby*.

3 Charles Stuart Papers, Hugh Trevor-Roper to Charles Stuart, 25 December 1967.

4 Charles Stuart Papers, SIS to Charles Stuart, 21 February 1968.

5 The recollections were not 'pirated', but willingly provided by Stuart.

6 Charles Stuart Papers, SIS to Charles Stuart, 26 March 1968.

7 Charles Stuart Papers, Hugh Trevor-Roper to Charles Stuart, 12 and 23 April 1968; SOC.Dacre 10/45, Charles Stuart to Hugh Trevor-Roper, 15 April 1968.

8 First published in the *Spectator*, 26 April 1968.

9 Philby's friend Ian Innes 'Tim' Milne and their colleague Desmond Bristow were among other wartime recruits who chose to stay on, but such decisions were not made known, and staff often appeared to work for the Foreign Office.

10 Roy Herbert Thomson, first Baron Thomson of Fleet (1894–1976), was a Canadian business magnate with extensive interests, including ownership of *The Times* and the *Sunday Times*, which published the Philby story in weekly instalments. Thomson hosted a dinner at the Savoy Hotel on 31 October 1967 attended by American and British business leaders. During an extraordinary speech, George Brown accused Thomson of dishonesty and urged the *Sunday Times* 'for God's sake stop [...] it is about time we stopped giving the Russians a head start on what we are doing' (Peter Paterson, *Tired and Emotional. The Life of Lord George-Brown* (London: Chatto & Windus, 1993), pp/ 197–200). The phrase *in vino veritas* referred to Brown's consumption of alcohol to ease the strain of high office.

11 'Not' was omitted by the printer from the original publication of this essay, much to Stuart's consternation.

12 In late 1944 Philby was appointed head of Section IX, which handled SIS's anti-Communist work. Philby's former superior Felix Cowgill, the head of Section V, had expected this post, and no persuasion could stop him from resigning in his disappointment. Cowgill was betrayed by his old patron Valentine Vivian, who nominated Philby for the appointment, and by Philby himself, who took it regardless of his colleague's aspirations. The double-cross by his young deputy must have deflated even Cowgill: *et tu Brute*.

13 In the *Encounter* version of *The Philby Affair* Trevor-Roper had dated this episode to 'Late in 1943', and written that the paper was submitted for clearance to Philby 'in view of the Spanish interest': *Encounter* 30/4 (1968), p. 20.

14 Colonel-General Franz Halder (1884–1972) was Chief of the Army General Staff from 1938. Halder dithered between loyalty to Hitler and resistance before his dismissal on 24 September 1942 as a scapegoat for the faltering Russian campaign.

15 *Erewhon* (1872), a utopian novel by Samuel Butler.

16 The paper was dated 5 June 1943.

17 Colonel Guy Randolph Westmacott was educated at Eton and Christ Church, married the only daughter of the second Baron St Oswald, and won the DSO with the Grenadier Guards in World War I. A member of White's and

the Turf, in June 1944 he was appointed by Menzies to a post at General Montgomery's headquarters, where he could act as an intelligence conduit between SIS and the Allied Expeditionary Forces; *Who's Who 1941*; Jeffery, *MI6*, p. 540.

18 Charles Stuart Papers, Hugh Trevor-Roper to Charles Stuart, 6 May 1968. By 1945 Mark Johnston was working for MI5 and frequenting the Dorchester Hotel, where Lord Swinton tried to recruit him to his staff. Aeneas Alexander Mackay (1905–63), thirteenth Baron Reay and Chief of Clan Mackay, was a frequent correspondent of Trevor-Roper's. Another friend, the biographer Freddie Birkenhead, complained that, 'although I have spent as much time at the bar of White's as most people, no one has ever asked me to join the SIS' (SOC.Dacre 1/2/12, letter of 25 September 1968).

19 Jeffery, *MI6*, pp. 475 and 585–6.

20 Charles Stuart Papers, SIS to Charles Stuart, 26 April 1968.

21 Charles Stuart Papers, SIS to Charles Stuart, 24 April 1968, Charles Stuart to SIS, 2 May 1968.

22 Charles Stuart Papers, SIS to Charles Stuart, 10 September 1968.

23 SOC.Dacre 1/2/43, Charles Stuart to Hugh Trevor-Roper, 16 September 1968.

24 First published in the *Spectator*, 27 September 1968, above a prominent advertisement for *My Silent War* which described the book as 'brilliantly introduced by Graham Greene'. This opinion contrasted sharply with the verdict on Greene in Stuart's essay.

25 Walter Krivitsky, a Soviet intelligence officer who had been working illegally in the Netherlands, defected in November 1937 and sought refuge in the United States. He fell from a window to his death in 1940. Victor Kravchenko (1905–66) was a Communist Party member and Soviet official who defected to the United States in 1944. Two years later he published *I Chose Freedom*, a best-selling denunciation of Stalinist Russia.

26 This alludes to Vivian's bizarre suspicion that Trevor-Roper had visited Ireland in 1942 not to go hunting, but to betray Ultra to the German Legation in Dublin.

27 In August 1968 Warsaw Pact forces invaded Czechoslovakia to stop an attempt at liberalisation: afterwards there was an influx of KGB officers.

Bibliography

Unpublished Sources

Bodleian Library, Oxford University, Papers of Sir (D'Arcy) Patrick Reilly:
MS. Eng. c. 6882, c. 6888, c. 6918 and c. 6925

Christ Church Oxford, Lord Dacre of Glanton Papers:
SOC.Dacre 1/1/F, 1/2/1, 11, 12, 25, 43; 6/4 and 34; 9/13 and 15; 10/7, 20, 28, 30, 31, 42, 44, 45, 46, 48, 49, 54; 12/24; 13/29, 58, 59

King's College London, Liddell Hart Centre for Military Archives:
Liddell Hart Collection 15/15/162 and Davidson Papers 4/1

The National Archives (TNA), Kew, United Kingdom:
ADM 223/298
HW 14/35 and 36; 19/331, 333 and 347; 34/5 and 23
KV 2/757, 4/ 97, 98, 100, 120, 170, 188, 191, 196, 217
WO 208/3787, 4701, 5095, 5096, 5097

Nuffield College Oxford Cherwell Papers
K295/1–12

Charles Stuart Papers (in private possession)

Published Sources

Abshagen, Karl Heinz, *Canaris*, trans. Alan Houghton Brodrick (London: Hutchinson & Co., 1956).
Adamthwaite, Anthony P., *Europe and the Struggle for Leadership: Britain and France, 1945–1975* (London: Bloomsbury, forthcoming).
Akhmedov, Ismail, *In and Out of Stalin's GRU: A Tatar's Escape from Red Army Intelligence* (London: Arms and Armour Press, 1984).
Aldrich, Richard J., *The Hidden Hand: Britain, America and Cold War Secret Intelligence* (London: John Murray, 2001).

—— (ed.), *Espionage, Security and Intelligence in Britain, 1945–70* (Manchester: Manchester University Press, 1998).

Andrew, Christopher, *The Defence of the Realm: The Authorized History of MI5* (London: Allen Lane, 2009).

——'Intelligence in the Cold War', in Melvyn P. Leffler and Odd Arne Westad (eds), *The Cambridge History of the Cold War. Vol. II: Crises and Détente* (Cambridge: Cambridge University Press, 2010).

Andrew, Christopher and Oleg Gordievsky, *KGB: The Inside Story of its Foreign Operations from Lenin to Gorbachev* (London: Hodder & Stoughton, 1990).

Andrew, Christopher and Vasili Mitrokhin, *The Mitrokhin Archive: The KGB in Europe and the West* (London: Allen Lane The Penguin Press, 1999).

Australia, Commonwealth of, *Royal Commission on Espionage: Transcript of Proceedings* (Sydney: Commonwealth of Australia, 1954–5).

Batey, Keith, 'How Dilly Knox and his Girls Broke the *Abwehr* Enigma', in Ralph Erskine and Michael Smith (eds), *Action this Day: Bletchley Park from the Breaking of the Enigma Code to the Birth of the Modern Computer* (London: Bantam, 2001).

Baumgartner, Gabriele and Dieter Hebig (eds), *Biographisches Handbuch der SBZ/ DDR 1945–1990* (Munich: K.G. Saur, 1996).

Baxter, Christopher, 'Forgeries and Spies: The Foreign Office and the "Cicero" Case', *Intelligence and National Security* 23/6 (2008).

Bennett, Gill, *'A Most Extraordinary and Mysterious Business': The Zinoviev Letter of 1924* (London: Foreign & Commonwealth Office, History Notes 14, 1999).

Bennett, Ralph, *Behind the Battle: Intelligence in the War with Germany, 1939–45* (London: Sinclair Stevenson, 1994).

Benton, Kenneth, 'The ISOS Years: Madrid, 1941–3', *Journal of Contemporary History* 30 (1995).

Bertrand, Gustave, *Enigma ou la plus grande enigma de la guerre, 1939–1945* (Paris: Librairie Plon, 1973).

Blake, George, *No Other Choice* (London: Jonathan Cape, 1990).

Boeselager, Philipp von with Florence and Jerome Fehrenbach, *Valkyrie: The Plot to Kill Hitler* (London: Phoenix, 2009).

Borovik, Genrikh, *The Philby Files: The Secret Life of the Master Spy – KGB Archives Revealed*, ed. and with an introduction by Phillip Knightley (London: Little, Brown, 1994).

Bower, Tom, *The Perfect English Spy: Sir Dick White and the Secret War, 1935–90* (London: Heinemann, 1995).

Boyle, Andrew, *The Climate of Treason* (London: Hutchinson, 1979).

Boyle, David, *With Ardours Manifold* (London: Hutchinson, 1959).

Bristow, Desmond with Bill Bristow, *A Game of Moles: The Deceptions of an MI6 Officer* (London: Little, Brown, 1993).

British Security Coordination: The Secret History of British Intelligence in the Americas 1940–45, introduction by Nigel West (London: St Ermin's Press, 1998).

Brown, George, *In my Way: The Political Memoirs of Lord George-Brown* (London: Victor Gollancz, 1971).

Browne, Thomas, *Hydrotaphia, or Urn-burial* (1658).

Buchheim, Hans, 'The SS – Instrument of Domination', in Helmut Krausnick, Hans Buchheim, Martin Broszat and Hans-Adolf Jacobsen (eds), *The Anatomy of the SS State* (London: Collins, 1968).

Canaris, Wilhelm, 'Politik und Wehrmacht', in Richard Donnevert (ed.), *Wehrmacht und Partei* (Leipzig: Verlag von Johann Ambrosius Barth, 1938).

Carter, Miranda, *Anthony Blunt: His Lives* (London: Macmillan, 2001).

Cave Brown, Anthony, *Treason in the Blood: H. St. John Philby, Kim Philby, and the Spy Case of the Century* (Boston, MA: Houghton Mifflin, 1994).

Cavendish, Anthony, *Inside Intelligence* (London: Collins, 1990).

Cecil, Robert, 'Legends Spies Tell: A Reappraisal of the Absconding Diplomats', *Encounter* 50/4 (1978).

—— '"C"'s War', *Intelligence and National Security* 1/2 (1986).

—— *A Divided Life: A Biography of Donald Maclean* (London: Bodley Head, 1988).

—— 'Five of Six at War: Section V of MI6', *Intelligence and National Security* 9/2 (1994).

Chester, Lewis, Stephen Fay and Hugo Young, *The Zinoviev Letter* (London: Heinemann, 1967).

Cockerill, A.W., *Sir Percy Sillitoe* (London: W.H. Allen, 1975).

Cookridge, E.H., *The Third Man* (New York: Berkley Medallion, 1968).

Costello, John and Oleg Tsarev, *Deadly Illusions* (London: Century, 1993).

Cradock, Percy, *Know your Enemy: How the Joint Intelligence Committee Saw the World* (London: John Murray, 2002).

Curry, John Court, *The Security Service, 1908–1945: The Official History* (Kew: Public Record Office, 1999).

Curthoys, Judith, *The Cardinal's College: Christ Church, Chapter and Verse* (London: Profile Books, 2012).

Davies, Philip H.J., *MI6 and the Machinery of Spying* (London: Frank Cass, 2004).

Deakin, F.W. and G.R. Storry, *The Case of Richard Sorge* (London: Chatto & Windus, 1966).

Dear, I.C.B. (ed.), *The Oxford Companion to the Second World War* (Oxford: Oxford University Press, 1995).

Dulles, Allen, *The Craft of Intelligence* (London: Weidenfeld & Nicolson, 1963).

Elliott, Nicholas, *Never Judge a Man by his Umbrella* (Salisbury: Michael Russell, 1991).

—— *With my Little Eye: Observations along the Way* (Norwich: Michael Russell, 1993).

Encyclopaedia Britannica (London: Encyclopaedia Britannica, 1955).

Erskine, Ralph, 'Eavesdropping on "Bodden": ISOS v. the Abwehr in the Straits of Gibraltar', *Intelligence and National Security* 12/3 (1997).

Erskine, Ralph and Michael Smith (eds), *Action this Day: Bletchley Park from the Breaking of the Enigma Code to the Birth of the Modern Computer* (London: Bantam, 2001).

Felfe, Heinz, *Im Dienst des Gegners: 10 Jahre Moskaus Mann im BND* (Hamburg: Rasch und Roehring Verlag, 1985).

Foot, M.R.D., *SOE in France: An Account of the Work of the British Special Operations Executive in France, 1940–1944* (London: HMSO, 1966).

—— Obituary of Professor R.V. Jones, *Independent*, 19 December 1997.

—— *Memories of an SOE Historian* (Barnsley: Pen & Sword, 2008).

Foot, M.R.D. (ed.), *Secret Lives: Lifting the Lid on Worlds of Secret Intelligence* (Oxford: Oxford University Press, 2002).

Fourcade, Marie-Madeleine, *Noah's Ark* (London: George Allen & Unwin, 1973).

Garraty, John A. and Mark C. Carnes, *American National Biography* (New York: Oxford University Press, 1999).

Gerwarth, Robert, *Hitler's Hangman: The Life of Heydrich* (New Haven, CT: Yale University Press, 2012).

Geyer, Michael, 'National Socialist Germany: The Politics of Information', in Ernest R. May (ed.), *Knowing One's Enemies: Intelligence Assessment before the Two World Wars* (Princeton: Princeton University Press, 1986).

Gibney, Frank (ed.), *The Penkovsky Papers* (London: Collins, 1965).

Gilbert, Martin, *Winston S. Churchill. Companion Volume V, Part 3: The Coming of War, 1936–1939* (London: Heinemann, 1982).

Gordievsky, Oleg, *Next Stop Execution* (London: Macmillan, 1995).

Groscurth, Helmuth, *Tagebücher eines Abwehroffiziers 1938–1940 mit weiteren Dokumenten zur Militäropposition gegen Hitler*, edited by Helmut Krausnick and Harold C. Deutsch with Hildegard von Kotze (Stuttgart: Deutsche Verlagsanstalt, 1970).

Harrison, E.D.R., '"Alter Kaempfer" im Widerstand. Graf Helldorff, die NS-Bewegung und die Opposition gegen Hitler', *Vierteljahrshefte fuer Zeitgeschichte* 45/3 (1997).

—— 'British Subversion in French East Africa, 1941–42: SOE's Todd Mission', *English Historical Review* 114/456 (1999).

—— 'The British Special Operations Executive and Poland', *Historical Journal* 43/4 (2000).

—— 'Kim Philby: The End of a Myth', in Alistair Horne (ed.), *Telling Lives: From W.B. Yeats to Bruce Chatwin* (London: Macmillan, 2000).

—— '*The Last Days of Hitler* revisited', *Spectator*, 17 March 2007.

—— 'On Secret Service for the Duce: Umberto Campini in Portuguese East Africa', *English Historical Review* 122/499 (2007).

—— 'Hugh Trevor-Roper und *Hitlers letzte Tage*', *Vierteljahrshefte fuer Zeitgeschichte* 57/1 (2009).

—— 'British Radio Security and Intelligence, 1939–43', *English Historical Review* 124/506 (2009).

—— 'J.C. Masterman and the Security Service, 1940–1972', *Intelligence and National Security* 24/6 (2009).

—— *The Young Kim Philby: Soviet Spy and British Intelligence Officer* (Liverpool: Liverpool University Press, 2012).

—— *Secret Service and Resistance to Nazism* (forthcoming).

Hassell, Ulrich von, *Vom Andern Deutschland* (Zürich: Atlantis Verlag, 1946).

—— *Die Hassell-Tagebücher 1938–1944 Aufzeichnungen vom anderen Deutschland*, edited by Friedrich Freiherr Hiller von Gaertringen (Berlin: Siedler Verlag, 1988).

Heinemann, Winfried, 'Der militaerische Widerstand und der Krieg', in Militaergeschichtliches Forschungsamt, *Das Deutsche Reich und der Zweite Weltkrieg* 9/1 (Munich: Deutsche Verlags-Anstalt, 2004).

Hennessey, Thomas and Claire Thomas, *Spooks: The Unofficial History of MI5* (Stroud: Amberley, 2009).

Hinsley, F.H. and C.A.G. Simkins, *British Intelligence in the Second World War. Vol. 4: Security and Counter-Intelligence* (London: HMSO, 1990).

Hinsley, F.H. and Alan Stripp (eds), *Codebreakers: The Inside Story of Bletchley Park* (Oxford: Oxford University Press, 1993).

Hinsley, F.H. with E.E. Thomas, C.F.G. Ransom and R.C. Knight, *British Intelligence in the Second World War: Its Influence on Strategy and Operations. Vol. 1* (London: HMSO, 1979).

Hinsley, F.H. with E.E. Thomas, C.F.G. Ransom and R.C. Knight, *British Intelligence in the Second World War: Its Influence on Strategy and Operations. Vol. 2* (London: HMSO, 1981)

Hinsley, F.H. with E.E. Thomas, C.A.G. Simkins and C.F.G. Ransom, *British Intelligence in the Second World War: Its Influence on Strategy and Operations. Vol. 3, Part II* (London: HMSO, 1988).

Hoare, Oliver (ed.), *Camp 020: MI5 and the Nazi Spies. The Official History of MI5's Wartime Interrogation Centre* (Richmond: Public Record Office, 2000).

Hoare, Samuel, *Ambassador on Special Mission* (London: Collins, 1946).

Hoehne, Heinz, *Canaris: Patriot im Zwielicht* (Munich: C. Bertelsmann Verlag, 1976).

Hoehne, Heinz and Hermann Zolling, *Network: The Truth about General Gehlen and his Spy Ring*, trans. by Richard Barry, introduction by H.R. Trevor-Roper (London: Secker & Warburg, 1972).

Hoettl, Wilhelm, *The Secret Front: The Inside Story of Nazi Political Espionage*, introduction by Ian Colvin (London: Phoenix Press, 2000).

Horne, Alistair (ed.), *Telling Lives: From W.B. Yeats to Bruce Chatwin* (London: Macmillan, 2000).

Howard, Michael, *Grand Strategy. Vol. IV: August 1942–September 1943*, in J.R.M. Butler (ed.), *History of the Second World War United Kingdom Military Series* (London: HMSO, 1972).

—— *British Intelligence in the Second World War. Vol. 5: Strategic Deception* (London: HMSO, 1990).

Jacobsen, Hans-Adolf, 'The *Kommissarbefehl* and Mass Executions of Soviet Prisoners of War', in Helmut Krausnick, Hans Buchheim, Martin Broszat and Hans-Adolf Jacobsen, *The Anatomy of the SS State* (London: Collins, 1968).

Jeffery, Keith, *MI6: The History of the Secret Intelligence Service, 1909–1949* (London: Bloomsbury, 2011).

John, Otto, *Zweimal kam ich heim: Vom Verschwoerer zum Schuetzer der Verfassung* (Düsseldorf: Econ Verlag, 1969).

Johns, Philip, *Within Two Cloaks: Missions with SIS and SOE* (London: William Kimber, 1979).

Jones, R.V., *Most Secret War* (London: Hamish Hamilton, 1978).

Kahn, David, *Hitler's Spies: German Military Intelligence in World War II* (Cambridge, MA: Da Capo Press, 2000).

—— 'How the Allies Suppressed the Second Greatest Secret of World War II', *Journal of Military History* 74/4 (2010).

Klemperer, Klemens von, *German Resistance against Hitler: The Search for Allies Abroad, 1938–1945* (Oxford: Oxford University Press, 1992).

Knightley, Phillip, *Philby: The Life and Views of the KGB Masterspy* (London: Andre Deutsch, 1988).

Krausnick, Helmut, Hans Buchheim, Martin Broszat and Hans-Adolf Jacobsen (eds), *The Anatomy of the SS State* (London: Collins, 1968).

Kroener, Bernard R., *'Der starke Mann im Heimatskriegsgebiet': Generaloberst Friedrich Fromm. Eine Biographie* (Paderborn: Ferdinand Schoeningh, 2005).

Lankford, Nelson Douglas (ed.), *OSS against the Reich: The World War II Diaries of Colonel David K.E. Bruce* (Kent, OH: Kent State University Press, 1991).

Laqueur, Walter, *World of Secrets: The Uses and Limits of Intelligence* (London: Weidenfeld and Nicolson, 1985).

Leffler, Melvyn P. and Odd Arne Westad (eds), *The Cambridge History of the Cold War. Vol. I: Origins* and *Vol. II: Crises and Détente* (Cambridge: Cambridge University Press, 2010).

Leggett, George, *The Cheka: Lenin's Political Police: The All-Russian Extraordinary Commission for Combating Counter-Revolution and Sabotage* (Oxford: Clarendon Press, 1986).

Leverkuehn, Paul, *German Military Intelligence* (London: Weidenfeld & Nicolson, 1954).

Lukes, Igor, *On the Edge of the Cold War: American Diplomats and Spies in Postwar Prague* (Oxford: Oxford University Press, 2012).

Mackenzie, W.J.M., *The Secret History of SOE: The Special Operations Executive, 1940–1945*, foreword and notes by M.R.D. Foot (London: St Ermin's Press, 2000).

Maddrell, Paul, 'Einfallstor in die Sowjetunion: Die Besatzung Deutschlands und die Ausspähung der UdSSR durch den britischen Nachrichtendienst', *Vierteljahrshefte fuer Zeitgeschichte* 51/2 (2003).

Masterman, J.C., *The Double-Cross System in the War of 1939 to 1945* (New Haven, CT and London: Yale University Press, 1972).

Matthew, Colin, 'Charles Harborne Stuart', *Christ Church Report* (1991).

Milne, Ian Innes 'Tim', *Kim Philby: The Unknown Story of the KGB's Master Spy* (London: Biteback Publishing, 2014).

Modin, Yuri with Jean-Charles Deniau and Aguieszka Ziarek, *My Five Cambridge Friends* (London: Headline, 1994).

Montagu, Ewen, *The Man who Never Was* (Oxford: Oxford University Press, 1953).

Mueller, Rolf-Dieter and Hans-Erich Volkmann (eds), *Die Wehrmacht: Mythos und Realitaet* (Munich: R. Oldenbourg, 1999).

Mueller-Enbergs, Helmut, Jan Wielgohs and Dieter Hoffmann (eds), *Wer war wer in der DDR? Ein Biographisches Lexikon* (Berlin: Christoph Links Verlag, 2001).

Muggeridge, Malcolm, *Chronicles of Wasted Time 2: The Infernal Grove* (London: Collins, 1973).

Myers, Ernest (ed.), *The Extant Odes of Pindar* (London: Macmillan, 1904).

Naftali, Timothy J., 'Intrepid's Last Deception: Documenting the Career of Sir William Stephenson', *Intelligence and National Security* 8/3 (1993)

Neue Deutsche Biographie (Berlin 1969–).

O'Grady, Jane, 'Sir Stuart Hampshire', obituary, *Guardian*, 16 June 2004.

O'Halpin, Eunan, 'The Liddell Diaries and British Intelligence History', *Intelligence and National Security* 20/4 (2005).

Orlov, Alexander, *Handbook of Intelligence and Guerilla Warfare* (Ann Arbor: University of Michigan Press, 1963).

Otto, Reinhard, 'Die Zusammenarbeit von Wehrmacht und Stapo bei der "Aussonderung" sowjetischer Kriegsgefangener im Reich', in Rolf-Dieter Mueller and Hans-Erich Volkmann (eds), *Die Wehrmacht: Mythos und Realitaet* (Munich: R. Oldenbourg, 1999).

Oxford Dictionary of National Biography, entries for John Henry Bevan by John P. Campbell; Anthony Frederick Blunt by Michael Kitson revised by Miranda Carter; Guy Burgess by Sheila Kerr; John Cairncross by Richard Davenport-Hines; Lionel Kenneth Philip Crabb by Richard Compton-Hall; Andrew Sydenham Farrar Gow revised by Hugh Lloyd-Jones; Richard Gambier-Parry by A.O. Blishen; Nigel Arthur de Grey by Nigel West; Herbert Lionel Adolphus Hart by Tony Honore; Alfred Dillwyn Knox revised by Mavis Batey; Guy Maynard Liddell by Nigel West; Donald Duart Maclean revised by Robert Cecil; Edward Phillips Oppenheim by William A.S. Sarjeant; Harry

St John Bridger Philby by James Craig; Arthur Cecil Pigou by David Collard; Morgan Goronwy Rees by Kenneth O. Morgan; D'Arcy Patrick Reilly by John Ure; John Tressider Sheppard by Noel Annan; Percy Joseph Sillitoe revised by Anthony Simkins; Hugh Francis Paget Sinclair revised by Christopher Andrew; John Alexander Sinclair revised by Dick White; Oliver Strachey by Ralph Erskine; Roy Herbert Thomson revised by Robin Denniston and Denis Hamilton; Edward Wilfrid Harry Travis by D.R. Nicoll; Valentine Patrick Terrell Vivian by A.O. Blishen, Frederick William Winterbotham revised by C.S. Nicholls; Peter Maurice Wright by Peter Martland; Greville Maynard Wynne revised by M.R.D. Foot.

The Oxford English Dictionary, prepared by J.A. Simpson and E.S.C. Weiner (2nd edition, Oxford: Clarendon Press, 1989).

Page, Bruce, David Leitch and Phillip Knightley, *Philby: The Spy who Betrayed a Generation* (London: Andre Deutsch, 1968).

Paterson, Peter, *Tired and Emotional: The Life of Lord George-Brown* (London: Chatto & Windus, 1993).

Pechatnov, Vladimir O., 'The Soviet Union and the World, 1944–53', in Melvyn P. Leffler and Odd Arne Westad (eds), *The Cambridge History of the Cold War. Vol. I: Origins* (Cambridge: Cambridge University Press, 2010).

Philby, Eleanor, *Kim Philby: The Spy I Loved* (London: Pan Books, 1968).

Philby, H. St J. B., *Arabian Days: An Autobiography* (London: Robert Hale, 1948).

Philby, Kim, *My Silent War* (London: MacGibbon & Kee; New York: Grove Press Inc, 1968).

—— 'Autobiographical Reminiscences', in Rufina Philby, Mikhail Lyubimov and Hayden Peake, *The Private Life of Kim Philby* (London: St Ermin's Press, 1999).

Philby, Rufina, Mikhail Lyubimov and Hayden Peake, *The Private Life of Kim Philby* (London: St Ermin's Press, 1999).

Pidgeon, Geoffrey, *The Secret Wireless War: The Story of MI6 Communications 1939–1945* (London: UPSO, 2003).

Pimlott, Ben (ed.), *The Second World War Diary of Hugh Dalton, 1940–45* (London: Jonathan Cape, 1986).

Preston, Paul, *Franco: A Biography* (London: Harper Collins, 1993).

Rees, Goronwy, *A Chapter of Accidents* (London: Chatto & Windus, 1972).

Rees, Jenny, *Looking for Mr Nobody: The Secret Life of Goronwy Rees* (London: Phoenix, 1997).

Report of the Royal Commission to Investigate ... Agents of a Foreign Power (Ottawa, 1946).

Roberts, Frank, *Dealing with Dictators: The Destruction and Revival of Europe, 1930–70* (London: Weidenfeld & Nicolson, 1991).

Robertson, K.G. (ed.), *War, Resistance and Intelligence: Essays in Honour of M.R.D. Foot* (Barnsley: Pen & Sword, 1999).

Rositzke, Harry, *The KGB: The Eyes of Russia* (New York: Doubleday, 1981).

Saunders, Frances Stonor, *Who Paid the Piper? The CIA and the Cultural Cold War* (London: Granta Books, 1999).

Schellenberg, Walter, *The Schellenberg Memoirs*, ed. and trans. by Louis Hagen, introduction by Alan Bullock (London: Andre Deutsch, 1956).

Schudel, Matt, 'Espionage Writer Anthony Cave Brown, 77' *Washington Post*, 28 July 2006.

Seale, Patrick, 'Professional Discretion', *Observer*, 22 September 1968.

—— 'The Shy Philby I Knew', *Observer*, 15 May 1988.

Seale, Patrick and Maureen McConville, *Philby: The Long Road to Moscow* (London: Hamish Hamilton, 1973).

Shulsky, Abram N., *Silent Warfare: Understanding the World of Intelligence* (New York: Brassey's, 1991).

Simpson, A.W. Brian, *In the Highest Degree Odious: Detention without Trial in Wartime Britain* (Oxford: Oxford University Press, 1994).

Sisman, Adam, *Hugh Trevor-Roper: The Biography* (London: Weidenfeld & Nicolson, 2010).

—— 'Letter to the Editor', *Journal of Military History* 75/3 (2011).

Smyth, Dennis, 'Screening "Torch": Allied Counter-Intelligence and the Spanish Threat to the Secrecy of the Allied Invasion of French North Africa in November 1942', *Intelligence and National Security* 4 (1989).

Snow, C.P., *Science and Government* (London: Oxford University Press, 1961).

Solomon, Flora, *Baku to Baker Street: The Memoirs of Flora Solomon by Herself and Barnet Litvinoff* (London: Collins, 1984).

Der Spiegel, 'Moskaus groesster Spion', *Der Spiegel*, 29 January 1968.

Stafford, David, *Britain and European Resistance, 1940–1945: A Survey of the Special Operations Executive with Documents* (London: Macmillan, 1983).

Stafford, David (ed.), *Flight from Reality: Rudolf Hess and his Mission to Scotland, 1941* (London: Pimlico, 2002).

Stevenson, William, *A Man Called Intrepid: The Secret War* (New York: Harcourt Brace Jovanovich, 1976).

Stöver, Bernd, 'Der Fall Otto John: Neue Dokumente zu den Aussagen des deutschen Geheimdienstchefs gegenüber MfS und KGB', *Vierteljahrshefte fuer Zeitgeschichte* 47/1 (1999).

Straight, Michael, *After Long Silence* (London: Collins, 1983).

Stuart, Charles, 'The Philby Phenomenon', *Spectator*, 26 April 1968.

—— 'Trade Secrets', *Spectator*, 27 September 1968.

Sweet-Escott, Bickham, *Baker Street Irregular* (London: Methuen, 1965).

Trevor-Roper, H.R., *The Last Days of Hitler* (London: Macmillan, 1947).

—— 'The Mind of Adolf Hitler', in H.R. Trevor-Roper (ed.), *Hitler's Table-Talk* (London: Weidenfeld & Nicolson, 1953).

—— 'Hess: The Incorrigible Intruder', in David Stafford (ed.), *Flight from Reality: Rudolf Hess and his Mission to Scotland, 1941* (London: Pimlico, 2002).

—— *Letters from Oxford: Hugh Trevor-Roper to Bernard Berenson*, ed. by Richard Davenport-Hines (London: Weidenfeld & Nicolson, 2006).

—— *The Wartime Journals*, ed. by Richard Davenport-Hines (London: I.B.Tauris, 2012).

—— *One Hundred Letters from Hugh Trevor-Roper*, ed. by Richard Davenport-Hines and Adam Sisman (Oxford: Oxford University Press, 2014).

Trevor-Roper, H.R. (ed.), *Hitler's War Directives, 1939–1945* (London: Sidgwick and Jackson, 1964).

Twinn, Peter, 'The Abwehr Enigma', in F.H. Hinsley and Alan Stripp (eds), *Codebreakers: The Inside Story of Bletchley Park* (Oxford: Oxford University Press, 1993)

van der Vat, Dan, 'Anthony Cave Brown, Journalist and Writer of Books on Espionage', *Guardian,* 17 October 2006.

Vronskaya, Jeanne and Vladimir Chuguev, *The Biographical Dictionary of the Former Soviet Union: Prominent People in all Fields from 1917 to the Present* (London: Bowker-Saur, 1992).

Wavell, Field Marshal Earl, 'Rommel', in Field Marshal Earl Wavell, *Soldiers and Soldiering or Epithets of War* (London: Jonathan Cape, 1953).

Wegner, Bernd, 'The War against the Soviet Union, 1942–1943', in Militaergeschichtliches Forschungsamt, *Germany and the Second World War. Vol. 6: The Global War* (Oxford: Clarendon Press, 2001).

Welchman, Gordon, *The Hut Six Story: Breaking the Enigma Codes* (Harmondsworth: Penguin Books, 1982).

West, Nigel, *A Matter of Trust: MI5, 1945–72* (London: Weidenfeld & Nicolson, 1982).

—— *The Friends: Britain's Post-War Secret Intelligence Operations* (London: Weidenfeld & Nicolson, 1988).

West, Nigel and Oleg Tsarev, *The Crown Jewels: The British Secrets at the Heart of the KGB Archive* (London: HarperCollins, 1998).

Whitwell, John, *British Agent*, introduction by Malcolm Muggeridge (London: William Kimber, 1966).

Who's Who 1941 (London: Adam and Charles Black, 1941).

Widen, J.J., 'The Wennerstroem Spy Case: A Western Perspective', *Intelligence and National Security* 21/6 (2006).

Wildt, Michael, *Generation des Unbedingten. Das Führungskorps des Reichssicherheitshauptamtes* (Hamburg: Hamburger Edition, 2003).

Winter, P.R.J., 'A Higher Form of Intelligence: Hugh Trevor-Roper and Wartime British Secret Service', *Intelligence and National Security* 22/6 (2007).

Winterbotham, F.W., *The Ultra Secret: The Inside Story of Operation Ultra, Bletchley Park and Enigma* (London: Weidenfeld & Nicolson, 1974).

Wires, Richard, *The Cicero Spy Affair: German Access to British Secrets in World War II* (Westport, CT: Praeger, 1999).

Worden, Blair, 'Hugh Redwald Trevor-Roper, 1914–2003', *Proceedings of the British Academy* 150, *Biographical Memoirs of Fellows*, VI (2007).

—— 'Two Letters on Treason', *New York Review of Books*, 9 January 2014.

Wright, Peter with Paul Greengrass, *Spycatcher: The Candid Autobiography of a Senior Intelligence Officer* (New York: Viking Penguin, 1987).

Index

References to footnotes are indicated by n.